AN INDIAN ENGLISHMAN

AN INDIAN ENGLISHMAN
MEMOIRS OF JACK GIBSON
IN INDIA 1937–1969
Edited by Brij Sharma

Copyright © 2008 Jack Gibson

All rights reserved. No part of this book may be reproduced, stored, or transmitted by any means—whether auditory, graphic, mechanical, or electronic—without written permission of both publisher and author, except in the case of brief excerpts used in critical articles and reviews. Unauthorized reproduction of any part of this work is illegal and is punishable by law.

ISBN: 978-1-4357-3461-6

Book available at http://www.lulu.com/content/2872821

CONTENTS

Preface	vii
Introduction	1
To The Doon School	5
Bandarpunch-Gangotri-Badrinath	17
Gulmarg to the Kumbh Mela	39
Kulu and Lahul	49
Kathiawar and the South	65
War in Europe	81
Swat-Chitral-Gilgit	93
Wartime in India	101
Joining the R.I.N.V.R.	113
Afloat and Ashore	121
Kitchener College	133
Back to the Doon School	143
Nineteen-Fortyseven	153
Trekking	163
From School to Services Academy	175
Early Days at Clement Town	187
My Last Year at the J.S.W.	205
Back Again to the Doon School	223
Attempt on 'Black Peak'	239

To Mayo College	**251**
A Headmaster's Year	**265**
Growth of Mayo College	**273**
The Baspa Valley	**289**
A Half-Century	**299**
A Crowded Programme	**309**
Chini	**325**
East and West	**339**
The Year of the Dragon	**357**
I Buy a Farm-House	**367**
Uncertainties	**377**
My Last Year at Mayo College	**385**
Appendix	**409**

PREFACE

John Travers Mends (Jack) Gibson was born on March 3, 1908 and died on October 23, 1994.

In some ways, Jack was the last Englishman in India. He came ten years before independence and stayed on 47 years after it, rendering dedicated service to the country of his adoption. Jack was the last English Principal of Mayo College; he was the last English President of the Himalayan Club. He was the last, and for most of the time the only English resident of Ajmer, formerly a very British enclave in the heart of Rajasthan. He was the last Englishman to be accepted completely as a friend by almost all the former ruling houses of that chivalric region. He must have been just about the last Englishman to have been honored by both the British and Indian Governments. Jack's life exemplified the good; he lives on in the hearts and minds of thousands of Indians whose lives touched his.

As his students at Mayo College we are privileged to have known him and on his 100th birthday we celebrate his life by publishing this book, and recording the many fond memories his students and colleagues had of him at http://www.jtmgibson.com

Gibson's collection of letters *As I Saw It* published in 1976 covers more than 700 pages and he found it difficult to find a publisher for it in the UK. Eventually he had to underwrite its publishing costs and it was issued by a Delhi publisher who had also issued a Geography textbook by Gibson. He had little secretarial help at the time he put it together and had to go through the proofs which were full of errors. Many still remained.

We were fortunate to find Brij Sharma, a journalist based in Bahrain to help us edit *As I Saw It*. Sharma belongs to Dehra Dun where much of his childhood and youth was spent. And while not a product of Doon School, he has known its campus, the surroundings of the city and much of the mountainous terrain described in Gibson's letters.

In preparing this condensed version most of the material which would sound dated has been deleted – Gibson's efforts in relation to the various examination boards, his annual letters to parents except for relevant extracts which have been retained here and there, his comments on immediate political events, his accounts of various cricket and other sports matches with other schools, the reviews of Shakespeare performances at the school, and his sometimes tedious and repetitious accounts of his successive skiing, mountaineering and hiking diaries. But nothing which vividly narrates an event or incident, and no cameo of an important visitor, friend or servant, and nothing that shows Gibson's love of nature, animals and birds has been left out. Nor his accounts of India's fairs, festivals, marriage ceremonies that he attended or hunting expeditions he went on. What emerges is an account of a life lived to the full.

Anvar Alikhan
Yogen Dalal
Amitabha Sen
March 2008

INTRODUCTION

Teachers in the mould of Jack Gibson are not to be found any more. Certainly not in India. He was an adventurer who wanted his students to share his multifarious interests and made sure they did. He was no less concerned with their academic excellence and character-building which every teacher ought to. Above all he was fair, just, kind and liberal, with not a hint and not a trace of racism in his thoughts and actions. And this at a time when Indians, in their surge for independence which seemed to be almost within reach, were beginning to dislike Englishmen. He made friends with many of the Indian politicians we know as greats today – Nehru, Shastri, Dr Rajendra Prasad, Zakir Hussain and Abul Kalam Azad among others. He had little patience with the majority of politicians of India, though, and with the corruption he had begun to notice in public life. Yet he loved India and after reading this collection of letters one is not surprised he was honoured both by his Queen with an OBE and by the President of the country he had adopted as his own with a Padma Shri.

Jack Gibson was 29 when he arrived as a housemaster and geography teacher at Doon School in 1937, three years after the school was opened. And from the beginning plunged himself into all the activities which he had enjoyed during his own schooling and trips to the skiing resorts of Switzerland. Doon School faces the lower ranges of the Himalayas. And apart from hiking, climbing and mountaineering in the snow-bound regions of the higher Himalayan ranges during successive vacations he introduced his students to pursuits which were either novel or in their nascent stages in India of those days – canoeing for instance, or fencing or boxing. He also experimented with Shakespeare performances by schoolboys wearing Indian dresses.

In later years, as age caught up with him, his wanderlust found release in scouring Rajasthan in his Jeep – he was welcome at all the princely courts in the state for the simple reason that all of them were Mayo Old Boys! Visits to Sikkim and Bhutan in comparative luxury came near the end of his career, a sort of spurious solace that he was still mountaineering.

The proximity of the Doon School to the Indian Military Academy opened around the same time as he arrived in India brought him in close touch the military class as well which culminated in his taking leave of absence from the school to start a military training college for the young in a Dehra Dun suburb. This was eventually shifted to Khadakvasla near Pune and renamed the National Defence Academy.

During World War II he joined the Royal Navy and even went up to Muscat where his father had been while working as a surveyor in India and that was a nostalgic moment. During this time he also wrote a history of the Royal Navy but we are not told whether it was published. He had a 'girl' back home called Friede, who was two years his senior, and they did consider marriage but nothing came of it when she refused to move to India. By the time, after 17 years with Doon School, Gibson arrived at Mayo College in 1954, he was a confirmed bachelor and this may have prompted him to stay on and, after retirement, settle down in India. He had few family ties in Britain apart from a sister. But he must have wished he had his own children. In the event he had begun to lavish his paternal affection on Deb Burua, a Mayo boy who was doing well in further studies in England, and just before he retired he had taken two Tibetan refugee boys under his wing.

While as a Housemaster in Doon School he had only a limited scope to show his administrative abilities. These first came to the fore when he took charge of the nascent NDA and then another similar outfit in Nowgong in central India. By the time he arrived at Mayo as Principal, it was an institution on the verge of closure, with few students and saddled with debts. It is to his credit that he put the school back on its feet within a space of two years, supervised the building of new wings and blocks, began to invite school-leavers from Britain on short stints as teachers, slogged to improve academic standards and finally oversaw the rise in applicants to the point that by 1960 he considered it necessary to introduce a system of entrance tests which was to be copied by the Doon. Till the end he looked for a balance in the number of candidates who came from the rich and the business classes and those who came from the middle class. He also acted as a true ambassador for the college by not only writing features on it in the Indian Press but also making contacts with big business houses to have his boys placed at a time when the era of institutions with specialist courses, from where these houses could draw prospective employees, had not yet dawned.

He was 60 when he retired to the house he had bought in Ajmer. He named the house Shanti Niwas or the Abode of Peace and was even active in his years of retirement. So much so that another book narrating his years there followed in 1984. Gibson died in October 1994, having spent 55 years in India.

Brij Sharma
March 2008

1

TO THE DOON SCHOOL

Gibson arrived in India (Bombay), travelling by ship, on 21 January 1937 to join The Doon School as a Geography teacher. He was 28 at the time. Almost from the moment of arrival he was confronted with the stark reality of the East-West divide and realized that the English were hated among the educated classes. Interestingly, he had begun to read Forster's *A Passage to India* on the way out. These were the closing years of the British Raj, years of political turmoil, Congress agitations and Mahatma Gandhi's calls to rid India of the British.

Gibson, from the start, was a pro-Indian person at heart, in sympathy with the Indians' political aspirations. While this thread runs through the book, Gibson's mindset is evident in the first chapter itself. The chapter also has intimations of Gibson's other interests which he indulged to the full during his lifelong stay in India – hiking, climbing, skiing, canoeing and of course witnessing the Indian fairs and festivals. The beginning on this last score was made when on a visit to Delhi, Gibson, against sage advice, decided to mount a minaret of the Jama Masjid to watch the congregation of the devout for the festival of Eid.

23.1.37 *The Doon School.* Here I am, safely arrived, and will try to record the crowded impressions of the last few days. I finished the awful job of packing in time to see our arrival at Bombay. India gradually grew out of the ocean, fishing boats first, and then a line of hills, and then Bombay itself with the Taj Hotel making an impressive focus for the view. Tips handed over, invitations exchanged, and goodbyes said, I landed to find my bearer with a letter from Jack [my cousin, J. S. R. Spelman]. He was in hospital with a cracked vertebra from a toss hacking to a hunt and I took a taxi and went to see him. He was very cheery and expected to be up in a week. I was to catch the Frontier Mail that evening, so did not see much of Bombay. I had to leave most of my luggage to come by goods as I hadn't enough money to pay for it by passenger, and I travelled second class. However there was only one other in the compartment, a pleasant young Gurkha officer, and he got out the next morning.

Yesterday I spent in the train through Central India, rather monotonous, but an experience. At tea time an Indian got in and we talked: most interesting, but depressing. I am already shocked by the extremes of squalor and magnificence, of subservience and pride in the country, and I think the English are hated. My companion was a doctor from Lahore and an ex-member of the Congress party who had been to gaol twice. He asked about the political situation in Europe, and I asked him what would happen in India if there was war in Europe. He said it depended greatly on whether England and Italy were on different sides. In any event the outlook for the English was not bright. I got him on to what he thought were the shortcomings of the English in India and what he had to say made interesting and depressing hearing.

To start with there was what I myself noticed from the moment of landing in Bombay: the way the average Englishman, and probably worse, Englishwoman, treats the Indian. Any sensitive person would react to it, and I don't wonder the 'ruling race' is disliked. Then there were various specific 'wrongs', some difficult to understand or excuse, others probably necessary. The Communal Award is considered an attempt to disintegrate nationalism by keeping the various groups separate and hostile. I don't know whether this was planned, or the award was made because it was impossible to work any other scheme, but what it comes to now is that the Hindu appeals to the Hindu as a Hindu, and the Moslem to a Moslem as a Moslem, and neither to the other as Indians. Other complaints were the high salaries paid to officials, that Indians are not allowed to form an Indian Defence Corps, that British Consuls, for instance in Canada, do not treat the Indian subjects of the Empire on the same basis as the white subjects, and that any member of the Empire can serve in the Indian Civil Service, while Indians cannot compete for the Civil Services of other Dominions. Dr. Dev, my companion, said that I ought to write down my ideas now and see how they changed, under the influence of the ruling caste atmosphere, in three years' time. Funnily enough I had just been reading *A Passage to India* where such a change is described. I liked Dr. Dev in spite of all his criticisms, and I hope we shall meet again.

We got to Delhi at 7:30 p.m. and had an hour to spend before the train we changed into left for Dehra Dun. Garthwaite, also from *Carthage*, and a forest officer from Burma on a visit to Dehra, and I set off in a tonga - a more-than-dangerous two-wheeled trap that went at a tremendous speed in the most unexpected directions - to see the sights. The driver expected us to visit the local brothels but we disappointed him and got out and walked when we reached the bazaar. It was very picturesque in the flares and electric lights, and we bought some rugs for the train at Rs.3 each, and then explored, nearly getting lost down a series of alleys where I rather expected to get my throat cut at any moment.

Each street or section of a street is taken up by those selling one sort of goods, like medieval Norwich with a Parmentier Gate, a Madder Market, and so on. One seemed to be where our tongawallah (I'm picking up the jargon already) wanted to take us: eating-houses with rather attractive wailing music below and windows with less attractive beauties above.

When we got back to the train I paid the extra and went on first to avoid the crowd in the second and to be able to travel with Garthwaite. On arrival at Dehra Dun Foot met me at the station and I had breakfast with his family after a very welcome bath. I had no idea that the dust would be so bad, and they say that it hasn't yet begun to rise and blow properly!

On the way up to the school we passed bullocks with their horns swathed in coloured turbans, peasants in all sorts of dresses, bearded and unbearded, trousered and bare-legged, turbaned, fezzed, mules, goats, cows, sacred bulls, dust, noise, cross-legged men sitting smoking hookahs, sitting on the ground round a little fire, sitting on beds dragged into the street, sitting in their stalls—niches two feet from the ground let into the wall, dust, women with their faces covered, dust, cows, bicycles, motors, tongas, a motorcycle, noise, dust. I can't convey it all, and in a week I suppose I shan't notice them. They will have become as ordinary as the Austin 7, the tramps and harvesters and lorries, the flocks of sheep of the English scene.

I breakfasted with old Mrs. Foot, young Mrs. Foot and the H.M., and also saw the newly-arrived Adrian George Foot. I liked them all. The bungalow I am to have is palatial after my quarters at Ripon: two bedrooms with bathrooms, drawing room, dining room, study and various lobbies, veranda, porch with room for two cars, and servants' quarters apart.

This afternoon, the Foots took me for a drive through the jungle by one of the forest roads. We saw lots of deer and monkeys, a great wild cat and the droppings of elephants, but no tiger. I was struck by the white-ant hills, something like the architecture in the film *Metropolis.* I disgraced myself by going to sleep in the car on the way home.

I can't get this letter finished. It's now the 26th. On Sunday Miss Welby, the Hospital Sister, arranged a shooting expedition with picnic lunch and tea. There were only two guns and the beating was done by villagers. You should have seen and heard them: legs as hard and shiny as polished wood, and they shouted and grunted as they beat. Nothing happened till the very end of the drive when two birds came out of each end of the wood. Martyn and Clough [two masters of the Doon School. Martyn, a house master, is referred to as John in subsequent letters] turned outwards to fire and miss, and a whole flock of jungle fowl and pea fowl came across in the middle and escaped without a shot being fired at them. However it was all great fun.

Yesterday was another good day when the Cloughs took me up to Mussoorie. Unfortunately, it was cloudy and we could not see the great peaks, but there were lots of snow-covered hills, and where we were, at 7,000 feet, there was snow on the northern slopes. Among the people you could plainly see Mongolian types with straight black hair and flat faces, and others had gold ring in their noses and ears. We went a bit by rickshaw, and the poor coolies, five carrying two people, ran wherever they could and sweated and panted uphill. I got out and walked, uphill for shame and downhill from fear. The coolies nearly all die before they are 40 from T.B., strained heart, or other diseases. Both are animals, those who have to live like animals and those who drive them to it.

Last night I dined with the Foots and we were disturbed by a sacred bull breaking into their garden. Foot and I armed ourselves with ice-axes, but by the time we got there the animal had gone. Today the boys came back before breakfast. They seem a good lot, and tomorrow we start work. Until my house is ready I'm staying with John Martyn. He has lots of books and is a good companion.

7.1.37. *From my mother.* I can't believe you have really gone and there won't be the Easter holidays to look forward to your coming back. In case you ever feel a bit homesick I want you to keep this and when you read it to know that we are constantly thinking of you and believing in you. You will make mistakes - everyone does - and I expect sometimes will feel that things are going wrong, or are very difficult; well, even if you can't quite believe in it, try saying a short prayer. You will live more in the public eye than ever before, remember, and your words will carry more weight possibly than they have done.

I am sending you one of your prep school reports, when you were seven: (Mathematics—Progress is slow, French—Very inattentive, English—Fair. Headmaster's Report—I don't think he quite realizes yet what a great amount of work is before him. He is old enough now to take his work far more seriously). When you feel inclined to be impatient with your boys, read it!

15.2.37 *The Doon School.* I have bought a very smart looking second-hand Buick, cheap (£60) because it's expensive to run: 26 h.p.; but the difference in capital outlay between it and a less expensive one to run (the next cheapest was £100) allows of a lot of extra petrol. On Sunday I took Khastgir [Art Master at the Doon School and then one of India's leading artists] and four boys to Chakrata and the car went very well till stopped by a landslide across the road. All along, the road was being mended by coolies who lived in hovels of reed and sticks: a contrast to the steam-roller from England. Chakrata was under snow, and the same word is used in Hindi for snow and ice, so three of the boys, who had never seen snow before, were surprised to find that they sunk into it.

Last night Foot had the housemasters and me to dinner to discuss various problems. All sorts arise, different from what you would expect in an English School. One is whether you should wear slips when having a bath. Thinking that this was not really cleanly, Martyn, the other day, told his house to do without. This caused a discussion at the tops of their voices all over the place, and several refused to have any more baths. They are used to being shy of nakedness, but a boy, last term, was found going round the house with a sword in his hand threatening little boys and making them expose themselves. We hope that this sort of thing should stop when it becomes natural to see each other.

24.2.37. *The Doon School.* Last weekend I took two of the staff, Sprawson and Clough, to Delhi. We crossed the Siwaliks, as spikey as the top of King's Chapel, and the rest of the drive was hot and dusty. I was struck by the cruelty of life: poverty, flies and disease: starved animals, a horse down on the road between the shafts, overloaded donkeys.

On Sunday morning Colonel Battye [a member of the Committee of Imperial Defence who had befriended me on the voyage to India], with whom I am staying, took me sightseeing. After lunch we watched the finals of the Prince of Wales Cup polo. The Viceroy was there.

Monday was the Muslim festival of Id. People thought it would be impossible for me to get into the Jama Masjid but I had no difficulty though I had to cover my shoes and was locked in a little room or balcony overlooking the great courtyard. It was a wonderful experience. When I got there people, 25,000 of them, were coming in and finding a place without anyone to direct them and without the pushing you would get in an English crowd. They spread their prayer mats and sat down in well dressed rows. Suddenly there was silence except for the children who were there in large numbers, and all stood up. The colours were as good as a field of mixed tulips. Then, for a quarter of an hour, they all went through their devotions, standing, bowing, kneeling, and prostrating themselves, everyone together like a perfectly drilled army with no words of command. It was most impressive: turbans and fezes all suddenly lifting, bare feet in perfect lines. After lunch I said goodbye to Battye who had been so good to me, giving up two days of his holidays to take me sightseeing, and came back to the school.

We are going to make a relief model of India and I want to show the curvature of the earth as well as the build of the land. We have a table 3½ feet square on which to build it and I propose a circle of radius 4 feet showing about 33 degrees of latitude from Tibet to Ceylon. I have yet to work it out accurately, but I think the centre will rise about 5 inches from the edge of the model. We can't use clay because it would crack in the hot weather, so will use circular layers of cardboard.

10.3.37. *The Doon School.* Another good expedition last Sunday, up to Chakrata again, from where I had my first clear view of the high Himalayas: stupendous. We had no sooner started back than the car broke down. There was no one to put it right and no other way of getting down so we had to stay the night in the empty officers' quarters of the Beds & Herts. Peters, the Station Staff Officer, gave us an excellent dinner after which I talked to him of the problems of Indianisation. These are very tricky. Indians are not admitted as members of the Dehra Dun Club: a foolish rule that ought to be changed. The regiment is stationed there in the winter and has two Indian officers attached to it. If either wanted to join the club the Regiment would have to put him up, and if he was refused the whole mess would have to resign, so they get out of the difficulty by not suggesting they should join and pretending that they don't think they want to do so.

29.3.37. *The Doon School.* Here I am in my own bungalow in charge of 60 boys, 41 of them new, several of whom have never been away from home before, and the rest, the Pilgrim Fathers, old boys, from other houses to help me look after them. John has been very generous and given me some of his best. I have bought a dachshund with a long pedigree, very intelligent, but rather shy at present. I like them best of the small dogs and I hope he will be fun. I've called him Archie.

13.4.37. *The Doon School.* In my bad moments I feel it's damned silly to have come out here to work so hard. Everybody on the estate works too hard, the pace being set by Foot who does an enormous amount but looks worn out. I've had some rotten tummy upsets (had to go to bed with a temperature of 103 one day), but most of the English staff have suffered in much the same way, and you apparently get over it in time.

The map to show the curvature of the earth has been a failure because the cardboard layers would not lie flat even when glued and nailed down, so now we shall have to think again. We had a first round of inter-house hockey matches last Saturday and I find myself very keen that my boys should do well, and laugh at myself because I always felt that housemasters at Haileybury attached too much importance to success in games. How ripping it must be at Puck's Hill [my home in Norfolk] now with the bulbs coming out, and the primroses and gorse, and the fresh green of the silver birches. I suppose the robins, chiffchaffs and willow warblers have just about begun to sing; and how I would love a sail in my boat at this moment with a fresh breeze and water to stick my legs into. However, there are lots of good things going here, though they aren't such fun without you to share them with. I have a fantail flycatcher in the garden with a lovely song, and would like to hear old F. [in my letters I referred to my father and mother as F. and M.] exclaim "By Jove, wasn't that ripping'. You must come out here next year and enjoy it all with me.

29.4.37. *The Doon School.* I found the heat making me irritable in class. Anyway, I went off last weekend with John, and now feel much better. We drove in my car to Rishikesh. The road was pot-holes, boulders, river beds, or dust six inches deep; either one or the other or several at a time. From there we turned up the valley of the Ganges and went to Devaprayag, some 50 miles by a road that makes you gasp and beats the mountain roads of Switzerland hollow. No one is supposed to start up it after 3 p.m. and we only got to the gate at 4. However we persuaded the policeman in charge to let us go, by flourishing a letter with the Maharaja of Tehri's crest on it, and hinting that it was his special invitation. Actually it was only a reply from his secretary to our enquiry whether the road was open; but it did the trick. The road was built two years ago for the pilgrims to Badrinath and Gangotri. The river flows in a gorge that is usually narrow, but here and there widens enough for a village to be built on the spur of a hill or its base. There were lots of rapids and it looked as though it would make exciting canoeing. The road started soberly enough, but soon got onto the hillsides, and how it stays there I don't know. I felt climber's giddiness at times, and we could only go about 12 m.p.h., so arrived after dark, which made the last bit more exciting than ever.

When we got to Devaprayag, the local scoutmaster, a very decent chap, who runs a camp in the summer for the pilgrims, put us into quarters overhanging the river which was a roaring torrent and lovely music to sleep to. We had to start back at 8 a.m., so were up at 5:30 for a bathe and a walk round the village, built on a spur between the Bhagirathi and Alaknanda. The drive back was as good as the drive up, and before we left the river we had a most enjoyable swim, diving off a rock ledge and letting the current swish us downstream. We had a very good lunch served by my bearer, Ahmed Ali, whom we had taken with us, and then slept, and bathed again, and rested and basked in the sun and listened to the birds and watched the butterflies, and read. Then back here, happy and feeling much better.

6.5.37. *The Doon School.* I did eleven one-minute rounds of boxing today with the best eleven boys in the school and as I couldn't hit hard I had to rely on speed. Some of them are getting quite good, and fencing is coming along too. Indians have very supple wrists and should be able to be very good fencers.

Social duties in India differ from those in England. Here, instead of waiting to be called on, at any rate if a junior newcomer, you are expected to go round leaving cards in little boxes marked 'Not at Home' outside people's gates or front doors. I have been doing this for some time and am now getting asked to dinners by the local bigwigs. I'm not good at making conversation and don't always enjoy these occasions.

An amusing thing has happened. John Martyn joined the Left Book Club and the police have come up searching his bungalow for seditious literature; plainclothes men asking questions of his bearer and so on. Isn't it preposterous! Nehru's private secretary and his sister had dinner with us the other evening and told us that all their correspondence is opened. You can have little idea of the atmosphere out here, and, my goodness, it must be ghastly in a fascist country.

20.5.37. *The Doon School*. The weather is pretty hot now—over 100 in the shade most days, but not so bad when thunderstorms freshen up the air. I stand it all right, and we comfort ourselves by reading the weather reports of 115 at Delhi and 125 at Lahore. I am sure climate has a lot to do with character. The heat is bound to make people slack, especially to live up to ideals that entail extra effort, and I was wondering this morning how much India owes to the reservoir of energy that Europe must have been.

10.6.37. *The Doon School.* The day before yesterday evening the monsoon broke. Most impressive. All day it had been very hot, with a dust haze in the air. At 9 p.m. the lights suddenly failed, then came on again, and then went out. Everything was very still. Then a wind came from nowhere and I said to myself "This will tear the mosquito net round my bed on the lawn," so out I went to bring it in. I had hardly got out before everything was blotted out with flying leaves and dust and even small stones. My bearer joined me and somehow we got the bed under the porch, the storm working up in fury all the time. The noise of the wind was terrific, but there wasn't time to be frightened. A great tree crashed down where we had been a second before. We didn't hear it fall because of the noise of the storm: only saw its branches appear on the ground by our sides, and even they might have been mistaken, in the dust and confusion, for the twigs and branches flying through the air. I realized that this was more than an ordinary storm, and made off to the boys' quarters. As I passed through my bungalow I saw that everything was covered in dust, and what could blow about, all my papers, was sailing around. Fortunately, most of the boys have torches against snakes when they go outside in the dark, and all was black except where lit by beams of torch light.

By the time I got into the house the dust storm, which can only have lasted about five minutes, had finished, and there was a lull. Then the rain came down and the wind got up again. Things were flying everywhere outside, and thank goodness the boys didn't go out to stand in the rain as they usually do when the monsoon breaks. I don't know whether it was in the first dust storm or in the rain storm that most of the damage was done, but the roof came off in strips and the corrugated sheets blew for distances of 10 to 150 yards across the playing-fields. One great beam of hard wood 2½ inches square and 10 feet long, attached to a sheet of iron, blew 70 yards from the house. We didn't see the extent of the damage till yesterday. Steel telegraph poles were bent double, wires down everywhere, and trees uprooted. Most of the upstairs bedrooms were flooded by rain coming through the ripped roof. The Dame's flat was an absolute shambles: all her papers blown everywhere and a lake on her mattress. We moved the boys to my bungalow where they slept on cushions and things on the floor, and the Dame had my bed. It was a proper cyclonic storm. I expect F. has been in many, but the first experience of one is memorable.

When term is over John and I are going into the Himalayas, taking our skis (what hopes?), and are going to try to cross from Gangotri to Badrinath.

2
BANDARPUNCH-GANGOTRI-BADRINATH

During the first summer holidays, barely five months into his stay in India, Gibson decided on exploring the higher Himalayas, almost within sight of Dehra Dun, in the company of John Martyn, a fellow school master. They even carried skis though in the event they found no occasion to use them. The two-month trip took them from Mussoorie to Gangotri via Harsil [associated with the romantic figure of British deserter John Wilson in Victorian times] reaching up to Mana, the last village on the Indian side. On the way they met and often interacted with pilgrims and holy men. From the source of the Ganges they crossed over to Badrinath and thence to Naini Tal. During this trip they walked 400 miles. Part of the terrain had been covered by some eminent climbers as well, including Eric Shipton who came to stay at Doon School, and H.W. Tilman, while great plant collector Frank Smythe, author of the 'The Valley of Flowers', was also in the neighbourhood.

It was the first time Gibson had encountered such high mountains though he had climbed and skied in Europe. And there were usual hiccups which make the narrative exciting – trouble with recalcitrant coolies, food shortages at high altitudes with no habitation in sight, the bureaucratic delays in the arrival of their permit to cross the Inner Line or the restricted area between India and Tibet and a nasty accident when Martyn fell almost 400 feet and was nearly killed. Interestingly, among their Nepali sherpa coolies were Rinsing and his brother Tensing, who was later to find fame as the first man on the Everest in 1953 under the name Tenzing Norgay [1914-1986].

30.6.37 *Dhanaulti Rest House*. The end of term was like all ends of term and arrangements for this trip have had to be made in a frightful rush. We have to get permission to cross the Inner Line, a sort of boundary on the Indian side of Tibet. To prevent the political complications if anyone gets shot by the Tibetan frontier guards or chucked into prison, the governments of India and the native states round Tibet have a secondary frontier across which no European is allowed without a permit, which makes it possible to keep an eye on him. We had to do everything in such haste that the permit hadn't arrived before we left, but we have a telegram from the Dewan of Tehri Garhwal saying that there will be no difficulty for us crossing the line.

We bought all our stores and clothing for the porters, in a great scramble, popping down to the bazaar in Dehra Dun when we remembered something else we needed. The most important item of our luggage is the calico money bag with 397 rupees in coin. We transported all this, and our skis, by bus to Mussoorie where the road stops just below the town, and baggage has to be carried up by coolies. Our bus was quickly surrounded by a mass of these who had to be kept off by a policeman who often raised but did not use his staff or lathi, and the baggage was taken to the headquarters of the Survey of India. Major Osmaston, a member of the Survey, has helped us enormously. He knows the area we are going to, having been on the survey that covered it, and has lent us tents, and made copious notes on what to do, what to take, and how many porters are needed. He is now on leave in England, but has left his two Sherpa porters, 'tigers' who have been on Everest expeditions, behind at Mussoorie for us to take over. They are Rinsing and Tensing [it was not I think, until he had climbed Everest that the spelling was settled as Tenzing], and it is taking us time to recognize one from the other. They are great fun, and splendid men. Our porters are carrying up to 50 pounds each and have agreed on 16-mile marches for Rs.1/4 a day. Indians make them carry 80 lb. for up to 25 miles a day for 12 annas.

We slept Monday night at the Survey and at 6 a.m. on Tuesday loaded up and distributed two yards of mackintosh sheeting to each porter, and started off here in the rain. John and I walked with umbrellas stuck into our rucksacks - quite effective. We hadn't had time for a proper breakfast and walked the 16 miles on a plate of porridge and some chocolate. It was 5 p.m. before the porters arrived and we had a real meal.

Bandal Gaon Dharamsala. I found a scorpion in my sock when I got up this morning! The walk along the ridge from Mussoorie was very lovely. Ridge walks are always exciting, but this one was especially good. To the north were the hills, ridge behind ridge, with now and then a glimpse of the snows, on the other side the Doon with great watercourses, dry and full, running across it and beyond the sharply serrated Siwaliks, and beyond them the plains. How good to smell pine again and to hear the Alpine tinkling of animal bells.

Today we have left the Doon behind and branched into the hills through forests of evergreen oak, covered to the tips of the branches with thick moss. Here and there we came on banks of wild strawberries, welcome for their moisture but without much flavour. As we dropped lower towards the valley of the Bhagirathi the land began to be cultivated.

The dharamsala here has a covered veranda in front from which open off rooms without any ventilation but the door. The floors are covered with dried mud on which you find anything from fruit stones to fish bones. There is no furniture; a contrast to Dhanaulti with its great pillared veranda, luxurious spring beds, and dressing tables with looking-glasses. The water supply is nearly a mile from the village and has to be carried from a small spring in the mountain side. Not knowing how far it was, I went to see whether it should be boiled or not. On return I found John talking to a Deputy Commissioner of Tehri State, a decent fellow who sent us across a shoulder of mountain lamb and a jungle fowl. Later in the evening we saw a man grovelling at his feet and kissing them all over in spite of his efforts to prevent it. It was one of his coolies who said he could go no further and was praying for permission to stop.

Nagaon Dharamsala. We had a good night last night, though a bit hard on the lower ribs and hip bones. We came down to the valley of the Bhagirathi, glissading down scree slopes, and have sweated up it all day in great heat. The fields are full of peasants working, the women with their ears and noses hung with silver and gold ornaments, and their thin arms and ankles surrounded with bracelets. The valley is full of birds and great butterflies, and if it wasn't so hot would be as lovely as anywhere I have ever been.

We arrived here about 4 p.m. The dharamsala has pleasantly carved pillars and looked very attractive until we got inside and found how dirty it was; however we decided to use it as it would be dark by the time our tents arrived. We have just seen a paradise flycatcher with its long white tail waving and curling in the air after it as it flies. There is a temple with peepul trees, one of which has a low platform round its trunk on which to sit in the shade.

3.7.37. *Dunda Dharamsala.* We hardly slept at all last night, being kept awake by bed bugs and ticks that crawled out of their holes in the mud walls directly it was dark. I was amused to see that the sadhu who shared the veranda with us had no scruples about killing them when he caught them. Today we have had a splendid walk. The valley has closed in except for little opening here and there, where there are villages, and we walked all day along the side of a gorge in rain that kept us cool and made everything smell fresh. We are gradually rising and have reached pines and walnuts again and found some great pink gentians this morning. This dharamsala is above the village and spacious and clean.

4.7.37. *Kot Forest Bungalow, Uttarkashi.* We went a short stage today and are now in a bungalow that is very unkempt but contains the luxury of beds to sleep in, and commands a fine view of the valley. Our way was mainly through rice fields with the world and his wife at work in them: an animated scene reminding you of a picture by Bruegel: people bending over in lines, and transplanting or thinning out, or ploughing, with a continuous noise of grunting and shouting at the oxen. Uttarkashi is a beautiful place with stretches of grass on and around which are numerous temples. In it have settled many sadhus, most of them highly educated, often with a degree from a European university, who have come here to contemplate. There are great numbers of butterflies, brilliant deep blues, orange with light blue borders, and black and white underwings. One we saw had a wing stretch as great as a lark and a body the size of a cocktail sausage. A muscle in my thigh is giving trouble and we are going to have a rest day here tomorrow.

5.7.37. Had a night disturbed by pain in my hip. I hope it clears up. Tomorrow we leave the main valley to go up a tributary coming down from the Bandarpunch region to visit a lake called Dodi Tal at 13,000 feet.

6.7.37 *In the rain, under an umbrella at about 8,000 feet on the way to Dodi Tal, waiting for the porters to arrive.* An awful blow last night. A telegram arrived form the Tehri Secretary to the Durbar to say that we must not cross the Inner Line until permission arrived for us to do so from the Government of India. It's very sickening as we have leave to cross on the Badrinath route and only came this way on the assurance by the Dewan that it would be all right. However we shall go to Dodi Tal, wait there till our pass comes and have a crack at Bandarpunch. Today we have come up about 4,000 feet, to start with through scenery that John says he has never seen bettered, even in Kashmir. Here we are on a little level patch, and 100 yards on, the path has fallen away in the rains, so tomorrow, we shall have to find a way across or above the land slip.

7.7.37. *Dodi Tal.* Last night we had an excellent supper of stewed apricots that we had bought from some villagers on the way up. They were taking them down to Uttarkashi to sell, a man and his two wives in their best clothes with pendants, six earrings to each ear, heavy silver bracelets and decorated jackets. The villagers are all suffering because their cattle have foot-and-mouth disease, and last night we had a deputation wanting us to give them medicine to cure it. It was sad to be able to do nothing.

Today has been mainly through thick forest and up and down round great clefts and gullies. There are lots of leeches and snakes and we have had to be careful not to step on a cobra. We have had several scrambles where the path had been washed away down a precipice. We got here about 4 p.m. to find it rather different from what we had expected. A guide book gives the height of the lake as 13,000 feet, but our aneroid makes it just over 10,000, which is much more likely. We had hoped for a plateau lake from which it would be possible to see Bandarpunch and possibly start the climb, but this is shut in on all sides by cliffs of about 3,000 feet, except a narrow gap where a stream flows out from it: very beautiful, but it's going to be a job to get at Bandarpunch. The lake is full of trout and we wish we had something to catch them with, but we had a bit of dietetic luck today, having come across a number of wild raspberry bushes whose fruit was as good as any you can buy.

Our porters have done very well today considering the difficulties of the path, and are now, some of them in a tent, and the rest in a little stone hut by the lake. This has a doorway that you have to creep through and no windows or chimney, but they have a fire going in the middle of the floor and are cooking their evening meal with the smoke coming out through chinks in the walls and the grass roof. Here comes supper cooked by the Sherpas.

8.7.37. Back at Dodi Tal after a hard day we are all sitting round two fires, one for drying clothes, and the other for cooking. Another fire is burning in the hut and the blue smoke coming through the roof and the tumbledown building and lake look very picturesque, like the drawings I copied so unsuccessfully at Mowden [my preparatory school]. Sentimental, but I like it.

9.7.37. *In camp beside the Hanuman Ganga, 10,800 feet.* A good day. When we got to the top of the ridge the weather was kind and we had a splendid view of Bandarpunch in front of us, so we have dropped down to this torrent which starts from a glacier coming down from Bandarpunch. We are encamped on a little alp surrounded by streams with the torrent below us and flowers all round. We are a bit worried about food shortage as we are such a way from any village, and three men have gone down the torrent this afternoon to try to find a village.

10.7.37. *Camp I, 14,400 feet.* We are on a little moraine right under Bandarpunch. We started through thickets of rhododendron still in flower, along the left bank of the Hanuman Ganga, till we came to a gorge to get round which we had to cross the torrent. It was not quite as fierce as yesterday when one of the porters trying to wade it nearly got washed away, but it was still frightening. I crossed it, then the Sherpas hand in hand with a rope by which the rest came across. From there across meadows rich with flowers, and shallots which we ate, then up and down moraines and across snow fields, here. One of the porters found a nest with eggs like a plover's at 12,000 feet, but we could not see the birds anywhere.

11.7.37. *Camp II, 17,300 feet.* Yesterday evening we sent the porters back to the Hanuman Ganga camp as they were not much good on snow, but the Sherpas have been wonderful. The event of the day has been John's fall. He slipped on a steep snow slope and fell about 400 feet, head over heels and in all directions, losing his rucksack and bedding. We thought he was done, but he managed to get his ice-axe in and stopped himself just before he would have gone over the end of a hanging glacier. He was marvellous and came up as though nothing had happened. Rinsing went down and collected his rucksack and bedding, while Tensing and I went on and dug places in snow for the tents. We are now on the summit ridge, but too far from the top to make it in a day. The weather is still kind.

12.7.37. *Camp I again.* The weather has broken, but not before we had time to find that we could not reach the summit from Camp II, and had to be content with a peak of something over 18,000 on the summit ridge. After breakfast, of which I could eat little, getting into our frozen boots, and roping up, we started along the ridge. The rock scrambling was easy, but we had to cut steps all the way up the snow ridge. The Sherpas did most of the hard work as I was not up to it and John had had no experience. We reached our little peak at 10.30, and, as clouds were gathering all round and fresh snow would have made a descent from Camp II very dangerous if not impossible, we called it a day. Disappointing, but also fairly satisfactory to get onto the mountain at all for the first time.

13.7.37. *Camp I, 2.30 p.m.* John and Tensing have gone down to fetch porters to move our camp down, while Rinsing and I have made an unsuccessful search for John's hat, which is a serious loss with the sun so hot.
6.30 p.m. We have spent an anxious afternoon. There has been no sign of the porters or of John. We are putting up the tents again as it is

no good leaving here with only an hour's more daylight. I pray for a clear day tomorrow, as a search in the mist would be very difficult, and if John comes up and we go down we might miss each other. Rinsing and I have both sat yodeling from time to time and looking at each other. It does not make it any easier that neither can speak the other's language.

14.7.37. *Camp, Hanuman Ganga.* No sign of John or Tensing this morning, so Rinsing and I started down carrying as much as we could and both anxious. That was obvious without an interpreter. Visibility was good and we searched with my glasses everywhere. We reached the opposite side of the torrent to the camp about 1 p.m. and shouted for information. All that we could find out across the roar of water was that John was not there, and the five porters who were, were starving. We made off down stream to the great tree that overhangs the torrent and found his and Tensing's tracks along the bank. They ended near the tree and I had a horrible fear that he had slipped off it, that Tensing had tried to save him, and that both had been washed away. Rinsing would not cross the tree, so I put on a rope and got across all right, taking food for the porters. From them I was thankful to learn that John and Tensing had been into camp the day before and had gone off again in search of food. The three men we had sent down the river had found it impossible to get down the gorge and had returned the next morning and gone back to Dodi Tal and the village beyond: two days there and two days back. It was all the porters' fault. They had not brought supplies for as long as we had told them to, and had overeaten.

I decided the best thing to do was to recross the river and go up again to Camp I with Rinsing and fetch all our supplies which would have lasted everyone for three days, by when those who had gone back should have returned. Rinsing had put up a tent by the tree, and into this we dumped everything we had brought down. We set off in drenching rain. It was an awful lug up and I wasn't looking forward to a night in wet clothes at 14,000. Then suddenly—you can't think how unexpected and what a relief—we came on John and Tensing having tea under a rock. They had missed us while in a gorge we couldn't see into, and only saw us far below when they got into the camp. There they had breakfast, and then carried down the rest of the stuff, and were resting when we met them. A great bit of luck that we didn't miss them and go onto find the site of Camp I empty of tent and food.

After tea laced with brandy we started down and crossed to this side by the snow bridge. As we approached the camp we could smell roasting flesh from a mile off, and this could only mean the return of the porters with food and a mountain sheep, as instructed. It was exactly that and the kidneys for supper were the best I have ever tasted.

16.7.37. *Camp, Hanuman Ganga.* One of the porters who went back for food heard that our pass across the Inner Line had come, so tomorrow we shall start for Harsil instead of returning to Uttarkashi by that broken, snake-infested path.

17.7.37. *In camp at 11,200 feet, we don't know where.* We have climbed out of the Hanuman Gorge and walked along the ridge northwards, looking for the track that crosses the Bumsar Pass and goes on to Harsil. The mist came down, and we lost the track along the ridge. One of the porters is sick: a naughty old man and it may be put on and we can't make out whether it is mountain sickness, strained heart, too much mutton or pneumonia. In hopes of a cure I have given him brandy, camphorodine, cascara and aspirin.

18.7.37. *In camp at 13,100 on track to Harsil.* We are in the land of shepherds, and have been all day. We found our track this morning— had only missed it yesterday by about 100 yards in the mist. We also found a shepherd with his flock, all of which had colds and were running at the nose, and he directed us. He was a fine old man with his two sons, and three great dogs with broad spiked collars to protect them from panthers. The porters all had a smoke from his hookah.

I am writing by candle after supper, and we have watched the sunlight die away, changing the pastures from green to brown and purple, and the snows from white to rose, and then to a dull white against a grey-blue sky, with away in the far distance the soft colours of hills to far off to be seen in more than outline. It has been a glorious experience.

19.7.37. *In hidden Asia—we don't know where, at 9,300 feet.* We set out along the path pointed out by the shepherd and found ourselves climbing, which did not agree with the map. This did not worry us much as it had already been wrong in several places. Eventually we reached a pass 14,600 feet high with rows of cairns and little stone sleeping huts built along the top. We set off with some glissading on the way, till we came to more pastures where this erratic track once again disappeared, and once more the mist came down thick. Suddenly we came to the tracks of a large animal and its hot and steaming droppings. The Sherpas acted that it was one that clawed you, but we could not translate their name for it. They were frightened and went with their ice-axes at the ready, and I held by stick with its iron spike to use as a spear. However we saw nothing of the animal or animals, but supposed they were black bear. Then the mist cleared and we were confronted by a great cliff of whitish rock on top of which was another cliff of hanging glacier that must have been 300 feet thick. This beat us completely as we ought not to have been near any great mountain, and we decided that we must have got too far round to the east or north-east of Bandarpunch. The stream from the glacier flowed south-east and we decided that it could only flow into the Bhagirathi and that our best course was to try to follow it. We have dropped down to just over 9,000 feet, but on the way the torrent has swelled to unfordability.

Later, We were issuing orders to the porters to go slow on food when one of them brought a report that he had found a bridge over the torrent that meets ours, and a track going down stream the other side of the bridge. A better supper has been put on to cook, including smoked sausage from which the green mould has to be removed.

21.7.37. *Forest Rest House, Harsil.* We arrived here safely yesterday. The path from the bridge soon turned up into the hills again and we could not tell whether this was to round a gorge or leading to more sheep pastures. While we rested on a col the mist suddenly cleared, and below us we saw the Bhagirathi valley. It was a good moment. We descended past banks of luscious and enormous wild strawberries with a really good flavour. We rejoined the pilgrim road, shaded first by great walnut trees, and then by deodars and firs. We feasted on walnuts at a village and gathered apricots, not ripe enough to enjoy raw, but excellent stewed last night, and better still cold for breakfast this morning.

As you approach Harsil the river bed widens to about 250 yards of sand flats with derelict tree-trunks, washed down in floods and left high and dry, looking like seals basking on the sands at Blakeney [an English village on the Norfolk coast]. At Harsil the river is again in a narrow channel and the flat valley bottom is high enough above flood level for cultivation and habitation, and the village stragglers along among pine trees. You come first to a street of Tibetan dwellings inhabited by traders and full of goats and sheep saddled with little leather bags, the women with their hair in many plaits; then comes the Indian village.

This is a magnificent bungalow, though in need of cleaning and repairs. It was built about 80 years ago by a fellow called Wilson whose name is still a byword here. He was given the agency for the forests and came and lived with five wives from the hills. He certainly had an excellent taste in architecture. The building is round a courtyard with upstairs balconies running all round, and upstairs and downstairs verandas facing outwards up the valley. All the eaves, beams and pillars are pleasantly carved, and round the house is an orchard whose fruits we hope to enjoy. The courtyard and its surroundings are now used as a trading centre, and half the rest as the offices of the local forest officer. The other half is the Forest Rest House where we are installed on the veranda, as it is none too clean inside.

Our main anxiety is whether our pass to cross the Inner Line, which we have already done, has come. We have sent a porter back to Uttarkashi to collect the others and the rest of our provisions and the pass.

22.7.37. *Gangnani Dharamsala.* Yesterday evening the Forest Guard at Harsil had a note from the Forest Ranger here that unless we had our pass we were to come back. These forest officials apparently act as state police. Both the Political Agent and the Dewan assured us that there would be no difficulty over the pass, but here we are on the way back, and the Forest Ranger has gone off into the forests. We don't altogether enjoy being treated like schoolboys who have broken bounds, but we have been reconciled to it all by our visit to the hot spring here. The water comes out hotter than you can bear and runs through cooling pans into two great baths which we had to ourselves. It was most reviving and the first time I have swum in hot water.

There are large numbers of pilgrims on the road, a depressed looking crowd with not a smile among them, but decorative with their bundles and umbrellas. A blemish is the lack of lavatory arrangements, and they all use the sides of the narrow track. It is difficult to escape the smell. There is no flat ground anywhere for our tents, so we are in the dharamsala, full of pilgrims; but we are on the top floor by ourselves. It looks clean and we hope there are no bugs.

23.7.37. *Bhatwari Forest Bungalow.* Arrived here after a pleasant walk to find our pass had come, or rather is probably in a letter addressed to us which the Forest Ranger has.

25.7.37. Things are looking up at last. The Forest Ranger arrived late yesterday on his horse, and as we expected the letter contained the pass. This had been sanctioned by the Government of India on the 2nd, and the sanction wired to the State capital, and has taken ever since to reach us.

Yesterday a nearby village, having finished their harvest and sown their wet-weather crops, set off on pilgrimage to Gangotri. The procession, led by drums and trumpets, had in the middle a sort of ark carried on parallel poles and containing the image of their god. This morning, at 5 a.m., they started off again, much more enthusiastic than the regular pilgrims. They visited the temple, and as they came down its steps in procession, I got them to halt for a photograph. The women were all in bright clothes and the men with red and yellow marks on their foreheads. When they got to a level place the image was lifted out of the ark, and the men did a dance in front of it, while those carrying the ark would suddenly sway it from side to side till it hit someone on the head. We were told that this was a sign of the god talking to the person hit, but they didn't seem to enjoy the conversation as they ducked whenever the ark got near them. When this was over the god was picked up, rather irreverently, by the head, and they set off. We are still stuck here till our supplies arrived from Uttarkashi.

26.7.37. *Between Gangnani and Harsil.* We are at last on the way up again. Another good hot bath at Gangnani where the friendly sadhu remembered Major Osmaston. I'm smoking a cigarette offered by the shopkeeper, a good looking young Hindu who was reading the scriptures when we arrived. He smokes his cigarette through his hand, and explains that he can then offer it to another to take a pull. These are kindly people.

27.7.37. *Harsil.* The shopkeeper and his friend were Brahmins, and not knowing it was wrong, I examined the food they were preparing for supper. A Brahmin may not eat anything touched by anyone but a Brahmin, and I'm afraid by action spoiled their supper. It wasn't altogether to their disadvantage, as we paid well for the food, and it suited us as there were three pints of jolly good milk in the pot. We haven't had any fresh milk for a long time, and I told the Sherpas to use it for soup and cocoa. They misunderstood and cooked up a mixture of all three which proved smooth and delicious.

I have been looking through Rinsing's book of chits, and he has very good ones, especially from Shipton and Ruttledge. He was on the last Everest expedition under the latter and carried up to Camp VI. Ruttledge says he was among the best six.

As our men from Mussoorie don't like going on snow we are trying to engage fresh porters here. By the way, those animal tracks I wrote about in my last letter were wild boar.

28.7.37. *Camp, Bhaironghati.* A short walk from the open valley into one rugged and steep sided, smelling of pine needles and fresh cut wood. We now have 22 porters with 3 cwt. of ata for their food.

29.7.37. *Camp about 3 miles above Gangotri.* The 6½ miles to Gangotri were similar to yesterday with the Bhagirathi in a very narrow gorge, blocked here and there with great boulders at the top, so that you could cross it. The temple at Gangotri is fairly new and well proportioned, but crowded round with dharamsalas. We hope to reach the Gaumukh tomorrow, and have crossed onto the left bank of the river. The map wrongly shows the path on the right which is sheer cliff. Opposite Gangotri were ashrams and we had an interesting conversation with one of the sadhus in English. Their ideals are similar to those of the early Christian saints or the monks and hermits of any religion. Through study and contemplation they try to get into communion with, or to realize, God. They believe that God is immanent in everything, that He is a spiritual power not outside creation as a spectator, but a part of everything. The sadhu we talked to believed in reincarnation and his ultimate aim was a death when the spirit did not reincarnate but entered into God, or nirvana. He said that God was happiness and contentment, and his life was an effort to enter into this happiness by contemplation.

We visited the temple and rang the bell: a mark of respect to God, but even with our boots off we were not allowed right in, through we were given raisins and crystallized sugar: a gift, they said, from Gangaji. The new porters from Harsil are good.

30.7.37. *Camp, below the Gaumukh.* The day began with troubles with Mussoorie porters, some of whom have not been reliable. They said they didn't want to go any further, but we persuaded them to carry on. They are high-spirited when things go well, but easily upset, and continually wanting to sit and smoke. After they had agreed to continue, two of them had a fight about loads, all of which we have weighed and none of which are over 50 lb. They fought like girls, scratching each other, and leaving great weals on their faces. The one in the wrong, who got the worst of it, lay down and sobbed for twenty minutes.

The first four or five miles went very well, and we were up to alps and flowers again. We insisted on the party keeping together and kept them going for forty-five minutes, followed by fifteen minutes' rest before starting again. All was well till we came to a torrent we could not ford, where the Mussoorie men all downed loads. We got them to follow the stream upwards and fortunately got a glimpse of the Gaumukh which cheered them as we had said we would go no further than that. A climb of about 1,000 feet took us to the glacier snout from which the stream issued, and we crossed this easily. We are now encamped on a pleasant alp with a spring of clear water at hand. I have walked to the Gaumukh, a cave at the snout of the glacier which is covered with silt and stones and looks more like a moraine than a glacier. Round the cave, however, the blue ice shows, and lumps of ice go floating down the river as it issues from the snout. It is thrilling to be at the source of so great a river and at a place famous in mythology and religion to so many millions of people.

Tomorrow we must move food and firewood as far up the glacier as we can, but the Mussoorie porters say they have food for only one more day: a repetition of their behaviour in the Hanuman Ganga. We gave them money for a week's food only three days ago.

31.7.37 Camp, below Gaumukh. Not a bad day, and we hope we are now in a strong position, having established a dump of all our food, plenty of clothing, and lots of firewood at the end of the Chaturangi Bamak, the glacier we have to go up, at 14,400 feet. The pass at its head was crossed three years ago, by Shipton and Tilman from the other side. We at least have an accurate map as this area was surveyed last year and we have been given a rough print.

1.8.37. Camp at the end of the Chaturangi Bamak. Here we are where we dumped our stuff yesterday. We have said goodbye to the Mussoorie porters and, sadly, sent back with them our unused skis. As we crossed the Gangotri glacier we saw Shivling, an incredible spire, and we are surrounded by cliffs and peaks. I have never seen anything like it, and wish I had a rich enough vocabulary to describe it all.

2.8.37. Same camp. We have relayed up the Chaturangi glacier to something over 16,000 feet, and plan to move the rest of the camp there tomorrow. Another Tibetan has turned up, a brother of Bumpal Singh, and a splendid-looking fellow. He crossed the Gangotri glacier in the very early hours of the morning and will add considerably to the strength of the party. He has brought another 60 lb. of ata and it will now be unnecessary to rush things.

Shivling really is a breath-taking sight, its peak miles up in the sky, cut off from the world by a bank of mist. We think we have seen Shipton and Tilman's col, and if it was, it certainly deserves their description 'unpleasantly loose and steep'. The col that was seen by Birnie but not crossed was described as 'safe for laden porters if roped' and sounds more inviting. We have just heard a resounding avalanche fall from Shivling.

3.8.37. *Camp, 16,100 feet.* We all carried loads up here today, and there is now rather more than we can do in two relays as the three hill men from Harsil have gone back. The Tibetans are tremendously strong. We have retrieved treasure probably abandoned by the Survey: a tin of glacier mints, a tin of ginger-nuts and some oatcake.

4.8.37. *Same camp.* We relayed to the head of the Chaturangi Bamak today, and are getting tired of this; like walking on Brighton beach, except that the stones are sharp and tear your boots, on a hot summer day at 17,000 feet.

5.8.37. *Camp at head of Chaturangi Bamak.* Our spirits weary of glacier slogging, have been entirely revived by the sight of an apparently easy col at the head of the Kamlindi Bamak. We breakfasted in the sun and Nilgiri Parbat (25,160 ft) looked splendid, with a long summit ridge from which the sides fell precipitously, giving it something of the appearance of a spade.

6.8.37. *Camp besides the Arwa River.* A splendid day, and we are safely over and down the other side. We were up at 5 a.m. in time to see the peaks change from grey to rose-pink, then white, and got away at 7. The going was good hard snow, and the weather all we could have asked. The only incident on the way up was my going up to my waist into a crevasse, but I was able to stop myself going further with my ice-axe.

The aneroid gave the top as 19,900 feet, and we had a splendid view of Kamet. On the Gangotri side there was no snow to speak of below 18,000 feet, but on this side it lies down to about 16,500, and was soft and tiring to walk in. We came down to a wide field of ice full of crevasses which made the going slow. John was in great form all day, but the descent gave me a splitting headache now cured by aspirin. The Sherpas have been splendid, and the Tibetans too. They all carried about 70 lb. Bumpal encouraged us all with cries of 'Shabash'. On the way up this was well, but over the col, under an overhanging cornice, when he let out an echoing series of shabashes, I was afraid they would bring down an avalanche on us.

7.8.37. *Camp at the confluence of the Arwa and Saraswati.* The hills this side are bare of vegetation and the country barren. There is no wood and the Tibetans have made a fire of sheep dung. We are down to grass and there is a big flock around us. We want to buy one. The Tibetans say 'Not more than Rs. 5', while the shepherd is holding out for seven.

8.8.37. *P.W.D. Bungalow, Badrinath.* Here we are back among the pilgrims and their smells, but sitting in front of a roaring wood fire in easy cane chairs. We bought our sheep in the end, for Rs.6 ½ and rather unfairly saddled it with a load of ata which it carried down before being eaten. The walk down was pleasant, back on grass and among flowers, even better this side than the other: great sheets of potentillas, anemones, marigolds, Michaelmas daisies, and Grass of Parnassus.

Above Badrinath the Saraswati falls through a gorge with perpendicular walls 300 feet high and very close together, and the track crossed the gorge by a chock stone. Just below the gorge is Mana, the highest village up the valley with the narrowest rows between the houses. Our arrival in Badrinath caused quite a stir as we are the first party to have crossed direct from Gangotri. Badrinath has been described as 'the Mecca of Hindoo pilgrimage': also as a 'huddle of tin-roofed huts'. Lack of building space causes the huddle, and the tin roofs replace leaky wooden ones. Anyway, we like the place, and the people are very friendly. There is an extensive bazaar and we have been able to buy potatoes, dal, umbrellas, and pyjamas.

On arrival we went to the post office to enquire for the food we had sent up from Dehra, and were shown various cases belonging to Smythe, who is collecting flowers lower down the valley. We were growing anxious, when our parcel turned up.

10.8.37. *Badrinath.* Yesterday we explored Badrinath. We were not allowed inside the temple, but they cleared a way for us to see, and illuminated the image with flaming torches. It was studded with precious stones which flashed and sparkled in the torchlight. As John says, a religious teacher who wanted to enjoin an observance that would do the people good for centuries, couldn't have done better than to institute these mountain places as centres of pilgrimage.

After seeing Badrinath we hired horses and rode up to Mana and to the Vasudara falls. Passing along a narrow rock shelf under an overhang, laid flat along our horses' necks, John's rucksack jammed in the overhang. His horse got excited and might have gone over the edge, but he managed to wriggle off down its tail.

In Mana, because the passages between the houses are so narrow, the roofs are used as street corners, and as it was a fine day there were collections of men smoking and chatting on them. The women were working at handlooms or carting loads of wood, and nearly everyone carried wool and a little wooden spinner which they twizzle round, hanging in the air, making thread: what corresponds to knitting in this part of the world. While we were there all the children came running and laughing out of school, just as they do all over the world. On return here we saw our first newspaper for six weeks, and were glad to learn that the Congress had taken office.

Today we have walked with our lunch up a little valley under Nilkanta and had an interesting conversation with a hermit living in a cave. On the way back we called on His Holiness the Rawal Sahib, the Temple Priest and local bigwig. He is a South Indian with a peaceful and intelligent face, and wore European brown leather shoes and a thick double-breasted overcoat as a Madrasi finds it cold up there. His mouth and lips were red from chewing pan. He knows all the climbers who have visited Badrinath and is always ready to help them with food supplies and collecting porters.

13.8.37. P.W.D. Bungalow, Pandukeshwar. We had to spend another day in Badrinath while I recovered from a tummy upset, but got away this morning rather late. Since we crossed to Badrinath we have been in British Garhwal and noticed the better state of the road and bridges, and greater comfort and cleanliness of the bungalows.

14.8.37. P.W.D. Bungalow, Joshimath. This is an old towner village at the meeting place of two routes into Tibet, with some interesting houses and a temple. We heard yesterday, when we got here, that Smythe was to arrive at Pandukeshwar last night. A disappointment having missed him, but we had left a note for him at Badrinath, and hope he may be able to visit the Doon School on his way down.

15.8.37. *P.W.D. Bungalow, Pipalkoti.* Yesterday's walk turned out more adventurous that we had expected. There had been exceptionally heavy rain the night before, and all along there had been landslides burying or carrying away parts of the road. Shortly after Joshimath we had to wade up to our knees through a sea of mud, and eight miles from here the surface soil of a whole mountainside had slipped, the road with it. We had to climb 3,000 feet to cross round behind the mountain.

On the way we have met several bands of pilgrims whom we had spoken to on our way up to Gangotri. They had come round by Kedarnath and were going on to Badrinath, and seemed pleased to see us, shouting the words for 'God bless you! Hail!' We discussed the road and exchanged cigarettes for unripe peaches, and have changed our opinion of these pilgrims. Their long faces melt when you get to know them, and there they were, old women and old men, slithering down the rather hazardous mountain path, quite enjoying the adventure.

At Chamoli we had to say goodbye to our Harsil porters as they found it getting too hot for them and wanted to return via Kedarnath. They have done us very well and been cheerful all the time and both they and we felt sad to part. There were no other porters to be had, but a local lawyer arranged with a pack-horse owner to see us down the valley. He ordered lunch for us, but would not eat with us, explaining that he had nothing against doing so, and had often eaten with non-Brahmins when at College but that he would lose caste by doing so up here. Thus does public opinion, based on what has become senseless prejudice, tie up progress. Cow worship costs India millions.

17.8.37. *Lobha.* We left the valley of the Alaknanda this morning, exchanging descent in grilling heat for ups and downs across the ridges to Ranikhet. This village has fourteen ancient temples, all small and more like the shrines of saints inside a European church than a whole church. Everyone is eating peaches, but we can't find a tree with any on it, and have been unable to buy a ripe one. Frustrating.

18.8.37. *Dwarahet.* We have covered 48 miles in the last two days, fair going in this climate, but made easier today by glorious mangoes. I had no idea they were such a good fruit. From here we can see the lights of Ranikhet on the next ridge, and tomorrow will be our last day's walking as we shall be able to get a car to take us to Naini Tal to stay with the Cannings. We promise ourselves brimming glasses of beer on completion of the steep ascent to Ranikhet, and return to what is called civilization. As far back as Chamoli we were startled to read on a building in large letters the words OPERA THEATRE. Instead, however, of being a centre of the arts it proved to be the operation theatre of the hospital.

This trip has been a great experience. We have walked about 400 miles and after each day I have had the feeling that we have covered as much as a day in a car. The people here seem to find it difficult to believe that John and I are English, we don't know why. Perhaps it is my wide Italian white hat and John's balaclava which he has had to wear since the loss of his; or it may be that we carry our rucksacks instead of employing someone to do it for us; or that my shoes are out at the toes and in tatters on top, for I have been unable to buy any large enough to take their place. We certainly look very disreputable.

We saw lepers today, a woman with her hands all eaten away, and another worse one was a little child under a grass shelter, without any arms, and kept from straying by a great stone tied to one ankle. It had been taught to cry 'Paisa do' (Give money) to passers-by. These people who tolerate that sort of thing and use their horses covered with sores, always seem good-tempered and kind to their children, and are honest, apart from what they consider legitimate bargaining, though they don't go out of their way to be polite as they did in Tehri Garhwal.

22.8.37 *Melrose, Naini Tal.* It's luxurious to be back in civilization again, and finding all your letters has been a joy, though damped by the news of F.'s heart attack. You must both come out and spend the winter with me.

The Cannings are giving us a magnificent time: sailing on the lake, riding, dancing, bridge, tennis, fishing in the mountain tarns, and sitting up for a panther, the last without success. Archie has been ill while I have been away. He was in great form till Sister Welby, who was looking after him, left and put him in the care of the people from whom I bought him. When she got back they returned him, a bag of skin and bones with tick fever, and more than 75 ticks were picked off him. I am very angry with them.

27.8.37. *Melrose, Naini Tal.* We are just back from a fishing expedition. While we were having a picnic lunch some buffaloes that had been wallowing in a corner of the lake were driven out and back to their village by a peasant. Two army officers had left their rods and lines by the side of the lake and shouted to the herdsman to drive his animals away from them. He did his best, but one of the beasts got tangled in a line, and these two bullies went and knocked the man over for allowing it to happen. I felt furious but hadn't the moral courage to do or say anything. Everybody else took the incident as a matter of course. How can you expect Indians to do anything else than hate the English if they behave like that; and what makes them so behave I can't understand. It shows how easily we all become Nazis if we have the chance.

On the way back from fishing we nearly had a nasty accident. We were riding up a narrow path along the side of a hill and a girl's dog went after monkeys. She pulled up to call it back and her horse got restless and ended by putting its hind legs on the edge of the path which gave way. She screamed as it reared backwards, and we watched horror-stricken. The horse reared up slowly and slowly turned a back somersault over the edge. The girl got her feet out of the stirrups and as the horse was just pitching over she managed to stretch up and grasp the bough of a tree. There wasn't another tree for twenty yards either side. The horse went down the khud, looping the loop completely twice, and the girl was left hanging over space. We soon got her in, and she explained that she was a keen gymnast at school. Meanwhile a man ran down the khud expecting to find the horse dead. By extraordinary good fortune there was no more wrong with it than severe cuts and a broken saddle. The slippery wet ground must have saved its life.

19.10.37. *The Doon School.* We have a plague of ringworm and scabies this term—both probably the result of not washing properly. I go into the bathrooms to see that they are washing properly and find them with towels round their waists. Some have a prejudice against nudity—'My grandmother says I'm not to take naked baths'—but this seems to be dying down. All the intelligent boys are supporters of Congress and want, not dominion status, but complete independence. I sympathise, but as a member of the oppressors feel relations at times a bit strained.

Shipton, who is in Dehra for two days, came to tea and looked at my photos of our pass. It was not the one he crossed, so ours was a first crossing. He is smaller than I had expected, with very blue eyes and very interesting. He spent the afternoon digging in the garden with the boys.

The more I see of some Indians the more I can't help agreeing with the Old Koihais that they can be pretty poor. Last night we had a meeting of the Games Committee. I am very keen to have boys on it, as well as the present masters, so that they learn to run things for themselves and can also see how difficult problems are tackled. You would have thought this was obviously a good idea, but would the Indian staff members have it? No, they were afraid of being voted against by the boys. No argument would sway them, and to crown it all they didn't want my motion to be recorded in the minutes in case, if the boys did join later, it should be seen that they turned the motion down.

9.12.37. *The Doon School.* Term coming to an end, and the next excitement will be skiing at Gulmarg.

3

GULMARG TO THE KUMBH MELA

Christmas holidays in 1937 were an opportunity for Gibson to go to Gulmarg in Kashmir for a skiing trip in the company of some schoolboys. He had skied in Morgins in Switzerland and was not surprised when he won the championship of India in the straight race though he came only fourth in slalom. Gibson's account is one of the rare descriptions of a skiing adventure in India in the British times since the sport was barely trying to find its way into the country.

The following April was the rare occasion of Kumbh Mela in Haridwar, barely 40km from Dehra Dun, and thus an occasion for Gibson to get close to Indian India. The event was doubly significant in that this particular Kumbh fell only every 144 years, as Gibson discovered. Fully immersing himself in the spirit of the occasion, Gibson could appreciate the sentiments of the Indians assembled there, the sight of the sadhus or holy men and even took advantage of an elephant belonging to one of them to take photographs of the crowds. Gibson's again is a rare firsthand account of an Englishman's close encounter with a spiritually charged assembly – and a sympathetic one at that.

20.12.37. *Gulmarg.* We didn't motor to Kashmir in the end as it is half a day shorter by train. We left Dehra on Friday evening and arrived at Lahore on Saturday morning. There we picked up the three Doon School boys and got to Rawalpindi that afternoon. The scenery was dull: endless plains of light brown earth with corn coming up here and there and mud-walled villages; then the Salt Hills, usually reddish and very barren and dry. Rawalpindi has broad streets and a good bookshop. On Sunday, from 6 a.m. to 6.30 p.m. we drove in taxis the 200 miles to Tanmarg.

We arrived in Tanmarg as the last of the light was going. The cars were at once surrounded with shouting coolies who struggled to capture pieces of our baggage. Eventually 15 of them got hold of something, though ten could have done the job, and by much argument we had reduced the number from twenty. We ourselves rode up to Gulmarg on ponies, along a slippery path through pine trees and mist, arriving in time for supper.

There is good snow and I went for a short run this morning before giving the boys a lesson. They seem as though they are going to enjoy it all. Of course it's not Morgins [a Swiss winter sports centre], but the people here seem very welcoming, and it's something to be able to ski at all in India. What a country this is. The ascent to the top of the usual run from Khilanmarg down through the woods is only 1,000 feet. Do you climb it? No! You ride a pony and a man carries your skis. The run is good and I came down on fresh powder quite fast. Above is the mountain Apharwat, 13,500 feet high. Gulmarg is 9,000 feet.

We sleep in little wooden huts, each heated by a large stove, though, even so, pretty cold. The dining room and sitting rooms are in a separate building, and getting to them is worse than from the annexe to the Grand at Morgins, and when you get there the only way to keep off the draughts is to plant oneself in an arm-chair, which is an effective shield up to the neck.

1.1.38. *Gulmarg.* This season has been an exceptionally good one with lots of snow. Today was beautifully bright. During the good days I had some splendid skiing, climbing twice to the top of Apharwat and to Al Pathri, a few hundred feet higher, and coming down by some very interesting and steep gullies from the top, with fast open running in the middle, and woods to end up. Holdsworth, who climbed Kamet, is the spirit of touring and has taken me some splendid runs, both on the mountain and through the woods. I spent two nights up at the ski hut at about 10,000 feet, and it was very warm and comfortable. The hotel sent up a cook and we dined, five courses off a table cloth! I have never had such a luxurious stay in a skiing hut, and the boys and John who came up for the second night all enjoyed it. The boys have become quite good skiers.

The first day of the snow showers we had the straight race for the championship of India. I went in for it after some hesitation and won it. It was a bit of an effort with snow getting into my eyes and lungs as I panted. There were several good runners, including an S.C.G.B. first class from Murren, so I was pleased at winning. The next day we had the slalom and I didn't do so well. White won and I was fourth, but my time was just good enough to give me the combined result and the championship. I think I shall have to give up racing as I felt very puffed and my chest has felt tight ever since.

The day before yesterday we did a wood run in the falling snow and somehow went down the wrong gully and had a fearful time getting back reaching the hotel in the dark at 8 p.m. It snowed very hard indeed all that night and yesterday and last night. I have never seen such a fall: about five feet here and goodness knows what above. This morning it stopped and today has been lovely, but we are very cut off with the road to Srinagar not likely to be opened for at least two days. There was a scare of running short of food, so we all made a track down into the valley 2,000 feet below. We took it in turns to lead and had to plough through snow up to our waists even on skis. We have ordered sheep, rice, chickens and eggs which will be brought up on the track we have cut tomorrow, and we shall now have to stay till the roads in the Vale are cleared. We had very cheery Christmas and New Year nights.

13.1.38. *The Doon School.* It was unfortunate that the message telephoned from the hotel to Srinagar that we were 'tracking to Tanmarg' was translated in Srinagar that we were 'trekking to Tanmarg'. They thought that we had been driven down and would need all sorts of blankets and stores, and the Government nobly arranged to provide these. I hope we have been forgiven for the muddle.

We skied down from Gulmarg to three miles beyond Tanmarg where the road was open and we got into the hotel lorry that took us to Srinagar. Its petrol system had been affected by the cold, and a man sat on the mudguard feeding the engine petrol from an old oil can through a rubber tube. The Vale was covered with snow and the mountains enclosing it changed colour as the sun sank. The bare poplars, snow bound villages, and ice covered waterways reminded me of Holland, while the flighting duck and geese recalled the Norfolk coast. It must have been a tremendous job to clear the roads of snow, and I was very impressed by the speed with which it had been done.

17.2.38. *The Doon School.* Life in school goes on as usual, except that there is an epidemic of measles which now seems a more serious disease than it was when I had it at Haileybury. Foot has started an excellent adult education scheme. All the servants who want to do so can now learn to read and write, and are given time off to do so.

17.3.38. *The Doon School.* I feel more reconciled to life in the school. We had a great excitement yesterday evening. I heard a noise like someone jumping on my roof and rushed out just in time to see an enormous civet cat, five feet from nose to tail tip, disappear down a conduit. I blocked up the ends and then tried to drive it out into a net, but it wouldn't budge; so I asked John to bring his gun. By this time my whole house was watching the hunt. I could see the beast's eyes shining in the light of my torch, but it was very difficult to aim at it as you had to lie on the ground and put your head and the gun up the drain. John was in this position at one end, and I was with the torch, throwing stones up the other end, and then looking to see if the cat was stirring. I had just got my head well into the drain when there was a terrific report and debris ricocheting pellets, and bit of cat blew me out. John had seen the cat and shouted 'Look out' without realizing I had my head down the other end. Fortunately the drain had a bit of a curve in it so I came to no harm. John has a nest of them on his roof and they make a frightful smell, so he was entitled to be a bit bitter with them.

3.4.38. *The Doon School.* We have just returned from a very good holiday. I had no idea that there was such varied country so close to us—so close, that is, as the crow flies, but about a day and a half in time, or considerably further than Delhi. We spent the first night at Sulphur Spring and then set off towards the Mussoorie-Dhanaulti road, with the idea of sleeping at Dhanaulti. I had six boys, average age about 14, with me, and it was hot and tiring going along a smelly mule track. They soon started their laments for water, and I began to wish I hadn't taken them. When we reached the pine belt one of them even complained of the smell of the trees. This is one of my favourite scents, reminding me of Puck's Hill, and this last moan made me lose my temper. I told them that they were a scraggy lot who had been full of boasts of how far they could go, but when it came to performance, as with so many things they put their hands to, miserable wets and failures. This shook them a bit and the complaints subsided; but I was a bit anxious myself, for there we were on top of a ridge climbing to the crest of another ridge it joined, and no sign of water. However we had the luck to find a spring, and near it a possible camping site. We pitched our tent and stewed potatoes, onions, carrots, dried beans and mutton. This revived the spirits of us all, and we went to sleep to the sound of the wind in the pines.

The next day we decided to climb Top Tibba and to descend into the valley of the stream that meets the Song just north of Raipur. It was hot climbing, but there were no complaints for water, though someone did ask what was the point of mountaineering. I think he was answered as we reached the summit where we suddenly saw stretched before us the great Himalayan range from behind Simla to Nanda Devi.

We headed down the mountain, and lunched by a rock pool in which we all had a dip. We had three porters with us, and it seems my fate to engage those who omit to bring enough provisions: they said they had run out of ata. At every settlement we enquired for food, but there was none to be had. At one village we found a maiden pounding corn and I asked her 'Tum ata hai?" meaning 'Have you any ata?'. I should have said 'Tumhari pas ata hai?' for what I actually said meant "will you come?" and she took it as an invitation, blushed and fled. Trying to explain that I didn't want ata for nothing, but was prepared to pay or exchange it for potatoes, I shouted out 'Hum alu hai!'. This meant, not 'I have potatoes', but 'I am a potato'. The boys haven't stopped pulling my leg.

The next day, our last, we continued down the stream to Raipur. It was like a miniature Ganges gorge, with cliffs towering up to 2,000 feet above us till the valley began to open up, and it got hotter and hotter. On reaching the Kailunga canal we were fortunate to meet a lorry that promised to take us back into Dehra on its return from the forest with wood, and we bathed and rested until it came back. I wish you could see my garden: it's a joy.

Easter Sunday. 17.4.38. *The Doon School.* Last time I wrote I was off to Hardwar for the great mela or religious gathering. It only happens every twelve years, and this particular Kumbh only every 144 years, so it was very special. The Friday before last I slept the night in the Forest Bungalow at Motichur and early the next morning started for Hardwar. All along the road were streams of pilgrims either going, like me, to Hardwar or in the opposite direction on a visit for the day to the temples of Rishikesh and Lachmanjhula. Both on this visit, and my second on the great day of the Mela, the 13th, I was astonished at the variety of faces we saw. There was every kind of holy man, from the pontifical bespectacled philosophers who ranged from jovial, fat, catholic bishops in appearance, through the college don type, to the obvious ascetic right through Chaucer's collection of monks and friars and pedlars of charms. There were Old Testament sack-cloth and ashes types, the naked men, the semi-imbeciles, the sadhus with long hair tied in great bundles on their heads; and finally there were the common people, Hindus from all over India; people of all ages, babies on their mothers' backs, hillwomen with their silver ornaments, old women with dried and wrinkled breasts that hung flat against their chests, men with their heads shaved, and others with magnificent flowing white beards that would put to shame a Victorian lithograph of Moses. At the boundaries round Hardwar inoculations against cholera were being given. The crowd was so thick that I had to leave the car in charge of Ahmed Ali's brother. All the way the sides of the road and of the Ganges were lined with sadhus and beggars. Many of the latter were monstrous deformities: one had a disease that had caused one foot to grow 18 inches long and 6 across; another had a head no larger than Archie's; another a normal head, but a body not more than two feel tall.

He was a sadhu and spoke with intelligence. A good deal of it was revolting and I couldn't help wishing that those who blame the British for all the ills of India would open their eyes to this manifestation of their own shortcomings.

It was very hot and the crowds raised a dust that hung as a haze in the air. I was very impressed with the efficiency of the volunteers, many of them boy scouts, who were helping to manage the crowds. They enjoyed blowing their whistles as much as a Paris taxi-driver sounding his horn, but they stood in the heat and dust shouting instructions, distributing water, and keeping the crowd moving, half down one side of the way, and half down the other. Ahmed Ali and I walked for hours—we were looking for a good place to go on the 13th—visiting several pilgrim camps, watching bathing at the various ghats, and parties being entertained by conjurers and snake-charmers, and exhibitions of monstrosities. The buzz of conversation in loud voices, like the hum of a vast beehive, was one of the most impressive things. We found what we thought would be a good place to watch from, and drove back that evening in a thunderstorm that must have soaked hundreds of thousands of those at the mela. I was glad to see it lay the dust and turn the trees from grey to green once more.

[Back from the picnic, and in my bungalow once more] The Tuesday evening John and I started off for the great day. It was dark when we reached Hardwar, and we drove through the crowds on to Rori Island. Spaces that on Saturday had been empty were now densely packed and it looked as though it would be impossible to find anywhere to sleep. However, eventually we came to a more or less empty enclosure and drove into it. We spread our beddings beside the car and went to sleep. When we woke, we found that we were in the police enclosure, right against the road by which the processions were to pass. We couldn't have done better, and once in they couldn't turn us out; there was no other place to go and the roads were closed. We were very lucky to have got in under cover of dark.

The day took a long time to pass as the auspicious hour for bathing wasn't till 4 p.m., and we were awake by 5 a.m. Towards noon the crowd broke into the police enclosure and we no longer had John's car to ourselves. I was able to realize how uncontrollable a mob can easily and quickly become, how unreasonable and difficult to deal with. The police didn't attempt to clear their enclosure, but only to keep the road open down which the processions had to pass. They had to ride their horses and back them sideways and the movement wasn't popular, though it was entirely reasonable, had to be done, and was done with good humour.

John's car was soon a grand stand. There were three or four babies on the bonnet, one of whom christened it, three fat men on the luggage carrier behind, and men, women and children on all footboards and mudguards. A young army officer thought we were in need of help and was keen to clear the car for us; but I was angry with his arrogant manner towards the crowd, as the last thing we wanted was for them to feel any animosity towards us. We didn't want our cameras snatched or smashed. Ahmed Ali approved of the officer, and I'm afraid he doesn't think I'm really pucca. We were very glad we were not on the roof-top of a canal bungalow, the official place for European sightseers, as we saw much more.

We were much impressed with the behaviour of most of the people. They were friendly to us, happy, and kind to each other. Here and there would be a man standing and fanning those around him with great sweeps of his arm, often for a long and what must have been a tiring time. In intervals between shifting into a less uncomfortable and sweaty position, I read Jane Austen's *Mansfield Park:* anything less congruous it would be hard to think of; but what fun her writing is. Eventually the time came when the crowd surged and those in front stood up, and those behind cried 'Sit'—and somehow they all sat so that everybody could see. The first elephants arrived with silver howdahs and gay banners and the sadhus in their saffron robes, some with their hands held up in blessing. The processions went on till past midnight. There were sadhus on elephants, sadhus on camels, sadhus on horseback, sadhus on foot, and sadhus, perhaps for the first time, in garlanded motorcars. The first procession was of the obviously best-fed and most college-donnish type of sadhu. The next lot were entirely naked and had renounced the world and any stitch of clothing it might provide. It all seemed quite natural and though some of the crowd thought it ought not to be allowed in these days, others obviously thought it the spectacle of the day to see an elephant loaded with naked men followed by perhaps 5,000 others on foot. I was given every encouragement to photograph them. Then came others, some with swords and spears and banners. They ran and jumped and did sword dances and singlestick play that interested me and made me wish I had a movie camera.

Shortly after they had passed us the sadhus who were not walking got down from their mounts or cars and proceeded on foot across the Ganges to take their dips in the sacred pool where is Vishnu's footprint. I borrowed one of the elephants while it was waiting for its master's return and took pictures of the crowd from it. I hope they will come out, but there was a fearful haze of dust. The view was incredible: heads as far as you could see—more than a million. The processions were controlled by wireless worked by a member of the Corps of Signals on an elephant, and the organization was excellent. In the evening the countless fires with suppers being cooked, and the burning lamps of offerings floating down the river: I can't do it all justice.

How we got away I still don't understand; but we did, between two processions. Unfortunately, yesterday, there was a clash between the police and crowd owing to an outbreak of fire. Thank goodness we weren't there.

I wonder if my relief map will be finished before the next movement of the earth's crust alters it all.

29.4.38. *The Doon School.* I dined with the Foots last night, together with some parents. One of them, a mother, had been in England. She was very indignant at the appalling ignorance of most English people about India, and said that the average German, Frenchman, Swiss or Italian was more interested in her country. She was probably right. But I get a bit fed up with all the animosity one meets against the British. There have been and are a good many of them who did and do their best for India. However I think there is little doubt that the nationalist movement has far greater support than many people realise. It is not only from college students, but from serious old men and steady old women. They all want an independent India, and they mean to get it. Some government servants will talk to English people in support of British rule, but at home they keep a photograph of Gandhi and tell their sons about our shortcomings. They still however, respect some of us.

John and I are planning a quiet holiday in the Kulu Valley when term ends.

4
KULU AND LAHUL

Summer vacation in 1938 was spent by Gibson in the company of John Martyn on a trip to Manali, Kulu, Lahul and the higher reaches in the neighbourhood. On the way they visited the Golden Temple in Amritsar. The highlights of this trip were witnessing the construction of a cantilever bridge over the river Beas by villagers, meeting with the hereditary ruler of Lahul, watching a dance-and-music performance by the local Lamas and a meeting with the Kulu-based Russian philosopher-artist Nicholas Roerich [1874-1947] "whose appearance was dramatic". Gibson also describes in detail a local religious festival which involved the sacrifice of a goat though the entire ceremony ended in a funny fiasco. On this trip again John was seriously injured while glissading and had to be operated upon.

1.7.38. John and I have escaped from Dehra Dun at last. We left the day before yesterday afternoon and drove to Ambala. On the way we passed through a dust storm: interesting, as I had not seen a proper Punjab dust storm before. One experience satisfies me. Branches came down all over the road, though none on us, and we had to negotiate round one great tree lying across the Grand Trunk Road. Dust was followed by very heavy rain.

Yesterday we continued to Amritsar where we stopped to visit the Golden Temple: impressive and moderately beautiful in the great heat. The streets of the city were narrow, squalid and smelly. I can't understand how the shopkeepers, who must be making money, can be content to live in such conditions. I suppose they blame the British. Many thinking Indians say they can't do anything for themselves till they have got rid of us. From Amritsar the drive became gradually pleasanter as we rose out of the plains, and I am now finishing this off at Manali, where we arrived this afternoon.

3.7.38. *Manali.* We have found a fairyland. We have pitched our camp on some close-cropped turf under a great rock boulder, and are at about 6,000 feet. Behind the boulder are rice fields, and behind and above them, the other side of a little gully, and showing up their greenness, is a forest. All round our tents are boulders and fir and deodar and pine trees. On the flat land below us, between two torrents that flow into the young Beas, is a part of the village, and above us, the other side of the now narrow main valley are terraced rice fields, then forest and then snow peaks.

The weather is perfect and the birds as good as those of Puck's Hill. This is a centre of ancient civilization and near us is a temple said to be more than 1,000 years old. Several English families have settled in the valley and, like Wilson in Harsil, have planted fruit orchards, and Kulu fruit is famous all over India. On our way up we lunched with a Colonel Minikin and his wife. His father had planted an orchard and he had built a number of wooden bungalows in which people can stay for Rs. 5 a day. He and others have stocked the Beas and its tributaries with trout, and many people come here for the fishing. We get supplies of milk and bread from a Major Banon whose father married a Garhwali girl and also settled in the valley. Banon has no children, but some of his brothers, who have married Kulu wives, have. He is a very decent person with a pleasant voice and interesting conversation.

11.7.38. *Manali.* We continue to lead a very lazy and happy existence here, only marred for me, by having picked up some beastly skin infection on my feet. John goes fishing every day, while I sit about and read. The day before yesterday I had a splendid walk up the Manalsu, a side valley that joins the Kulu valley just above Manali. I did about 18 miles with a lot of up and down and reached about 10,000 feet. Archie came with me all the way. I started through the village of Manali which is very charming and dirty like most hill villages. The houses are like Swiss chalets with steep roofs off which the snow will slide, and shady verandas round the upper storeys. There are apricot trees in the gardens, and most houses have a hand-loom somewhere about outside.

The Manalsu valley is very wild and fine, full of great waterfalls and gorges. I came across a glade full of mini-vets, both black and brilliant scarlet, and bright yellow and brown, the males and the females, and I watched through my glasses a falcon feeding its young at a nest in a cliff; but the excitement of the day was when I eventually turned back. I was sitting on a fallen tree high in the forest not far from the edge of the tree line when suddenly, just behind me, there was a terrific noise, and down the hill plunged a large red bear, chased, if you please, by Archie. I was terrified that it would turn and kill him and had the greatest difficulty in calling him off, but these red bear are apparently timid and it was as frightened as I was. It was a fine sight seeing it bound down the hillside. Not long before, in Manali, Archie had been scuttling in all directions out of the way of cows.

Yesterday we witnessed a most interesting performance: the finishing of a cantilever bridge across the Beas. On each side of the river were two towers of squared stones bound with timber beams. From these two or three tires of other beams stuck outwards over the river, and it remained to span the space between. For this two very tall trees had been cut and squared and these were dragged through the forest to the bridge. There was a band—two drums and an enormous trumpet four feet long, and a smaller trumpet—and as they hauled, a team of about thirty men sang what might have been a sea shanty. An old man, too feeble to be much good on the rope sang a short refrain which they all took up as a chorus ending on a note at which they all heaved. It was as good as any Covent Garden opera, and I wouldn't have missed it for anything. They got the trees to the bank above the bridge, then there was a terrific job getting them down into position to shove across to the other side. It all seemed very inefficient. There was no one in charge. Everyone shouted instructions at the same time. One party was pulling, while the other that should have been pushing at the other end were having a rest; but everyone was thoroughly happy and enjoying it all. Eventually they got the two trees into position to cross the river. A stone on the end of a line was slung across, and the main rope pulled over the river by this. One party, on one side of the river, pulled, and the other on the far side pushed, with people sitting on the beam to keep its pulled end from dropping into the water. For nearly an hour this end was stuck under the supporting beams of the tower, before it could be eased up and over them. When the beam was finally across a man calmly walked it—worse, I should have thought, than any mountain ridge.

17.7.38. *P.W.D. Bungalow, Koksar.* We both had a splendid rest at Manali, but the last three days were very wet, the monsoon having arrived in force, so we decided to cross the Pir Panjal into Lahul, where it is dry, and we left Manali yesterday on our way to Patseo where we hope to see the annual fair. My feet are being a nuisance and we have taken a pony to ride in case they give out. We have walked through wonderful country and the change today as we crossed the Rohtang Pass (13,050 feet) was very striking. We are not on a pilgrim road this time, but a trade route with pack ponies, and sheep and goats with smaller loads. The ponies have attractive deep-noted bells, and many of the caravans we have passed have been on their way to Patseo. They will mostly carry wool and salt back to India. One that we passed was carrying up shoes.

Two children, attached to a caravan that was resting, showed us where the sacred snakes lived, on our way up the Rohtang this morning. Most of the children in these parts seem happy and are merry and bright-looking, with charming smiles and big brown eyes; but some, in the roadside villages, have learned to beg and greet one with 'Salaam Sahib, bakshish dena'. The two who showed us the snakes climbed a long way to do so, and asked for nothing. They greatly enjoyed the toffees we gave them. The snakes live under a stone slab which was strewn with offerings of flowers. We couldn't learn who first found them and called them holy, but we were told that they had been there for a long time.

I have just been to see a village on the other side of the river and found a party of girls and old women sitting by a stream doing each other's hair: a complicated business as they have a great number of thin long plaits with silver and amber ornaments. The girls were very good-looking. Above the village, under a cliff, is a little Buddhist monastery. The lama was away and I was shown round by an old woman with a large turquoise ring and a fine silver prayer-wheel. We have now left Hinduism behind. The last evidence was a little temple before the summit of the Rohtang by the spring from which issues the Beas.

19.7.38. *P.W.D. Rest House, Gondla.* We walked two stages yesterday because, when we got to Sissu, we found the bungalow filled by the Bors (he is the botanist at the Forest Research Institute in Dehra Dun), and a young cavalry officer up here to shoot ibex. He had a very cavalry moustache, and I lost face when I asked what we ought to do about one of our ponies which has developed sores. 'What, on the withers?' he said, to which I replied, 'No, on the backbone,' thinking the withers were somewhere down the beast's sides.

This bungalow was also occupied by the Superintending Engineer and the Sub-Divisional Officer. They travel in luxury compared to our dirty clothes and unshaven faces. Each has a pony beside him to ride up all hills, and bearers and khansamas and mehtars and babus; but I must say I was impressed by the S.E.'s work when his post arrived by special runner. Piles of forms to sign, letters to answer and comments to make on various schemes and suggestions.

We shared rooms last night, but are staying here today to let the others get on to Kyelang from where they turn back, and this morning we went to see the house or castle of the local thakur. This is a romantic part of the world as we realized on the flat saddle on top of the Rohtang where there suddenly appeared riding out of the mist a party of Tibetans, trotting, not in line but spread out haphazard. I wondered if they looked anything like the Asian hordes that invaded Europe in the Dark Ages. All along the road are Buddhist prayer-walls and chortens which you have to go round leaving them on your right. The castle is as romantic in its setting as any Rhine castle. The galleries and woodwork of the tower are of the darkest wood, while the outbuildings are either white-washed mud-covered stone, or plain grey unmortared stone. It is built on great mound commanding the road and the village. The Thakur is at present away, but we were allowed to go round inside after the ladies had been hurried off into purdah. It was pretty dirty and not so fine as outside, but there was attractive simple carving on the woodwork, a chapel full of images and utensils, with some manuscript books in long unbound leaves wrapped and tied up in cloth which we felt might be of great interest, and a hall containing armour—chain mail, arrows, etc. Obviously the old man lives a very simple life, much, I expect, as life has been lived for the last few centuries.

20.7.38. *P.W.D. Rest House, Kyelang.* Here we are in the capital of Lahul. The houses, square with flat roofs, look very modern in their architecture. People are confined to their houses for from five to eight months of the year when they apparently spend most of the time drinking home-brewed beer. It must be a curious life.

We have just been to visit the Rev. Peter who runs the Moravian Mission that has been established here for over eighty years. He is a German-Swiss and most charming, and had his sister with him. At present he is suffering from a boycott of Christianity over some argument with the local Buddhist bigwig, and he is without any servants. He is a fine-looking fellow and can turn his hand to anything, so isn't upset. When we found him he was making a chicken run, and when we left he was about to repair his sister's shoes. As with most missionaries, I expect that any good he does is largely in setting an example, here of good farming. Kyelang, though a disappointing town, has a post office, so this shall be sent off now.

22.7.38. *Patseo.* Yesterday we walked from Kyelang to Jispa along a hot and dusty track. The mountains on each side, however, rose to the snows precipitously and the views were fine. Patseo is a most interesting place, and on the way we met all sorts of interesting people: a large party of pilgrims, men and women, a party of Buddhist monks, and a party of village women. The first two groups were going to Triloknath and to Tandi where the Chandra and Bhaga rivers meet, a place sacred to both Hindus and Buddhists. The women pilgrims had a headdress new to us. The Lahul fashion is a filigree silver saucer behind, with great amber lumps at the sides. In Ladakh, from where these women came, the head is covered with a long flat pad that hangs down the back and is covered with turquoises—great big ones an inch and a half square sometimes, and sometimes also decorated with silver and gold ornaments. These as well as the amber side-pieces of lower down, are apparently heirlooms, and I was unable to buy any, though I was told they were on sale from China and Tibet in the autumn.

The men in the pilgrim party were twirling silver prayer-wheels and wearing long sheepskin boots and purple cloaks and tight trousers. Hats are a speciality: anything from a purple cross between a topper and a jester's cap to an ancient Homburg. The monks were an interesting party too. They wore red and were sitting drinking tea on a bright green patch of turf by the river. They greatly enjoyed the toffees we gave them (much in demand up here), but what interested them most, more even than our old map which they all crowded round, was the Bromo paper that John dropped by mistake. They couldn't make out what it could be for.

Among the party of village women was a very pretty girl. They all had turquoise headdresses and were crossing, one by one, a suspension bridge of ropes made from twisted and plaited twigs of birch. There was a flooring of two main ropes, two main side ropes as hand rails, all joined up with numerous cross ropes. The bridge swung perilously from side to side as one crossed.

Here, at Patseo, there are all sorts of people: from India, Ladakh and Tibet—not a great crowd, but groups in tents who come for a short time, until they have done their trade. The tent walls are either of stone or of piles of goat and sheep saddle bags, or of canvas. This evening we saw salt from Tibet being exchanged for corn from India, but more about the fair when we have seen more of it. We hope to do a bit of climbing here if the weather keeps fine.

23.7.38. *In camp at 14,000 feet, above Patseo.* This morning was clear and I went off to have a closer look at the fair. Sheep were tethered in long lines by leads off a single rope, and the wool buyers were going round feeling their fleeces. About 9'o clock we set off. We couldn't get any porters so were prepared, though not anxious to carry our stuff ourselves: but as the side valley we proposed to explore looked easy going to start with, we persuaded the pony men to load up and come with us as far as they could. The going was easy and the ponies reached here across various snow bridges, but our mountain, with an ice face on it some 3,000 feet high, is not possible from any way we can see. We dumped camp, persuaded the pony men to stay, and went off to explore. We crossed the glacier, intending to climb the peak marked in my very rough sketch map. This must be a bit over 17,000 feet. We had only got about half way when it started to rain, but carried on to a little col which the aneroid gave us 16,700 feet. I am very glad to find that I am much better acclimatized than last year when, at this height, I was puffing like anything.

25.7.38. *Patseo.* We had a terrific day yesterday. Breakfast by 6 a.m. and very cold breaking the ice of a little pond beside our tent, and later washing up in water that had again frozen over. We have no Sherpas to do all the hard work for us this year.

As the weather was still unsettled we sent our camp back to Patseo and decided to explore in the direction of the dotted line on the sketch map, and, if it came on thick, return to Patseo. However, it grew finer and finer and we decided to try to cross the ridge and come down to the Baralacha Pass. The climbing was easy, both on shale and snow, but exhausting because of the height. Eventually we reached a col at 18,400 feet from which we had a magnificent view. In front of us was a great snowfield, not on the map, hemmed in with peaks at about 19,000 and going away in a big glacier north-east towards the Baralacha La (16,000 feet).

By then it was 2.30, and although it meant a long day, we decided to go down that way. We kept to the side of the glacier to avoid crevasses, and it was a longer slog than we expected. We reached the Baralacha at 5.30 but couldn't tell whereabouts on it we were. We searched about and waded a number of streams in growing dark and anxiety, but eventually found the road to Patseo. It was 7.30 by the time we had wrung out our socks and set off with 12½ miles to go.

Just as the sun had dropped behind the mountains we came to Chunkun Lake (also called Suraj Tal). This reminded me of a picture I had greatly admired by Roerich. The river running into it crossed a wide plain and split into innumerable silver criss-cross ribbons. By the time we had passed the lake it was dark. Fortunately, we had a small torch. We got here at 12.45. I don't think I have ever been so weary; but a grand day.

26.7.38. *P.W.D. Bungalow, Jispa.* It rained again yesterday morning, so we decided to move down here, but before doing so we had an interesting look at the fair. In many ways it was like a country market in England with the same types of burly farmers, thin farmers, jovial farmers and sour-looking farmers. The brother of the Wazir of Lahul had come up to buy wool, and he explained it all to us. The sheep came down from Tibet with their wool on them and often carrying loads of salt. The wool fetches about a rupee and the salt about the same. Often the load of salt is exchanged for a load or just over a load of barley, or two loads of rice brought from India on other sheep. When the wool on a sheep has been purchased or exchanged, the sheep is sheared by men who stay up at Patseo while the fair lasts. They get something less than 1 anna for each sheep they shear.

The Thakur, brother of the Wazir, was doing business with the chief trader from Tibet who had come with many others through Ladakh, and wore a fine embroidered blanket over his shoulder something like a Highland plaid. They were sitting cross-legged in a tent before a Tibetan table—rather like a painted wooden footstool—and were drinking home-brewed rice-beer. I found it excellent with a clean, bitter, yeasty taste, though the Thakur said that barley-beer is better, and has promised us some. He told me that the amber side-pieces worn by women on their heads may be worth anything up to Rs. 100 a pair, but that composition ones are now imported from Germany.

We were pretty footsore after our long day, so are taking a day's rest. I have been darning my socks with a bodkin, having lost my needle, and pushing it through makes holes almost as big as the ones I'm trying to mend.

28.7.38. *In camp at 15,000 feet, above Jispa.* Our climbing is over and the 20,000 summit unattained, but we have greatly enjoyed ourselves. Yesterday we climbed up from Jispa just under 5000 feet, a frightful sweat as the two porters we employed proved broken reeds: that is they couldn't carry twice as much as us and keep up with us; so we had to carry half their loads ourselves and were very tired when we got here last night. Having found the mountain wall unclimbable from the Patseo side, we decided to have a look at it from the south. We crossed the Bhaga from Jispa by the swinging twig bridge. As you got to the middle, a foot or so above the swirling water, it threatened to turn you out like a hammock. The far side we met an old abbot with another monk attending him and carrying a load. He had a roll of parchment slung across his back, a yellow hat, and red skin boots and red cloak, and the two of them might have stepped straight out of Chaucer.

After a steep climb, we camped here, both too tired to sleep well, and only got away about 8 this morning. After a trying time over glacier covered with boulders we got onto a spur by which we hoped to reach the summit ridge. By two o'clock we had reached 18,000 feet and the top of one of three little peaks. We were both tired, and the way on was very steep ice on one side and slippery, loose overhanging slabs on the other, with few places for anchorage. It was disappointing, but we decided to go back. Anyway, we had had some good climbing and splendid views. On return here we lay naked in the hot evening sun, rolled in the snow, and then lay until we dried again.

29.7.38. P.W.D. Bungalow, Jispa. We have run very short of supplies and necessity has produced some wonderful dishes. Porridge oats mixed with butter and treacle and fried has been a staple diet something like Yorkshire parkin. An alternative has been dough made of country flour or ata and water, fried in butter to make a very edible hard biscuit. Best of all was powder milk, brandy and brown sugar with water as a hot drink.

The descent today was hot and uneventful except for a moment on the bridge, when I thought I was falling in. The best part was lying in a rill beside the road and letting the crystal water flow over and all round you—most refreshing. Tomorrow we move down to Kyelang. I can't get over the feeling that all this is unreal—I have had it ever since coming to India, and look at myself taking part in these adventures as a sort of outsider, feeling that my real life is still at home. I wish I could step out of the dream for a while and be with you all.

2.8.38. Kyelang. We have had a most interesting time here, beginning on the way down from Jispa. We called at the Thakur's house and were shown round and entertained by his son who goes to school in Lahore, his father being away. The house was most attractive with an upstairs courtyard—floor of white lime renewed daily—surrounded on the two open sides with boxes of flowers, and with painted doors leading into the living rooms on the other two sides. The reception room had wood pillars with broad, flat, carved and brightly painted capitals. The living room had bright, thick rugs and the charming Tibetan tables before which we sat on the floor and from which we were refreshed with biscuits and wine, homemade and very good: one dry and another sweet. The Gompa or chapel was beautifully kept, the walls hung with thankas (painted banners) and one side taken up with a row of Budhhas in front of which were numerous little brass bowls filled with bright small flowers. The rest of the walk was anticlimax, hot and dusty.

The next day we interviewed the Wazir, the hereditary ruler of Lahul, and he promised to arrange for us to see a Lama Dance. He was very small, sprightly little man with Mongolian features and a rather evil or slightly debauched-looking face. His family came up here from India and married some hundreds of years ago. He told us a good deal about Lahul and its customs, but not that when a boy of eleven, he had shot his aunt for annoying him. It's a funny place this in many ways. The Wazir is a second-class magistrate and administers petty justice under an Indian official of the I.C.S. who is now on his way up here to inspect. At the same time he can do just what he likes up to a point as it is his country. Some years ago his brother murdered a man—the eternal triangle—and a Commission came up to make an enquiry, but they could find out nothing as everybody denied any knowledge of the matter. Traders have been beaten up, and even the resident doctor, an Indian, but nothing has ever been officially found out, though it has been common knowledge who has been responsible. The Wazir holds a commission as a lieutenant in the Territorials. They know his reputation, but can do nothing without proof, which is not forthcoming. The authority for all this is Peter, the missionary: a first-class fellow.

There is a good deal of polyandry: perhaps a form of birth control, land being short. The Wazir has a winter wife in Kulu, and two summer ones here. Peter told us how, one spring, an old woman was throwing dust out of a great basket onto the snow round her house to make it melt more quickly. She slipped, fell into the basket, and it shot off down the slope like a toboggan. It crossed the river by a snow bridge and shot some way up the opposite bank, and then down again, and so on, to and fro, till the old woman fell out into the river and was drowned.

We complained of the poorness of our map—made in the 1880s—and Peter told us that there is a mountain range marked on it with Tibetan words for 'I don't know'. The surveyor had asked, one supposes, what it was called. Last year Peter got, by the first post over the pass, a request to hold a celebration service for the coronation of George VI. He couldn't understand this but told his congregation that, as a member of a republic, he didn't know much about monarchical customs and supposed the monarch changed his name when crowned, just as a monk changes his when he takes his vows. It wasn't till after May, when the bulky post of newspapers was brought up, that he learned of the abdication of Edward VIII.

Peter knows a lot about doctoring, is a civil engineer and runs the mission farm. He has a number of cattle and sheep and is sending the latter into India to fetch corn if this is continued to be denied him in Lahul.

The chief interest of the next day was our visit to the monastery 2,000 feet above Kyelang with the Gilberts. On our arrival we were greeted by music from drums, trumpets and cymbals. In the chapel were dozens of little rollers on end containing prayers and with prayers written on them. You brushed them with your hand and as they turned round it counted as saying all the prayers. The Thakur at Jispa had a prayer-wheel worked by flowing water.

The head Lama was an albino with a fine white beard and pleasant smile. When he was not screwing up his eyes, a habit of albinos, his expression was saintly. He wore a brownish cloak and his legs were bare. He has a great local reputation as a rain-maker. The second Lama was more austere-looking, and I thought much less inclined to approve of us. The monks and servants were all full of fun and responded to our smiles with broader smiles and laughter. After seeing the public rooms of the monastery—we didn't see where the monks lived—we were taken to the place where the dance was to be held. In the centre was a tall staff with a prayer flag. Round this was an area of flat ground about ten yards square. At one end was a covered balcony with a raised seat in the middle for the head Lama, and at the end was the entrance down a path from the monks' dressing room. Of the other two sides, one fell way in a precipice and the other was a bank from which the audience watched.

We sat on rugs placed for us on the bank, and the Lamas took their places in the balcony. They had on great hats like this: scarlet on top with yellow sides, and each played some musical instrument. The head Lama had a bell which he rang, the second Lama cymbals, the others drums and so on. There was another orchestra in a ministrels' gallery over the monks' dressing room. The music had a very distinct rhythm with a rather subdued tune. The master of ceremonies, in a fur hat like a borough councillor's directed from near the pole in the centre. Each dance was started by a blast on a whistle that sounded just like a botswain's. Many of the dance movements were beautiful, and the light relief active and amusing.

The general idea was to show the evil spirits of this world and the next, and how they harry people. Then came the Lamas to subdue them. You were shown what happened to the spirits of the dead, unless they were helped by the influence of the Lamas, and no doubt these dances help to keep up the prestige of the monks and win them offerings. All the dancers were masked and many of the masks and dresses were very fine. Colonel Gilbert said that it was the most interesting afternoon he has spent since his arrival in India.

4. 8.38. *Gondla* We have repeated the crossing of the pass over the ridge between the Bhaga and the Chandra as we thought the sweat of climbing 5,000 feet preferable to that of walking in the heat and dust. On the way up we visited another monastery. These are usually perched on the sides of hills and you see them above you, square-looking buildings, white and decked with prayer-flags. This one was comparatively new and the paintings were fresh and bright. The monks were all very friendly. Some were worshipping in the chapel, making obeisances like Catholics before the altar and chanting prayers. While we were there a file of women wood-gatherers passed on their way up hill to collect juniper. They were also chanting, a folk song.

We bought various things: a copper kettle and tea cup from Tibet, and some ear-rings from a woman outside. As we hadn't enough money to pay, we promised to send it by money order to the post office at Kyelang, and they were quite satisfied. This is a part of the world where one's word still holds value. Peter keeps a large sum of money for a Tibetan friend in the Post Office Savings Bank, and there are no signed documents about it—only his word that he will give it back when asked.

On the way down here we came across the local Gompa: quite deserted and very dusty, with brass jars tumbled about the floor in disarray, and some good paintings. In spirit it was rather like the interior of a gothic village church in a Cotman etching.

5.8.38. *Manali.* We double-staged back. The walk after is less interesting than the walk before. At Koksar we found the four chief Thakurs of Lahul assembled to welcome the I.C.S. officer who was to cross into Lahul the next day on a tour of inspection. We wondered whether they were there to make a case against Peter. We met the officer himself on top of the Rohtang, a fellow called Lal, with his wife and an Oxford friend. We liked them all very much, and he knew all about what was said to be going on. We did 21 miles yesterday—very pleasant walking.

We got back here last night pretty tired to a discussion about the mineral prospects of Kulu and Lahul. A man can wash six annas worth of gold out of the river here in a day's hard work if he wants to, and several people have spent their retirements searching for the source of supply. There are various silver and antimony mines left unworked up in the hills since the costs of transport, fuel and so on make them uneconomic.

8.8.38. *Manali*. Two days ago, we called on the Roerichs. The old man is a Russian artist who has settled lower down the valley. There is an account of his work in the *Encyclopaedia Britannica* and large collections of his work in New York and Prague. He has travelled widely in Asia and written of his experiences in a book called *Alte Himalia*, and here he runs an institute for the study of Tibetan languages and culture, herbal cures, and so on. He has been suspected of being a Russian spy by some. We had arranged to call by post, and were met at the door by his son with a pointed red beard and dressed so that one would have recognized him as coming from eastern Europe. He led us upstairs to meet his father, whose appearance was dramatic, and I felt must have been studied. Dressed in a light-coloured silk suit with blouse-like coat and knee breeches, he had a fine, white, spade beard, longer at each side than in the middle. He stood in the centre of a very dark room, looking, as John said, like some transparent figure. Our conversation ranged over many subjects: teaching, world affairs, religion, Tibetan mysteries, Trotsky. He seemed benign and most unlikely to be a spy. He was interested in telepathy and the feats of religious mystics, but most interested in peace and the preservation of culture in the world. Yet, there was something about him I don't understand. He calls himself H.E. Professor N. de Roerich. Why the H.E.? Banon says he gave himself the title and he is obviously attracted by titles in a way surprising for a philosopher. He gave us a pamphlet with two columns of things he has been called, mostly in American papers: The Messiah of Culture, the Teacher from White Summits, the Forerunner of the Era to Come, Apostle of World Unity, Prophet of Universal Beauty, and so on.

Yesterday we attended a local religious festival at a sacred hot spring, more enclosed than the one at Gangnani where bathed last year, and with a temple in which the village god is kept. The god of a village further down the valley had been brought up for a bathe in the hot spring, and we arrived as he was being addressed after his dip. There was still a goat to be sacrificed, a far more interminable procedure than sermons in Roughton Church. There was a great blowing of trumpets and beating of drums and smoking of incense and putting of flowers on the altar. The god was in the same sort of ark carried on two poles as the one we saw at Bhatwari last year, and again there was swaying of the ark from side to side, and when it touched a man the god was supposed to be holding conversation with him. Before the kid could be sacrificed, the god had to accept it, and this was shown, either by the kid shaking, or by one of the men touched by the ark crying out 'I accept the gift'. Everything was done to the poor kid to make it shake. It was covered with ashes, dipped in spring, had flowers stuffed into its ears, but it wouldn't shake—only bleated piteously. Two of the crowd became possessed and shook all over with violent trembling, but failed to utter the words of acceptance. The crowd was critical and humorous, shouting instructions and arguing with each other, much as the bridge-builders had done when we were last here. Gods are often treated with great familiarity in this part of the world apparently, being taken out and scolded when they fail to produce rain at the right time, or to stop it when there is too much. We left when, after about two hours of trumpet-blowing and possession by numbers of the crowd, the god had still declined to accept the sacrifice, and everyone was sitting down for a rest preparatory to starting the ceremony all over again in hopes of better luck.

18.8.38. *The Forest Rest House, Kulu (or Sultanpur).* These last few days have been a nightmare and I keep finding myself thinking that they can't really be happening, and that I shall wake up. The afternoon before we were to leave John and I went for a walk in the woods to do some glissading down a steep bank I had found, and had already had good fun on. I went down first, fast because it had been raining hard, and John followed. On his way he slipped and sat down, and got up at the bottom rubbing his backside. We both laughed, thinking he had taken a hardish bump, when suddenly he turned very white and I saw blood pouring from his shorts. A stone, or something, had slit his thigh, making a gash six inches long and very deep. I bound it with my handkerchief and helped him to a bungalow 400 yards away where the Gilberts were staying.

We sent for the local doctor, and he stitched up the wound. We asked whether to fetch the Civil Surgeon from here, but he was so sure that it wasn't necessary that we didn't. Two days later John's temperature rose to 104, so I shot off here for the C.S., an Englishman. He came back with me and stayed the night after deciding that the wound would have to be opened to drain, and that John should be moved here under his care for dressings, etc. The next day he was brought down in the Gilberts' car, but was too weak for operation, so that was done yesterday. He wouldn't go under the anaesthetic for an awful time and I had to take over from the old compounder and go on squeezing away at the bulb. His temperature has now come down, and the doctor is satisfied that things are going all right, but his dressings are an awful torture to him and he is delirious off and on. There is no trained nurse, so I'm getting handy with bed-pans and blanket baths.

5
KATHIAWAR AND THE SOUTH

In January 1939 Gibson was invited as a state guest to the Maharaja of Mysore's annual Keddah or elephant-catching expedition, a doubly important event since the Viceroy was to be the chief guest. The trip was also to result in visits to some other princely states whose wards were Doon students. It was the twilight of princely India and Gibson was to witness all the pomp, panoply and protocol which were about to pass into history. The trip was amply facilitated by a legacy of £500 left by an aunt just before he embarked on it.

Limdi in Kathiawar was one of the stops where Gibson had an occasion to go for blackbuck shooting from a car. There was a detour to Rajkot to visit former colleagues at the Rajkumar College, an institution for Saurashtra princes. Then he was a guest of the Porbandar ruler, visiting salt works among other sights. On arrival in Bangalore, capital of Mysore state, he was taken under his wing by the Dewan Sir Mirza Ismail and wryly observed: "All efforts concentrated on making a success of the Viceroy's visit, and there is a vast amount of window-dressing."

At the Keddah he was placed next to the Maharaja of Bikaner and also came to know Ivor Jehu, who was to quit as the last British editor of 'The Times of India' in 1950. After visiting Seringapatam, associated with the exploits of Tipu Sultan, Gibson returned to Doon

School taking in Cochin and Goa. Barely two years in India and he had covered quite a ground.

9.9.38. *The Doon School.* John was so much better at the end of August that I could leave him in charge of his bearer with the doctor visiting him twice a day. The drive back was very hot. At a fair at Saharanpur I bought some very attractive wooden bowls for only a few annas each and they will make really large and useful ash trays into which you can knock out a pipe.

28.9.38. *The Doon School.* If only public opinion had been better informed and people had determined to stand for justice—both revision of the Peace Treaty and opposition to Japan's aggression—then I think there would have been less likelihood of the war that now seems to be coming. It would be ironic if I had to fight to support an imperialism with which I am not in sympathy, so I bury my head in a sand of jobs to do here.

14.10.38 *The Doon School.* I think my geography is now going fairly well. I have got the boys used to looking things up for themselves in books in the library. Some of them have a genuine regard for the West, but I don't suppose any of them like being controlled by us. The reason they support us is that when British control is removed the reactionary states will disappear faster than the kings in Europe after the French Revolution; and the newspapers mislead the public with stories of loyalty to the empire.

I'm coaching football this term, there being no one better available. The Indian boy hasn't as much 'go' as an English boy, and I'm concentrating on improving this—getting them to get to the ball first instead of waiting for it to come to them, and to conquer natural reactions like turning their backs in a charge.

The house garden is gradually taking shape—sweet peas up already. Some of the boys have grown very keen while others have dropped out. I have a member of the Board of Governors coming to see me this afternoon to look at my servants' quarters. They are a disgrace: a tiny room without chimney or glazed window: eight feet square for a family. Foot has tried to get the Governors to do something about this, but when he brings it up they say: 'It is what is customary'. I'm determined to get them improved or to send in my resignation.

7.11.38 The Doon School. We have had a meeting of local schoolmasters here to discuss the possibility of forming an Assistant Masters' Association. They were all quite keen on the idea as long as it involved tea parties and they didn't have to pay anything or do anything. We could all talk and understand English, but because of the spirit of nationalism that is everywhere, some of them spoke in Urdu or Hindi which had to be solemnly translated into English for the benefit of the South Indians and people like me.

I took some boys in the car to Nahan last Sunday over the most awful roads. I knocked the front bumper off on a boulder and stuck in the middle of a ford with the exhaust pipe under water, but the old Buick stood up to it well. The great thrill was being ferried across the Jumna. Driving onto the ferry there were only about six inches of spare between the wheels and the unrailed sides of the boat onto which you drove along planks laid at the correct breadth of the car. Men go across on buffalo skins blown tight and looking like prehistoric monsters.

I'm pleased with the football team which has won seven out of eight matches.

6.11.38. From my aunt Catherine. Before I forget, do note that soar means to move upwards like an eagle. Sore means tender, afflicted in some way; viz. sore throat. Do you teach the English language? Doesn't spelling matter?

25.11.38 The Doon School. It is wonderful that Aunt Maude has left me £500. I haven't met her since Cambridge days when I went over occasionally and she gave me a tumbler of port to drink with lunch. This will make it possible for me to come to you next summer. The other excitement is that I have been invited as a State Guest to Mysore for the Keddah in January through the kindness of Colonel C.O. Harvey who wrote to the Dewan or Prime Minister, Sir Mirza Ismail, about me. You remember the film *Elephant Boy*—well this will be the real and actual thing: a drive of elephants into a stockade in the jungle, and then taming them. The Viceroy will be there and there will be a State

Banquet and all that sort of thing. It ought to be a terrific experience. Aunt Maude's legacy will again come in very useful for the journey.

16.12.38 *The Doon School.* This afternoon I'm riding out to a village called Tunwalla where we have started helping in Rural Reconstruction work. Some of the boys who had finished their exams went out last night and are camping there and starting to dig a tank to hold water for the villagers for three weeks.

On Boxing day John and I are off to Limbdi in Kathiawar for the duck shoot we missed last year. From there I hope to sail down the west coast to Cochin, and so to Mysore. I am greatly looking forward to Jill's arrival and am so glad she has someone to come out with. I advise her to wear an engagement ring so that she won't be mistaken for a member of the fishing fleet.

2.1.39 *The Guest House, Limbdi.* John and I have spent two days in the train, mostly going through desert before we arrived here. Passing through Rajputana you would catch glimpses, every now and then, of a hill with a fort on top commanding the barren plain. Where water was available there was cultivation. Kathiawar is very flat, but much more fertile than Rajputana, and there are acres and acres of cotton fields, and here and there a certain amount of wheat. We arrived here on the morning of the 28th December and were whisked off to the Guest House which is very comfortable with marble bathrooms and so on, and we have been kept going with a continual round of entertainment ever since. On the 29th we were taken round Limbdi town, and called on the Thakur Sahib in the morning. The town has a fine main street at the head of which is the old palace, now used as the secretariat. On the way there we passed a row of palaces belonging to members of the ruling family. They are about the size of a medium country house in England and interior decoration varies from Victorian marble effects to up-to-date chromium furnishings. The Thakur Sahib, who celebrated his silver jubilee two years ago, is a fine and benevolent old gentleman. He received us in his study, a little room lined with Hindu literature, and he talked to us about his visits to England. This morning he called on us here and told us of his hopes to visit Norway this summer to see the midnight sun. His sons are the Yuvraj, whose guests we are, Pratap Sinhji, the father of two boys in John's house, Fateh Sinhji, and

Ghanshyam Sinhji, the guardian of a boy in my house. We are looked after by Captain Rana, A.D.C. to the Yuvraj, a first-class fellow. In the afternoon Rana and the boys took us for a drive round Limbdi State which has an area of about 400 square miles. There are no perennial rivers and the water in the wells is usually brackish, so they have to rely on what they collect in tanks during the monsoon. We shot duck at one of these. Villagers waded into the water to put up the duck and we shot them as they came back to settle again. We also had some shooting at partridge and sand–grouse in the fields. The next morning Ghanshyam took us before breakfast after blackbuck. In this part of the world they shoot these with guns from a car. I thought this sounded unsporting, but it isn't so easy. The blackbuck feed on the grassy plains where it is too dry for cultivation, and you pick out one and chase it, having to shoot it while going at 40 to 50 m.p.h. I found it very exciting. We stopped for breakfast beside a creek and I had a shot with a rifle at a young crocodile sunning itself on the opposite bank, but missed. In the afternoon we had tea with Pratap Sinhji off a very lovely silver set hand-beaten here in the bazaar. After that Ghanshyam took us up in his autogiro and I took photos of Limbdi from the air.

The next day we went off to the Yuvraj's country house, having been joined by some people called Brett, and we had a great shoot of a stretch of water of 40 square miles called the Nal. This, with its reeds and cuts and dykes was very like a Norfolk broad. The reflections were wonderful and there was every sort of bird: flamingoes, pelican, storks, redshank and snipe.

I liked the Bretts. He had been here seven years ago and had remarked before he came that he hoped Limbdi wasn't too uncivilized. They sent him a telegram before he arrived saying 'Bring bromo' and met him at the station which is some way out of the town. He was led off on a camel to a mud village and dumped in a dusty shack which he was told was the Guest House. Ghanshyam had dressed up as the chowkidar, and brought him his tea, stirring it with his finger.

4.1.39. *Porbandar.* We arrived here last night after a dusty and bumpy drive of about 200 miles, calling on the way to Rajkot to see the Barrits and Sprawson who were at the Doon School before they came there to the Chiefs' College. The Thakur of Rajkot was not a good ruler, so this was a good state for making trouble, partly engineered by members of Congress from British India. The Thakur was forced to accept a popular government, and they are now trying to achieve the same in Limbdi. Perhaps we are seeing the end of an era: people with three, four or more cars, luxurious houses, servants galore, whisky on silver trays in the middle of the forest, country houses with fountains and swimming pools, illuminations, rifles, guns and cartridges at one's disposal; mud villages, but on the whole happy-looking villagers, Congress agitators, mostly college students—it's all a great experience. I have been trying to see as much as I can of the life of the people. Though dusty, some of the villages are very clean and well kept, while a few are dilapidated. The peasants look better fed than those in the Doon. If there was more water the country would be very rich, and as it is, large parts of it produce good crops of cotton, wheat and millets. The villages have schools and dispensaries, and there was a fine hospital at Limbdi, but dirty inside.

Here in Porbandar, everything is on a larger scale as the state draws wealth from its port and from famous quarries as well as the land. On New Year's Eve in Limbdi the villagers had danced for us. They were great fun, very graceful and in picturesque clothing. Some of the dances, with jumps and kicks, reminded me of Russian folk dancing. The people are very attractive-looking. The men have longish hair with side curls and bright waistcoats, and look like Gilbert and Sullivan pirates. The women wear little waistcoats that cover the breasts but leave the stomach open. If they are young and good-looking this is very alluring.

We got to Porbandar in the evening and were given one of the villas for guests overlooking the sea. The Guest Master was a Parsee with the most perfect Court Chamberlain manner.

6.1.39. The next morning we called on H.H. the Maharaja and were then driven round to see the city and port. The latter had Arab dhows lying in the creek, and bales of salt and groundnuts on the wharves. There is no deep anchorage and big ships have to lie about a mile off shore and loaded by tender. I had hoped to sail to Bombay from here, but there is no ship available, so I fly this afternoon. In the evening we went to try to shoot a panther, but neither that night nor last night did one come to its kill.

Yesterday morning we visited the salt works and saw all the processes from panning to crushing. Then we went to see a coconut plantation that looked like a picture from the South Sea Island, and so on to lunch with H.H. after a visit to the school where they were learning English by the direct method and starting geography with their immediate surroundings, in the most up-to-date and approved methods. The palace had all the big stuff: fountain in the hall, silver dinner service, silver chairs for sixty guests, and H.H. was charming. He has planned all his buildings and the architecture is excellent. He is also a musician who composes western music, and he captained the first Indian cricket team to visit England. From what I saw, I should think he is also a very good ruler. He plays a round of golf at 7'o clock every morning, and any of his subjects who wish to see him come up and speak to him on the course. I asked him what happened when he was addressing the ball, and he said he was used to it. He sees people at the palace from 10 to 11, and is in his office from 11 to 1.30 every day. He had a long minority rule, and I wonder how much the English influence during this period has to do with his being such a model ruler.

In the afternoon we visited the quarries which have long been famous, but are now being hit by competition from reinforced concrete. The stone is an attractive off-white limestone, almost cream, and we watched them splitting it, the exact sized blocks required, with hatchets. Then we went on to H.H.'s country house, a gem, with fountains and greenery that contrasted with the dry hills around. Finally we sat for the panther that didn't come.

This morning we went over the men's and women's hospitals, and the gaol: the former the last word in operating tables, X-ray apparatus, and sterilization plant, and the latter very clean with prisoners looking healthy and at work cooking, and making clothes and carpets. Must stop. Plane off in half an hour. This letter has cost me a sea bathe!

10.1.39. *Mysore.* The best part of the flight was across the Gulf of Cambay and down the coast from Bhavnagar to Bombay. The river mouths, the boats lying on their sides on the sands, the hills rising steeply from the coastal plain, the sinking sun shining on the sea, and the groves of palm trees where all in the best purple passage vein. In Bombay Jack met me and took me out for the night to the Jackal Club, the headquarters of the Bombay Hunt. The next morning we got up at

5.30, and, in the breeches of a man with an even larger backside than mine and boots just too long, I went off with four others on an early morning hunt. We didn't get much of a run, but I have not enjoyed anything before quite like the hounds working across hillocks silhouetted against the rising sun. Part of the going was very rough and steep, and I was glad that the only place we had to go fast was down below where it was fun to canter over the paddy fields and bunds dividing them.

I left Bombay on the afternoon of the 7th and arrived in Bangalore the evening on the next day. It's not easy to tell you about Bangalore and Mysore yet, as I've seen so much and my ideas aren't clear: gaols, hospitals, factories, reservoirs; but today I had as interesting an experience as I shall ever have—the opportunity to see benevolent despotism at work at close quarters. The Dewan, Sir Mirza Ismail, with whom I am staying, took me in his car with him on a tour of inspection from Bangalore to Mysore. Also in the car were officials with note books open to take down instructions which were frequent and much to the point. He has an amazing eye for detail; for instance he spotted a sign-board where the post had been painted as far up as the board, but left unpainted behind the board. Instruction: 'That sort of thing is inefficient—to be remedied'.

13.1.39 The State is very go-ahead, very well organized and the people seem satisfied. The factories I have seen all seem well run: electrical engineering shops, soap factories, silk manufacture, and sandalwood oil refineries. There are purification plants for drinking water for the towns, and the roads are up to western standards. In Bangalore I met a most interesting Polish Jew who runs the state electrical engineering institute. He has gone eastern in dress and philosophy, and though involved in it, doesn't fully approve of all this westernization. There are snags in all simplifications, but sentimentally I do like handicrafts and rural life, rather than machinery and cities, and there is little doubt that the west has become too complicated and unreal. I think that one can be happier on a horse than in a car, at a play than in the average cinema, making things oneself rather than turning handles; but I suppose it's impossible to reverse the way life seems to be going even if we are to arrive at a sort of insect fascist world.

Porbandar gaol was clean, but the prisoners still wore iron fetters on their legs, which I didn't see in Bangalore where they were allowed pocket money and where the only complaint the Superintendent had was that there weren't enough 'lifers', so they couldn't turn out carpets quickly enough to fulfil orders.

All efforts are concentrated on making a success of the Viceroy's visit, and there is a vast amount of window-dressing. I wonder if any Viceroy ever sees India as it really is; but the occasion does serve as a spur to the completion of projects that might otherwise hang fire in the way things do in this country. On the way here, Sir Mirza ordered all the walls to be washed in grey or brown instead of glaring white that was being used. The workmen involved must have cursed, but it will certainly be an improvement. Such is power.

I have before me a Programme of the Visit. Every movement and its exact timing is laid down, with lists of those who will be present at each place, the number of cars to be provided, who will sit in them and the spaces to be preserved between them and the accompanying troops of Lancers and Bodyguard, and the exact route to be followed. For your edification I give a few extracts. 'Lunch will be served for the Viceregal party and the Dewan in a pandal near the Rural Welfare Centre at 12:30 p.m. Lunch for the maids and valet and the Viceregal Staff will be served in the train...The procession route will be closed to traffic by the City Police from 4 p.m. to 7 p.m.... In the middle of the platform will be an ornamental pavilion for the reception of His Excellency the Viceroy by His Highness the Maharaja. On the platform to the south will assemble the invited officers of the State and the leading citizens and merchants of Mysore (List IV). The principal sirdars and officers who are to be presented (List V) to His Excellency the Viceroy will take up a position behind His Highness the Maharaja and in a line with Hon'ble the Resident's staff. Durbar uniform will be worn by all officers entitled to wear it. Europeans not entitled to it will appear in morning dress with decorations...at 10.30 a.m. His Excellency the Viceroy will receive a visit from His Highness the Maharaja...On alighting from his car. His Highness the Maharaja will be met by the Hon'ble the Resident in Mysore and an A.D.C. to his Excellency, who with the deputation, will lead His Highness up the stairs. The Political Secretary will receive his Highness the Maharaja at the head of the stairs and conduct him to the Ball Room, which will have been arranged as a Reception Room by the Toshakhana officer accompanying His Excellency the Viceroy. Two golden chairs will be placed on a golden carpet at the eastern end with lines of chairs running east and west on either side of the room, those on the south for the Staff of His Excellency the Viceroy, and those on the north for the retinue of His Highness the Maharaja. His Excellency will receive His Highness the Maharaja within the Reception Room at a distance of one pace from the threshold, and will conduct His Highness the Maharaja to a seat at his right hand…A salute of 21 guns will be fired from the Palace Battery on His Highness's arrival at and departure from Lalitha Mahal…At 11.30 a.m. on the same day, His Excellency the Viceroy will return the visit of His Highness the Maharajah at the Palace…His Excellency will leave Lalitha Mahal by motor car at 11.20 a.m. under a Royal Salute of 31 guns fired from the Palace Battery…His Highness the Maharaja accompanied by His Highness the Yuvaraja, the Yuvaraj Kumar and the Hon'ble the Resident in Mysore, will receive His Excellency the Viceroy as His Excellency alights from the car at the steps of Kalyan Mantap inside the Courtyard of the Palace and will conduct His Excellency to the Reception Room in the Amba Vilas Hall and to a seat at His Highness the Maharaja's right hand…After a short conversation Captain Rajkumar C. Desaraj Urs, the Dewan and the principal sirdars and officers will be presented to His Excellency by the Hon'ble the Resident and at the time of presentation to His Excellency the Sirdars and Indian Officers will offer nazars of five gold mohurs each, which will be touched and remitted.' And so it goes on for thirteen pages.

Yesterday Eagleton, the professor of English at the University here, and I were driven round the country. We visited Seringapatam where we saw the Fort, Sultan Tippu's Summer palace, his tomb, Scott's Bungalow, and various temples and mosques. Tippu lies with his father Hydar Ali in a magnificent Gumbaz where funeral dirges are still played every day. The walls of the Summer Palace are decorated with paintings, some of which show his defeat of the British. You would have been amused by one picture of a water-carrier emptying his skin of water over the exploding powder store, while the British general looked on with his finger in his mouth, obviously not sure what to do about it. The Hindu temple at Somnathpur is now unused, so one can go right into and round it. It struck me as being over decorated at first, and a bit fussy, but the perfection of detail is astonishing. Except for the floor, I don't think there was a square inch either inside or outside, and it is a large temple, that was not intricately carved.

Last night I dined with the Todhunters—he is Private Secretary to the Maharaja. You will be amused that I keep being told that I look like G. VI. Today the Viceroy arrives and there is the State Banquet, and tomorrow the elephants.

17.1.39. *Mysore.* The reception of the Viceroy was very grand, and the procession of lancers and gilded and silver carriages drawn by beautiful stepping horses that all it should have been. In the evening, there was the State Banquet and we were all introduced to their E's, and I had a short conversation with H.H. after the dinner. I also met a number of other interesting people, and danced with Linlithgow daughters. I couldn't go to the ceremonial visits and return visits the next morning as I have no morning dress. I wish I had known that I should be asked to go as it would have been very interesting to have witnessed the traditional ceremonial. However I went to watch the fire-crossing ceremony at the palace in the evening. For this the villagers from around bring their cattle and drive them across lanes of fire, straw burning in trenches: a religious ceremony of cleansing. I think almost the most astonishing sight I have ever seen was the palace lit up with what were said to be 80,000 bulbs outlining the domes and turrets and gateway: a fairyland picture. After the fire-crossing we went to the Brindavan Gardens for a display of fireworks, and dinner and dancing at the Sports Club. The gardens are below a dam at a great reservoir and have hundreds of fountains kept playing by the weight of the water behind the dam, many coloured by electric bulbs from underneath.

The next day we went out to camp in the jungle for the Keddah. I was driven by Sir Mirza with a Mr. Jehu of the *Times of India* whom I thought very good value. Though there were tents in the camp, it wasn't my idea of camping. Their E's had long baths with hot and cold laid on, and even the small fry like myself had comfortable beds with spring mattresses. In the afternoon we watched an elephant drive. One herd had already been driven into the stockade, and as they didn't want to capture any more, this lot was simply driven past us to show how it was done. We were along the high bank of the river and the herd was driven down the opposite bank, up the river past us, and then back into the jungle. We were behind palisades of bamboo and had to speak in whispers so as not to attract the attention of the elephants. First you heard the shouting of the beaters in the distance in the jungle gradually growing louder and nearer. The tree-tops were shaken by monkeys fleeing from the beat; and H.H. Bikaner, who was next to me, got very excited and told everyone to keep their heads down. Then there was a volley of shooting and we were afraid that the wild elephants had broken the line of the tame ones driving them. Suddenly, about 300 yards away from us the herd plunged into the river from the opposite bank. They tried to cross and get up our side, but were prevented by having rockets and buck-shot fired at them, so they turned up the river and came right past us within 30 or 40 yards, a herd of about 50 and a wonderful sight. They were all sizes from tiny babies to a huge tusker. The babies were lifted and helped and pushed along, and it was a fine sight when the big elephants heaved themselves out of the deeper water over submerged rocks.

Yesterday, with intervals for refreshment, we spent all day watching the roping in the stockade. The captured herd was in a stockade several acres in extent and surrounded by a great ditch and wooden pillars. Four or five men on tame elephants would ride into this stockade and drive the herd towards the roping stockade, and when three or four of them had been driven into this, the gate was lowered. It may sound easy, but it wasn't. You should have seen them breaking away and heard them trumpeting. Next came the excitement of roping the wild elephants, of their attempts to escape from the stockade, and their struggle with the ropes. Tame elephants with mahouts on them were let into the stockade and these separated one of the wild elephants and pushed it where they wanted it, while the mahouts tried to slip ropes over its head, and men on their feet came into the stockade through gaps in its pillars and, sheltering behind, between and under the legs of the tame elephants, somehow got ropes round the legs of the wild ones. How they did it without getting hurt I don't know. Once roped, the wild elephants strain and heave to get free. We saw two ropes broken—great applause!—but once tied with several they are pulled and pushed by the tame elephants along a barricaded way to the river to wash themselves, and then they are moved to the jungle where they are tethered by the legs and the process of taming begins.

It's now time for breakfast, and then I return to Bangalore and go on to Cochin from where I hope to go by sea to Bombay, and so home.

19.1.39. *Mangalore.* This is a marvellous part of the world. I left Bangalore on the 17th evening and woke up yesterday morning in a different country, having crossed the Western Ghats through the Palghat Gap. The Malabar coast is spread with coconut trees with their graceful slant and green tops against a blue sky, with paddy fields, either with the second harvest since last rains being reaped, or the third crop a vivid green; with patches of water covered with water-lilies or backwaters with narrow high-prowed boats being sailed with square sails or punted along. Why is it that quanting is one of the most graceful movements? Most of them are very handsome, with beautiful features. They are very dark and the men seldom wear anything above the waist, nor many of the women either. They all seem to move with great grace.

When I got to Cochin I found no ship to be had, but I'm very glad to have seen the place. It is being developed as a first-class harbour and port. Many buildings in the town have a pleasant Dutch style of architecture, and there is a Jewish Synagogue belonging to a community that settled there in 70 A.D., and the church in which Vasco da Gama was first buried. I spent yesterday looking round and had dinner in the local hotel. Since early this morning I've been in the train, passing through scenery that prevented me sleeping. Tomorrow I go aboard a ship for Bombay.

Later, I have fallen in with a person from Naini Tal, an interesting and good fellow named Howard. It is curious how parsons are so often true to type in curious little ways. He has a canon's tummy and a rather parsonic voice, but is very human, and though over fifty looks much younger. We went round Mangalore together this evening and visited the tile factory. After being broken and mixed, the clay came out of the machine looking like a great filament of toothpaste, and then had the firm's mark stamped on it.

21.1.39. *Goa.* The more I see of this part of the world, the more I like it. Howard and I spent a comfortable night at the Mangalore Club, and set out before dawn the next day for a sail up the river. You know what it is like: the noises of the water and the sway of the boat, the reddening sky and then the silver water as the sun gets up. Add to these, palm trees outlined against the sky or water, and boats with square sails or boats being quanted by men whose grace of movement is unblurred by flapping clothing, and you may have some idea of what it was like.

We were aboard the steamer by 8.30, and the voyage up the coast took till early this morning. Yesterday we called at several little ports, lying off shore while boats brought out passengers and merchandise which were loaded into the ship. I had two enjoyable bathes, diving off the side, which must be the highest I've ever done, but seemed much easier into the sea than into a restricted swimming bath. The long-shore sailors who manned the boats all looked so healthy and happy, quite different from the natives of the plains. The agility with which they climbed the rigging and the song they sang as they handled the cargo or pulled on the oars were all such fun.

We decided to stay here for a night as there is another steamer to Bombay tomorrow, and it seemed too good an opportunity to see Goa to miss. We landed at Marmagao and came round here to Panjim by car through country similar to that I have already described, and I saw men climbing coconut trees for the first time. They do this with a rope round them and the tree, and as they go up their movements are like a knees-bending exercise.

Old Goa is now almost deserted owing to malaria, but has three splendid sixteenth and early seventeenth century churches and some great monasteries all kept going by a few priests. One of the churches contains the tomb of St. Francis Xavier, a silver coffin and stand in late Renaissance tailing into Baroque, on a marble and gilt plinth. His body, except for an arm which is in Rome, is exposed to the public every 12 years, and his shrine is visited by many pilgrims whose offerings, I take it, help to keep these deserted churches in repair. They have magnificent carved and gilt reredoses from floor to very high ceiling. There were also fine chandeliers and seventeenth-century paintings of early evangelists in India being martyred: interest enough for a long stay, but we were only able to get a general impression. The Baroque architecture of the many churches in and around Goa seems to fit excellently with the landscape. Panjim is modern Goa, and quite attractive. Old Goa tells the story of the ravages of heat and malaria: great churches and a cathedral with only a handful of priests to say or hear Mass; huge monasteries emptied of their monks and nuns; great colleges falling into ruins. It had a curious melancholy atmosphere.

30.1.39. *The Doon School.* Here I am back again, and term starts tomorrow. The voyage to Bombay was along a shore less beautiful than it had been further south, but here and there we passed islands fortified with huge walls all round, the strongholds of the Mahrattas, and looking very suitable for the back scene of some pirate romance. Jack gave me lunch in the Yacht Club in Bombay and I came on here that evening.

6

WAR IN EUROPE

With the Second World War looming, Gibson's sister Jill arrived in India on a holiday in early 1939. It was a largely uneventful year with usual runs up to neighbouring hills and lakes – and an expedition to explore the vertical caves near the mountain resort of Chakrata. Fencing was another of his passions which was coming to the fore. Gibson was also getting involved in some useful projects. One of these related to improving the educational and moral level of the school servants through an Adult Education Society. The other was the school student's adoption of a nearby village of Tunwalla to carry out various projects beneficial to the people. The efforts ranged from the screening of educative lantern slides to showing the villagers how to prepare compost. With the War coming and consequently the hopes of Indians rising in terms of getting rid of the British, Gibson was not oblivious to the sentiment and had some pragmatic comments to make on what the Indians really thought of the British. Gibson also took a vacation to England – his first since arrival in India. And seems to have found a lady love while there since his sister wrote to him soon after, suggesting he should invite Friede over.

[Early in February my sister Jill arrived at the Doon School to stay with me. I was able to leave it to her to report home, and I quote from some of her letters, preserved, like mine, by our mother.]

15.2.39. *From Jill at the Doon School.* I have learned to drive Jack's car. He drives at terrific speed, and I'm really rather terrified, but he hasn't killed anyone yet. He says that I'm to do all the letter-writing now that I'm here.

22.2.39. People are continually calling at the bungalow: Chinamen, Tibetans, men from Kashmir. They come with enormous parcels on their bicycles and spread their wares on the veranda.

28.3.39. Yesterday being Sunday, Jack planned one of his expeditions for boys. We took four and went to visit the parents of one of them at Patiala, about 160 miles away. We started at 7 a.m. and cooked breakfast on a primus on the way: scrambled eggs, bread and butter, strawberries and cream, and ginger beer! After crossing the Timli Pass over the Siwaliks, the drive was through the plains. The road was tarred most of the way, but only in the centre so when we passed anything we had to get off onto the dust and mud at the side. The trees which shade the road were just coming into leaf, and there were mango trees in blossom with a very heavy scent. After lunch in Patiala we went round an old fort, and saw the place where the Maharaja keeps his concubines. The last, who died last year, had over 200. They go into the building, and never show their faces outside again. Pretty ghastly! Our journey back took longer than planned owing to various mishaps. First the oil was found to have leaked and we had to get some off a bus driver, then we had a puncture, and then something went wrong with petrol flow. We got back at 10 p.m. all pretty tired.

27.4.39. The inspectors were pleased with Jack's work. They wrote 'Geography is very well taught in this school' so he is happy. His map of India goes on, and we went to find out about wood pulp the other day, to fill the spaces between the contour layers and build up the peaks of the Himalayas.

[I now return to extracts from my own letters.]

2.3.39. The Doon School. On Friday we went down the Jumna from Dhakpathar to the headworks of the Jumna canals on rafts—about 32 miles. It was at times exciting. At one place a mixture of cross winds and currents broke the lashing and I thought the raft would come to pieces, but it held together and was mended.

9.5.39. The Doon School. At a meeting of the Adult Education Society School Management Committee it was decided to carry out a literacy census of all the servants in one house as a test of how the work of the school, irregular attendance, classes whose members are of very different capacities, and other difficulties that have been experienced were discussed. It was decided to try to meet these by starting classes within houses to be held by boys, each boy taking one class a week. Apart from the work of its school, another problem the Adult Education Society is concerned about is how to encourage school servants to set aside part of their earnings as savings. At present there is a general exodus to the bazaars on pay day. We have also heard that some servants on the estate exact a tribute from others whom they claim to have helped to their posts. Finally there is the problem of indebtedness. The Society is considering whether it would be possible to start some form of co-operative savings bank, and some form of Servants' Club where they could meet when they have finished their work, instead of having to foregather in sometimes undesirable places in the bazaar.

On Saturday evening members of my house showed at Tunwalla lantern slides of different parts of the world. The lantern can be run off a car battery and is very handy for this sort of work. These pictures were followed by others showing how to avoid malaria and tuberculosis, and the evening finished with a display of physical training and tumbling which the villagers seemed to enjoy.

16.5.39. The Doon School. Last Saturday Hyderabad House gave the weekly entertainment at Tunwalla and performed a chemical play involving loud explosions which were a great success! The next morning they were up at 3 a.m., and dividing into groups, completed the digging of a compost pit by 8'o clock.

1.6.39. The Doon School. I'm in the process of booking a passage by K.L.M. Just think of it, I shall be home before the end of this month. You mustn't mind if I look a bit of a ghost. The hot weather always does that. I shall have to be back here about September 3rd.

[At the end of my time in England, John drove Jill and me across France to Marseilles, and from there he and I sailed to Bombay.]

3.9.39. P.W.D. Bungalow, Khalgat, by the Barbada. We got to Bombay just before Hitler marched on Poland, and left before we heard whether G. B. had declared war or not, so we don't know what is happening. It looked, however, as though war was certain, and I went to the Navy Office to enquire how to join, but they showed no interest whatever, and told me to get back to my job of teaching. We stayed in Bombay for two days while John's car was serviced for driving to Dehra Dun. Yesterday we set off. The first part is over bad roads, so we didn't do badly to cover 280 miles. The country was green and peaceful and it seemed out of tune to find bridges guarded and to be questioned to make sure that we weren't Germans. We didn't come across any difficulties from floods or swollen rivers till we were stopped this morning by the Narbada which has been up over the bridge for five days. Here we wait till it subsides, and if it does not we shall have to go back 100 miles and put the car on a train.

We have been for a walk and visited a Bhil village. They are the aboriginals of this part of India and some are handsome with clear-cut features and long black hair. They use bows and arrows to shoot small game and birds for food, and were very polite and pulled out a charpoy for us to sit on and made excuses for the shyness of their children who were afraid of us because the last Europeans they had seen had been doctors who inoculated them.

9.9.39. The Doon School. Safely back. We were delayed another day by the Chambal, and had no time to look at Gwalior or Agra. I shall try to get some sort of military training next holidays to fit myself for whatever I may be wanted for eventually.

22.9.39. *The Doon School.* It looks to me as though the war will be a long one, and the longer it lasts, the greater will be the change in ways of life at the end of it. I think we ought to frame our peace terms now. If we don't, and we win, we shall only have a repetition of the mistakes made at Versailles: terms neither generous nor possible to keep.

23.10.39. *The Doon School.* I have just returned from a weekend camp with 30 of my boys. We went by bus to the Timli Pass, unloaded our bicycles there, and descended the other side on them. I got a very clear idea of the difficulties of mechanised transport: punctures, broken chains, jammed brakes, and falls in all directions. If I hadn't been rather worried I would have laughed like anything. We arrived at the foot of a hill leading up to Khara Canal Bungalow, where we were to stay in the dark to find the road washed away. The buses which had followed us arrived with the beddings, cooking utensils and food, and we had to carry these up, only to find the bungalow locked when we got there. Then I found three boys missing, one of them the heir to Rampur who has joined us from Wellington and is very 'precious'. I organized a search party, but they turned up as we were setting out, and I have more or less decided never to go for a bicycling trip again.

My early enthusiasm to learn Urdu has evaporated under the strain of keeping up with my work. Running the school as a democracy takes a lot more energy than it would by efficient bureaucracy, and in spite of our ideals, democracy doesn't work perfectly as the boys don't take over enough responsibility—they think it means the right to criticize rather than the duty to carry on the government: and that seems to be true of Indians in general.

10.11.39. *The Doon School.* Elsie has gone sick, and I have had to combine the duties of schoolmaster and matron. I never want to have to check another week's washing: 96 handkerchiefs, 70 pyjamas, 60 sheets, 63 pillow cases, 70 bath towels, 300 kitchen cloths, etc. and now the head cook has become ill. I have bought a 1937 B.S.A. for Rs.425. It goes ten times as far to the gallon as the Old Buick which I keep for occasional picnics.

26.11.39. *The Doon School.* Last night I took a party of boys to Tunwalla. The villagers are interested in getting anything they can out of us, but the job is to get them to be interested in doing something more for themselves. What it amounts to is that we must rouse them to discontent with their present conditions, and that, of course, in the long run will make it more difficult for privileged people like ourselves to live in comfort dependent on people producing things while living at a very low standard. After a play and sing-song, Hunter Boyd organized a demonstration of compost making. The Chinese have been doing this for centuries, and H.B. thinks the future salvation of India lies in composting.

The energy that will be released when the war comes to an end, if it is a short one, may be turned to national reconstruction instead of being allowed to grow bitter in unemployment. I wonder what will happen to India and the capital invested in the country. I don't see how we can say that we are fighting for democracy and not be ready to grant it to India and the rest of the dependent Empire. It is obvious that India is not ready to govern itself well and also that a good deal of British influence is at work determined that it shall not become so. We have taken a lot out of the country, and put a lot into it, and I don't suppose it possible to draw a balance, but we must realise, and people at home must be made to realise, that our time as rulers is coming to an end if we are ready to apply to India the principles we claim as our right.

My ear has started to give trouble again and I plan to see a specialist in Lahore on the way back from Gulmarg next holidays. There is quite a large party of us going up to ski: Foot, John, about eleven boys and myself. It all seems a bit unreal, we going off to enjoy ourselves, and you contending with the problems of the war.

This afternoon I have started fencing again. Cricket has now started, so I shall get a bit more time to myself.

11.12.39. *The Doon School.* Roger Nicholson—I think I told Jill he had married in Naini—is just off to rejoin his regiment. I went to drinks with him and his wife on Saturday evening and stayed on to dinner. General Auchinleck was there and is said to be one of the coming men of the army. I found him most interesting. I have Eric Shipton and a friend coming to stay with me and use my bungalow while I am up in Gulmarg. They were in the Karakorams when they picked up the news of the war on their field wireless. They hurried back, but have found nothing important to do in India at present, and are working up maps on what they had been able to survey.

16.12.39. *The Doon School.* I have turned into a sort of general merchant and provide anything from warm underclothing to ski boots and rucksacks. I've just approved the menu for 'Golden Night': Tomato Soup, Fish and Mustard Sauce, Samosas, Roast Goose & Apple Sauce, Peas & Potatoes, Chicken Curry and Pilau, Vegetable Curry & Pilau, Cheese Souffle, Pakoris, Christmas Pudding & Whipped Cream, Fruit Salad, Dessert. We don't do so badly, but not most usually as well as this!

2.1.40. *The Doon School.* I'm back at the Doon School having taken a lot of hard exercise and feeling very fit. We had very little snow at Gulmarg which was most disappointing for the 13 boys and other beginners. Instead of gentle slopes and the easy runs through the woods we had to struggle up to 13,000 feet for snow and then found it lying at very steep angles uncomfortable to learn on. The boys hardly had a chance to realise what fun skiing can be, and only experienced it as a terrific sweat. However, one of them, who came last time, did very well and climbed to the top of Apharwat several time and came down under control—very creditable—and I think most of them enjoyed the holiday. John and I certainly did. I got some skating and went through most of the turns at an orange, but found myself more out of practice on ice than snow. We played ice hockey with brooms, sticks not being available, and four of us skated some simple combined figures.

14.1.40. *The Doon School.* Glennie, Biddle, Shipton, Mott, John and I have been on a visit to the caves in the limestone beyond Chakrata from where we walked 14 miles among the ridge-top to Bodia where there is a Forest Resthouse that we made our centre of operations. Half a mile away there is a group of caves which we spent two days exploring. There were galleries extending a long way underground, and we went down two posts of over 80 feet deep opening into caverns with passages running out of them. It was an eerie feeling, hanging onto a rope ladder in dark space faintly lit by a torch attached to one's forehead.

Then I went to Lahore to see Dr. Dick about my ear. Nothing wrong internally, but a big fungus infection on the drum. After seeing him I called on various parents, and then caught the evening train back here. I got the impression that most parents are only interested in their son's examination results as a step in the race of life, and that the general education we try to give here, though they render it lip service, cuts little ice with them unless their boys do well in the School Certificate and earn a piece of paper that will help them to get a job. This means that many boys leave at 15 or 16, and what we hope to do for them is only half completed. The trouble is the terrific scramble for the sort of job our parents want their boys to get, and the feeling that the sooner you can get into one, the safer you are. There is no tradition of staying at school till you are 18; the discipline of school life irks the average boy; and the average parent sees little point in it. It will be difficult to persuade people that there is, until there has been time for our old boys who have stayed on to show their mettle. Another impression that I got was that everything we do is taken very much for granted, the attitude being, 'Well, they wouldn't do it if they didn't get something out of it.' Only one boy thanked John and me for our efforts over Gulmarg.

2.2.40. *The Doon School.* The expedition to Rainka Lake was fun. While driving onto the ferry boat at Paonta, the boat, not properly made fast, pushed off into the river a bit and the back wheels of the Buick were left hanging over the stern with the car resting on its axle. It was a frightful job to get it onto the boat and one of the tyres burst in our efforts to do so. Eventually, having done so, and changed the wheel, we drove off into Nahan. We stayed the night at a little Rest House at a village called Kolar and the next morning drove about three miles up the bed of a dry river, and then set off on foot over a steep pass to get to the lake. We had engaged a porter to carry lunch and extra clothes and he looked rather weedy, and we had asked him whether he was really strong. He seemed determined to prove that he was a good deal better than any of us, and took us up over the ridge at a terrific pace. We climbed 2,000 feet in 40 minutes. The lake was different from what we had expected; very lovely but not so wild. There was a temple at one end with a number of sadhus living close by, and a fair ground where, at the end of the autumn harvest, the people from the hills around come and trade and dance for two days. The ground was covered with bits of the glass bangles the women wear, and there were great ovens at which you could imagine throngs of fair-goers refreshing themselves. The lake looked more African than Indian. Round it were palms and wild orange trees, and at its edges tall reeds. Its water was very dark and in it floated shoals of great black fish anything from one to three feet long rather the shape of a tench. There were mallard swimming about, but the lake is holy and shooting and fishing forbidden.

24.2.40. *The Doon School.* The old Buick was packed up. It broke down again, and although I loved it deeply, I felt it was too unreliable as well as frightfully expensive; so I have bought a second-hand Ford V 8 tourer, and am paying for it by monthly instalments. Monday was a holiday for Mohurram, so on Saturday we set off for Agra, four boys and I, in the Ford. It went very well, 70 m.p.h. with ease. We stopped that night at Meerut and saw the film of Edith Cavell. I think the Germans were within their rights to shoot her, though foolish to do so. If a woman does in war what a man would be shot for, I see no reason why she should escape the penalty on account of her sex. The next day we drove through the doab between the Ganges and the Jumna, irrigated with water from tube wells run by electricity generated by the falls on the Ganges canal. We inspected a tube well which much impressed the boys. In the afternoon we looked round the Fort at Agra, and in the evening the Taj Mahal.

The first view of the Taj through the gateway is astonishing, and then there isn't much more; but you don't need more—only to sit and look at it. Then we drove out to Fatehpur Sikri, deserted after 17 years occupation, and arrived in the dark. We got up at dawn and looked round, and I think it is the most wonderful thing I have seen built by man. All in red sandstone, except for a white marble tomb in one of the courtyards, its architecture is generally simple, though some of the carved decorations are superb. We came back by Delhi and visited Akbar's tomb at Sikandra, another very fine building. We passed through Muttra, where we are now told we ought to have visited the museum, but only saw a garish temple, and Brindaban, Lord Krishna's garden, now hot, full of flies and tiresome; through Delhi, where we didn't have time to stop, and so home.

8.4.40. *The Doon School.* Yesterday I went to the mela (fair) at Tapkeshwar, one of the holy places near here. There were thousands of people with roundabouts and all the fun, sweets cooking, and everybody enjoying themselves. There was the squalid side too: lepers waving their stumps of arms and other beggars. It must have been like that in Europe in the past.

12.4.40. *The Doon School.* We have just had our half-term break and I took about half my house—the rest went to scout camps or on Historical or Scientific Society expeditions—to the banks of the Ganges above Lachmanjhula. One day we drove up to Devaprayag, and on another boated, dragging the boat up the rapids, and then shooting them in it. It all seemed so far away from this bloody war. It seems to me more and more important that we should make a promise that can't be misunderstood to clear out of India as soon as we can. If we are really fighting for the ideals we claim it will be the end of the British Empire whether we win or lose. I don't know how many people feel ready for that, but if they don't they have no right to blame the Germans for their ambitions, even if they may criticise their methods of fulfilling them. If we are to hold India, we shall have to institute proceedings as repressive as those of the Nazis in their occupied territories, and I don't see that doubts as to what will happen to India without us are a moral justification for clinging on to it against its will. People in England don't have any conception of the bitterness of feeling against the English by the ordinary politically conscious Indian. Much of their feeling may be unreasonable, but sentiment often is, and it's there. All this too about the wonderful loyalty of the Princes is rot. They are kept in artificial positions of medieval grandeur by our protection, and of course they welcome our presence in the country.

24.4.40. *From my sister.* Why don't you write to Friede and ask her to come out to you? I liked her, Jack. You said that you wouldn't be able to give up enough time to looking after a wife, but a girl doesn't want to be with her husband all the time, and if she had children she would be satisfied. You'd still have the holidays together.

28.4.40. *The Doon School.* We have been having the Adult Education Society sports, and the boys all served their own supper and washed up. I enjoyed seeing the heir to Rampur working hard with a dish-cloth. This would have been impossible three years ago, and it really is rather encouraging.

21.6.40. *Rawalpindi.* I have been invited to Chitral by Set White [an officer of the 9th Gurkhas who was commanding the Chitral Scouts]. The term is now over and John, Holdy and I are at Rawalpindi on our way to Swat. I applied for training as a pilot, but was told I was too old and no one seems the least enthusiastic to make use of me, so I'm going off to climb and fish, and to get physically fitter.

[Set White already had Tenzing with him in Chitral and had asked me to bring Rinsing, who therefore came with us to Swat.]

7
SWAT-CHITRAL-GILGIT

In the summer of 1940 Gibson was invited by an army officer friend posted in the north-west frontier province of Chitral to spend time with him. This was an opportunity for him to not only visit remote outposts of the Empire, bordering Afghanistan and Russia, but also do a good amount of climbing in snow-bound regions there. He was prudent enough to take Tenzing's brother sherpa Rinsing with him. On many occasions he was a guest of the ruling tribal chiefs – as in Chitral itself since the ruler's brothers were his students. There was also a good amount of polo playing. Interestingly, in Gibson's letters one encounters places – Chakdara, Swat, Gilgit, Dir among others – which are merely names on the map for many Indians today, occasionally springing before their eyes in Press reports of Pakistan army skirmishes with militants.

24.6.40. *Mankial Village, Swat.* We motored up from Rawalpindi to Saidu, the capital of Swat, the day before yesterday. From Rawalpindi on there were bare hills and bearded men. The bridge over the Indus and the fort at Attock looked very romantic, and the road passed through many cantonments with names famous in frontier history. The drive over the Malakand was all that one expected of the NW Frontier. The fort and cantonment stand on the ridges and tops of gaunt dark hills with the road winding up from the plains and down to the Swat valley through bare, steep and forbidding country. The Swat valley, in contrast is green and fertile.

There is a different atmosphere in the valley from anything I have struck before. Many people have the hook nose and sharp features of the NW and a good number carry ancient rifles, and belts of cartridges slung across their shoulders. Dotted along the valley at intervals of about six miles are forts of wood, clay and stone: very romantic-looking, but no good against modern armaments. They have towers at each corner of square walls about 40 feet high and look splendidly forbidding on the top of some spur.

We arrived at Saidu for lunch and were welcomed by Ataullah Khan and the Waliad, the Ruler's eldest son. Swat was recognized as a State in 1916 when the tribesmen, among whom there had been continuous fighting before, came together under the rule of a chief who was given the title of Wali (or Ruler), though his people call him Badshah (or King). He is a fine-looking man and very capable, but apparently very autocratic and stern. Anyone who makes a nuisance of himself is shot. His son, the Waliad, is charming, and has built himself a very lovely house furnished in excellent taste. We bathed in marble bathrooms, in glaring contrast to the poverty outside. I don't know whether it is a comment on this, or just custom, but when we went out for a drive with him in the afternoon we were attended by two revolver bearers with belts stuffed full of ammunition, while there are always about six soldiers on sentry go round his house. Even we, as we walked up the valley, had to take a guard of four with rifles.

Yesterday we motored a further 35 miles up the valley to the end of the motor road, and then walked on some six miles to a village called Branial—a name that we were told is Sanskrit in origin, and like various ruins we have seen, a reminder of the Buddhists who 1,000 years ago lived in these parts. Today we have walked a further 13 miles, and tomorrow turn east, away from the main valley, towards a pass at the foot of Mankial, the mountain we hope to climb. I'm sitting on the roof of a house in the village. Shortly I shall go to sleep on it. The savour and the smoke rising from our cooking dinner, the roar of the river, and the comic opera soldiers make it difficult to realise what is going on at home.

25.6.40. We are encamped in the most perfect place about six miles and 2,500 feet above Mankial village. At one village they gave us maize bread: thick chapattis with a crust on the outside and soft inside: very good indeed. We walked up through pine and deodar and meadows with here and there a great bush of briar rose that scented the air all around. Here we have a crystal spring just below our tents and behind us a Gujar village from where we were supplied with bowls of most excellent lassi, rich and refreshing. Mankial peak is still behind a great cliff in the foreground and tomorrow we plan to reconnoitre, so shall have another night in this delightful spot.

26.6.40. We climbed between five and six thousand feet today through scented pine forests ringing with bird song, then through fields of iris, potentilla, anemone, saxifrage, primula and columbine well into the snowfields and glaciers with their windswept silences. We shall probably have to climb a very steep couloir onto the summit ridge which should then not be difficult. Tomorrow, with the help of Gujars, we shall carry a camp up about 3,500 feet, and then another 3,000 or so the next day. We were guided up today out of this valley and onto the snow by a Gujar who took us a quick and easy way we should never have found for ourselves. Although old, he went wonderfully, and with him came a youngster who played the flute. The party was completed by Rinsing and a guard with his rifle: another old man who seems to enjoy it all. We had two splendid glissades on the way down and, back in camp, were refreshed with more lassi, after which I had an ice-cold bathe.

The following week was spent by Gibson and company in climbing the Mankial peak.

9.7.40. *Lower Mess, Drosh, Chitral.* On return to Saidu Sherif we spent a day of comfort and then John and Holdy went off to Kashmir, while I set off to join Set White in Chitral. This involved a return to Malakand where I spent the afternoon and night of the 6th. Major Walshe lent me the account of the siege and relief of Chakdara by Winston Churchill: very interesting to read and follow on the spot. His long, well balanced sentences are always to the point and vividly expressed, and he has a fine eye for country and the interesting details of vegetation and animal life. At night we sat on the edge of the fort, looking down to where all the fighting had been, and hearing, now and then, a bugle call. A good deal of rubbish has been written and filmed of outposts of empire, but there is something about them when you get there.

On the 7th I left Malakand and had a very hot and long journey to Dir by Post Buses. At Chakdara, where there was a two hours' wait, I had a swim in the Swat River, and then for about 70 miles went on at an average speed of 10 m.p.h. in a bus crowded both inside and on the roof. Yesterday a Gurkha officer and I crossed the Lowari Pass over the Hindu Raj and out of Dir into Chitral which is lovely country. The valley down from the pass to the main valley of the Kunar River reminds me vividly of Switzerland, and I enjoyed the walk very much. From Ashret a lorry bumped me along to Drosh. This is a delightful place. After breakfast I motor on to Chitral.

11.7.40. *Chitral.* I am staying with the Lowises—he is A.P.A. [Assistant Political Agent], Chitral—and they are both very good fun. Tomorrow I go for two days to stay with H.H. the Mehtar, till Set White returns. The drive up here, through rather barren mountains, had wonderful views of Tirich Mir. I played my first game of polo the day I arrived, am playing again this evening, and have been practising before breakfast. I feel like a beginner at ice hockey: that I could hit the ball if I had more control of the direction in which I approach it. Last night we dined with the Mehtar. He is the eldest of fifteen brothers of whom two are at the Doon School, while he is about 40. In the old days rival brothers were all murdered, and one of the problems of the State is to find uses for these now. One is in the Air Force and another in the Army and the State is not rich enough for them all to live on it in the style to which they are used.

17.7.40. *Baronis.* H.H. and his Doon School brothers looked after me very well when I stayed with them. He used to be very active and a good polo player, but has become paralysed on one side of his body, and has turned his attention to religion and eating. He is a keen chess player, and though I managed to make him think once or twice, I wasn't up to his standard. On my return to Lowises, we set off up here. Our two days ride so far has been great fun. When we arrive at our destination the whole village turns out to welcome us and the band, usually two horns and two sets of drums, strikes up. Then the men dance. There is a good deal of work with arms and hands, and in those that I enjoy most, hopping and jumping and touching the toes in the air—very light and graceful.

19.7.40. *Bunt.* Yesterday we had a short ride to Roshun, and today came on here. I haven't been so contented and happy for a long time. The evening polo was followed by morakka: we all sat cross-legged around a square of rugs and ate pilao while there was music and dancing. An old man, slightly cracked, sang while he danced with sword and shield. There is a certain amount of insanity in these parts, but it seems very harmless. The polo ground here, lined with poplar trees outside its walls, is beautifully situated, and between the chuckers the boys of the village had a shooting competition with bows which shoot stones from a little pad held by two parallel bow-strings.

3.8.40. *Gupis, Gilgit Agency.* We stayed several days at Mastuj from where I last wrote, and then crossed into Gilgit. The usual pass is the Shendoah with a lake on top, but Set and John Edelman wanted to see the Chamar Khand so we went by that. We stayed four days at Pandour where the Chitral Scouts played the Gilgit Scouts at polo. There is a little lake enclosed between old moraines, and full of fish. Between polo matches we had great fun fishing and swimming there, and living on trout and the fruit of the valley. Tomorrow we start up the Yasin Valley and back into Chitral to visit some of the higher passes into Afghanistan.

4.8.40. *Yasin.* We had a grand game of polo yesterday. Afterwards we had supper with the Raja of Gupis who has a small octagonal one-roomed house with a platform outside, in the middle of an orchard. Two flutists and duffs (a soft drum) played very attractive music. Today we had a hot walk on here where we were met with a gift of enormous and luscious apricots from the Raja.

8.8.40. *Yarkhun Valley.* Yesterday we crossed the Thui Pass back into Chitral. On top of the pass (just under 15,000 feet) we were met by a postman with the mail for the Scouts and a letter for me from Jill. This ended 'I wonder whether this will find you in a military training camp or on top of a mountain'!

15.8.40. *Rosh Gol.* The crossing from Yarkhun into Turicko by the Bhangol Pass was shorter and easier than we expected. At Bhang, which we reached by one of those hanging bridges made of birch twigs across the Yarkhun River, the Scouts did some recruiting, and the villagers danced and sang folk songs in the evening. The next day we climbed steeply over rock boulders to a camp on grass beside a high summer village of shepherds. The shepherds, kindly and hospitable, gave me curd to drink from wooden bowls with wooden spoons that were very attractive in their simplicity.

We had an easy walk up to the pass the next day and I climbed a little peak to photograph the view. The descent from the Pass was the usual rock-hopping mixed with easier going. Another postman met us at Rich, at the foot of the pass. From Rich we walked down the Turicko Valley to Zhanglasht where we were welcomed by Muzaffar-ul-Mulk, H.H.'s second brother and Governor of the Province. There we spent our first rest day for some time and played polo by moonlight. I scored a goal with four successive hits down the field. One of the delicacies Muzaffar gave us to eat was young chuker caught by sparrow hawks. They were delicious. There were the usual singing and dancing, and especially good was the duck dance imitating a flight settling on water. Muzaffar has a story-teller who tells him stories in Persian every night until and after he has gone to sleep. From Zhanglasht we had a long walk including 3,000 feet of up and down into the Tirich Gol. On the flat top of the little pass, at over 11,000 feet, was a polo ground.

Today we have walked up Rosh Gol, a tributary of the Tirich Gol, and are on our way to climb the Kotgaz Pass across the Hindu Kush and on the boundary of Afghanistan. Russia will be only about fifty miles distant across the Wakhan, and Chinese Turkistan not far off. We came through fantastic scenery today: first a barren valley weathered to all colours and shapes, with earth pillars like some Walt Disney fairyland. Now we are on a delightful alp with silver birches, fresh springs, the smell of pines, and glimpses through the clouds of peaks up to 23,000 feet. John Edelman was recalled by telegram from Zhanglasht to rejoin his regiment as soon as possible. He left this morning intending to ride the 85 miles into Chitral in the day. He had been hoping for this and I liked him immensely. [He was killed shortly after arriving in North Africa.]

18.8.40. The day before yesterday we climbed up to 14,000 feet and camped in a windy, but otherwise perfect little valley with a green grass floor laced with rills of crystal clear water. Yesterday we started off on an overcast morning to climb the Kotgaz Pass. We toiled up it, partly on scree that slid back with every step you took, partly over ice in which we had to cut steps, and partly up rock that was so rotten that you had to take great care with every hand and foot hold. Set trod on a rock that looked as firm as a house and it went crashing down, but fortunately he stayed with us. The views were superb. The whole climb took us 11½ hours.

In the following week Gibson and company did some more climbing in the area, reaching ridges of up to 18,000 feet.

23.8.40. *Gokhir.* I cursed myself for having used up all my colour film—but it always happens like that. The local cobbler is making me a pair of sheepskin boots. I'm tired of my nailed battleships and my gym shoes are worn out. Tomorrow is our last day's walking, and the next day we ride into Chitral.

24.8.40. *Baronis.* A rather dull walk down here—anti-climax—but a postman has arrived with letters. In reply to my enquiry whether I could train as a pilot I am informed that I could lecture to those being trained. If I have to go on teaching I don't think I can do better work than at the Doon School.

8.9.40. *The Doon School.* A short letter to let you know that I'm safely back and the boys returning as I write. The journey was pretty beastly. Eric Shipton has gone as Consul General to Kashgar. Foot's speech to the boys on 'Loyalty' came into the hands of the police who concluded that the school must be a hotbed of disloyalty, and he has been asked to report any boy making seditious remarks. It's hard to comprehend such a lack of balance and sense of humour. The police cannot be unaware that millions of people in the country are saying the same things that Foot complained of, and can they suppose that these sentiments are not bound to be reflected in any school? How could you report to them a boy with youth's enthusiasms and radical outlook for expressing opinions which we may regret but which suppression will only inflame?

8
WARTIME IN INDIA

Those were the days when Gibson could boast of driving from Lahore to Doon School between lunch and dinner! The highlight of 1941 was the performance of 'Merchant of Venice' for which the Nawab of Rampur, whose son was at the school, lent some magnificent court apparel. It was also the year when Gibson went on a trip to Almora, part of the way on his motorcycle, visited the dance academy run by Uday Shankar in the company of Doon School art master Sudhir Khastgir, later to be an eminent Indian painter, and found time to meet a couple of western sadhus who had set up an ashram not far from the town. One of them gave him a copy of the 'Bhagvadgita' with his commentary, which Gibson found time to read. His foray into Hinduism was complete with visits to some hill temples in the neighbourhood and on the way back a detour for the Kumbh Mela in Allahabad.

22.9.40. *The Doon School.* The doctors have been fussing with my stomach and have now decided that I have had amoebic dysentery and have now got colitis, sprue, and an enlarged and barely working liver—nothing to worry about as the sprue has been caught in its early stage, and they say I should be quite O.K. in six weeks.

9.10.40 *The Doon School.* Though the British Government and its puppet in India were very clumsy in not getting the support of the Congress before declaring war on Germany, I think the Congress is now losing the respect of clear-thinking people. Of course there are still enormous numbers who follow it blindly, and they may make serious difficulties, but more and more Indians support the war effort and are ready to be more friendly with the British. The change of tone in this school even is remarkable. The boys in my house are subscribing more than twice what was suggested by the School Council to the local Spitfire fund.

We have just had an educational conference here. It was presided over by Mr. Sheshadri, Principal of Government College, Ajmer, an outstanding person. His speech opening the conference dealt very well with the chief problems of teaching in India: low pay and bad conditions of services for teachers, inadequate teachers, poor discipline, and the hold of politics over students. He is a Madrasi, but looked like an ancient Greek. I presided over the Geography section and we had some lively discussions. Too much time was wasted in moving votes of welcome, thanks and farewell. Indians love making speeches.

5.11.40. *The Doon School*. M. N. Roy spoke to the Crickets (John's society for discussions round the hearth) last night and then dined. He is a communist with a worldwide reputation, and knows Germany, Russia, and China well. He has just been expelled from the Congress for supporting the war against the Nazis. He dislikes being looked on as a supporter of the British in India because he supports the war effort. What a muddle everything is in. Nehru supported the war until we would not grant Congress demands, and his arrest is likely to rally people to the party just when it was losing popular support.

30.11.40. *The Doon School.* We have now entered on a policy of wholesale repression of the Congress. It's not easy to see how this could have been avoided. The Congress attracts all those young Indians with vague but enthusiastic ideas of a united and free India. The Government dare not give them the control that their numbers in a democracy justify for it fears British interests will not be properly looked after.

20.12.40. *The Doon School.* We had an exciting experience in the forest the other day. We were shooting jungle fowl and were in fairly thick stuff with little clearings here and there, and I was watching the tops of the trees as the beat approached. Suddenly I looked down and there, not 20 yards away, was a very large male tiger standing staring at me. It all seemed very natural, and I thought to myself, if he comes for me I must hold my fire till he gets within five yards. I had only sevens in my gun. However after what seemed some time, but was probably only a few seconds, he turned, and with a deep roar went off back into the jungle. Not till then was I really frightened and I found myself trembling. I shouted to Holdy who was about 40 yards off in the direction the tiger had gone. He said afterwards he was surprised to hear me yell 'Look out, Tiger' instead of the usual 'Look out, Murgi'. The tiger ran across in front of him, and then turned back and charged through the line of beaters without hurting any of them. It moved with incredible grace and speed and made another very deep roar. I have always wanted to see a tiger, and at last I have done so. We felt we had had a really good day, even if a lot of murgi had escaped in the excitement.

25.12.40. *Gulmarg.* We drove up here in my Ford via Sialkot, where we looked over the sports factories, then through Jammu and over the Banihal Pass which, at 9000 feet, is the highest I have done by motor as far as I can remember.

New Year's Day, 1941. *Gulmarg.* I've skied every day and gone to bed tired after bridge every evening. I have been asked to edit the Ski Club of India Annual this year, so shall have a good deal of writing to do in the coming months.

26.1.41. *The Doon School.* I have been to Peshawar to see the doctor who specializes in stomach disorders. He carried out a series of tests, and although he could find no amoebae, he thinks they are at the bottom of my troubles and has ordered a course of injections. These may affect the heart, so I'm to stay in bed: rather a bore when I'm feeling better than for some time past. I had a very interesting time in Peshawar and went up the Khyber and the Kohat passes and visited villages and arms factories in tribal territory where they make revolvers and rifles of soft steel. The villages are all walled and have watch-towers and it really is unwise to be on the roads after dusk. I had always thought that this Frontier business was something of a newspaper and cinema stunt and I was a bit surprised to find that it really was a dangerous and romantic part of the world with the bazaars full of people and products from all parts of western Asia. It was tempting to buy all sorts of strange clothes and utensils as mementos.

Actually it's not unpleasant to be forced to lie in bed for a fortnight. I'm reading a good deal, and at present am on *Gibbon's Decline and Fall of the Roman Empire* and enjoy his balanced sentences and caustic remarks. It does seem a pity that mankind is apparently unable to benefit from past experiences and the knowledge and philosophy of individuals. So much of what we are suffering today is a repetition of political, economic and religious problems already experienced in the Roman and other civilizations.

We have just had a letter from the Board of Governors saying that we are doing work of greater national importance here than we should be in any military job, so I suppose we shall go on with it and I do feel that though we are only a minute part of the life of India, we may have, one of these days, an appreciable effect. At any rate we are free of communal difficulties and our boys are growing in that self-respect which is the cure for many of the futilities of politicians in this country.

I drove Fluffy Best back from Peshawar and we did the 300 miles between Lahore and Dehra Dun between lunch and dinner, averaging 50 m.p.h. including all stops. I had two days at a fishing camp before these injections started with her, Betty Hinds, Flinty, John and Holdy. Fluffy disgraced herself by cooking one of Holdy's big fish before he had weighed it.

5.3.41. *The Doon School.* John made a rude remark about the number of daffodils that have flowered this year in the house garden, so I sent him the following:

> I wandered fretful as a child,
> An envious and resentful cove.
> Leaving my garden, bare and wild,
> I passed by Kashmir's scented grove,
> Where, peeping with a jealous eye,
> I saw what I would fain deny:
> A Ring of golden daffodils
> Around the fount, beneath the trees,
> Where golden fish with flapping gills
> Glide silently above the lees
> Of summer's withered lotus blooms:
> More kindling to a rival's fumes.
> Eleven saw I, and beside
> What filled my lustful heart with sorrow,
> A host of buds that prophesied
> No vacant plot like mine, tomorrow.
> A gardener could not but be green
> With envy at the things I'd seen.

Old Foot has given me more than my fair share of fat boys and dullards from the new boys, and I'm afraid we are going to have a longish period of being second-rate. It's not much compensation for working up one's house to being what I like to think is the best, if the reward is to be given the worst material to average it down again.

19.3.41. *The Doon School.* One lives in a sort of dream world, and nothing seems to matter very much. At the back of one's mind is a misty conception of what it must be like at home, and a realization that the life one lives here can't last.

John and I were fishing on the banks of the Ganges last Sunday when some curious men in grey breeches and black riding boots appeared. We couldn't think who they could be, till John said, 'They must be Italian generals', and the Alice in Wonderland part of it all was that they were. There are 29 in Dehra at the moment, and they are let out of their camp occasionally to show them, I suppose, that India isn't as described in enemy propaganda. I've been asked to arrange some fencing with them, and the officer in charge says he will let me know which are the black-shirts, so that I can take the button off my foil for them. The black-shirts are not liked by the regulars. We are in the process of digging trenches in the school grounds as an air-raid precaution.

8.4.41. The Auk, who is now C. in C., came round the school yesterday and I asked him if he would speak to Admiral Fitzherbert with regard to my doing some training next holidays with the Indian Navy.

30.4.41. *The Doon School.* A sunbird has built, just in front of my bedroom window, a little nest of faded honeysuckle flowers, hanging with an entrance in the bottom half, and a little porch built over the entrance. I have another dog. Said to be a dachshund, when it arrived it proved to be a black bitch, a mixture between a dachs and a Labrador. However it is a delightful creature, and I have called her Melly—short of Melangee. Most of my energy at the present is directed into producing *The Merchant of Venice* in aid of war funds for Indian soldiers disabled in the present war. We have a rehearsal every evening and are doing the play in the Open Air Theatre that John and the boys have built. I am having Indian dress and Indian music which I think not only technically correct (Shakespeare dressed Caesar in a doublet), but likely to be very splendid as the Nawab of Rampur is lending us some magnificent court apparel; you never saw such lovely silks, embroidery and gold lace. Some rehearsals have been very promising, but last night we had an awful one, and the night before we were driven in by a storm.

3.6.41. *The Doon School. The Merchant of Venice* went off better than I had dared to hope, and we raised over Rs.1,150 on the sale of tickets. As a pageant alone the dresses made the show a fine spectacle. The boys knew their parts and spoke so that everyone could hear. I didn't have to prompt once, though I thought I was going to have to do so when Antonio says 'I am dumb'. He always forgot that line in rehearsals, and every time I had to prompt, everyone laughed! The

Rose Bowl was a perfect place for the play, and one day I would like to do *A Midsummer Night's Dream* there. We had a torch dance as a sort of interlude in the scene where Lorenzo fetches Jessica.

Here is part of what Dr. Amarnath Jha wrote in criticism of the play "A clear crisp evening; the floor of heaven thick inlaid with patines of bright gold; tall trees in luxurious foliage; the atmosphere marked by concord of sweet sounds; all ages from the whining schoolboy to the soldier full of strange oaths... in such a night, in such appropriate setting, the boys of the Doon School produced *The Merchant of Venice*. A minimum of property was used; the stage in the open air was the last word in simplicity. The actors were word perfect. The performance went through from start to finish without a hitch. High praise is due to the producer for his attention to detail and the boldness of his decision to use oriental costume and oriental music..."

30.6.41. *The Doon School.* Holidays have begun. John and Holdy have left for Kashmir, and I am going up to Almora with the Foot family to take things easy. Uday Shankar has his school of dancing there, and there are a couple of Englishmen who have become Sadhus whom I am looking forward to meeting. John's and my houses have been rented to the I.C.S. probationers for the holidays. There are now thousands of Italian prisoners here, and the prices of all foodstuffs have gone up.

10.7.41. *Snow View, Almora.* I enjoyed my time in Dehra Dun and was able to clear up a lot of odds and ends I have wanted to deal with, but had no time for before. Also, leaving later than usual, I was able to watch my mangoes ripen. It was a good year for them and their flavour was excellent. I gave a lot away. One day I went up to Mussoorie to lunch with the Nawab of Rampur and met the Maharaja of Kapurthala and a number of other interesting people. I suspect these princes are living out of their century, but I enjoyed a very good meal.

Almora is a most promising place for a holiday. I took my motor bike by train to Kathgodam and from there came up on it the 80 miles through the hills, a lovely ride, even the soaking I got in a thunderstorm at the end. I have met Boshi Sen, a scientist who is experimenting on crop production, and his American wife Gertrude. He will be most interesting if I can get to know anything about his work. He is growing

Star Grass from Africa. This grows very strongly and fast and may become of great importance in checking erosion which is such a problem in heavy-rainfall areas. Some 17 miles away in the hills are the English sadhus: a Major Alexander and Shri Krishna Prem. Alexander was a doctor, and the other, whose English name was Nixon, was a professor of English at Lucknow University. I hope to walk out and meet them one day.

We are all wondering if it is too much to hope that Hitler has at last overplayed his hand in his Russian adventure. When the news of his invasion came, I said "This will be the end of Germany".

25.7.41. *Almora.* I am enjoying this quiet holiday enormously. The smell of the pines reminds me of Puck's Hill, and the wind in them is like the noise of the sea. I am working on editing the S.C.I. (Ski Club of India) Annual, but the collection of material is difficult with people scattered by the war. I shall probably have to copy the example of Arnold Lunn in the S.C.G.B. Annual, and write most of it myself.

4.8.41. *Forest Rest House, Binsar.* I have just started on a short trek with two lightly laden porters and very flexible plans. I had thought of going to the Pindari Glacier, but hear that the valley one has to pass through is full of cholera, so have decided against that. Walking out here from Almora, it was good to get into the swing of the road again. I got wet in the rain, and am now sitting in front of a roaring fire. This is a lovely bungalow, perched on top of a hill at 7,500 feet.

7.8.41. *Pannanala, Before breakfast.* I stayed at Binsar on the 5th as it was raining hard, and yesterday came here along a ridge through forests of ancient moss – and fern-covered trees. This is the place where the two English Sadhus live with the widow of the vice-chancellor of Lucknow University as their guru. After the last war, when Nixon was in the air force, they were up at King's together and, dissatisfied with the way life in the West was developing, they decided to come and see what they found in the East, one as a doctor in the I.M.S. and the other teaching. Eventually they found what they wanted, and have settled down here. I don't know enough about Eastern philosophy to describe theirs to you, but they accept Christ, the Buddha, and others as manifestations of God, and do not believe in any dogmatic creed. Their aim is to achieve balance and to know God through mystical experience and contemplation. When I met them it was obvious that they were exceptional, not in the cranky way most English people out here would expect, but in a good way. The ashram, known as Mirtola, is a pleasant place with a large garden and orchard. They grow most of their food as well as their tea, and to their relatives at home who cannot understand them they are a doctor with a dispensary and a tea planter.

I saw another side of Hinduism on my way here yesterday when I visited Jagdishwar, where there are a number of fine ancient temples. Many of them are to Shiva, and the place is stiff with lingams. It was also crawling with priests, worst than any continental verger intent on his tip. The site of the temples was beautiful, but a little sinister, and made me think of the groves condemned in the Old Testament; and there have probably been human sacrifices there in the past.

Later. *Bhatgaon Forest Rest House.* I spent this morning at the ashram which is a mile from Pannanala. We talked all the morning and they told me something of the technique of achieving balance in life, and of contemplation. It is not a thing that happens quickly, and I am probably too impatient, but I have no doubt that a period of contemplation, prayer, quiet hour, call it what you like, every day can be very helpful. After lunch with them I walked on by little hill tracks down hillsides, along streams, and through rice and millet fields to this bungalow. I am so often surprised how well the sites of so many bungalows have been chosen in this country. This one, at the end of an open space, is surrounded on three sides by running water and sheltered by pine trees.

10.8.41. *Mukteswar.* I came on here on the 8th, a long and tiring walk in rain, up and down, and in and out of hills and valleys. I had not, before, realized the extraordinary extent and complication of the foothills: miles and miles of them. Here there is the Imperial Veterinary Research Institute, and I have been going round all the labs and seeing how they trace bacteria, toxins, protozoa, fungi, and so on. It is very cut off, with no motor road, but they have made themselves tennis courts, a little golf course, and a delightful club. All the same, they suffer, I gathered, from the usual drawbacks of a small community.

13.8.41. *Almora.* I walked in yesterday from Mukteswar and had tea with the Boshi Sens who have Ian Stephens, assistant editor of *The Statesman,* staying with them. He is writing an article on Uday Shankar's Culture Centre and I found him very interesting. There was a letter from Jack from Bombay waiting for me saying that they urgently want fifty officers for the R.I.N., so I am writing about it.

27.8.41. *Almora.* I have been learning something about Indian dancing under Uday Shankar and have enjoyed it. Khastgir has been staying with us and has done some sketches of me and Melly which I am sending you. Salim Ali is also here, and his book on the common birds of India has just been published. However, many of the birds up here are not common, and are not in it, so we hope he will do one on hill birds.

I have been reading the Gita with a commentary on it by Krishna Prem. It is astonishing how much it has in common with teachings of Christ. I had hardly heard of it before, and I don't know why it isn't a set book in all schools. Here are people in India who have been thinking the same things about God, reality, truth, whatever you like to call it, for thousands of years, and we are apt to think of them as ignorant heathens.

14.9.41. *The Doon School.* I came from Almora to Bareilly on my motor bike, about 185 miles, and when I got there felt so stiff that I wondered however Jill managed two days running of 200 miles each. My precious map, that I have spent such hours on with the boys, had the rain through the roof on to it in a storm while I was away, and a great deal of it will have to be done again.

23.1.42. *Rampur.* I am now about at the end of a very interesting trip. The Kumbh Mela at Allahabad was fun from the river down which we went in a boat, but too dusty on shore. I don't know how many millions of people were there, but less than usual as travel by rail was restricted owing to the war. Many, however, streamed in on foot. The processions of Sadhus on elephants and on foot were similar to those we saw at Hardwar three years ago. My next stop was at Benares where I again saw most of the sights from the river: temples, burning ghats, and bathing ghats with their umbrellas. I visited the university. It seemed good, but not much like Oxford or Cambridge, and the students were more like a collection of older schoolboys.

Then I went on to Patna and Bhagalpur where the Collector, Prideaux, had the room next to mine at Sidney Sussex. I was fascinated by the ruins of an old rackets court, and by the cemetery with its many monuments, mostly pagan in shape, to generations of people from Britain, most of whom seem to have died young, and many in childhood. I copied some of the inscriptions.

From Bhagalpur I'm on my way back to the Doon School via Rampur where I have joined Holdy and H.H. has laid on black partridge shooting from elephants—not all that easy as they sway from side to side as they walk through the grass, but exciting and amusing.

9
JOINING THE R.I.N.V.R.

In July 1942, with WWII in progress, Gibson joined the Royal Indian Naval Volunteer Reserve, having been granted leave by Doon School. Between learning about signals and semaphores and undergoing an anti-submarine course, Gibson explored the Bombay neighbourhood by way of minor shooting or climbing expeditions, including an offshore trip with some Indian fishermen. His stay was interspersed by trips to Doon School where he managed to complete a large relief map of India modelled in plaster of Paris on which he had been working fitfully ever since his arrival in India.

7.5.42. *The Doon School.* I'm still looking for something to do next holidays, but haven't heard of anything yet. I would like to drive a lorry on the new road to China, but don't suppose I shall fall into anything as interesting as that.

25.5.42. *The Doon School.* I have now got permission to go for the duration of the war if I can get a combatant job. I have sent in an application to join the R.I.N.V.R. It will be an awful wrench to leave this place. I have put into it a sort of invested capital of work which is only just beginning to bear fruit: all the information I have collected about the geography of India, and so on. If I go I shall have to leave all this with nothing to show for it but a half-written textbook, but I dare say it's a good thing to prune my roots before they take too tight a hold.

9.6.42. Things move very slowly. I didn't get acknowledgement of my application for a fortnight and I'm to go for my medical board at the end of this week, and if I get through, to an interview in Bombay in a fortnight or so. As the time comes I realise that the pruning of my roots may be good for eventual growth, but is a painful process at the time.

26.6.42. Term is over and the boys gone home. The place is empty and quiet, the rain is falling steadily and I'm full of sorrow. The boys gave me a ripping goodbye and a book of British Paintings with all their names inscribed. The term ended with success in music and swimming rather marred by finding that three of my boys had broken into the Tuck Shop on the last night. I suppose the little blighters don't realise that 'a raid on the tuckshop' is the same as stealing. Do you remember when you caught me pinching sweets from a shop in Brighton? I think I have certain advantages as a housemaster, having experienced most of the problems I have to deal with as a boy myself.

9.8.42. *C/o The Navy Office, Bombay.* To go back to my first visit to Bombay for R.I.N. interview: I stayed with Jack and Kay, and all went well and I was told that I would probably be wanted back about July 27th. It was then the 5th, so I returned to Dehra Dun with visions of a comfortable week putting things ready for the Vyases who are taking over from me, and perhaps of having a look at Bandarpunch from the source of the Jumna above Jamnotri which I have long wanted to visit. However I think I told you that one of the things that I most regretted leaving unfinished at the Doon School was the relief map of India. I found that there were two or three boys in Dehra for the holidays who were willing to help, so we got down to it: two hours before breakfast then till a late lunch, and then tennis or a ride in the evening. It took longer than I had expected. The modelling in plaster of Paris went at about the speed I had planned, but the painting was a tricky business as we had to give it a fist coat, leave that for a day to dry, and finally paint the rivers and lakes. It had to be done in sections working outwards as the map, seven feet by seven and a half, is too big to be able to reach all over it from the sides. It was a long and laborious business, but we finished it on the 25th and we all felt it had been worth while. One photo I took, while the paint was still wet, shows the Western Ghats reflected in the Arabian Sea.

16.8.42. The last day at Dehra was the worst. Melly knew what was happening and sat disconsolate on a pile of paper I had thrown away. She has been a ripping companion, always full of fun and life, much better than Archie who was too aristocratic and highly strung. I had an interesting journey from Delhi to Bombay with Peter Fleming whom I found very interesting to meet for the first time. Celia Johnson, his wife, is Mrs. Dyson's niece and I expect you remember seeing her in *Pride and Prejudice* many years ago.

15.9.42. When I got to Bombay I was put to teaching English to a class of C.P.O.s who were to become Warrant Officers at the Gunnery School. This was a considerable disappointment but the authorities pointed out that it was only temporary job and allowed me to do my short course in gunnery at the same time, which had great advantages. Being up at the school I could always put in a bit of extra time and get someone to clear any of my difficulties. Anyhow I came out top of my lot in the course, and I hear all my class got through their English exam, though, if that is so, the examiner must have accepted a low standard.

For my first week in Bombay I stayed with Jack and Kay at Pali Hill. We used to ride before breakfast and bathe in the evenings and I enjoyed it very much. Meanwhile I searched for a flat near my work, and I found one at last and have been sharing it with a fellow called Oppenheim. I suppose he is a Jew, but he's not the musical comedy sort, and I like him. I have managed a couple of concerts which I enjoyed enormously, one a Beethoven chamber music evening and the other orchestral. My chief relaxation is going out to Pali Hill on Sundays, or for weekends when there are no Divisions. Last Sunday we went for a long ride along the sands, all rather like a Norwich School painting, through a little village with boats lying about and fish hanging out to dry—more pleasing to the eye than the nose—and then along hard wet sand from which the horses were reflected. The monsoon is now more or less over and the sea has subsided, so bathing isn't such fun and surf-riding has come to an end.

I have again been offered the headship of the Chiefs' College I told you about, and this time they have said they will keep it for me till the end of the war but I am very happy at the Doon School which is first-class, while Raipur might not be, and Doon School have been good about letting me go and making up my pay.

20.9.42. For the next three weeks I shall be additional to a mine-sweeper. The idea for additionals is that they should pick up as much useful knowledge as they can. After that I take it that I shall go and complete my courses. I have left the flat I was sharing and moved into the Mess where there was room and which is much more convenient for my work, and I have joined the Bombay Yacht Club where you can still get a glass of beer at a reasonable price.

Yesterday I had an afternoon off and Kemmis Betty, a Gulmarg skiing friend in the Army, and I took a country craft and sailed to Elephanta Island. We went up on the flood with a fair wind and had been told that the tide turned at 5 p.m.— I couldn't get hold of a tide table. At 7 p.m. we were still tacking off Elephanta against the still incoming tide.

I gave up teaching which I thought more important than anything else for two reasons: first one can't get on with anything until this war is finished and all our efforts must be towards finishing it the right way; second because I hold views now described as old-fashioned liberal ideas and don't feel justified in working for them behind the shelter of those who are fighting. That is why I am so keen to get into some job that isn't just sitting in an office.

17.10.42. Last time I wrote I was just off to stay with Jack and Kay for four days to get over the effects of a go of dengue fever. Jack had a month's leave and they were in a shack at Marve (a little fishing village not far from Bombay) almost on the beach outside the village. One morning we paddled in the dark up the creek in dugouts to see what we could shoot on the edges of the flats. The mists and noises were just like Blakeney and the shooting no better. On another morning we drove inland to where there were marshes and paddy fields and shot very wild snipe till we had enough for lunch. This we ate beside a pond surrounded by incredibly tall palm trees and covered with water lilies. India is such a mixture of what is lovely and what is not. Not far off was the carcass of a dead buffalo with attendant circling vultures, but fortunately we were to windward.

One day I went out with the local fishing fleet. We sailed so as to arrive at high tide, and they then put down their nets and waited till low tide. Our nets were attached to moored buoys, though it is more usual to use great beams 50 or 60 feet long. While the tide was ebbing we lay under the sail on a deck made of split bamboos tied together so as to roll up. I like the fishermen. Most wore gold ear-rings, some very heavy and intricate, and some had on silver belts made of beautifully wrought pieces about half an inch square. When hauling in the nets they sang a shanty that would have pleased father and which was more tuneful than some of his. The catch was mostly what they hang up to dry and turn into Bombay Duck.

1.11.42. I'm just back from listening to plain-song in Bombay Cathedral. I love Gregorian music, and they sang it very well. The Cathedral is not beautiful—badly painted Victorian gothic—but I shut my eyes and listened. I sat and thought of the churches of Europe and Christian tradition, and what a mess we seem to have made of it; but the music was lovely and the incense reminded me of rubbing brasses in St. John Maddermarket.

15.11.42. I'm now on my short course of signals and finding it very interesting. There is too much to digest in the time, but it's fun how it is all worked out, and the ingenuity of the people who invent codes and ciphers is more than Heath Robinson. We start work at 6.15 in the dark with flashing practice which I can only yet read at about six words a minute. I do hope I eventually get to sea but there are a great many people waiting for very few ships: rather a shock after all the talk of urgent need we heard before I joined.

30.11.42. I'm on my anti-submarine course at the moment and find my complete lack of knowledge of electricity rather a handicap, but after a week am just beginning to see daylight. I've only got navigation and a week's gas to go. The great thing is to escape any long course which would probably be followed by appointment as an instructor, and I'm trying to come first in several.

22.12.42. Last week we were doing pilotage and chart work on charts of the Red Sea and African coast and sailing directions for West Africa. On Sunday three of us went out to the old Portuguese fort at Bassein and found it a most interesting place. It is a deserted city about a mile square with its wall still standing and many of the churches and public buildings in about the same state of ruin as Castle Acre.

3.1.43. On Christmas Day I went out with a friend from the Mess to explore a lake where we thought we might find some duck, and to climb a hill called Bawa Malang, known to the English as Cathedral Rock. The lake was covered with teal, quite 300 of them, and we decided to come out on the next Saturday with our guns. We didn't get to the top of Cathedral Rock though it is only 2,500 feet high. There is only one way up it, and that we didn't hit.

I had work on Saturday morning and the other fellow couldn't get away till Sunday, so I went off on Saturday evening by myself, having arranged to meet at 11 the next morning. I slept very comfortably in a field at the foot of the hill and woke with the idea of getting to the top in an hour to see the dawn. I'm afraid old age is creeping on for I found it quite a struggle to get up in an hour and a half, but it was well worth the effort for the view from the top: the sea with all its inlets to one side, and the Western Ghats on the other. The hill is sacred to both Hindus and Muslims. The top is a small tableland, once fortified, which must have been impregnable.

20.1.43. Navigation was followed by gas, a short and quite interesting course in which I got back to the top again after my disappointing result in navigation, and then, thank goodness, courses were over. I was give ten days leave and spend them in Dehra Dun. Having been away so long I realized, perhaps more clearly, how lovely a place the Doon is. The first day I rode one of John's horses out to Tunwalla where I looked at the village school. You must tell Mrs. Burton about the school, for the money she sent helped to build it. I rode down the lane I have often bumped along with a car-load of boys. There was the tank we built with quite a crowd drawing water, and to one side the school. It looks delightful and the children who were having their midday interval were eager to show me everything in it. One little boy whom I remember lying for quite a year with a gangrenous leg came up walking with the help of a stick and smiling at his recovery. Surely, if only the energy that goes into making this war can be conserved after it for remaking places like Tunwalla, then so much could be done in the Tunwallas of the world.

On the way back to Bombay I wondered what was awaiting me, and it's better than I could have hoped for. I have been appointed to a sloop as asdic and signals officer and should be at sea very shortly. They had expected an expert, but I hope will bear with me until I get into the swing.

10
AFLOAT AND ASHORE

The next two years were years of official peregrinations for Gibson as an RINVR officer. His assignments took him to Persian Gulf [evidently Oman], where his father served as a surveyor, to Ceylon more than once, apart from postings in Bombay, including on a 'stone frigate' on Malabar Hill. In Bombay he also made friends with the eminent Parsi Sir Dinshaw Petit, a fellow volunteer reservist. His passion for hiking took him to the "highest point in Ceylon" on Christmas Day in 1943 and to Adam's Peak the following year.

It was also the time when he and Friede – his sweetheart – discussed prospects of getting married though Friede, who was two years older to him and 38 at the time they were mulling over the idea, was not very enthusiastic about it, not being keen to come to live in India.

In 1944 Gibson also completed a history of the Indian Navy in his spare time and forwarded it to Delhi in the hope of its being officially printed but was to discover that a commissioned – though less detailed – history was already with the authorities, as informed to him by the other author in high dudgeon. He does not tell us what happened to his work but evidently it was not printed.

In January 1945 Gibson found he had been posted to the Inter Services Pre-Cadet Training College in Nowgong, in the central Indian district of Bundelkhand.

1.3.43. I am enchanted by the sea: its stillness and beauty. Only one of its moods I know, but I wish you could have watched just now a line of four dhows slip past heeled over ever so slightly by the evening breath of air, their sails full—two great lug-sails, a mizzen and a lovely top-sail that tapered away to a point like a great banneret.

13.3.43. Here [the Persian Gulf] we are where Father once was, and I wonder if he was ever actually in this spot. We arrived yesterday and in the afternoon I trolled a mother-of pearl spoon for an hour or so and caught three rock cod, a sea salmon of sorts, and a long silver thing like a thin mackerel. After that I scrambled about the little cliffs: barren volcanic rock with clear water at their feet. I enjoy it all and feel at last, after a long period wondering whether I was right to escape from the Doon School, that I am doing something useful again. There is another keen fencer on board, so plenty of exercise. I have a magnificent cabin and feel quite like a schoolboy again with his first study, and have forgotten the pangs I felt for my bungalow and garden.

We are back for a few days and then shall be off in another direction. 'Join the navy and see the world'. Jill asks if I have a division. Yes, I do, and this morning we were inspected by the new Admiral. You know my awful habit of forgetting names when I introduce people, well, I had heard that he was fond of asking men's names and where they came from, so I warned my division that if I rechristened any of them and gave them strange homes, they were to stick to them; then, when the old boy came along I had all their names on the tip of my tongue, but couldn't remember what my division was called! He must have thought me a complete ass.

Easter Sunday, 1943. To my sister. The R.I.N. has expanded at such a rate that there have passed in both men and officers who are not really fit for their jobs. If only I knew a bit more about the sea and had had more experience, I think I would make a better First Lieutenant than a technical officer. I'm fairly good at handling men, and I inherit Mum's flair for organization. I find it a bit irksome at times to have much younger men, who don't do their jobs any too well, senior to me, but on the whole I'm very happy.

30.5.43. Today I went by bus, very overcrowded, to a little place along the coast where there is excellent bathing, and had some of the best surfing ever. I met a fortune-teller who told me that people thought I was wealthy but that I cared little for money. After that compliment I stopped him, fearing I should have to pay him, so proving him wrong.

26.7.43. I had a long letter from Friede the other day. She is now a regulating P.O. in the WRNS. I wish I had asked her to marry me years ago instead of waiting to see what India was like, and then waiting to see what would happen in the war. Now I suppose it's too late, but I feel envious of all these people with families.

17.8.43. The other day a letter I wrote to you on 3.7. came back with a blast from the naval censorship authorities because it had been posted ashore. I didn't know how this happened, but suppose the messenger must have shoved it into a civil pillar box to save himself the walk to a naval post office.

27.9.43. *The Doon School.* Here I am in Dehra Dun on leave. It makes lying in bed in the mornings even pleasanter to hear people doing P.T. outside, and increases the feeling of luxurious holiday to see John Martyn, with whom I'm staying, going off into school after breakfast while I settle down to read the paper; and except for the famine in Bengal and threatening more generally, especially in the Deccan, the news gets better and better.

I am afraid my letters have been very dull. First there have been no excitements, and second, if there had been, I don't suppose I should have been able to tell you about them. We have been engaged mostly on convoy work which has taken us here and there – my first time south of the equator, my first experience of a coral island [Adu Atoll].

28.10.43. [*From Colombo*] Life is full of dull and apparently trivial work. For a whole month signals have been accumulating undealt with, waiting for my return. I have now dealt with them, but there are still many corrections to books that I have to make myself: a loathsome and soul-destroying occupation, for you spend hours getting them up to date, and you have no sooner done so than they are superseded and you have to burn the copy you have spent so much fruitless labour on. On the other hand, if you are slack and leave the book uncorrected until someone wants to know something that should have been corrected, and you are done.

In the place of the First Lieutenant who was so inefficient we have a very young (22) chap a very keen and intelligent Indian, who I think is going to do a lot of good.

30.11.43. I don't know if they try to make you bloody-minded in the R.I.N., but that's what I feel at the moment. We have just had a signal transferring me to Bombay to a training establishment and appointing in my place a fellow who hasn't been to sea for four years. In the past ten months I've served under four different captains and four different executive officers, and there have been far too many changes in the ship's company for efficiency.

7.12.43. One of the things I have enjoyed during the refit has been running the sports. Our hockey eleven is first-class and too good for me to play in. The last time I suggested that I might do so the secretary said 'I think you would be more useful as a referee, sir'!

9.1.44. I'm afraid it's a long time since I last wrote from the Naval Hospital in Colombo, and I'm now in another Naval Hospital up-country, but leave tonight on my way back to Bombay. Here is an account of what I have seen and done. I left Colombo cured of dengue early in the morning of December 23rd and got into the train to Nuwara Eliya. For the first time I was able to see a bit of the interior of the island: a fairyland, at any rate this part of it.

I arrived in the evening to a five-miles drive from the station. The air was cold and damp and I was glad of tea and toast in front of a log fire. The hotel was a bit of a mausoleum full of ancient women and hard-faced men, but I had a pleasant room and made friends with two planters and their wives, very different, but each typical of the planting community. I think I would like the life of a planter. It is open and healthy and you are more or less your own master so far as everyday organization goes, but the labour situation is now very difficult. Wages have to be paid whether the labourer works or not. If you have to get rid of him he must be given a month's notice and may do no work during that time; and when you have got rid of him it is difficult to find anyone to take his place. To protect their own people the government has put a stop to Tamil labour coming from India

The day before Christmas was wet and cold, but Christmas Day was sparkling and fine and I walked up to the highest point in the island. The day after Christmas I started the blasted dhobie itch which has put me into hospital again – oh the diseases one can pick up in the east! I got so raw that I had to give up walking and golf, and eventually the doctor sent me here to hospital.

Here I am, back in Bombay fed up with being back here to a job I see little prospect of liking. The better I do it, the more they will want to keep me in it, which is little incentive for trying.

[On 15.1.44. I Joined H.M.I.S. *Feroze,* a 'stone frigate' on Malabar Hill, and was put in charge of the Divisional Course for officers joining the Service. Each course lasted a month and covered, among other things, such subject as the history of the Service; parts of a ship and its internal organization; different classes of ships, rates and ranks in the R.I.N. and other Services; dress, customs and ceremonial; responsibilities and duties of different officers; advancement of ratings; complaints, discipline and punishments: service documents, correspondence and security; stores and returns and visits to ships, the dockyard, and Castle Barracks. The victims varied widely. There was a full colonel joining, if I remember rightly, the Regulating Branch of the R.I.N., there were those who had served as ratings in the R.N. and had seen much more service and knew much more than me, as too had several Gunners from the R.I.N., and there were youngsters fresh from School or University. It was not easy to suit everybody.]

19.2.44. *From Friede.* And now for the major problem you have set me. Do you realise how old I am? I expect you have forgotten that I am two years older than you. Had you thought of that? And that it is a very long time since we've seen each other. I haven't got myself attached, mainly because I'm not a very susceptible female and I have very definite ideas on marriage. Unless I can marry the sort of person I want to, I don't want to marry at all. How can I possibly say, after such a long absence, whether you are that person? We will both have changed in many ways even if not fundamentally. That we should have many things in common I don't doubt. Marriage has to be partly intellectual and partly emotional to satisfy me. Anyway, as I said before, I am old, I've gone very grey and thin during this last year. I think the blitz on London may be doing something to us all at this late date. My idea of amusement is no longer a good party, but a good dinner with an interesting companion followed by good seats at a theatre or concert. Which is proof of my age I think! Savouries rather than sweets. I haven't lost my sense of the ridiculous thank God, nor my interest in people. But it's no good trying to explain things in a letter—just sail your ship up the Clyde if you think it's worth while and come and see me! And India—I don't even know about that. My chief longing, when this war is over, is for the quiet of a cottage in an English country village and the coming of Spring and Summer which I seem to have missed these past four years. Just now I'm utterly weary. But I should very much like to see you again.

20.2.44. *Bombay,* Time passes pleasantly enough. I have been reading up the history of the Indian Navy, mostly in a book by C. R. Low published in 1877, now out of print and borrowed from the Asiatic Society library, and also in various reports. It is most interesting and there is far more to it than I had realized. I was very excited to find a report by Admiral Mends, Father's distant cousin, or whatever he was who came to inspect the Service in 1872.

Today I have been umpiring a cricket match between Doon School old boys and an R.I.N. team. We, my loyalty was to the former, gave the latter a good beating. Vasant captained the side and several boys from Kashmir House played and did well. All the old boys remark on how grey my hair is going, so be prepared; but I'm feeling very fit.

Last night I played chess with Sir Dinshaw Petit, also a V.R. officer. He is one of the fabulously wealthy Parsees and lives in a mansion as fine as any I have seen. On the sea's edge, the salon or whatever it should be called is open, except for fluted pillars, to the garden running down to the water. At night you can't see the garden, but can hear the waves and imagine them at your feet. It is paved in black and white marble and at the end opposite to the sea there are let into the wall each side of the entrance aquariums full of rainbow fish, lit from beneath. The lighting is indirect from niches in the walls in which are magnificent jades through which the light shows. He gave me a very good dinner with Scotch whisky, now almost a rarity, and ended off with brandy that was softer and better than any I have tasted. I beat him at chess and much enjoyed the evening. I think he is probably lonely and not a happy man in spite of his charming wife and wealth, and he has continual pain from gall-stones. What a curious thing life is.

3.3.44. *Bombay.* I gave a birthday party last night in an empty house being prepared for more officers. Four P.O.s came and piped in all the guests who came dressed as pirates. Someone brought a fiddle and another a banjo and we sang and danced. I had made up a treasure hunt in about half an hour. 'Music like me so they say was first played in the U.S.A.' was easy for the swing, but 'If you find me as quick as it, you'll be conducted by your wit' was, for some reason, found difficult for the lightning conductor. All rather childish, but everyone seemed to enjoy it.

We were inspected during the week by the Commodore in charge of Instruction. I tried to make him sympathise with my desire to escape from here, but got no change out of him. I don't like the job, or some of the people I have to do it with. However, I'm now trying to write a short history of the Indian Navy which I'm finding fun. I'm also trying to get on top of the subject I'm supposed to teach, but it's so vast that I often get asked questions that I can't answer: how many torpedo tubes has such a class of destroyer, and so on. As I'm honest about my ignorance and try to find out the correct answers it doesn't do me any harm, but I could do better than dictate inaccurate notes which is all the authorities appear to want from me.

14.3.44. *Bombay.* I've now taken on as sports officer as well as my instructional duties and for the first time there are some chances for exercise offered to the officers under training. I was asked for suggestions for improving the messing and I have written in a long screed. I know it's only butting against a wall and won't do me any good but I feel so angry at the inefficient and probably dishonest way some things are done that I have had to loose off steam. For example, the officers under training are charged Rs. 20 a month for their share of a room boy who looks after four of them and is paid Rs. 30 a month. The profits must be big, but no mess accounts have been published for three months.

28.3.44. *Bombay.* I wonder if you have had any skiing. I long for some and practice in the lorry on the way to games. Sudden swerves and alterations of speed are more or less like unevennesses in the snow.

Two Sundays ago I took a party of officers under training to Bawa Malang. We were given a Ford Wagon as it was a more or less official expedition to work out future cross-country training. I'm glad they are beginning to take seriously the need for officers to be physically fit. Have just had a break in this letter to fence with a young fellow just out from England. He is good, and it is fun to fence with someone who makes you think.

30.3.44. *Bombay.* We had a great weekend last Saturday and Sunday. I took three of the officers under training and Iyer, an old Kashmir House boy who is in Bombay doing an apprenticeship in electrical engineering, and we crossed the harbour by ferry. On the way we got into conversation with an old fellow who looked the typical I.C.S. official, which he proved to be "one of the advisers to the Governor. We told him that we were going to look at the fortifications along the coast about which I have been reading in connection with the history of the Indian Navy. I said that we hoped to spend the night at Alibag Rest House. He had apparently booked this for himself, but kindly let us share it, though he had gone there for a bit of rest. He not only did that, but introduced us to the Collector who placed a police bus at our disposal. This made the whole expedition as we were able to cover much more ground than we could have done in country buses. The Collector, Roland Davies, asked me and Collins, the I.C.S. official, to dine with him, while Collins put his cook at the disposal of the rest, so we all did very well.

Just before dinner we killed a Russell's Viper, the most deadly of snakes and a very fat and big one, just outside the bungalow. We got up with sunrise on Sunday morning and set off in the police bus to Revadanda, a Portuguese fort on the site of the very ancient port of Chaul: the first Indian port mentioned in European literature by Ptolemy in 200 or so B.C. Though not so imposing as Bassein,

Revadanda has extensive walls and some seven roofless ruins of churches. From there we sailed across the Kundalika river creek to Korlai Fort which has changed hands between the Portugese, Marathas, Angrias and British. This is on the top of a great rock ridge running out into the sea and commanding the entrance to the creek. There were still a number of guns in their emplacements, the remains of wall cupboards, and memorial tablets in Portuguese Latin; and we thought how interesting it would be to excavate the place.

20.4.44 *Bombay*. I've finished my history of the Indian Navy at the cost of several nights up to one or two in the morning, and now I have started on notes for officers out from Europe on the races, languages, conditions of life and so on of the ratings they will have to look after. My History has gone up to Delhi and I hope they will print it.

I suppose you may have seen in the papers that there was an explosion and fire in the docks here last week-end. We stood by to help but were not called on. I took photographs from our roof. On Sunday a party of ten of us went for a cross-country expedition, walking across Salsette Island and visiting the Buddhist caves at Kanheri. After throwing stones to frighten them away, we bathed in a lake in which crocodiles were floating and I felt some relief when everyone was out.

26.4.44. *From Commander (Sp.) G. E. Walker.* Either someone has led us up the garden path, or we have been travelling on parallel courses; anyway we have both written brief histories of the R.I.N. – mine was an order, obeyed in my spare time, and I'm wondering if yours was too. Mine had already been sent up for sanction to print as a Training Pamphlet when yours arrived. I have had the two of 'em placed side by side before the technical advisers to the Powers that Be, to choose between them, amalgamate them, or what the hell else they fancy. Yours is much fuller and a more scholarly business in every way than mine; but there you have the bulge on me, being (my spies tell me) an historian by profession, whereas I'm only a p.b. lawyer. Anyway, I have refused to have anything further to do with either of them until the authorities have decided which they want to use. But I had to write, in case they should choose mine – because I started off my introductory note with a disclaimer of any original research in almost exactly the same words as yours; and while I freely admit to being a plagiarist, I hate being blamed for it when I'm not being. And the coincidence would have been too striking; though in point of fact my introductory note was written five weeks ago, and I didn't see yours till yesterday. Having got that off my chest. I now revert to my spies. They tell me that you are tall, slim, left-handed, and a fencer. Are you then the John Gibson who succeeded the Lloyd-Winder-Coates triumvirate and captained the new generation in the following year? Because if you are, I know you well, and have fought with you both foil and epee on many occasions.

8.6.44. *From Roland Davies.* [Tehmasp Kotavala had lent me his Norton motor-cycle, and I had ridden on it, unaware that powered vehicles were not allowed there, to Matheran, where, not in uniform, I was arrested.]

I was very amused to read of your misfortunes at Matheran. It is a pity that the police respected you too much to try out the lock-up where you might have languished, or, as our friends say rotted in jail for your misdemeanour in not taking out a licence for your exercise, a journey very few people have been able to make. Bertrand Russell says that no one should have a vote who has not been in jail or married (he qualifies doubly on each count I believe). I have written to the D.S.P. not to pay official notice, but he will probably send you a certificate of merit.

26.10.44. *The Doon School.* It was wonderful to arrive back in the Doon and look out of the carriage window in the early morning: crisp air, mist in the hollows, the hills in the background, and blue smoke arising from morning fires. I had a day's shooting last Wednesday with Quarries: two of them and Sir Douglas Stewart and myself. We got 19 jungle fowl and 4 pea fowl, and in one of the beats a fine big leopard came out between me and the next gun. As we were in fairly open country I got an excellent view: the first time I have seen one since I came to India, though not quite as exciting as the tiger that stopped and looked at me some three years ago.

The plan is to send me to a new training place that is being started for those who are expected to make good officers but at present are handicapped by weak English, lack of self-confidence, poor physique and so on. It sound as though it might be interesting, and I have had a letter from the colonel in command in which he writes: 'Your duties will be studying and helping British and Indian youths. By means of exercises across country of short and long duration to develop character and personality. Supervising map reading, English, general knowledge, discussions, etc. It is an experiment and an interesting one. We want enthusiasts.'

Last night we had a dinner party for ten in pre-war style—best glass, candles, sherry, port and Madeira—but one lives in a curious uncertain atmosphere these days. There is much unrest and dissatisfaction about, and life in India will not be happy until the political troubles are settled. At present our promises of independence are not believed. The British feel insecure and the weaker ones that they must make what they can while they can, and so there is all this beastly corruption. I don't know what I shall want to do after the war. I think come back to the Doon School.

17.11.44. *To John Martyn.* In Delhi I called at N.H.Q. and found that they had done nothing about my going to sea, so I persuaded them to send me to Bombay via Nowgong so that I could see what sort of a place it was. I was given a very pleasant welcome on arrival and stayed with the commandant. There is a considerable river onto which we plan to get naval boats, and I shall prefer to work there to any job the service is likely to offer me ashore. Nowgong will be valuable experience in a new sort of training.

20.11.44. My new job will be right in the wilds on India's central plateau. There will be three companies, each under an army, air force and naval officer. My company won't assemble till early January, so I'm free till mid-December, and have managed to fix up a month at sea. You had better address all future letters to Kitchener Inter Services Pre-Cadet Training College, Nowgong, Bundelkhund, Central India.

21.12.44. I have been having a most interesting time: three weeks in H.M.I.S. *Rajputana* while she was doing a work up with her new C.O., and then an Australian ship for an operation in the Bay of Bengal that might have been exciting, but wasn't, though it was all very interesting. Finally, I found myself with two or three days in Ceylon waiting for a ship for India and took the opportunity to climb Adam's Peak or Shri Pade, the sacred footprint.

I started for Adam's Peak before dawn and I got down at Hatton with little idea of what I ought to do next. There had been no time to plan or get hold of a map. I found I had to take a bus for 12 miles and it was so full that I made myself comfortable on the roof to the amusement of onlookers and feeble protests from a policeman. At the bus stop I found there were about ten miles to walk and 3,000 feet to climb to the top of the mountain. I wanted to be there for dawn so engaged a coolie and set out at 16:30 after buying some provisions and having a tea of bacon and eggs. To start with we walked through tea gardens, quiet except for bird song, and a purling stream.

Eventually we started to climb, in places steeply by steps cut in the rock. We were about 1,000 feet below the summit when night fell. It became too dark to go on without a torch or lantern and it was too wet to sleep outside, so we had to use a pilgrim shelter. There were bugs all right, but I hadn't bargained for it being so cold. I had to give the poor coolie whose teeth were chattering my Burberry and from time to time we got up and flapped our arms and jumped about to restore circulation. At 0400 I could stand it no longer, and we roused the keeper of the shelter to make us some hot tea. We reached the top at 0600 warmed by our exertions and took shelter in a little priest's room beside the temple. It is a very fine hill, impressive in its isolation. There were enough pilgrims to greet the sunrise to make one feel virtuous to be among them, but not so many as to be a nuisance. I returned to Colombo by goods train, persuading the guard that I was an intelligence officer who had to get there as soon as possible.

11
KITCHENER COLLEGE

In early 1945, soon after he had joined in Nowgong, Doon School asked him back. Bundelkhand was the back of beyond and with only 39 cadets in the school, there was ample time to explore the neighbourhood with gun and rod. There were ruined forts on hilltops, a river and Gibson also made a visit to the then not-so-well-known temples of Khajuraho. He was informed he would be relieved in June and decided to visit England, partly to explore the possibility of getting married. Meanwhile his sister Jill had already married an old friend of Gibson's, a naval padre by the name of Humphrey. In the event his own marriage plans did not work out. Friede and Gibson were together for ten days in October 1945 but she did not want to come to India. Since he was going back to Doon, Gibson also had to decline an official invitation to write a war history of the Royal Indian Navy.

7.1.45. *Nowgong.* Here I am in front of a roaring wood tree. Much of my work is out of doors and I shall get lots of exercise and fresh air. Already I have a magnificent appetite and feel that I'm putting on weight. The training scheme that they have worked out seems to me first-class. Apart from some classroom instruction, it starts with what is more or less glorified scouting, and work up to long and interesting schemes. At present I have 39 cadets under me, with an Indian Army Captain—a jolly and helpful Punjabi, a commissioned R.I.N. Gunner—

ex R.N. who was in *Hindustan,* and three British sergeant-majors to help. Next month another company of about 45 will be added.

I share a large old-fashioned bungalow, a very pleasant house with a long formal garden stretching to the road, high rooms and red tiled roof. At the well two white-bullocks work a leather bucket by walking up and down a ramp while a small boy guides the rope with his toes. Nowgong has a nostalgic air, something like what I found at Bhagalpur. It was for a long time an important military centre, and there are a number of what were fine bungalows, now falling into ruin. The old club, a very fine building in the 'chalao punkawalla; brandy pani lao' style is now a police training school. The old mali remembers the days when it was the scene of dances for upwards of a hundred officers and their ladies with regimental bands playing, and seems to regret them.

15.1.45. *Nowgong.* I had tremendous difficulty getting any pay for the time I was on leave and at sea, as a signal had not been sent to the C.N.A. and no one knows on what books I was born. I stood behind tables arguing with babus for a whole day and a morning and no one yet knows who is going to pay me while I'm here. The bank manager has taken to sending me telegrams when he gets no remittance from the navy.

22.1.45. *Nowgong.* The setting sun is just in line and on a level with my door and its light is streaming in and killing that of the fire I have just lit. The garden stretches for about fifty yards to the well, and down the centre runs a paved path with formal beds each side, then lawn, then hedges and the drive in and out. There are groups of trees, pleasantly irregular and breaking the formality. So much for my immediate surroundings. There is one largish river within four miles, still full of water and in places about 300 yards wide. We plan to have two whalers on it. There are dams across it here and there from which canals lead off, and we hope to keep the boats in a reservoir above one of these. There are great boulders in the bed of the river on which they could easily be wrecked. Here and there are ruined forts on hill-tops, and the rocky hills and great boulders make a different countryside from anything that I have been used to.

28.1.45. *Nowgong.* Last Thursday, Mr. Downing, the commissioned Gunner who is one of my company officers, and I went to explore the river where we hope to keep two whalers, for about eight miles between two dams and had an interesting and hard day. In difficult places we made less than a mile an hour, and twice we had to swim the river. We eventually got to the car which was waiting for us with our lunch at the second dam, at 1730. After a very welcome meal I had half an hour's fishing while Downing took my gun. I caught a 15-pound mahseer which I had to land by myself. I shouted for help, but no one heard me, except apparently the fish which ran every time I shouted.

19.2.45. *Nowgong.* Foot has asked for my services back at the Doon School where they are getting short-handed. I am ready to go. The policy in the navy is now the reasonable one of only sending to sea those who are likely to stay on after the war, and if I am to go on teaching it will be those of much higher potential at the Doon School than here—or do you think that should not count?

3.3.45. *Nowgong.* My chief relaxation, as you must have gathered, is to get away with a gun or fishing rod. On Tuesday there was a holiday and a party of us went to the ancient Hindu and Jain temples at Khajurao. The carvings are wonderful, though some of them are what we call obscene. Perhaps they took a more natural view of life in those days.

4.4.45. *Nowgong.* My half stripe came through yesterday as from March 31st.

15.4.45. *Nowgong.* The authorities are so pleased with the results achieved here that they are looking for a permanent home where it is possible to work all the year round, possibly not far from Bombay in the Western Ghats. I find it all first-class experience, but not what I would want to spend too long at: not enough intellectual interest.

23.4.45. *Almora.* Last Sunday before leaving for Almora I set out on a scheme with one of my companies which I will describe to give you an idea of one part of the life we lead. The scheme was called 'Famine' and the story was that two parties, one American and the other Japanese, had been wrecked on opposite sides of a Pacific Island. This was an area in the neighbourhood bounded by rivers. All that was known to the parties was that there was a food dump at a lighthouse on the island between 11 and 12 miles from where they were wrecked, and that there was only a very limited supply. The parties were dumped at their starting places, where they were supposed to have been wrecked, at 2030 on Sunday evening, a dark night. They had tossed up which was to be the American and which the Japanese, and they both had enough food for one meal only, salvaged from the wrecks. I was the lighthouse keeper, an old man, who, having spent all his life saving people from the sea, had no sympathy with war and had even grown a little peculiar in his lonely old age. The scheme started with a race to the food dump, and the Americans got there first, having sent an advance party of their strongest marchers who covered the 12 miles in just over two hours—extraordinarily good going. I was on top of a little hill, having hung up a lantern that could be seen from miles around. When the Americans arrived I refused to tell them where the food was, or to allow them to carry it off for the rest of their party, or to tell them how to escape from the island, until they had made two promises: to cease fighting while they were on the island, and to maintain absolute silence from within 15 minutes of rejoining their party and explaining these conditions which they had to accept on behalf of all; this till 0930 the next morning. This was to make them think; should they have to ask their way they would have to use signs. Having extracted these promises, I told them that there was a second large food dump at a gulf (a reservoir) about eight miles up the island. In two days time the tides would allow ships to approach the island and sail up the gulf, and I would signal from the lighthouse for relief, but they would have to survey a channel up the gulf. I kept them talking a good time in hopes that the Japanese would arrive and an interesting situation arise, they having promised to fight no more but being in possession of the food. As it was, they saw lights shown by the approaching Japs and were able to get away. When we discussed the scheme on return, this was a lesson not to give position away at night in this way. The Jap party arrived after 2 hours 40 minutes, also very good going, and were duly disappointed to find almost no food left. On condition of telling them how to get off the island I told them the same story and extracted the same promises. I then returned to the college, picked up rations for everybody for the next two and a half days, and set off for the reservoir. The rest of the scheme was spent charting the river till lunch, with the afternoons free.

24.4.45. *From my sister.* You have probably gathered by now that Humphrey and I have been seeing a bit of each other and when I stayed at Great Melton we decided to get married. Dear old Jack, it is so lovely and I'm terribly happy.

7.5.45. *Almora.* It's wonderful to be in the hills again, and I'm already feeling a different person; but I'm beginning to feel my years and I can't run up hill as I used to. I have already visited various old friends from 1941: the Boshi Sens, Drummonds, and Brewster, the artist. Uday Shankar and his school of Indian Dancing have left Almora for Bombay as he couldn't make things pay here. Next Wednesday I take my companies across the valley and up a hill called Bandani Devi, about 5000 feet of climb and descent.

A very nice letter from FOCRIN arrived yesterday in which he said he thought I had made the right decision to return to the Doon School as he realized its work was of great value. He also wrote, 'You will probably be pleased to hear that it has been agreed that you should be granted 61 days leave in the UK immediately on relief from Nowgong before you are released back to the Doon School.' I want to marry Friede. There won't be much time to fix things up when we have had a look at each other and decided for or against, two months will be so short.

18.5.45. *To John Martyn* [acting Headmaster of the Doon School while Foot was on leave]. My dates are still uncertain, but as far as I can tell I shall be available for next term after leave in England. I do want to get back to my old house. Salim Ali came through here last week on his way to Lake Manasarovar. He was kept waiting by Donaldson for hours on his veranda when he called. Why do people do such bloody silly things?

Jill is being married this August to an old friend of mine who has been a naval padre for most of the war and is now taking over his father's living, a lovely place near Norwich. I hope to marry Friede and bring her back with me to the Doon School, but that is all very much in the air.

I have just spent an hour bird-watching with Archie Bryson who is up here on leave. We discovered two minivets building a nest on the branch of a pine tree—most fascinating. Archie tells me that so many celebrities in Delhi go out to observe bird life on Sundays that it is almost more interesting identifying them than looking at birds.

5.6.45. *Almora.* Some days ago I went on a reconnaissance for a new scheme. I drove a military lorry along a ridge at about 9,000 feet with views of the snows on one side and wild low hills on the other, and we saw a serow. On return I found that the lorry I had driven out had gone down the side over the edge of a cliff on its way back. I now have to explain to a court of enquiry either why I drove against rules, or, if I did so for safety, why I let the driver go back. Fortunately, he wasn't killed or badly injured. Yesterday we had quite a good earthquake—enough to shake you off your feet when it started. No more damage than a few cracked walls.

18.6.45. *Almora.* I had a children's party here last week, about the only way I could think of to return hospitality. I told my cadets that I hadn't time to think of anything myself, and gave them a morning to get something ready. Perhaps a curious way of training for the fighting forces, but it made them think, plan and build, so not so bad. They were very good. They put up a miniature obstacle course and three swings, and made up a rhymed treasure hunt. The party was a great success—said to be the best ever in Almora! No one broke a leg or arm, and some of the children were amazingly acrobatic. The greatest success was a bed turned upside down and swung from a tall tree by its four legs. It held about ten at a time and swung not only forwards and backwards, but sideways, so that I was afraid that the children would be sea-sick.

Nehru has come out of gaol here. He is a fine person and how we can have kept him shut up beats me.

21.6.45. *From Captain Passmore Edwards.* A bunch of your lads joined here early this month and are all doing well. Their bearing stands out compared with the direct entries and everybody has noticed this and commented upon it. I had occasion to write to Col. Donald Portway a few days ago, and mentioned that I had been visiting you. He replied that he knew you well as a member of the Cambridge Fencing Club.

22.6.45. *Almora.* I am taking this week-end off, the first for a long time, and five of us are going to Naini Tal to sail against them. We have called ourselves the Almora Shipless Sailors.

7.7.45. *Delhi. To John Martyn.* Yesterday they said I should be off today. Today they say I shall be off tomorrow. Leave passages have a low priority, and I'm told the most effective way to get off is to put up American badges and write in block capitals on top of the signal granting passage 'Must go'. I can see no reason why I should not wait at the Doon School, but I can't let you know even the approximate date of my return. Everything is in the air except myself.

Sunday morning. I was told that they wanted me to write the official war history of the R.I.N. which would have been very interesting with latitude to go places and do things, but I explained that I had to get back to the Doon School. Of the journey down:

> Two elderly colonels from Naini
> Disapproved of that man from the briny
> Who filled up with trunks
> The floor and two bunks
> And reduced a large space to a tiny.

4.8.45. *Shenley Military Hospital. To John Martyn.* The flight home included three days in Palestine for what they called 'deacclimatization'. This was fun as it did not count as part of the 61 days leave and allowed us to visit Jerusalem and Bethlehem from Tel Aviv. The mixture of Christian creeds seemed allied in one thing: to exploit their sacred places. In Jerusalem the narrow covered King David's Street with old men with long beards and big bellies on ridiculously small donkeys seemed to fit in with expectations.

My tummy has continued to give trouble and by the time we got to England I was passing pus and blood so decided to take things in hand forthwith. I reported to the medical authorities in London and they have sent me, after four days' visit home, to this hospital near St. Albans. I've been here for a fortnight and am in the middle of a cure that involves 65 injections of some wonder drug called penicillin, one every three hours night and day. This will probably make it impossible for me to be back with you by October, and I suggest you count on me for January.

11.8.45. *Shenley Military Hospital.* I've now completed my injections and started on 12 days of pills that make you feel sick. Thank God the Jap war seems to be over. I was lying in bed next another Gibson, the brother of the dam buster, when the news of the atom bomb came over the wireless. We both wondered if that was the end of civilization.

23.10.45. *Puck's Hill. To John Martyn.* I have waited to write till my medical board. They seemed to think that I ought to have another month's leave and that a sea voyage back would do me good, so the present arrangement is that I catch the first convenient ship after November 20th. I shall return single. Friede stayed with us for ten days and we decided not to get married. I'm disappointed, but I dare say she was right. She didn't want to come to India, and I felt rather cool after all these years.

30.12.45. *Petit Hall, Bombay.* We were in Bombay harbour by midnight of the 20th-21st. I'm just off to Dehra Dun to see what needs doing to my bungalow and to plant the bulbs I brought from England, then I return here for the formalities of my release from the navy.

24.1.46. *Barkot Forest Rest House.* Here I am having five days in the jungle before once again getting down to work in the Doon School. The chief excitement during my final visit to Bombay was watching the reactions to the Government order by which all notes of Rs.500 and above were cancelled. They had to be declared and exchanged. In this way it was hoped to catch the people who had been dealing in the black market and those who had been evading income-tax by not declaring and banking their profits, but keeping them in paper money instead. A lot of people must have been caught as notes for Rs.1000 were on offer for sums as low as Rs.500 in small notes. However, whether the government will reap much advantage I don't know, for besides selling concealed notes at a loss, people were giving them to friends and relations to declare, or sending them to banks in the Indian States or abroad. It will be difficult to check on declarations of small amounts as it is part of the Indian way of life to keep largish sums in cash hidden about the house. The Petits, for instance, had over Rs.350,000 in notes of high denomination which were not illicit or black money, and which were declared. When Din took me to the bank to do this, we found great queues waiting to get the official forms, and touts who already had them, selling them to those who were impatient.

I always find tipping a problem when I leave these big houses. There were over 70 servants—dining room, hall, bedroom, garage, wash-house, gardens—at Petit Hall, and when I left I felt rather like the person who gave the gamekeeper half-a-crown.

20.12.45. *From Mon Harvey, Commandant I.S.P.C.C.* The college is closed and that great feeling we had in Nowgong as a team of enthusiasts is a pleasant thing of the past.

12

BACK TO THE DOON SCHOOL

Gibson rejoined Doon School in 1946. The highlight of the year was his aborted attempt to climb Bandarpunch with Tenzing again for company. Galsworthy's 'Strife' was also performed before the summer holidays and there was a revival of contact with the school-adopted village of Tunwalla. At the end of the year there was a skiing trip to Kashmir and in January 1947 he was elected President of the Ski Club of India.

19.2.46. *The Doon School.* We are having an extraordinarily dry winter and I suppose that the forecasts of famine have reached the English papers. But for two short light showers there has been no rain since I got back here. The whole of north India is suffering and, in conjunction with a world wheat shortage, this may be very serious; and the country is already in a political turmoil over elections, the independence issue and the I.N.A. trials. The last has become, not a matter of right and wrong, but a political issue. I don't think you in England can realise how bitterly almost the whole people of India resent these trials. They no longer try to think whether a man was guilty of brutality, let alone breaking his word. They feel that the I.N.A. was a symbol of Indian resistance, and as such was good and right. Their argument is that people only joined the I.N.A. either to escape Jap brutality or because they thought it best for India, were the Axis Powers to win, that she should have some armed force. They claim that it was a patriotic movement by people who were convinced on good evidence that the Allies were beaten, and they were doing their best in the circumstances for their country. The government policy is now to punish only those proved to have used brutality to persuade unwilling people to desert to the I.N.A., but the general public want all sentences remitted. It is sad that behaviour that may have had excuses, but which I feel can hardly be called the highest, is being held up for admiration. I have just met Captain Badhwar who was hung up in a cage and suffered various other inducements to join the I.N.A. but refused to do so. An English officer who had been with him in the same prison camp told me that he was one of the bravest men he had ever met.

20.2.46. The papers are full of the R.I.N. mutiny. They call it a strike in these days of flabby thinking.

The Commandant of the Indian Military Academy has asked me to tell them of my experiences of training in Nowgong and Almora. They intend to introduce some of our activities there. It's rather like fate at work in a Greek tragedy to watch distrust of the British grow, just as they seem really to have woken up to their responsibilities to India.

25.3.46. *To Elsie Baker, Matron of my house.* After our conversation, in which I did not mean to be critical, I want to make clear what I feel about food for the boys. We must see that there is no waste, and we may be called on to cut down cereal consumption; but within the limits of what the Store supplies to us we should provide meals that are as attractive as possible to the boys. I know you do this, but it not enough to be satisfied yourself; it must also be plain to the boys that you are doing all you can for them. I know that they are irritating, apt to change their tastes, some of them greedy, others fastidious, but it is part of our job that they should be as satisfied as we can make them. The attitude of mind that is grateful for what is done for you rather than accepting it for granted or even criticizing it, is not natural to boys, and we must not be disappointed if we don't find it. I think that at times you do feel disappointed. This is natural when you take so much trouble, but don't feel resentful at their requests.

9.4.46. *From my sister.* I'm feeling very well and I don't suppose it will be long before I'm quite strong again. It was an ordeal, but once it's over you can't remember the pain and it seems a small thing to have suffered compared with such a wonderful gift and such boy to follow. Father had never seen you or me when we were tiny, and I think he was very impressed with the perfection of his wee grandson. Mum said she would never forget her first sight of you and Dr. Hinds saying, "Well done, a fine boy. I shall now cable the news to your husband that you were as brave as a sailor's wife should be.' Humphrey and I want you to be a Godfather. He's to be called Peter.

7.4.46. *The Doon School.* Jill asks what the future of the Doon School will be. Well one can't tell. It all depends whether there is revolution or civil war, or whether power can be handed over peacefully. The latter seems possible, but not, I think, probable. If power is handed over peacefully then I think the Doon School will have an important future.

I went out to our village at Tunwalla where they were having the children's sports day and exhibition of work done in the school. Tell the Burtons about this as they sent a subscription to help with the work. Eight years ago the village was filthy. Gradually, very gradually, real contact has been established between the Doon School and the villagers. The tank which we dug as our first bit of work is still useful, but the best thing we have done is the village school. There is now a full-time teacher, trained at our expense, and the difference in the village children is astonishing. Many of them are clean, quite a number can read and write, and all show much more intelligence in games and so on. The I.M.A. is thinking of adopting a nearby village for practical work in citizenship. I think the British in India have fostered progressive ideas, and it will be sad if their flowering is cut off in the bud. You would have enjoyed the evening at Tunwalla. There was an air of kindliness and many smiles. I tried my hand at Gray's metre:

> Eight years ago, I well recall the scene,
> The Doon School boys started to dig a tank;
> It's here today, familiar in the green,
> A sign we hope that snobbery and swank

> Are not the only attributes that are
> Justly ascribed the teaching in our school
> Where we believe that Brahmin and Chamar,
> Hindu and Muslim, East and West can pool
>
> Their special talents for the mutual good.
> The tank, the school, the happy children show
> Something of what in rural India should,
> And can be done, if we determine so.

I have started the production of Galsworthy's *Strife* which is to be acted by the staff and boys on May 25th.

12.5.46. The Doon School. Last Sunday, after fishing, I lay beside a stream and watched kingfishers hovering and then diving into the water. I thought of Davies' 'I also love a quiet place. That's green, away from all mankind'.

10.6.46. The Doon School. I'm sorry I've been so long writing but it has been a struggle to keep up with work. Producing *Strife* set me behindhand as it filled every evening till 9:30 or 10 p.m., after which I went back to a late supper and then tired to bed. I suffered a good deal of doubt during productions, but it turned out a great success. I was worried about how it would go in the open air theatre—good for the crowd scene in Act II, but difficult for interiors. By keeping the lighting concentrated on these and the properties very simple one wasn't the least worried by the trees around. I knew the play was a great one, and the actors did very well, but I wasn't sure how it would go down with the younger boys. Even the older ones, when we first read it in class and before we got down to acting it, thought it was dull stuff. However, it was listened to in absolute silence, no shuffling, always a sign that you've got your audience, especially when the seating is not very comfortable. Holdy was very good as John Anthony, and a boy, Ashraf, as Scantlebury provided excellent light relief without overdoing it, but best of all was Aamir Ali, once in my house and now on the staff. He has a magnificent voice and played the part of David Roberts most movingly.

We plan to try to climb Bandarpunch in July. I am delighted to have got hold of Tensing once again to come with us. Next hot weather will be my 11th successive one, and Arthur has agreed that I can come home from April to August next year. I am already looking forward to it. As one grows up and sees how much some, far too many, lose by not having a happy family life, I realise how lucky I have been and you both with your rather specially nice families.

3.7.46. *Bandarpunch Trip.* As you know, John and I were the first on the summit ridge in 1937 since when there have been several unsuccessful attempts to climb the mountain, so I am very keen to have another go, cost what it may in porters who, as well as tinned food, have increased greatly in price. We have had a good day out from Chakrata, and as long as it doesn't rain too much this should be a good party.

Gibson and party had bad luck in trying to climb Bandarpunch due to incessant rain, soft and deep snow, some members of the party pressed for leave and others running fever or hurting themselves. Eventually, they had to give up the idea on 19 July. His account of the trip is largely uneventful, studded with walks from one flea-infested and dirty dak bungalow to another. The trip, however, took them to Lakhamandal in the Jumna valley, said to have been founded by the Pandava brothers who legend says came up to the Himalayas that way with their dog. Among the pilgrims they met and talked to on their way down was a princess from Nepal, "a most sporting old lady, lame in one foot, now off to Gangotri." In fact Gibson recorded at one stage that "there have been exceptionally heavy rains and there are many landslides and bridges washed away. That accounts for our bad luck on Bandarpunch."

31.7.46. *Darasu Bungalow.* Last night Tensing and I went to try to shoot a wild boar which was ravaging the fields of a villager. He, armed with his kukri, and I with my rifle, were led at nightfall by the owner's son to field where we found a splendid structure for watching from. We were given milk richer than any I have tasted for a long time, and the man said that he would watch, and inform us when the boar came. We made ourselves comfortable on the hay on the wooden watch-tower and I stretched myself out and went to sleep. The boar never came, and at 5 a.m. we returned to Dunda dharamsala after a comfortable sleep disturbed only three or four times by suspicious noises. We have had an easy walk today, but tomorrow have 18 miles with 5000 feet ascent and 2000 descent before us, and we have been told the road is very bad and broken. We have hired a horse for two days at the exorbitant rate of Rs.33 to lighten the loads of the porters.

2.8.46. *Magra Forest Bungalow.* The forest rest house is beautifully situated, but very dirty. Half of it is occupied by an inspector of fruit who keeps his cow in the kitchen. I don't understand his way of life. He speaks good English, is very pleasant to talk to, takes two daily papers, which he has lent us, was a college friend of Vyas; and yet he lives surrounded by dirt, and has, since we arrived this morning and found him sleeping, done nothing towards earning his living. If only I could be Prime Minister of this state for five years I'd make it a model for the whole of India. It is naturally lovely, and only man's effort is needed: a university at Uttarkashi, fruit farms, youth hostels, roads, toy-making and other village industries: what could not be done.

15.9.46. *The Doon School.* I've been kept very busy. I have 24 teaching periods a week, two period of boxing instruction of 40 minutes each on both Monday and Tuesday afternoons, gardening with the boys on Wednesdays, and football on Thursdays and Fridays. This doesn't leave me much time for corrections or preparing interesting lessons, but I keep a'going and feel very fit.

28.9.46. *The Doon School.* For a long time I have wanted an improvement on the geography textbooks available. Most are written from an English point of view and centred round England instead of what we need, round life in India. I have started one of my own and had the first chapter printed as an experiment the other day. The printers here are all overworked and very bad about proofs. You correct one and the next printing has a whole lot of new mistakes, and my precious chapter has appeared with a number of commas in place of full stops.

Elsie Baker, my old dame as the matron is called here, is leaving us to join her sister whose husband has died. She has been difficult to manage at times, but has loved the boys and been a tower of strength and most efficient at looking after them. I shall miss her a lot, and hope that the Indian lady who is taking her place—as petite as she is enormous—will be as good. It is really these people, often in background, who make all the difference to the successful functioning of life.

1.11.46. *The Doon School.* Last week, in addition to my usual school duties and odd jobs as a housemaster, I had a general knowledge paper to set for the whole school, seven mid-term geography exams to set and correct, a paper to read to the Mathematical Society, and preparations to make for our half-term weekend holiday. We aim at having a general knowledge paper roughly every three weeks, and I am in charge of them, though thank goodness I don't have to set them all. I have divided them into seven sections: Current Affairs; Local Affairs (School rules, history and geography of the Doon, education, sports and games, and so on); the Humanities (Art, music, painting, literature): History; Geography; Science; and Various. The paper is set and the boys are given two weeks to find out the answers they don't know, and then have to do the paper in class, 75 questions a time. I get everyone to set questions on their own subjects, and then collate them, picking the best. In my geography exams I still peg away at trying to make boys think, rather than just mug up undigested facts, so a common complaint is 'Oh, we haven't done that before, Sir'.

Lately we have been boxing against boys in the Gurkha regiments who are very tough and go very hard, but are not all that skillful. If they land a lucky swing they may do a bit of damage, and I had two of my boys knocked out last week; but mostly mine are better boxers and more than hold their own with the straight hitting I have concentrated on teaching them. As our boxing is all voluntary I don't want to have our boys frightened away from it by expecting too much from them and having too many knocked out; but one reason why boxing can be such valuable training for boys is that it can help them to get over any tendency to funk, and also, when they see their skill defeating wildness, it puts up their self-confidence.

23.11.46. *The Doon School.* The news out here isn't good. For a time things seemed as though they might go well, but it now appears to me that the blood-bath the hotheads talked about so glibly and now, many of them, wish that they could avoid, may be very difficult to prevent. Personally I have lost much of my sympathy for the Muslim League. Nehru seems a constructive statesman and Jinnah an opportunist out to get all he can for his party.

15.12.46. *The Doon School.* I hope to be off to Kashmir for ten days' skiing, the first for five years. My house has done well this year with more distinguished work than any other, and has won the football and athletics.

27.12.46. *Gulmarg.* It is marvellous to be with glittering snow again, and to find that I can still ski. Holdy and I got away on the 21st, having booked two berths in a second-class compartment—we can't afford first. We arrived at Pindi at 2 a.m. and were met by Nandu who has come to Gulmarg with us to learn to ski. Five miles short of Tanmarg we came to an abandoned car, two empty buses and a carload of skiers who were gathering porters to carry their luggage. This was a splendid opportunity for the locals to get their own back on people who usually find themselves besieged by coolies wanting work and sometimes do not behave very well. The five miles cost us Rs.30. We got to Tanmarg at nightfall and I was thankful that Holdy, who was determined to push on to Gulmarg (four miles and 1,500 feet), could not find a single porter willing to make the trip for any price at all. We had to spend the night at the wayside inn, sharing the floor with crowds of others. The next day, Christmas Day, we climbed to Gulmarg, arriving at the hotel just after the morning carol service. I climbed the 1,300 feet to Khilanmarg after lunch and had a good run down. Skiing came back to me like swimming.

12.1.47. *The Doon School.* They elected me President of the Ski Club of India which pleased me very much. There was a crowd of very nice people there and the hotel was packed. We had five days' very good running, and the rest mostly wood running in falling snow. Most of the races had to be cancelled because of the heavy snow, but we ran the novices and Beta races, the latter for those up to but not better than

S.C.G.B. second class standard. When the English leave India there will be quite a number of Indians to continue skiing. On the last day of 1946 I took a party of 20, including one woman who insisted on coming though hints were dropped that perhaps she might feel out of it, to sleep at the Ski Club hut at Khilan. She retired early to bed where I hope she was unable to hear the songs that were sung.

13
NINETEEN-FORTYSEVEN

The onset of 1947 brought a sense of uncertainty to the English population in India and Gibson was not immune to this feeling though outwardly it was the same routine of trips for hiking, black partridge shooting and rafting. His pet dog Melly left a deep sense of sadness in him when he had to put it to sleep since she had been suffering from ulcers, which resulted in a poignant letter home. As Freedom approached for India there were reports of "awful massacres" in Punjab and even Dehra Dun was flooded with them, their number rising up to 30,000. With anti-Muslim feeling on the rise Gibson was appointed Liaison Officer between the military and civil authorities with regard to Muslim refugee camps in Dehra Dun and had to make daily reports of his on-the-spot observations. Later he was made a Special Magistrate. But with the socio-political scenario altering fast in India, he became unsure of his position and wrote letters to each parent at the end of 1947, putting across his dilemma whether to stay on in India or not and leaving the decision to their response.

24.1.47. *The Doon School.* Return from Kashmir saw me swept into a whirl of gaiety: cocktail and bridge parties, dances at the club and at the 2nd Gurkhas, croquet and beer on Sunday morning, and tennis in the afternoon. There is, I suspect, a certain feeling of devil-may-care about among the English population out here nowadays. No one has much of an idea of what his future may be, and it's a bit difficult to take life seriously. I left this round of light heartedness last Monday to go and stay with the Raja of Katiari, the father of one of my boys, for a duck shoot, Holdy coming too, and we got back this morning. He is a zemindar and one of the great landowners in the U.P.

We went to a lake seven miles long and a mile broad, part of an old river course. There were only five of us with guns, and of course we could not cover it, but there is a great pleasure in being on water, gliding through it in a boat and listening to the drops falling off the punt pole, or sitting in a butt watching the changing lights on the water and the shadows and reflections of clouds and listening to the noise of the fighting duck with the chance of a shot every so often.

The second day, while part of the party went by jeep, four of us rode across country to a place where we hoped to shoot big and crocodile. We saw two small mugger on a sand-bank, but a wind got up and this always drives the croc bank into the water. The beat for pig was unsuccessful, though a fine herd of nilgai (blue bull) came out. Though they do great damage to cultivated fields and are really antelope, they are not shot in these parts because of their name and the cow being sacred. What I most enjoyed was the ride, though I had a mishap. One of my leathers broke while I was galloping. For half a minute I thought I could manage, and then off I came. It is curious how you don't hurt yourself if you are going fast and can manage to roll instead of bumping, and I wasn't even bruised, only a bit stiff at the end of the day from riding twelve miles or so for the first time I have been on a horse for six years.

I have never stopped in the centre of the Ganges plain before, and it isn't till you do so that you realise its immense stretch. Level as far as you could see, it was covered, except for sandy patches left by the river, with corn and mustard. They plant both crops together here and harvest the mustard before the wheat. They seem to accept a certain wastage as I noticed the horses were turned loose to graze the young corn, and we walked through it while shooting, though I remarked that I understood that doing this was one of the causes of the French Revolution.

9.2.47. *The Doon School.* During the war we housemasters agreed to a limit of eleven years for holding a house, so as to give a chance of promotion to the rest of the staff. John has now given up Hyderabad House.

18.2.47. *The Doon School.* Last week I had to get the vet to put poor old Melly to sleep. The ulcers she has suffered from for the past year without allowing them to damp her spirits, for right to the last she was full of fun and the joy of life, had got so bad that everyone felt it was kinder to put her away. As I wrote the note to the vet she crept under my desk in the same dejected way as she did five years ago when I left to join the R.I.N., and I was sure that by some extraordinary instinct she knew that something was wrong. It is curious that one should get so attached to an animal and even more that the animal should get so attached to you, for I did not feed her and cupboard love does not explain it. I feel quite lonely without her running out to greet me when I return from school, and both Samuel and my mali were in tears when we buried her. She had a most charming and lively character and I can recall many amusing episodes we have come through together: time when, out fishing, she has insisted on crossing every stream to be by my side, and has got almost washed away; trips up the hills when she has scrambled up the most forbidding cliffs until some rock, too high for her, has defeated her, and I have had to push or lift her up; rides through the Doon when she was scampered by my side and kept up even when I was cantering and arrived at the end of a 15-mile hack fresher than me; there was, too, the famous occasion when I was out for a bicycle trip with a party of boys. The pace and the hard road were too much for her, and I put her in the rucksack on my back. She remained with her nose poking out for some time, and then got bored. I suddenly felt a struggle and a lurch and she was turning somersaults on the road and scattering the party. Bicycles clashed and boys fell off, but Melly seemed none the worse. She was also a good watchdog and ratter, and loved to come out on a shoot, though there she was a nuisance as she was not trained to retrieve and wanted to chase things. She was awfully good with children and let them push and pull her about, but some people she didn't like and in a funny way they were always people who had something about them I didn't like myself.

25.2.47. The Doon School. Last Thursday we had a holiday and Holdy and I went to try to shoot black partridge in the sugarcane. The villagers were making gur or unrefined sugar. Two oxen attached to a long pole walk round and round turning the mill which has the canes fed into it by a girl or old man sitting in a hole in the ground so that he doesn't get his head caught by the pole. The mill is a glorified vertical mangle, and the juice that runs out is collected and boiled: the resulting syrup then solidifies into candy. The fresh juice is delicious to drink and we had many glasses during the day, but not a bird came out of the growing cane.

30.8.47. The Doon School. Here I am once more. I am writing on my veranda. It is 7.30 p.m. and dark outside. From my sitting-room comes the sound of one of the gramophone records I brought back with me: Schnabel playing Mozart. From the mango trees on my lawn comes the singing of crickets, and from the swimming bath, some fifty yards away, can be heard the frogs croaking. It seems peaceful and languorous. The curtains move in a tiny breeze which keeps one cool. One can lean back and sip a glass of whisky brought by an attentive Samuel. The gramophone stops and from some way off I can hear a flute played by some village boy. This is the life of the Lotus Eaters, the life that makes the retired Anglo-Indian in Cheltenham long to live, if only for a while, his life in India again. But this is not the India he would remember, I am not sure, but there is something about the gardens and bungalows that suggests a tide overflowing them. Is it only the exuberant growth of the monsoon? But they do not seem as well tended as they used to be, and the streets and many of the bungalows are full of refugees. I think the greatest shock was our carriage on the train from Delhi. Many trains from the Punjab have been delayed or stopped, and they were short of carriages. They therefore had to make up a train from some that had been lying waiting repair in the yard after being occupied by refugees. Our first-class compartment had had cooking fires built on the floor, and the filth in the lavatories was indescribable, but it was all there was to travel in. From Saharanpur we came on by bus. In the changing colours of sunrise I thought of the days fifty years ago when English visitors to Mussoorie travelled along the same road in tongas and bullock-carts. What changes will now come to the social scene out here I don't know, but the physical beauty of the country will remain.

Although there have been awful massacres in the Punjab, we hope they will be avoided here, but how much the all-India character of the school will be altered we don't know. Eventually we may lose a number of our boys from Pakistan, but at present we expect most of them back. I think my leave was the happiest four months I have spent in what begins to be a long life—do I see F. smile? Most of all I enjoyed Puck's Hill, cutting wood, painting the house and doing odd chores.

4.9.47. *The Doon School.* It's beginning to be difficult to see how the civil government will be able to carry out its functions: already they can't move the food and coal they want on the railways. Yesterday there were rumours of trouble on the Dehra Dun line and half the passengers got off and returned to Dehra from about ten miles out on their journey. Others armed themselves with stones from between the sleepers, and others had guns poking through the windows. All trains now run with armed guards. You will probably see all this sort of thing in the papers, so I tell it you; and there is no need to worry over me. I'm fairly good at looking after myself, and I know you will be happier if I let you know exactly how things are, as I see them.

Both Hindus and Muslims must bear part of the responsibility for what is happening, but basically, I feel it is caused by the extreme poverty of the people of whom there are so many living on the borders of starvation, so many with nothing to lose, that any excuse for mob violence is welcomed. We, the British, have failed to change an almost universal poverty. We have been able to keep the lid on the seething pot, but it has boiled over from time to time, and some of our administrators have played on the divisions between Hindus and Muslims. Whether we could ever have united them I don't know, and we've had to hand over a divided India. The agitation that achieved Pakistan has further embittered Hindus and a great movement of population has started: what may be one of the greater tragedies of history. Since August hundreds of thousands of Sikhs and Hindus have been fleeing from West Punjab. First came the wealthy who could get away quickly. Dehra is full of them, and they have bought up all available property and houses. Then came the poor who are still flocking in, destitute with nothing to live on and full of hatred. Feelings are being inflamed against our local Muslims, and they, in their turn, are having to fly in the opposite direction. The government does not approve of this transfer of people, but the embittered refugees with nothing to lose encourage it.

14.9.47. *The Doon School.* We had to put off as many boys as we could from returning to school on the 7th owing to a breakdown in the main water supply, and I went to Delhi to fetch those from Madras who had already started. I woke at Ghaziabad to see a line of corpses stretched side by side on the platform, and in Delhi, where I spent two days in the station, with an umbrella my only weapon, I had to watch the killing of harmless hawkers. I tried to remonstrate, but a Sikh officer in uniform threatened me with his bloody sword. Meanwhile the Baluch regiment was drawn up outside waiting to entrain for Pakistan. It was unpleasant, but the boys got through all right, including the Muslims. A very decent Indian officer, Brigadier Yadunath Singh, took the first batch in his compartment with him while I waited for the second lot.

There are some 30,000 refugees here in uncomfortable quarters in a crowded camp or wandering round. Many are armed. At present, however, things are quiet. There is a curfew from 6 p.m. to 6 a.m. I've had 11 very happy years here and I'm glad here now that things are a little difficult. John is safely back from Kashmir. They wanted to kill his bearer in the East Punjab, but he managed to persuade them that he was a Christian and not a Muslim. The school servants of both communities are all here and everything on the estate is normal except for the lack of boys, of whom there are only forty.

21.9.47. *The Doon School.* This has been a week of tension in the Doon. Most of the refugees want to settle down peacefully, but the population is already thick, and the problem is where to settle them. Meanwhile, there are gangs, how strong is uncertain, supplied with automatic arms and transport. They visit villages and persuade the villagers to help them sack the houses of the Muslims and share the loot. Those Muslims who escape flee into the forests. Though the resident Hindus of Dehra don't approve of all this, most of them acquiesce so as not to expose themselves to the accusation of lacking sympathy for those who have suffered as badly in the Punjab. The governments of India and the U.P. have spoken through Pandits Nehru and Pant and plainly said that their policy is that Muslims who are loyal to India must be protected and allowed to dwell peacefully in India.

In the school there has been some nervousness, but with a long tradition of working together our Muslim and Hindu servants remain friendly and co-operate in patrolling the grounds at night. We have had one poor old tailor murdered a little distance outside the school, and have now moved those who live outside into safety here. This afternoon I brought up Nizami, the stenographer, and his family. It was a sad business with his bundles of belongings, and he had to leave his library behind.

I am starting today as a sort of liaison officer between the military and civil authorities with regard to Muslim refugee camps in the city. I went down to inspect one this morning. In the building and ground of a school for 300 day students are some 900 refugees. There are no proper latrines and the stench was horrible. I can't describe everything, but here are four typical little pictures for you. I went out to see Miss Stehelin at Tunwalla early in the week. There she was, by herself in this troubled countryside, an old woman, but a source of confidence to the cultivators around her and the workers on her seed farm. No question of leaving; she was determined to stay and see how she could help. One evening last week there was a scare at one corner of our estate and I was called. There was obviously some tension between our servants and the people in the village on the other side of the road. I took Gurdial Singh, a Sikh master, and we crossed into the village. A gun went off somewhere in the dark. We contacted the villagers who were afraid of our Muslim servants, and told them they had nothing to fear, and the shouting has stopped. This morning I went to the Muslim refugee camp with an English Lt. Colonel in the Medical Corps. He had offered to serve on in India, but has been informed that he is no longer required: this in these critical times. A fourth little picture: Holdy and I digging our gardens and sowing seeds: we wonder if we shall see the fruits of our labour.

Here follow extracts from the daily reports [20 September to 9 October 1947] Gibson filed as liaison officer between the military and civil authorities, basically outlining the problems faced by the refugees, remedial measures being taken to protect Muslims, restoring morale, helping to provide food and security, arranging burials for newborns who died and many other unpleasant but essential duties.

7.10.47. The Doon School. The troubles had just begun in Dehra when I last wrote to you. At first they seemed the result of the influx of destitute and desperate refugees, but since then it has come to seem that they are carefully planned and organised. For myself, I'm doing what I can to help. As one of those who thought India should be independent I must stay and abide the consequences; but what I do resent is suffering odium for the sake of the Muslim League of which I have always disapproved. I offered my services in any way they could be used and have been made a special magistrate to help with the Muslim refugees. In these camps are not to be found, in general, the people who wanted Pakistan who are responsible for what has happened, but the poor and the peasants. In helping them I incur the hostility of many Sikhs and Hindus who think all Englishmen favour the Muslims.

14.10.47. To my sister. Things are quietening down because the local Muslims are leaving as and when they can get transport. It is not the official government policy that they should be driven to do so, but it is happening. Though revenge is no solution, it is little use to preach. What is wanted is the resettlement of those who have had to move from Pakistan,. I think that new colonies should be carved out of the less productive forest and all vacant areas, and handicrafts, dairying, poultry farming and anything that can be organized fairly quickly should be started. Once the people have a chance of a settled life and work to occupy them, they would give up wanting to loot and murder.

A pistol or revolver, I'm not sure of the difference, was issued to me, and I have learned something new. I must not sleep with it under my pillow as that is, apparently, the first place an enemy will look for it. I have to tie it round my waist and keep it down the bed. Not much of a companion. The school is a dream-like oasis of peace and sanity. We have a fair proportion of our Muslim boys back with us, and the Muslim servants are all working happily with their Hindu colleagues. One goes into school and tries to believe that this good work must go on. We have put so much into it and feel so bound up with it, that it would be heart-breaking if it had to come to an end.

10.10.47. *From my mother.* I am sending you off on Monday a box of medical supplies: blankets, towels, soap, vitamin tablets and some sheets to tear up for babies' nappies, and as much lint, cotton wool, gauze bandages, triangular bandages, etc., as I could get hold of.

8.12.47. *The Doon School.* M's parcel of blankets arrived last week. You really are splendid to have thought of sending them. The Muslim refugee camps have now all been closed so I passed on the parcel to the wife of the District Magistrate who is collecting for refugees from the west. She was very genuinely touched, and your sort of action does more for good international relations than any amount of talk about good will. Your gift will be really helpful as it is now definitely cold and many of these poor people have no more than the cottons they stand in.

From my end-of-term letter to boys' parents. May I end this on a personal note. I had hoped when I returned from my leave to an independent India to play my small part in that new life and progress for which we all work here. These past few months have not been as happy as I had hoped. In the Doon School we have always believed and acted in accordance with policies with which some of my countrymen do not agree. The unhappy events connected with the partition of India, a step I have never believed was right though I recognize it may have been necessary, have forced one to wonder whether one's faith in liberalism is justified. Furthermore, there is a tendency in India today to put the blame for everything that goes wrong on the British. In these circumstances an Englishman's position at the moment as a servant of India is not an easy one. I believe that the British in India have often made mistakes and been guilty of wrongs and that British rule has been subject to selfish, commercial, individual and narrowly imperialistic influences. But I believe that there have been innumerable upright and honest people from my country, who have served India to the best of their abilities, and considering the limitations imposed by history and human nature, there is no cause for shame in general at Britain's connection with India. We may all regret recent events but I have no doubt that the independence of India is morally right, and I hope to be able to continue to work here and to watch the fruition of those plans for India's happiness and greatness that have been so much discussed. But the work I must be able to do here is something more than just lecturing in classrooms and seeing that bedrooms are kept tidy. To be of full value I must have the understanding and trust of boys and parents. That is why I have written these things rather difficult to say. While I feel this sympathy and trust I shall be glad to continue at the Doon School; if they disappear my work here will be barren and I should do my best to disappear too.

14

TREKKING

Encouraging responses to his letter from parents and old boys prompted Gibson to stay on in Doon School. The summer holidays again led to a trekking trip in the Himalayas – Dodi Tal, Harsil, Nela Pass and the valley of Baspa. There was visit by Lord Mountbatten to the school. Gibson also began to write a text-book of Geography which was eventually published some years later.

19.1.48. *The Doon School.* The letter I wrote to parents at the end of last term has evoked some very encouraging replies and these, together with various letters from old boys saying that they hope I shall stay in India have decided me that I should do so, though what the future holds one has little idea. Gandhi is a wonderful person—as difficult to understand as God, but we hope that his fast will work the miracle that is needed to make people start thinking in a new way.

My boys have acted before the school *The Shepherds' Play* that they did for the house at the end of last term. I adapted one of the York Mystery plays somewhat similar in spirit to the plays acted at religious festivals out here and it seems to come off very well.

9.2.48. *The Doon School.* As you say, the most appropriate comment on Gandhiji's death is that it may work the miracle he was striving for during his last days and bring about communal unity. F. has often said that the world is in need of a new religion. I wonder if he is to be beginning of one; not in the way that already many simple people out here look on him, as another God, but as I think one can look on many of the great men of history—Buddha, Socrates, Christ—as manifestations of the divine in man. If the world would follow his teaching of simple living, love, and search for truth, lessons that have been given, followed, and forgotten before, we might see the beginning of another golden age. His death has made a startling impact on people all over the world.

The day before the Foots left, Lord and Lady Mountbatten paid the school a visit. They were both charming and he was brilliant, giving the boys one of the best speeches I have ever heard. Boys and masters were captivated and moved. I wish we had had more like him out here instead of some of the old pomposities we have suffered from.

My inflatable landing craft has arrived, and I hope to make a trip down some great river next cold weather.

29.3.48. *The Doon School.* The final round of boxing last night between Tata and Jaipur was the best school boxing I have seen for a very long while. I had arranged to give the judges supper at the end, and expected a few extra visitors, so had told Samuel to prepare for 15. Actually more like 30 turned up. Samuel coped as usual, but they made rather a hole in my limited supplies of liquids. Everyone is feeling the pinch of rising costs. The school spent Rs.80,000 more than its income last year, the staff are asking for higher salaries, and fees will have to be put up.

The majority of the members of the Dehra Dun Club have left, and most of them wanted to sell the buildings and share the proceeds. A resolution to this effect was passed last year while I was in England, but I have always thought that the Club should be handed on as a running show to the citizens of Dehra Dun, and as a member of the committee supposed to carry out the resolution I find myself in an awkward position. M's second parcel of medical stores has arrived and been handed on to the refugee organization. It was much appreciated.

29.4.48. *The Doon School.* I have decided I can't afford another go at Bandarpunch as porters have become so expensive. Instead I shall do some quiet walking in the hills.

9.5.48. *The Doon School.* M's telegram saying that F. had had another heart attack came on the last day of term in the middle of my giving out journey money. This seems to be a time for shocks. Six years ago, while I was doing the same thing, the news came through that Hitler had invaded Russia, but that time it was splendid news for I felt sure that it meant the eventual defeat of Germany. I do hope that by the time you get this the old heart will have settled down. What I am much worried about is whether you will be able to go on living at Puck's Hill. If it seems best you must not hesitate to sell it. I think of it as a home to come to when I finish out here, but I fear that that is now an impracticable dream. I am waiting for a reply to my wire asking whether I should fly home.

11.5.48. *The Doon School.* The day before we had had a very hot and stuffy night and there was a haze hanging in the air in the morning. I said at breakfast that it felt to me as though there was going to be an earthquake. I repeated this at lunch, I don't know why, but I had a feeling, and at 2 p.m. there was one: only slight, but it quite frightened me when it started. However, I wasn't able to foretell the thieves who stole the battery and tools from my motor-bike yesterday from right in front of my bungalow. There is a lot of stealing going on in this area these days, probably the refugees; and it will get worse as they exhaust the small funds they brought away with them. The latest expression is 'since the British quit on us.'

21.5.48. *The Doon School.* I have spent a good deal of time during the last three days hanging round the telephone in the hope of getting a call through to M. Three or four times I have seemed on the point of making contact, but each time something has gone wrong. However, M's cable that has just come saying 'Don't come improving' has settled my doubts, and I'm now off in three days with John and Gurdial and two boys. We plan to go first to Dodi Tal, then over the Bumsar Pass to Harsil, and then I shall continue over the Nela Pass into the valley of the Baspa, a tributary of the Sutlej described as 'quite the most beautiful valley in the Himalayas, full of big trout fat as butter'. I shall be out of reach of post and telegraph for three weeks and do hope that all will go well with you.

We grew a lot of vegetables for the school in our house garden last term and seemed to be sending almost daily 50 lettuces or 10 lb of carrots or 5 lb of tomatoes. I have just had the princely sum of Rs.50 from the school store for all this, and they say it is more than they would have given in the bazaar, though they admit our quality was better. This is the return on the work of a mali, manure, seeds, and five or six boys one afternoon a week. I don't know how anyone makes market gardening pay, though rice is now Rs.60 for a bag that used to be Rs.20. Everything is going up in price, and everywhere there is thieving by the poor who can't afford the prices.

25.5.48. *Chapra.* Yesterday we walked from Mussoorie along the ridge and down to the Aglar river, and then on to the Forest Rest House at Deolsari. I developed blisters on my feet, something I haven't suffered from since that time I walked from Norwich to Braintree where I arrived carrying my boots which were too painful to wear, and was turned away from the Hills' house (they were out) by a maid who thought I was a tramp. Today my feet are better and we have had a splendid walk through woods full of wild roses whose scent blended with that of the pine trees, and we have gathered a supper of wild yellow raspberries.

29.5.48. *Hatchery Camp.* The two boys with us are Pratab and Jai Singh whose parents are both in Europe. They have already kicked through the toes of their gym shoes and I have spent most of my spare time the past two days mending their shoes and darning the holes in their stockings. We were unable to buy more gym shoes in Uttarkashi but found some sandals with no heel straps. While a mochi (shoemaker) sewed on straps taken from my rucksack I sat darning stockings and he told the boys what a hard life he led and how unfair it was being born an untouchable.

2.6.48. Camp below Aincha Pass at about 11,700 feet. Yesterday evening John shouted and pointed to a large animal lolloping over the snow about half a mile along the ridge. I couldn't get out my glasses before it disappeared, but we thought it must have been another red bear. The first thing we did this morning was to look at its tracks and there were the footprints of the Abominable Snow Man! It must have been a bear.

John and the boys now have to leave us and Guru and I have decided that there is too much snow for the porters to cross the Bumsaru Pass. Last night was very cold at only 13,000 and we haven't enough clothing to keep the porters warm, so we have come with John and the boys to this pass from where they will go westwards to the Jumna and we east to the Bhagirathi. Below us were great patches of mauve and white rhododendron, and silver birch trees, curved by the weight of the winter snow, glistening in the sun. Everywhere were primulas—yellow, dark, purple, mauve and rose—and gentians and king-cups.

On the pass we met a sadhu crossing from Jamnotri to Badrinath and he was surprised to see Englishmen, as have been other people on our way. They thought we had all been sent home. After arriving here I went out with my gun and shot a monal which is not ready to eat.

4.6.48. In camp on the Diara Plateau at 10,900 feet. Guru and I left John and the boys yesterday morning and had a pleasant walk very steeply down through woods with glades blue and white with anemones and past great clumps of white clematis growing on bushes or trailing over trees. Today our route seemed clear enough to start with, but soon split into innumerable forest tracks. We set direction by compass and struggle up through wild forest. This was not popular with the porters, but had the advantage that we probably saw more than we would have on a path. There were many monal which spread their red fan tails as they dived down past us, and we nearly stepped on a clutch of young ones. There were huge white lilies and different orchids, and rhododendrons, some almost pure white, others bright light pink or mauves. Eventually, we got onto a road which led us to a pass at about 12,000 feet, and, over this, we found ourselves on the most wonderful stretch of downs: miles of rolling country between 12,500 and 10,000 feet that would be splendid for skiing, and is now covered with dwarf iris varying from light blue through mauves to dark blue. The sheep and their shepherds have just come up from the valley, their dogs with great iron-spiked collars to protect them from panthers and sometimes very fierce and frightening to us and then men with bunches of primulas in their caps. The views of the mountains were breath-taking. On our left and behind us was the Bandarpunch range, then Srikanta, the Gangotri group and Jaonli. A thousand feet below the sheep we came to a settlement of cowherds and decided to stay there for the night.

9.6.48. *Camp, Jalandri Ga, 14,000 feet.* I don't know when my pen will catch up with my boots. The day down from the Diara Plateau to the Bhagirathi and on to Ganganani was uneventful, a good deal through chir pine country with its pleasant scent. I was looking forward to meeting again the sadhu John and I had made friends with in 1937, and both of us needed baths in the hot spring, but the old sadhu was away and the place was not as simple as it used to be. There were five pandas or priests hovering round like vergers in an English cathedral, all expecting tips, but the hot water took away all our aches and pains, and we washed our filthy clothes in the overflow. The next day we walked to Harsil where it was fun to meet again two of those who had accompanied John and me in 1937; also they keep chicken and we consumed 25 eggs in three days—all we could get. Guru, who has to return earlier than me and wanted to see the Gaumukh, has gone on to Gangotri, while I am on the way to the Nela Pass.

The evening we arrived the Forest Guard asked for some medicine for his little daughter who had dysentery and I gave him some Tessol. The next morning she was dead and we were horrified that he might have given her an overdose, however, he came to tell us that when he had got home the night before she was almost gone and he couldn't get her to swallow any medicine. He wanted some more for his son who also had dysentery. I gave it him, but strongly advised him to take the boy to a doctor. The nearest is three days away.

Left alone with his porters, Gibson managed to cross the Nela Pass [17,300 feet] the following day. But generally had a miserable time thanks to dirty weather and heavy snowfall.

12.6.48. *Camp at Chitkal.* This little village might come straight out of fairyland. The houses are of carved wood and are built on stones or boulders so that they are raised a foot or so off the ground to keep them dry when the melting snow runs down the hillside. I have just had supper of chappatis and sardines, rice and boiled rhubarb which we found growing wild on the way.

14.6.48. *Chitkal.* Yesterday I went 12 miles and over 3000 feet down the valley in search of trout-fishing, taking one porter with me. The fishing was a wash-out as the water was too rough and dirty all the way, but the walk of 24 miles as well worth while. I wanted to see what 'quite the most beautiful valley in the Himalayas' was like, and though I would not myself single it out with such assurance, it certainly was very lovely: groves of deodars, of walnuts, of apricots, water rills with irises along their sides cultivated fields and bright green pastures, with always magnificent mountains rising each side.

The men wear headgear similar to the caps of Kulu and Lahul, a very becoming round cap with a bright velvet turn-up on one side. In Kulu the cap is shallow and white and the velvet is bright red. In Lahul the cap is brown and the turn-up only edged with green. Here the cap is also brown, but deeper, and the turn-up is a glowing rich purple. In Chitral and Swat they wore long white wool bags rolled up to form a round cap with the roll round and below the crown. In cold weather all these turns and rolls can be pulled down over the ears. It would be fun to make a collection of the different head-dresses and shawls worn in the Himalayan valleys, where I suspect that each has an individual style, but they are probably mixing now as there is more movement down the plains than there was once.

We met and talked to a number of men, many with frank, open and smiling faces. One showed me a letter typed in English, beginning 'Dear Madam'. It was to his daughter-in-law regarding her husband's pension. He had been a subedar in the Indian army and had been killed during the war, and the letter was from the Ministry of Pensions in Delhi. I tried to translate it for him, but could not think of any Hindi for 'Form of Claim' which the letter said must be procured and filled up. You would have thought that the fellow in the Ministry might have done something more sympathetic than to send a letter in English to an illiterate peasant two long days' march from the nearest post office. He might at least have enclosed the form. Before going off down the valley for help, the man took us to his house for a smoke, and there he showed us his beehive. It was built into the side of the house and had been broken into by a bear which had eaten all the honey.

I'm blown up with wind after eating, I suppose, my first fresh vegetables for some time. We gathered them yesterday, a sort of spinach which threatens to turn me inside out. I feared the porter who shares my tent might have fleas and bugs, but it is I who am the bad companion. Though the women and children here come back from the forests laden with staggering burdens of firewood, the men seem to do very little, and the porters have spent most of the day gambling with them: a dice game I don't understand but which involves a great deal of shouting. The counters they use are one-rupee coins issued by Wilson of Harsil, and I have bought two.

Tomorrow we start from here over a pass across the Dhaula Dhar called the Borasu, and then down the Tons Valley and across the lower hills to Chakrata. I have employed two Chitkal men to guide us over the Borasu as my Harsil porters are a bit nervous after our experiences on the Nela. Three of the Harsil men went with the Swiss expedition that was up in the Gangotri area last year. This has both advantages and disadvantages. A lone climber like myself, compared to a national expedition, feels rather as I imagine a true amateur must in the Olympic Games. One can't do things on the grand scale that the porters are now used to. The Swiss provided them with complete climbing outfits which is much beyond by means. I can only lend them my spare clothing on the high snows.

15.6.48. *In camp in the Zupkia Nala at 13,500 feet.* We retraced our steps up the Baspa valley for a mile or so this morning, and then turned south up this nala. The first part of the walk was notable for irises, thousands of them filling the air with their fragrance. How can I describe this to you? Smell has not been analysed as thoroughly as sound, and I can give you no note for their scent, though perhaps that of ripe pears come somewhere near it. Even musical notation can't define all sounds, which perhaps shows that intellect is still behind the senses. I wondered about this and thought of Beethoven's Sixth Symphony as I saw two cuckoos flying and listened to them calling. One had broken its call into the treble cu-cu-koo, while the other still give the pure two noted call.

The porters are now busy gambling accompanied with cries to fate as they throw the dice. I played for half an hour and lost one anna after what was considered a run of bad luck, so I don't think they will ruin themselves. One of them yesterday won three rupees which he spent on arrack in Chitkal last night. He seems no worse for it today, but has had his leg pulled a bit. Wilson's token rupees have written on them 'F. Wilson—one rupee—Hursil' and must have been in circulation for nearly 100 years. I wonder if those who were paid in them ever got any value in return for them.

16.6.48. *In camp in fairyland in the Harki Doon at 11,450 feet after crossing the Borasu Pass (16,900ft.)* How I wish you could be with me to enjoy this wonderful place. Today has been one of the best in my life. We started up the Zupkia glacier before sunrise and heard the plaintive cry of a large bird the porters call 'Bumri'. They said it came from Tibet and was very large and good to eat. The cry was something between that of a kite and a curlew and similar to that of a monal, several of which we have seen here.

The pass was not difficult and the first flocks of sheep and goats had crossed it last week leaving a track in the snow that made it unnecessary for us to have brought the men from Chitkal. I like to find my way with the help of a map, but was afraid of delay as I'm getting short of time and money. The Chitkalis thought they were in on a good thing and had told us that it would take four days to get across. When they found that we walked for more than four hours a day, they wanted to go back, but they came to the top of the pass which we reached at 10 a.m. and returned from there. The descent was good going and we got down first. Tobogganing on the frying-pan was even more fun than glissading. Once off the snow, after about ten hours, we walked on grass and flowers, many of these the deep blue primula with a white centre and a scent like hyacinths. The valley came down in steps, first a steep drop, then for 400 yards, or so a flat stretch where the river flowed gently and spread into numerous channels and little lakes. The different blues and greens of the water were lovely, and beside one lake was a huge boulder with a shepherd's stone shelter built under the overhand. We were tempted to stop there, but there was no wood, so we went on. Below the next steep step silver birch and rhododendron in full bloom began and the valley suddenly opened out into a great amphitheatre where three other valleys meet: the Harki Doon, whose beauty I had heard of and which I was very keen to visit. It beats all my other expeditions. We are encamped beside the river of grass thick with primula. The other side of the river is a wood of fine old gnarled silver birch and blue pine all in fantastic shapes, as in a Japanese paining; and what makes the resemblance even closer are the huge moss-grow boulders that lie all about. Beyond the wood a steep bank leads down for more than a hundred feet to a flat valley through which flows the Tons and on which is pastured a great flock of sheep and goats. The other side of the valley the mountains rise to hanging glaciers, snowy domes and fantastic rock pinnacles. All around is a ring of snow peaks, except to the west where the hills gradually fall away and the valley seems to open out. Against the setting sun the softer outlines of these hills merge in blues and mauves, a painter's rather than a photographer's landscape.

17.6.48. *Same Camp.* Yesterday evening we visited the shepherds and bought a lamb, part of which we had for supper and the rest for breakfast today. The kidneys were delicious—the first fresh meat I've had for three weeks. I ought to be ashamed that I was glad there was no one I had to share them with! I'm just going to have a night-cap of hot goat's milk. It's excellent to drink, without the strong favour of the English variety. When we went to fetch it the goats all gathered round us and licked our boots for the salt sweated out through them.

18.6.48. *Camp at 10,400 feet above Oshol, the highest village in the Tons Valley.* I've just darned my socks and mended two holes in the seat of my shorts, so for the rest of the trek I shall look like a Dutchman. This has been another red-letter day. The two porters who went down the valley yesterday to buy more food returned after dark without having been able to procure anything, and we are now out of sugar, fats, flour and ata. We had decided to start down early today, but there wasn't a cloud in the sky when we woke, and this was too much of a temptation for me. I and two of my band climbed to 15,700 feet to get the view I wanted so much to see. We were off by 5 a.m. and at the top of a little peak on the ridge by 9, which wasn't bad going. The great moment, however, was that of our arrival on the summit ridge. We were surrounded by a ring of snow peaks for an arc of 150 degrees. We counted nine peaks that must have been over 20,000 feet, and the most splendid view of the Bandarpunch group. We got back to camp at midday.

19.6.48. *Datmir Forest Rest House (7000 ft)*. The Forest Bungalow is filthy and all its windows broken. The last official visitor came three years ago. My porters are having a dispute with the villagers over the price of the ata and ghee they have bought. It is all a matter of three or four annas, but causes much shouting. I intervened to pay the amount in dispute myself—anything for peace. The local people are terribly poor and their clothes are all rags. They pay me the deepest salaams and all want medicines for anything from V.D. to malaria or swollen limbs. Great triumph: a man has just turned up with two pounds of the honey of wild bees: most welcome as we still have no sugar, but it entails further bargaining. The villagers have a balance and one weight of a seer (about 2 lb.). The divisions of a seer are arrived at by weighing it against stones and then dividing and subdividing the stones in the weighing pans. While I have been writing this it has been decided that I owe Rs.5-8-0 for 2½ lb. of the honey.

20.6.48. *9 a.m. On the road down the Tons.* Looking back up the valley to the country we have left, early this morning as the sun rose, it cast slanting beams through the grey clouds and lit it in a silver haze pierced by the peaks and pinnacles: it was like what Bunyan must have imagined Pilgrim saw ahead of him beyond the Delectable Mountains. The red flowers of the tree rhododendrons are not withering, but still look like the glowing ends of torches in their clusters at the tips of each bough.

Later, at Naintwar Forest Rest House, 4,900 feet. Heat and flies, but this is a pleasant bungalow among pine trees. When one stays at these Forest Rest Houses one signs the book and puts down any remark one sees fit to make—usually 'Many thanks'. The last Englishman to sign at Datmir was Philip Mason when he was Secretary for War. He wanted to cross the Borasu, but says there was too much snow—it was November. The bungalow books make good reading with records of expeditions, and people one has met.

22.6.48. Ringali Forest Rest House (7500 feet). An officer named Roper Caldbeck (a Norfolk name?) has used this bungalow for several periods of a week or so and obviously looked on it as ideal for his leaves. He gives accounts of shooting serow, thar, goral and panthers as well as the weather at different times of the year.

23.6.48. In camp at 9,400 ft. some 9 miles out of Chakrata. For breakfast we bought milk from a Gujar who asked what chance there was of the British coming back. I told him 'None' and he seemed sad and to think that there was no future for his people. I hope he is wrong, but he isn't the first person I have heard regret the departure of the old regime.

24.6.48. Chakrata. We were up before dawn. The sky was covered with thick cloud across which lightning flashed, and then it started to rain. Very welcome, as it means that Dehra Dun will be cooler. I am waiting in the bus for the 10 o'clock gate. It has been a magnificent trip. I do hope I have been able to pass on some of the pleasure in this letter, 30 sheets; it must be the longest I have ever sent you.

15

FROM SCHOOL TO SERVICES ACADEMY

The year 1948 was to be another year of change for Gibson. First he was offered headmastership of a public school in Ghora Galli in Pakistan – a "tempting proposition" which he declined since he did not want to leave India. Later in the year he was offered the position of Principal of the proposed Inter-Services Wing of the Armed Forces Academy to be based in Clement Town on the outskirts of Dehra Dun, [which was to grow into the National Defence Academy in Khadakvasla] and in 1949 Gibson joined it on two-year leave from Doon School. Before leaving for the new assignment he had an occasion to join a hunting party and killed his first tiger. It was also a year of tragedy when he lost his father just before joining his new post. Among the visitors to the school before he left were the UP Governor Sarojini Naidu and India's Governor-General C. Rajagopalachari.

30.5.48 *From my father.* If ever there was a time to write to you, now is that time, with nothing to do all day but sit back against the top of the bed and contemplate the universe wondering what could have been done in the past to improve it and how many years, months or days will be granted me in which to prepare for the end. The latter does not worry me much. I read the proofs of your geography chapters with great interest and wished I could have had the same sort of thing to start me on my surveying career.

6.7.48. The Doon School. There's such a chatter of mynas going on in the jaman trees outside that I can't hear myself think. At the moment the trees are loaded with berries, green until they ripen to a dark purple, almost blue. The green ones, attacked by insects, drop off and make it difficult to mow the grass. The ripe ones make excellent vinegar, or with plenty of sugar, a very good jelly. The mynas come to roost every evening at about 1915 and make a noise very like a huge flock of starlings. I don't mind it in the evenings, but when they start up again at 0430 I'm less pleased. I have considered frightening them away with my gun, but the malis say they do a lot of good.

John has a new car, a Singer, that cost him Rs.10,000, for which you could almost have bought a Rolls before the war. I do wish I could afford a car again, but at present prices I don't see any hope, and I don't know how long the old motor-bike will last—it wasn't built for the rough roads of India. I spent this morning gathering my mangoes. What a deep and primitive pleasure it is, climbing trees and gathering fruit.

25.7.48. The Doon School. We had Mrs. Sarojini Naidu here the other day—very charming and she insisted on having one of my water-lilies for her hair. She couldn't have paid a greater compliment to a keen gardener! She is Governor of the U.P. and asked me to lunch: very good food and she was in great form. Yesterday Sathe, the first head of my house, turned up with his newly married and very charming wife. He is just back from China and is due to go to Kashgar as India's Consul General. There he will find Eric Shipton. It was very touching that the Sathes should come and stay with me and call it their first bit of honeymoon.

29.7.48. To Salim Ali. It's ages since I heard from you, though I have heard rumours of you from time to time. One was to the effect that Loke had presented you with a station-waggon for your work with birds. This filled me with envy! On a trek from which we have just returned I found a nest at 12,900 feet.

3.8.48. *From Salim Ali.* I have been hearing a great deal about the Harki Doon for years, and have been dreaming of visiting it during some nesting and flower season. From your description of the nest and eggs, they were probably an Upland Pipit's. Yes, it is quite true about the station-waggon. It has made all the difference in the world to life and movement in camp. Why not try to join me for a couple of weeks in Bastar. I am expecting to find evidence of a theory regarding the spread of Malayan forms to the Western Ghats and Travancore across the peninsula by way of the Satpuras. The Malayan element is very marked in the bird fauna of Travancore.

12.8.48. *Sat Narain Fishing Bungalow.* Last Saturday John motored me up to Mussoorie to see an aged couple who want a free passage home—a job I have been lurked in for on behalf of the High Commission for the U.K. It's sad work as the authorities are not generous with passages.

21.8.48. *The Doon School.* Holdy and I went to Delhi last Wednesday for a meeting of the Committee of the Ski Club of India. We have got Pandit Nehru, who years ago was a keen winter sportsman in Switzerland, to be our new Patron-in-Chief and Mangat Rai as next President. The war in Kashmir makes it impossible to know whether we shall be able to meet in Gulmarg next winter, but there seems some chance we may as the Army is keen on training officers and men to ski, and they may make it possible for us to go up.

6.9.48. *The Doon School.* Fed up with correcting geography exercise books yesterday, I went off at 5 p.m. with a small boy on the back of my motor-bike in search of one of the bench marks at the end of the base line Colonel Everest measured in the Doon in 1835—part of the main Indian grid. We found it after a bit of search. I had hoped for some sort of an inscription, but it was a small square cement and brick structure with steps leading to the top which was pierced, I suppose for a plumb line.

My daily interest at tea-time is watching my ducks have their food. The older ones are greedy and show no paternal or maternal feelings, chasing their young away from the dish. Meanwhile a little grey squirrel or tree rat has taken to joining the feast, and the ducks all chase him. It's most amusing. He gets pecked sometimes but does not seem to mind and puts up no counter-offensive.

26.9.48. *The Doon School.* I have had a letter from the Rahim's father, who is now Commissioner of Lahore, suggesting that I should go to Pakistan to be headmaster of a public school at Ghora Galli. A tempting proposition, but I have said 'no' for various reasons: I am happy here and don't want to move; we have lately lost several senior masters and too great a dispersal would be bad for the school; and I feel it would not be right at the moment to leave India for Pakistan. Though they make the English very welcome there, I think we are wanted here, and shall stay until I feel we are not. All the same it's good to have been offered the job.

22.10.48. *Sabhawala Forest Rest House.* Fourteen boys and myself have just arrived here to join another party of 11 who came yesterday. My party is on its way down the western Doon from the source of the Asan river to its junction with the Jumna during our four days half-term break. Some of us carried guns and three teal, flying high, tempted a costly fusillade. Cartridges are now Rs.50 for 100.

26.10.48. *The Doon School.* About shooting and fishing I am in two minds. They are an excuse to explore places one would not otherwise visit, and there is great satisfaction when one brings down a high or difficult bird or lands a big fish; but it is beastly when a wounded bird looks at you with frightened eyes or a big fish cries out, as they sometimes do, as you unhook it. What is the answer? To be a vegetarian I suppose, as it's no better to let others kill your food round the corner.

It's more than three weeks since I last wrote and I must go back to tell you about Founder's Day. Rajaji was apparently greatly impressed and made an interesting speech which seemed to me typical of Hindu thought: not cut-and-dried in its conclusions, but looking all round questions and weighing up this and that, balancing one thing against another, so that in the end it often seems to come to no conclusion. Members of the Congress Party have always been shy about acknowledging any good in the Doon School as they reckon that they represent the people while the school caters for the rich, so we weren't sure what sort of a message the Governor-General would have for us. He walked and drove round with John and was apparently quite bowled over by what he saw (we had put on examples of various school activities), and in his speech he more or less admitted it. He said that the school filled him with hope and should be a model for the rest of India. Then he paused to qualify what he had just said. The school was very good and there ought to be more schools like it, but it was too expensive and you couldn't have such places without too heavy expenditure. Teaching was likely to go on in English, though they might not approve as nationalists, but how else were boys from all over India to understand? The English had left India physically but their influence remained and could not be got rid of. It was like a halter round their necks, but perhaps he ought to call it a necklace. In such a way he spoke; not a stirring speech like Mountbatten's, but a kindly, quizzical, questioning talk. Lots of old boys turned up—majors and prosperous businessmen. How quickly they grow up, while a schoolmaster tends to remain the same from twenty onwards. After they left I found on my table a cigarette box with a card 'To Jack from Kashmir House old boys'. Very touching and the sort of thing that helps to keep the wheels going round.

There is one more bit of news. Last week Brigadier Mahadeo Singh, Commandant of the I.M.A., came along and asked me if I would take on the job of headmaster of the new junior wing that they are starting for the Indian War Academy. I suggested to John that the school might give me leave for two years so that I could start the thing going and then come back here which is where I really want to be. This would suit them as they quite naturally want an Indian for the job, but haven't yet found a suitable one. John agreed and I put the idea to the Brigadier who liked it. That is where the matter stands at the moment. Quite possibly Finance may turn me down as I have said that I cannot afford to go for less than I get here. If they do, I shan't worry as the job will be an awful headache to start with, but it is nice to have been asked.

29.11.48. *The Doon School.* Will you and can you lend me another £100. I have taken on this new job for one year and I shall have to have a car for it. I can't afford it but have already given the order for a second-hand jeep. I am to be Principal of the Inter-Services Wing of the Armed Forces Academy. To start with this will be in Clement Town, some six miles out of Dehra Dun, while the I.M.A. will continue functioning as it is and will train the army cadets when they leave the I.S.W. The naval cadets will go on to Dartmouth, and the Air Force ones to further Air Force training. Eventually, the I.S.W. will move to a new centre that has yet to be built near Poona. We shall take in cadets between 15 and 17 years old and have them for two, and later three years. It was at first planned that they should be older and stay longer, but that has been altered as the naval cadets would then be too old for Dartmouth. It is an experiment with two ideas: to give service officers a wider academic training, and to make the three services more aware of the problems and methods of each other. I shall be responsible for the academic training, starting it off, getting it working, and then handing over to an Indian who meanwhile will be chosen and trained. They want to start it at once, and it will open in the first week of January. I greatly wonder how much will be ready—books, playing fields, laboratories, lecturers—everything is being scrambled together in a hurry, and I am trying to organise my side while finishing off the team's work here. I went up to Delhi last week to be interviewed by the Defence Minister and the C. in C. and they appointed me that evening. After this term I shall take a week's holiday at Christmas in the jungle with Holdy. We have one of the best blocks in the Doon and should get some good shooting possibly a tiger. When I took on the job I said I must go home for at least three weeks. There is a vacation from mid May to early July, so expect me some time then.

Telegram received 30.11.48. Father died peacefully Nov. 29th. Mum and Jill's best love.

30.11.48. *From my mother.* You will have had the sad cable which Jill and I sent off yesterday. I'm afraid it must have been a terrible blow to you, as for a time we were so hopeful that Father was making progress. He has been so cheery and patient. He was a wonderful husband and father. I think everyone that knew him well loved him. I can't put it all into words but you will understand.

5.12.48. *The Doon School.* I have just had your letter of November 30th and the cable saying 'Don't come'. I'm glad, if it had to be, that it all happened quickly. He would have liked it to be that way. I do wish you would come out here. The complete change would help in readjustment. What is in my heart doesn't go down on paper, but I know how you will be feeling and I think you will also know how I wish I could be more help to you. I think all sorts of things I remember about him, and perhaps the happiest memories are those of Morgins. He always got a lot out of life, and he always did his job. I hope I shall be able to live up to him.

12.12.48. *The Doon School.* My new job will be interesting, though it will be largely administrative and I shall miss much of the human interest of teaching and running my house. Last week the I.M.A. had its annual passing-out parade attended by all sorts of V.I.Ps. I had talks with the Prime Minister, Admiral Parry, Air Marshal Sir Thomas Elmhirst, General Russell and others. Nehru, I am convinced, is a great man, though whether his moderate outlook will prevail against the extremes of communism and communalism is a matter that is still to be decided.

Thanks awfully for the wire that you have put £100 into my bank. The jeep is due to arrive this week. It is very sad to think of Puck's Hill having to be sold, but I can't think of any alternative. I shall feel I no longer have a real home.

2.1.49. *The Doon School.* I got there on the evening of the 23rd and that night a tiger killed, so on the 24th we had a beat for it. The shikaris had put up three machans (seats in trees), and we drew lots for them. I had been listening to the beat and watching the ground in front of me for about half an hour when as luck would have it, I saw the tiger making its way in my direction. I first saw it about 70 yards off and could hardly believe it was the tiger, it seemed so dark in colour. You don't seem to see the yellow when it is head on to you. It came on about ten yards and then paused and turned its head sideways, giving me a view of the shoulder which is the best target. I fired and bowled it over—not a bad shot as it proved afterwards on examination, but just not right to kill it outright. I was using the 405 Winchester given me by Mr. Canning. The tiger got up and all I could see through the undergrowth was its flank, so I fired again and hit it in the stomach and broke its further hind leg. It then crawled through the undergrowth for about ten yards and was invisible, but could be located by the movements of the shrubs. I was afraid that I had made an ass of myself and had a wounded tiger in thick undergrowth—a most dangerous thing. However, it lay quiet for some time, so we got out of our trees and proceeded to investigate. It was impossible to see it, so one of the shikaris climbed another tree, while I stood on the ground covering him with my rifle, and from the tree he fired a gun into the place where the tiger was. This produced an awful roar and an undignified scuttle and scramble up the nearest trees. I followed the shikari up his tree and from it got a view of the tiger's back as he lay on the ground. I put a final bullet through him and finished him off. It was exciting, but I felt, when it was all over, sad to have put an end to such a magnificent creature. He was a moderate size, but in splendid condition and with a very fine head. This was my first tiger shoot, and I was sorry that Holdy didn't get him as he has been trying for years, but has never had the luck.

I start on my new job tomorrow. How I wish I had made a fortune and could come back and live at Puck's Hill—but it's no good crying out for the moon.

Here follow technical and administrative details of the Inter-Service Training, a movement inspired by Field Marshal Sir Claude Auchinleck when commander-in-chief. Eventually the outfit was to move from Dehra Dun to Khadakvasla near Pune and renamed National Defence Academy.

In an examination in 1949 a number of cadets were caught or found to have been cheating, and I spoke to the whole Wing as follows: 'I want to speak to you about this business of cheating in examinations. I know that many of us do not look on taking help from our neighbour as an action of the same meanness as, shall we say, stealing, and if someone cheats to save himself from relegation of withdrawal, I know there are those who think his mistake was not in cheating, but in being found out. I do not agree. If a person cheats in order to secure a higher place in the order of merit than his neighbour who has not cheated, then I think you will all agree that there is something mean about it. So what I want to explain to you is why we will not allow people to accept help from their neighbours, even if it is offered. I want first to make a distinction between work done in an examination and work done during preparation. In preparation it is permissible to ask for explanations and help from other cadets in your company. Our object is that you should understand what we are trying to teach you, and if another cadet can help you to do so, so much the better. The important thing is that you should not copy his work without understanding it, and that is why I ask my pupils to write "Helped" at the end of work that they have not done by themselves. I can then test whether they fully understand it, and help them further if they do not. I have noticed in my French class here that cadets are apt to help each other when I am asking them questions, and when I complained one of them said that they were learning to work as a team. This is a sound idea, but there is a proper time for it, and you have also to learn to stand on your own feet, and not to need to rely on others. And now I come to why we will not tolerate cheating in examinations. They are partly a test of the success or failure of our methods of instruction. If results are arrived at by unfair means and appear better than they are, then we shall be deluding ourselves and supplying the Army, Navy and Air Force with officers of a lower calibre than we should. If I allow a cadet to pass out from here who cannot think for himself and who has to rely on others to do his work for him, then I am cheating your country. From your point of view, if you want to develop that self-confidence that an officer must have to be successful, you will learn to work on your own, and in an examination you will observe the rules, just as you would in a game of football or a boxing match. The Commandant has asked me to tell you that he will not tolerate cheating and that anyone caught in future will be much more severely dealt with than those this term. I will try to see that temptation is not placed in your way, and that seating arrangements make it impossible to copy; but the important thing is that you should make up your minds that something that you realise is not really straight is something you will not let yourselves be tempted to do.'

It was not easy to get the cadets to view examinations in what we considered the right perspective, and on a later occasion I spoke to them again. I said: 'I do not want you to feel that once you have finished an examination in a subject that the subject is finished with and can be dismissed from your interests. Perhaps the most fundamental work that human beings have to do is to grow food from the soil, and we can all imagine the feeling of relief with which the labourer comes to the end of a hard day's work and put aside his plough; but he would be a very poor farmer if, having done this, he allowed the field that he had cultivated to become choked with weeds. Part of your work here is to cultivate your minds, and you would be just as foolish if after examinations, you ceased to take further interest, and allowed them to become unfertile. There is a very general tendency, not only among you cadets, to feel that once an examination is over, work is at an end. This is partly because, in the country at large, examinations have been widely used more as an end than as a means. Once someone has his degree he feels that he has qualified himself for a job, and he takes no more interest in real learning. This is not what we want here. All that you are learning here is designed to help you to be better officers and citizens of a great country, and if you do not continue your interests in, shall we say, History or Applied Physics, you will reduce your value and efficiency as officers and citizens. You will not be able to maintain a detailed interest in all the branches of learning covered here: but we are trying to give you an all round understanding of man's search for truth, and the fundamentals of general knowledge from which foundation you can later develop any specialized knowledge that suits your particular interests and capacities. What is important is not that you should do well in our examinations only, but that you should develop technical skills and the ability to think clearly, and should become citizens of wider understanding and interests than you would have been without the opportunities offered you here.'

At the end of my time as Principal of the J.S.W. I felt that life there, in spite of early difficulties, was showing very healthy progress, and that the bearing of the cadets made obvious the value of the service training that they were getting. There had been admirable variety in their concerts and socials. Clubs and Societies were functioning well, and we had had a number of stimulating addresses by eminent visitors. In my handing-over report to the Commandant I wrote: 'My time at the J.S.W. has been an extremely happy one, and I have felt it a very high honour to play a part in the development of this new institution...and in building up a way of life in planning which there has always been room for different points of view.'

16
EARLY DAYS AT CLEMENT TOWN

In January 1949 Gibson joined as Principal of the Joint Services Wing of the National Defence Academy in Clement Town on the outskirts of Dehra Dun. His letters at this time are full of teething troubles he was facing – lack of staff and equipment, bureaucratic hassles, low standard of candidates and so on. Soon after joining he suffered a personal setback as well when he had an attack of Bell's palsy which left one side of his face out of action though he was cured within six months. Dr. Sen of Delhi University he praises in one of his letters is the eminent historian Surendranath Nath Sen, who was to produce a scholarly account of the Indian 'Mutiny' eight years later on the occasion of its centenary year.

The vacations in these two years were spent by Gibson in pursuing his usual hobbies in the company of his colleagues and students – a trip down the Ganga on a rubber landing craft he had imported, skiing in Kashmir and another abortive attempt to climb the Bandarpunch.

In early 1950 he also made his first visit to Mayo College in Ajmer, not realizing his life would be tied up with it in later years. This first visit was as an observer at the headmasters' conference there.

16.1.49. I.S.W., Clement Town, Dehra Dun. Here I am after a very hectic fortnight, in my new home. It is one long row of rooms running from north to south with a front veranda on the east. Most of the week 2nd to 8th I had to spend in Delhi sitting on selection boards to choose more academic staff for this place. The selection is still going on, but I came back here as the cadets arrived from the 8th to 10th since when I have been hard at it trying to get some sort of academic instruction going with a skeleton staff. There are only three of us at present, though the Services are at full strength and will have to do most of the work till my staff turns up.

I had an interesting time in Delhi, but didn't find it a place where you could get much done in a hurry. The wheels of government rotate slowly, and when there are several different departments involved, as there are here, it takes a good deal of time before the cogs connect and anything comes out of the machine. Mahadeo Singh, Brigadier but likely to be upgraded to Major General shortly, is Commandant of the two Wings, and I am responsible to him for the academic training at the I.S.W.

30.1.49. The Military Hospital, Dehra Dun. Here I am laid up with Bell's Palsy, the left side of my face out of action. At first they thought I might have polio, but that, thank goodness, is ruled out. I seem to get a tiny bit better each day, but it is slow and tedious and I ought to get back to work. I have a stream of visitors to cheer me up.

27.2.49. I.S.W., Clement Town. I'm still under daily electric shocks at the hospital and orders to go slow, which I do, though it's much against the grain with all there is to do here. However, during the last fortnight I've interviewed all the cadets individually, and tomorrow I start lecturing to see how it goes.

24.4.49. I.S.W., Clement Town. I'm hoping to get leave for four weeks in June to come home and see a specialist about my face. I don't suppose he will be able to do any more than the very good one in Delhi, but it improves so slowly. This afternoon I drove over to Tunwalla to see Miss Stehelin. She is having to build herself a new house as her present one is falling down. She exists very bravely, and I think happily, on a tiny pension. I was hoping to buy some of her strawberries, but they have done very badly this year. She used to gather at least 100 lb. a season. Though her father and grandfather I understand were both generals, she and her father were born in India and she won't take the trouble to get a British passport.' Next Sunday the C-in-C., General Cariappa, is visiting us, so I shan't get the day off.

24.5.49. *I.S.W., Clement Town.* We are winding up our first term here. I'm a bit worried at the low academic standards of the cadets, but they are all so keen that I hope we shall be able to get them on and not have to turf any of them out. We have a long way to go before we can offer anything like as good an education here as the boys get at the Doon School, though it costs the Government more than three times as much to train a cadet here as it costs the parents of a D.S. boy. We have an Inauguration Parade on June 4th which involves endless preparations. My face is improving and my fear that I shall spend the rest of my life looking like the village idiot recedes—or is that vanity? I shall be getting home for four weeks early in June.

13.7.49. *Delhi Station.* I had a good flight back to India, the best part over the Alps just at sunset when the summits were tinged with an Alpine glow and the valleys filled with feathery clouds. The Mischabel group with the Matterhorn behind woke memories of my two Easters at the Britannia Hut in what now seems another life. How carefree and what fun it was. The most annoying part of the trip was losing my wallet at Heathrow. It had been given to me by Phil Taylor, the skipper of the Cape Teriberski, after my trip with him from Hull, and I have used it ever since: however there wasn't much money left in it. When they weighed my luggage they asked for £30 and my face fell so far that they allowed me to take the heaviest bag by hand, and I only had to pay £6-11-0.

25.7.49. *I.S.W., Clement Town.* I am very fit and everyone says how wonderfully my face has improved. I'm having difficulty with my staff—all the better ones are being offered better jobs with better pay. Indians are attracted more by pay than by the circumstances of life, and I wish we could avoid these continual changes.

14.8.49. *I.S.W., Clement Town.* I'm just back from Delhi where I had to go to interview candidates for posts here. The visit was fairly successful, though the standard of some of the candidates was pretty low. With the great expansion that is going on in the country it is difficult to find enough good people to go around. At the interviews for a historian we had to help us a Dr. Sen of Delhi University and I was most impressed by him. He had a detailed knowledge of all period and countries and was expert at bowling out imposters. I was thankful that I didn't have to answer some of the questions he put and felt his scholarship spoke well for Oxford where he took a degree.

Things go along well enough here though all sorts of difficulties crop up unexpectedly. The latest is that the electric supply company now say that they can't let us have enough power to run our workshops. General Williams, the Engineer in Chief, is coming tomorrow to try to solve the problems. Another difficulty is to get the money out of Government for a generating plant for the labs. This usually takes months, but we need it at once. Then, I have two clerks in my office, both good and one outstanding, but they haven't the qualifications laid down, and if I have to get rid of them I shan't get anyone nearly so able, and I'm fighting for special permission to keep them. We are having very heavy rains and a spring has emerged outside my office and threatens to undermine it. In my bungalow I first hear the distant roar of the rain in the forest, and the note gets higher as the rain approaches, and then the air is white with it. Everything is damp, but it won't last many weeks longer and it has compensations in the greenery all round and the magnificent cloud effects. On our way back from Delhi we had first a burst tyre, then a second puncture which we had to mend on the spot. Life has its little trials, but I find it well worth living.

22.8.49. *I.S.W., Clement Town.* Last Monday was a holiday for Independence Day and it rained all day, so I spent it in my dark room enlarging photos I took two years ago, and there are lots of earlier ones I haven't yet had time to touch. Some of my paper is six years old, going back to the time I last did any serious enlarging.

21.9.49. *I.S.W., Clement Town.* We have had a lot to do for the past fortnight as they suddenly sent us a new batch of cadets, and these had to be examined and graded and put into classes with those who arrived in July.

27.9.49. *I.S.W., Clement Town.* The vice-chancellors all wanted me to give more time to their particular pet subjects, but in the end all went off well. They criticized our lack of equipment and teaching staff (the fault of government departments in Delhi who take three months to do what an individual with authority could accomplish in as many weeks) but gave us a pat on the back for what we have managed to get going. The Committee has recommended that I should be asked to stay on here for a second year. Next July would be the time I would like to move, so that I can get my garden going, but I've become very interested in the work here, so if they keep me I shan't moan. The financial people and those who think only Indian nationals should be employed in government jobs want to be rid of me at the end of this year, so I don't know what will happen.

10.10.49. *I.S.W., Clement Town.* For our half-term break I took a party in my rubber landing craft down part of the Song to the Ganges, and then another party down the Ganges to Hardwar. On the way we saw a huge mahseer leap clear of the water—a thing I have never seen before. I had no luck with my rod, and I think they don't feed after a moonlit night. Our main camp was at the Forest Rest House at Ranipur, near Hardwar. There were plenty of jungle fowl, but it was difficult to drive them through the thick forest. On two evenings cadets sat along a streamside hoping for a shot at a pig or deer. They found this exciting as they heard both pig and deer as well as panther but none came into the open. This morning the cadets helped to hoist our naval mast which has been sent from Bombay to help give the place an inter-service atmosphere. It cost over £1,000 to get it here as the railway line had to be re-laid in places to get it round the corners, but I think you can't measure the importance of the idea in terms of money.

25.10.49. *I.S.W., Clement Town.* On Friday I attended Founder's Day at the Doon School. It went off very well. John, in his report, had mentioned that some old boys weren't particularly good correspondents, and Sir Homi Modi, Governor of the U.P. and the Chief Guest, whose sons are or have been at the school, started off about one of them who is now in America. 'I haven't heard from him once' he said, 'for the past three months...' pause while everyone laughed. 'No, not what you think,' he continued, 'I haven't heard from him once for the past three months without his writing to tell me how I ought to comport myself as a Governor.' Loud laughter. It was a most amusing speech, much more fun that what one usually gets these days. Then the school produced a Masque on Diwali in the open-air theatre—very beautiful with the lamps. Last night I judged boxing there, and of course this was where Mountbatten gave his brilliant address: a place of many associations.

27.11.49. *I.S.W., Clement Town.* I was in Delhi from the 15th to 22nd helping to choose my successor and more staff for next term. I hope I persuaded the F.P.S.C. to pick the right person to succeed me, Bhawani Shankar, my senior colleague here. Apart from the interviews, I barged into the offices of various people like the Defence Secretary and told them that we can't get decisions quickly enough from Delhi where our problems are passed from department to department and no one solves them. I was able to say things that someone needing to keep his job might not have liked to have risked saying, and I hope I have been able to do some good.

I stayed with the Saxtons and they looked after me royally. They took me to the Governor General's 'At Home'. Rajaji, though he himself lives very simply, keeps up the pomp and circumstance for state occasions. His Bodyguard, commanded by Govind Singh, one of my Kashmir House old boys, is of splendid men, all over six foot tall in magnificent uniforms. They lined the stairs and reception halls whose walls are covered with the portraits of ex-Viceroys. It was all very grand, and contrasted with the plain fare of nuts and tea provided, and the uncouth appearance of some of the Congress politicians in ill-fitting homespun. Government servants dressed in smart black and white. I met many old friends including old boys of the Doon School, who are doing very well. At the interviews it was embarrassing to listen to one after another of the candidates referring to what he had learnt from the Doon School and three of the short-listed candidates to follow me were old Doon School masters.

Last Friday I went to see the new University of Roorkee inaugurated by Pandit Nehru, with speeches by Sir Homi Modi and Pandit Pant. There was an exhibition of what the engineers have done for India during the past 100 year since the college which has now become a university was started.

My supper has just been brought in by a resigned Samuel who thinks it's time I went to bed. There's lot more to tell you, of the way monkeys have been raiding my garden, how large my tomatoes are, what a mistake it was to buy a second-hand jeep, of the letter Mrs. Saxton had from Lord Dunsany describing how he was in New Delhi when it was building and why none of the houses had wide enough verandas because Lutyens was only there in the cold weather and told those who complained that the sun was good for them, of the visit we had last week from a Swiss general and how I wore my Swiss Alpine Club badge and he was very pleased and we talked of the Porte du Soleil which he had skied down often, and all sorts of other things, but I must to bed.

19.12.49. *I.S.W.* The last three weeks have been a ghastly rush—concerts, parades, exams; generals, air marshals, cabinet ministers; and the jigsaw puzzle of next term's time-table to make up. Tomorrow I have to go to Delhi again to help choose more staff as our numbers are to increase by anything up to 250 next term. In January I'm off to Kashmir for 10 days' skiing which is really splendid and makes up for any trials. The Army is taking me as I am going officially to advise on skiing matters.

1.1.50. *Joint Services Wing, National Defence Academy, Clement Town.* Note that we have had our name slightly changed and I shall have to get new letter-heads. Tomorrow I'm off with Holdy to Kashmir. In Delhi I had a very interesting evening dining with General Cariappa who had invited the Auk. I wish the Auk could have visited this place for which he was mostly responsible, but the cadets would have been away. It is sad, but he is now rather at a discount in India as they think he favoured Pakistan when partition took place. In fact, he told me that he did his best to see that things were divided fairly, and it broke his heart to have to split up the army he had built up. He is one of my heroes. In Delhi I was informed that the Defence Minister wanted me to stay on here permanently and was trying to arrange for this with the Cabinet. It's a great compliment, but I really prefer my work at the Doon School, unbound as it is with red tape, and anyhow the politicians are likely to insist on having an Indian, and I think they would be right.

19.1.50. *New Delhi.* Am back from Kashmir where the skiing was splendid and I found I could do all my old turns; but the cold was intense—41 degrees of frost on two nights. Am just off to a conference in Ajmer.

1.2.50. *J.S.W., Clement Town.* Kashmir was great fun if rather tough. I enjoyed the Skiing immensely and was glad to find I could still wag my tail successfully and take pleasure in the thrill of running down fairly fast, though not with quite the dash of old days. The chief drawback to relaxation was the difficulty of keeping warm when you weren't Skiing. We lived in wooden huts built for summer visitors and draughts whistled in through cracks in the walls and floors. Holdy nearly lost his false teeth when his servant threw out the lump of ice containing them from his tooth mug, and many people had troublesome coughs and colds. The army had employed Swiss instructors for their ski school and one of them turned out to be the nephew of Herman Imseng from Saas. Do you remember him at Morgins where I once beat him in a race? I used to ski with him at Saas and had long talks about runs round there with his nephew.

The flight out of Kashmir was wonderful; up the valley between the High Himalayas and the outer Pir Panjal, and all along we could see splendid skiing country. It only needs enterprise and some road and hut building to turn Kashmir into an Asian Switzerland—not a new idea, but no one has acted on it yet.

From Delhi I went to Ajmer to attend a conference of headmasters at Mayo College, now run by Vyas, my old Kashmir House tutor. The school was started for Chiefs and no one who was not a noble was allowed to attend, and the Principal used to have up to six princes living in his house as special wards and charge them Rs.500 a month in addition to his salary. Those palmy days are now over, and no private pupils are allowed, while the school has been thrown open to commoners. The Doon School has exercised much influence on the old Chiefs' Colleges, but they retain a spacious atmosphere and Vyas did us all very well. The general public is still hesitant to send boys, but I think they are missing a good thing as these schools have large resources, the Mayo staff seemed good and keen and the building and ground are splendid. I was very interested to see a bit of Rajputana and a side of life which with its virtues and failings, is rapidly coming to an end.

John and I came back together, picking up my jeep which I had left in Delhi, and driving home from there. On the way we visited Sardhana, not far outside Meerut, where are a Roman Catholic Cathedral and the remains of a palace built by a romantic character, the Begum Sumroo. She lived in the second half of the 18th century, starting life as a Kashmiri dancing girl and marrying an adventurer from Luxembourg who, once a private soldier in the employ of the French East India Company, later did very well with his own private army which he hired out to local powers. When he died his widow took command of his troops and ended up as a sort of ruling princess. She became a Catholic, persuaded the Pope to appoint her chaplain a bishop, built him a cathedral in which she is buried beneath an ornate marble monument, and left money for an orphanage which is now run in her palace.

My visit to Ajmer was an observer of the conference of headmasters was well worth while. I was much struck with the boys there. Intellectually many of them are at present a bit backward, but this can be righted in time. I liked their good manners and bearing, and have no doubt that there is good material for the Armed Forces in such schools.

.27.2.50. *J.S.W., Clement Town.* At the moment I'm in a furious temper. Several months ago I pointed out to the authorities that all our big days here were of a military nature—usually ceremonial parades—and that if this was all we showed the general public they would associate our activities solely with this side of our life here, and the cadets would come to think it the most important side. In order to help the cadets to realise that one of the most important things for them to do here is to take advantage of the general education we give them, and also to let the public know what we are up to (it has been pointed out by several people that they do not know enough) I suggested that on one day a year we should invite those interested to spend a day here, look round the Lecture Halls and see all our different methods—visual aids, group discussions, labs, workshops, club activities, etc.—in the morning, attend some sort of function with an address by an eminent educationist in the afternoon, and witness a play by the cadets in the evening. The idea was approved by the Director of Military Training and we have been getting on with planning and play rehearsals; we have even got the Minister for Education to give the address. This morning a bombshell arrives from Delhi: the Ministry of Defence consider that the general public has ample opportunity to visit us on the occasions of our passing-out parades, and do not approve of our plans. I have written to Delhi to say that I am not prepared to have my plans interfered with by people who do not know what they are talking about.

We have heard that Bhawani Shankar has been appointed to succeed me, which is excellent. He is to go abroad for experience first, so I shall probably have to stay till the end of the year. I'm trying to make the forces of what is now a foreign power as efficient as possible, and I suppose this is right because India and England have the same ideals at heart and if we can work together the world will be a better place to live in for everyone; but there are difficulties ahead. Educational standards are going down because of language problems, and though there are first class men in the Congress they are far too few to run this huge country and there are a number of useless people in important places. This is leading to disappointment and discontent for which there is no vent except via communism, and that is being repressed.

23.3.50. *J.S.W., Clement Town.* My dachshund, Herman the German, went out one evening after supper and never came back. Some days later his remains were found close by in the jungle by small boys tending cattle. There wasn't much left but his head and little paws with which he used to dance so daintily. He must have been taken by a panther or hyena.

I have had to go to Delhi for a conference and found it full of rumours of war with Pakistan. Hindus have been attacked in East Bengal and there have been reprisals on Muslims in places in India, though the government is making great efforts to protect its minority, more successful one gathers than those of the Pak government. There is popular demand for an expedition to protect the Hindu minority in East

Bengal, and this, of course, would mean war. I feel that ultimately India and Pakistan should reunite. They are geographically and economically a unit and their separation was a disaster.

While in Delhi I went to look at the President's garden. His A.D.C., an Old Doon School boy, took me round, and it must be one of the more beautiful gardens in the world. My own garden hasn't done too badly, and I won the first and second prizes for sweet peas in the local Flower Show and the first for schizanthus. The latter, from Sutton's seeds, have blooms as large as tortoise shell butterflies—no one has ever seen such blooms, and I wonder if they are a freak. I am saving the seed to see whether they do as well next year.

20.4.50. *J.S.W., Clement Town.* The last weeks have been filled for me with rehearsals of *Julius Caesar.* Here is an extract from a report by one of the cadets: 'Now get ready for Act II Scene I. Everything all right? Lights, No—no—no—Stop. Get more passion into your words, you must live your parts not just recite them: Right, go on.' And here is another. 'Our principal had invited the actor, Mr. Elliot, to watch us rehearsing. Talking to the cadets at the end, he said he was tremendously impressed and that he had no criticisms, but a bagful of praises.' We did the play last Saturday before an audience of something over a thousand and it went better than I dared to hope: indeed I think was a real success. We did it in our open-air theatre and my first consideration was that it should be audible. It took a good deal of practice to get the cadets to speak, not shout, their parts, throwing their voices up to fifty yards. Another difficulty was to get them out of the Indian habit of reciting in sing-song. All Indians have a great feeling for rhythm and this, added to the temptation to use the metrical construction as an aid to remembering, gave rise, to start with, to a monotonous recital. But as the boys got to know their parts they began to be able to live them unhampered by the effort to remember, and by the time we put on the play the words, with a few minor exceptions, came across very well. I left the cadets largely to interpret their parts themselves, only making suggestions here and there. Anthony worked out somewhat different from what one might expect him to be, but not, I thought, an improbable Anthony. He was a mob orator, a little vulgar perhaps, but a sort of Goebbels who could play upon the emotions of the crowd; and when he did become quiet and solemn as in 'O! pardon me, thou bleeding piece of earth…' and 'This was the noblest Roman of them all', the effect by contrast, was all the greater.

The next problem was dress. I decided to use Bengali dhotis which are near enough to the Roman toga, and only for the battle scenes did we attempt the Roman short skirt and armour. To quote the reviewer: 'You cannot, in the same breath, preach the essential universality of Shakespeare and insist on period costume in Shakespeare productions. Mr. Gibson obeyed a sound instinct when he decided that what is very convenient is very right.' My dressing of the play came in for some criticism, but not, I think, from people with any imagination.

The next problem was the lighting. 'The Bowl' had not been used before for a play and no lighting had been installed except overhead for boxing in the arena, and the film projection box at the back. To get what I wanted I had to get sanction for this and that from different government departments: someone had to agree to the installation, someone else the expenditure, and someone else the labour, and we only got our full lighting three days before the show which complicated rehearsals. In the end it worked out to be adequate. The stage was lit by building projections up each side-wall with lights behind them, the arena had the overhead lighting, and the rest we did with a searchlight from the projection cabinet at the back of the auditorium. Shadows were a difficulty, and as I couldn't cut them out I used them for effect. For lightning, we flickered the stage lights, throwing the walls into silhouette, and this was very effective. Act V, which so often tends to be anti-climax, we took with no breaks between scenes and with the actors all round the place and in the arena, with the search-light playing on the actors in different places. It went very fast with lots of movement. I again quote the reviewer: 'As on the Elizabethan stage, so here, the actors were half the time in the middle of the auditorium and not at the far end of a theatre, and this made for rapid elocution without loss of clarity. Hence the astonishing fact that the whole play, with a few slight cuts, took only two hours and a half. Another feature of the modern stage which eats up time is elaborate scenic apparatus which has to be changed between scenes. Mr. Gibson decided to cut this by doing with a bare minimum of stage equipment and dispensing with curtains. How the open-air theatre could be bent to any purpose, and effects inconceivable on the closed stage achieved, was shown vividly in the battle scenes presented on the high ground on both sides of the stage. With the spotlight travelling to and fro, picking out moments of tragedy in fighting, and the stage merging into the amplitude of the space around—here, you felt, drama shaded off almost into life.' We had a very good audience on the night, and for several rehearsals had had interested spectators. General Wilkinson and others came from Delhi and wanted us to take it there, but we can't manage that.

10.5.50. *J.S.W., Clement Town.* As soon as term is over I'm off to have another crack at Bandarpunch. The party will consist of Bill Williams, the E. in C.; Gurdial Singh; Jagjit Singh, a cadet here and Gu's brother; Greenwood, an English Warrant Officer on our P.T. staff; and myself. We shall have Tensing with us, his brother Kinchok, and another Sherpa youngster. In the evenings the air is heavy, really heavy, with the scent of Queen of the Night, a little white jasmine-like flower with a voluptuous fragrance. Two trees in my garden have just completed their annual shedding of leaves and are now covered with new ones in the most delicate light green. India may have its drawbacks, but there are many compensations.

General Thimayya has now taken over as Commandant, and we are very lucky to have him. I think he will be stimulating to work under. The Defence Ministry want me to stay on while Bhawani Shankar is touring abroad. The letter you wondered whether I was right to write to Delhi did no harm, and the fact that the day I had planned went off so well convinced those who came that my original suggestion was a good one.

5.6.50. *J.S.W., Clement Town.* My bedroom is littered with parcels of tents, clothing and provisions all of which must be sorted into loads of the right weight. The Sherpas are living on my back veranda as all bedrooms are full.

Gibson was hankering after climbing the Bandarpunch and the following chapter is a very condensed version of his letters since in terms of description of scenery, terrain and problems of climbing it offers little variety to his previous adventures. Eventually he again failed to climb.

9.6.50. *Dharasu Rest House.* We got up at four this morning (I didn't get to bed till nearly two and thought of you in the old days packing for Switzerland). From the J.S.W. we drove to Rishikesh, Narendranagar, Tehri and here in a bus and a lorry. I was in the latter sitting on piles of boxes, tents and beddings among a group of our porters who spent part of the time picking nits out of each other's hair. I snuggled down among the softer packages and slept for several hours of the journey. Sleep, however, was interrupted frequently by breakdowns caused by the beastly petrol they are supplying nowadays—a mixture of petrol and alcohol made from molasses. In the cold weather this is all right, but in the heat it won't work and we stopped to clean the system and cool the petrol pump at least 14 times.

12.6.50. *Dodi Tal.* Here we are at my favourite old haunt a few feet below 10,000, and I'm feeling very fit. We had an enjoyable walk here: a stiffish 2,000 feet over open grass slopes dotted with dwarf gentian, delphinium and other flowers, and then a gradual rise through the forest; a winding in and out round valleys and spurs along a very broken road. However we had other excitements. Bill saw a panther just above him while I, who was ten yards behind, saw a sambur jump off in the opposite direction. The panther was probably stalking it, and our arrival may have saved it.

14.6.50. *Camp in Hanuman Ganga Valley.* All goes very well so far, and we are at about 11,000 feet. We had a good walk from Dodi Tal over the ridge at about 12,500 and then down into this valley which is the drainage of most of the southern glaciers of Bandarpunch. From the ridge we had fleeting glimpses of the mountain which is a fine one, and it would be very satisfying to get to its summit. The flowers are marvellous. I have often noticed how scents stimulate the memory and lower down were the briar roses with sweet-smelling leaves and deep pink flowers, as well as another with white flowers with a strong sweet scent which recalled Aunt Lizzy's house and Limpsfield covered with creeping roses.

15.6.50. *Base Camp.* A short march today to about 12,000 ft. and our old base camp of 1946; then sorting of clothes and stores to take up to Camp I tomorrow. Here is the cave where John and Tensing slept in

1937 while I and Rinsing, 3,000 feet higher, feared they might have been drowned in the Hanuman Ganga, and here too are our trenches that we dug round the tents in the rain in 1946. We have even used some of the firewood we then collected and left unburned, and have found several old tent pegs.

17.6.50. Today hasn't gone quite according to plan as I spent most of last night being sick and have had to rest today. Guru and Tensing climbed to within 300 feet of the ridge and dumped a tent, ropes and crampons there, and are now safely back. Greenwood has returned with Tensing's brother Kenjan or Kinchock—we can't quite make out his name so call him King John—and more stores. Bill is determined to get to the ridge at least and has pitched his tent some 1,800 feet below us. The General Sahib and his enthusiasm are a matter of great joy to the Sherpas and just a little anxiety to myself.

19.6.50. *Camp I*. Guru, Greenwood, Tensing and I climbed to about 19,500 feet this morning to find a site for Camp III and see how the mountain would go. All went well, and it looks within our abilities. This beastly petrol with power alcohol added works no better in the stoves than it did in the truck.

20.6.50. *Camp III, 19,000 ft*. Tensing, King John and Greenwood have made the top and got back here about an hour after I arrived. We are all very happy and satisfied—though four in my tiny tent is too many, and I fear the night will be uncomfortable.

21.6.50. *Camp I*. It snowed all night and by the morning it was clear that it would be madness for Tensing and me to try for the summit. Last night it had looked as though there was nothing left for me to do but to follow yesterday's party. Tonight we are all back at Camp I after a hard day getting down in trying conditions. I'm sad that I haven't climbed Bandarpunch after all my efforts, but there may still be a chance.

22.6.50. *Camp II*. In a fit of midsummer madness here we are back at Camp II with Bill. The morning broke beautifully fine and Bill was determined to get to the ridge.

23.6.50. *Camp I.* A disappointing day. It snowed all last night and off and on this morning. The plan had been for Tensing, King John and myself to do a second ascent of the mountain, accompanied to the top of the rocks by Jagjit and the third Sherpa. We set out, leaving Bill to look after the Camp in doubtful weather about 7 a.m. Some 30 feet below the top of the rocks Jagjit complained of cold fingers. We removed his gloves and warmed his hands, and then it began to blow and snow hard. Jagjit had done very well to get as high, and we decided we must descend. A disconsolate party returned to Camp II. It snowed hard the rest of the morning, and, as much fresh snow would have made it difficult to get Bill down, and would also have made the top of the Bandarpunch too dangerous to attempt, we decided to evacuate Camp II and are now down at Camp I after an arduous and somewhat unpleasant roped descent. So my chances of getting to the top are at an end. However, the mountain has at last been climbed at, I believe, the ninth attempt, and Bill has successfully climbed to 18,000 feet—not bad for a general officer.

25.6.50. *Camp T/G.* A very long day, perhaps my longest. We woke at 4 a.m., having decided to try for the western or White Peak of Bandarpunch, height 20,020 feet. I had thought of trying the summit ridge from the west, but Tensing was all for an attack up the south face, so there we went, and all went well for a time. We climbed 3,000 feet in the first four hours and then met vertical walls and ice-filled gullies. I fell off while leading up one of the former. A hand-hold I had tested gave way and as I turned in the air I had a fine view of the valley thousands of feet below. Tensing, who was directly below me on a broad ledge, fielded me cleanly, and both he and King John thought it a huge joke. By 11:30 the clouds had come down and it was no longer possible to see our route any distance ahead, so reluctantly, we decided on retreat. We were well over 19,000 and not far off our objective, so this was another disappointment; but it had been a fine climb and we all enjoyed it enormously.

7.7.50. *J.S.W., Clement Town.* We reached Narendranagar at 11 p.m. yesterday after a drive down 40 miles of mountain road with just room for the bus and no parapet between the side of the road and drops of upto 1,000 feet beyond. We left again early this morning and arrived here for lunch. It has been a wonderful trip and holiday.

17
MY LAST YEAR AT THE J.S.W.

During his final year at JSW Gibson went on an inspection tour of the two Lawrence Schools in India with a long pedigree – one in Sanawar near Simla and the other in Lovedale in the Nilgiri Hills, liking the latter so much he secretly wished to be its principal. During vacations there were a number of rubber boat adventures in the rivers near by and his time there ended with the production of 'The Hundred Days', based on Thomas Hardy's *The Dynasts*. Gibson left JSW for good in the summer of 1951, handing over to a dear colleague, Bhawani Shankar, before taking a flight to England on vacation. Shankar was to die not long after of leukaemia.

3.8.50. *J.S.W., Clement Town.* For the past eleven days I've been on an inspection of the Lawrence Schools at Sanawar and Lovedale started nearly a hundred years ago, one by, and the other as, a memorial to Sir Henry Lawrence. They were for the children of British soldiers serving or settled in India and with Independence they were handed over to the Ministry of Education which is now running them as Public Schools open to any child irrespective of caste or creed, though they are responsible for educating free a certain number of English or Anglo-Indian children entitled to this under the terms of handing over. We first went to Sanawar in the Simla Hills, and are now at the other end of India, to which we flew, at Lovedale in the Nilgiri Hills.

11. 8. 50. *J. S. W., Clement Town.* I had expected this inspection to be something of a jaunt and holiday, but actually I found the work demanded a great deal of concentration, and what with getting up to see P.T. at 0600, and attending concerts and social gatherings in the evenings, our time was very full. Sanawar is on top of a hill the whole of which belongs to the school. The buildings are excellent, but owing to the terrain, playing-grounds are few and rather small. The staff is mostly Anglo-Indian with an excellent English Principal. The difficulty with both Sanawar and Lovedale will be to change the atmosphere from an English to an Indian one. To do this they will have to have really first class Indians on the staff, and at Sanawar they haven't this yet, while at Lovedale they are beginning to collect some. At Sanawar there are some, and at Lovedale many Anglo-Indian or English children, while most of the staffs, though Indian citizens, are not culturally Indians, and this is bound to complicate the necessary change to an Indian outlook. For instance we found at Sanawar that the children (both schools are co-educational) were having their morning assembly in a Christian chapel, saying prayers kneeling, and singing hymns from a Christian prayer-book, though the prayers and hymns had been carefully chosen so as to be suitable to any God. At Lovedale we found that the head boy last year had been expelled for refusing to carry the Indian flag at a parade, because before that he had carried the Union Jack and he was damned if he was going to carry any other flag. By expelling him they have made him a hero in his own and his friends' estimation. They should have said, 'If you don't wish to carry the flag of the country in which you are living and which has made itself responsible for your education, please fall out of the parade', and I think the incident could have been got round without bitterness on either side. I felt that the atmosphere was happier at Sanawar than at Lovedale. At the former, though there will have to be some reorientation of outlook, most of the old staff who have stayed on, are devoted to the school, and are keen to make a good show of it under the new conditions. Carter, the Principal, has been there for many years, and the Government has very wisely asked him to remain, in spite of the rule that all government posts should be filled by Indian nationals.

At Lovedale some fifteen of the staff decided not to take Indian citizenship and have left, and the gap is not easy to fill. The old Principal has also gone, and at present the post is filled by a man from the Ministry of Education until a permanent man can be found. There are also there many more Anglo-Indian children, some of whom have the attitude that the school is theirs, and resent the introduction of Indian children. As against this, the Indians on the staff are better than those at Sanawar, and the acting Principal is a man with lots of ideas and enthusiasms. They have a first-class Art School, an excellent school band, and very good domestic science teaching. I bought a lovely picture of the Nilgiri Hills by Mukerjee, their Art Master, and was given a very striking black-and-white drawing by one of their boys.

I had a talk to all the older boys and girls, both Indian and European and mixed, and I suggested to those who looked on themselves as British that they could do a much better job of work than any High Commissioner sitting in Delhi; that they might well be grateful to the Indian Government for its courage in taking on their school rather than letting it gradually peter out, and that their ambition should be to pass on the fine tradition of their school to its future boys and girls. To the Indians I said that they could learn a lot from the older European boys and girls—how to enjoy knowing about birds and butterflies they could find around them, the joy of walking in the hills, and so on. I felt that my talk went down well, and I hope it may have done something to help resolve the difficult situation.

Apart from the inspections, it was fun to see more of India. In spite of the monsoon, the flight over the Peninsula was comfortable both ways, and Ooty is lovely. I ate mushrooms, strawberries, Brussels sprouts and beef, and felt quite like being at home. I visited a Toda settlement and on one evening we were shown a colour film of the Nilgiri Hills and their wild life which made me want to see more of this part of the country, and indeed I felt that it would be fun to be Principal at Lovedale and try to solve its problems which in some ways I am rather well fitted to do; but this is not on as I don't intend to claim Indian citizenship by domicile, and I still want to return to the Doon School. I have little doubt that the Doon School is one of the best in the world, and there is another in India, the Scindia School in Gwalior, that I suspect is also very good. I am interested in the great influence that the Doon School seems to have had on education in India. Wherever you go, people in the scholastic line ask you about it and you hear of those who have taken ideas from it. What worries me a little is that we have to demand higher fees than almost any other school as we get no outside help. The two schools we were inspecting are at present financed by the Government as well as having large endowments. They can therefore afford to charge considerably smaller fees than the Doon School, and this will eventually mean that we shall have to depend on the richest people, largely merchants, whereas I should like to have many more sons of Service people. On the way up to Lovedale we passed through Bangalore and called on Sir Mirza Ismail. He was still exactly as I remembered him in 1938, and we came on him gardening in his pyjamas and left him very smartly dressed after a tea party.

30.8.50. *J.S.W., Clement Town.* I'm still a geography lecturer short and it takes up all my time and energy to do his work as well as my own. I've been reading the accounts of the French Himalayan expedition in *Alpinisme*. They collected 6,242,201 francs from the public together with getting almost all their food and equipment free or at very reduced prices. My share of our Bandarpunch expedition was just over £100, and though it's satisfactory to have done it on our own, I feel a bit envious of those who are able to enjoy themselves in the mountains at other people's expense.

26.9.50. *J.S.W., Clement Town.* We have our mid-term break of 4½ days coming, and I'm looking forward to a blow of fresh air. I and Pathania, the Wing Adjutant and a very good officer, plan to take a party of cadets down the Ganges in my rubber boat from Devaprayag to Hardwar. As far as I can find out there are no falls in the river and I hope no rapids too swift for the craft. If we can make the descent it should be a wonderful one.

I have been offered the headmastership of the Hyderabad Public School. Financially I would be better off than when I return to the Doon School, but my heart is there, so I have decided not to accept it.

12.10.50. *J.S.W., Clement Town.* The half-term holiday was a great success, though I don't think I would willingly repeat our adventures. The first afternoon was taken up getting to Rishikesh. We were ready by 7 the next morning, the advertised time for the bus to leave, but had to wait exasperating hours till it was stuffed full and it started. We reached Devaprayag about 1430 and enlisted the help of a gang of men to carry the boat down to the junction of the Alaknanda and Bhagirathi, the Prayag or sacred meeting-place of the two great rivers that form the Ganges, where pilgrims take their dip hanging on to chains that prevent them being washed away by the swirling current. Here we inflated the rubber floats and launched her and set off about 1530. The locals thought that we were going to return by bus and let the boat float down to see how far it got, and they warned us that we wouldn't survive for long when we embarked. The first 100 yards were a bit unnerving as the water broke over the sides, however, we survived and felt more confident. I knew the boat could not sink, but was anxious about two possibilities. If one of the floats got ripped open we would have to abandon ship and walk the 50 miles to Rishikesh and more, and, more dangerous, if we caught on a rock, the force of the water might capsize us. The cadets all wore inflated like jackets, but these, I soon realized, had only a psychological value, for if we had been upset the danger would not have been from drowning but from being bashed to pieces. Anyway, we swished down the gorge through the most magnificent scenery, here and there between great black cliffs, and at other places past high shelving banks of sand. The movements of the water were most interesting. At places it welled up in great black humps, in others it swirled round in whirlpools in which we occasionally gyrated, finding it difficult to get the boat back into the main current. Here and there it rushed over some great submerged rock and we found ourselves dropping as much as three feet the other side, or going round a cliff-enclosed corner we were thrown against the rocks and had all we could do to fend the boat off. Twice we crashed against these but took no harm, and our admiration for those who had made the craft was great. Pathania did what steering was possible with great skill from aft, and I was in the bows with another stout paddle. We had covered 21 miles by the time it began to grow dark—an average speed of over 7 m.p.h. in spite of delays in whirlpools and back eddies. In places we had certainly travelled as far as 15 m.p.h.

We were fortunate to be able to land on a gentle shelving bank leading to a little village. As we had expected to get away much earlier and to reach Rishikesh in a day, we had brought no beddings, and even if we had done so they would have been wet through. We went to a shop and tried to buy some blankets, but none were to be had; however I saw several rezais (cotton quilts) draped over a bed in the yard and the shopkeeper let me borrow two. We spent, I won't say a warm and comfortable night, but at least a much less cold and uncomfortable one than we should have had without them, one on the sand below us, and the other over us. We huddled together as close as we could, but the top one would not quite stretch from end to end of the line and there was a good deal of tugging during the night. I know because I was at one end. There was a heavy dew and we wore hats to keep this off. However we had had a good supper and tea laced with rum as a precaution against chills, and we survived all right.

The next morning we were off at 0830 hoping to reach Rishikesh for lunch, but that was not to be. Instead of getting easier, as we had expected, the river became more difficult, and in places we had to let the boat down over impassable looking boulders on the end of one of my climbing ropes. I or Pat went in the boat to ease it over rocks and through channels, while the rest ran down the side hanging on as hard as they could. It was tough work. At once place even this was impossible and we had to carry the boat which weighs 560 lb. some 50 yards over the rocks at the side of the river where it was difficult to keep the rubber lower floats from getting torn. At one place, when we were all in the boat, Pat slipped and fell out and was nearly carried away by the current; but he was able to grab one of the life-lines tied on the side and we pulled him in safely. The most exciting place was almost at the ends of the day's run, between Lachmanjhula and Rishikesh. We saw a fierce rapid ahead of us and made frantic efforts to row to the bank, but the current carried us down too fast, and we had to take the rapid. The waves towered above us and broke in on us swamping the boat so that we were sitting in water over our waists. I shouted 'Bail, bail her out', while trying to tear up the rubber sheet over the floor boards. Pat thought I was using the phrase 'Bail out' in the Air Force sense and shouted 'Don't, don't. Cling on, cling on'. Fortunately we all did and the boat emptied itself. It does this very quickly for under the rubber sheet are only folding battens of wood wired together so that, empty, you can roll the boat up. The deck is usually kept above water level by the lower floats and any water you ship empties itself through drainage holes in the rubber sheet; but we had taken in too much for this and I was afraid the added weight might settle us too deep and floats would get torn. The boat is wonderfully constructed, and this didn't happen, so all was well. We beached it to make sure nothing was wrong and to top up the floats with air, and while we were doing this we saw a huge monitor lizard. The rest of the voyage was peaceful and beautiful. We had emerged from the gorge and entered the Doon; the river became broader and, as we slipped past the temples on its banks, the people bathing or worshipping turned to look at us. We came ashore at Rishikesh and while one of the cadets went for my jeep, the rest of us deflated and rolled up the boat.

25.10.50. *J.S.W., Clement Town.* The Doon School has had its Founder's Day with the President of India, Rajendra Prasad, as their Chief Guest, after he had visited us here in the morning and asked very pertinent questions. At the Doon School he made a rather uninspiring speech largely devoted to the importance of the school starting instruction in Hindi at once. This is quite impracticable at present, but as he has given his life to achieving an independent India with a national language, I suppose you can't blame him.

14.11.50. *J.S.W., Clement Town.* On the 3rd John motored me to Delhi where I had to attend a meeting about the future of this place and its move to Khadakvasla. There were four generals, the secretary to the Ministry of Defence, a bunch of finance birds and others. They all have so much else to think of and knew so little of various complications involved that I couldn't help thinking how much better it would be to let one person or a small committee get on with things, but it seems that the days of individual responsibility are coming to an end and that everything is now decided by groups of bureaucrats.

25.11.50. *J.S.W., Clement Town.* In another very fine and moving ceremony on the 23rd the King's Colours of various regiments were laid up in the Chetwode Hall. On the arrival of Sir Archibald Nye, High Commissioner for the U.K., a stirring Royal Salute was played. The Defence Minister made a felicitous speech tuning in with and summing up the spirit of the whole function, and we English who were present were all deeply sensible of the large-heartedness shown by India. Here were people many of whom had suffered hardships to achieve their independence and had been brought up to think of the British, in part at least, as foreign tyrants, and yet were prepared to do honour to them in this way.

The Colours were marched off to 'Auld Lang Syne' and I was delighted to see Ram Nath, one of the I.S.P.C.C. cadets now a Captain, carrying those of his regiment. There were tears in my eyes, not, I think, of regret for the old order, but of gratitude and understanding: understanding of the sense of loss that the regiments felt in handing over emblems that had meant so much, and gratitude for the generosity that paid them honour and for the resolve that the traditions they recorded should be maintained. I felt that it was good to find and honour virtue where it had been shown, rather than to deny it and magnify faults: a negative attitude to life which is so tempting in the difficulties of today. Here was an honourable burial of something that is past, and the promise, shown by the excellence of the parade, of hope for the future.

6.1.51. *J.S.W., Clement Town.* As soon as last term was over six of us went off to Khadakvasla to see the plans and the ground and whether we had any suggestions to make. On the way through Delhi I stayed with the American Military Attache who suggested that I should go and do a similar job to this in the States, but I told him my roots were too deep in India. Khadakvasla is very lovely, but distances between buildings are going to be rather great.

Isobel has given birth to seven puppies, six black and I have kept one, a yellow that I have called Pili which promises to grow into a lovely bitch. While Holdy was away the other day his two dogs came over the seven miles to see me. They must have made a plan together. It was rather touching, though I had to take them back in my jeep.

12.2.51. *J.S.W., Clement Town.* The Parrys have just been to stay with me for the weekend. We went down the Jumna some 15 miles, not in my rubber boat, but on a proper raft of logs, about 30 feet long and 10 broad being floated down to the market. It's very enjoyable trip and the Admiral made a list of 27 different birds he had spotted, among them three different kingfishers, the white-capped and plumbeous redstarts, the river and black-bellied terns, and a wall-creeper. I wish I could make a documentary film of life along the river. You start at the place where they have a boom to catch the logs that have been floated down the mountain torrents. Here they are pulled out of the water, slid while wet and slippery up log slides and stacked until ready for making into rafts for further transit. The stacks along the bank, with each log marked at the end with its owner's sign, make brilliant play of light and shade on a bright morning. The men who do the work are very tough—lifting the logs and steering the rafts down the river is hard—and they are an amusing lot, proud of their strength. In the evenings, when you would have expected them to be tired and glad to rest, they have wrestling competitions on the sand. As you go down the river you see fishermen casting bell nets, and numbers of ferries. Some of these are for people only, others for bullock-carts, and there is one large enough to take a bus. They are great flat-bottomed boats which get carried down by the current as they are paddled across, and then have to be hauled up the bank. The bullocks from the carts have to swim. Then you may see a funeral party with the pyre burning by the water's edge, or a wedding procession moving along the bank with the groom in bright silks on horseback. If you are lucky in a quiet stretch you may see some wild animal come down to the drink. Once I saw a string of camels wading across the river; and then there are all the birds.

9.3.51. *J.S.W., Clement Town.* I have just heard that I have been sanctioned leave home from the end of April. Will you please book seats for both of us for the Norwich Festival—good seats. I've got used to sitting in the best places, and intend to go on doing so, at any rate till my leave is over!

15.4.51. *J.S.W., Clement Town.* We had our half-term break a fortnight ago, and I took a party of five cadets down the Jumna gorge from the bridge across the river on the Mussoorie-Chakrata road to which the rubber boat had to be carried by six coolies. I had said I wouldn't make such a voyage again, but I thought the Jumna would be less dangerous than the Ganges as it is nowhere near so big nor the water so heavy; but it was more difficult, and we were without Pathania, who has been transferred, at the helm. There were more rocks above water than in the Ganges, and we had to do a good deal of getting out and easing the boat over them. At one place where we were going fast down what looked a harmless rapid the boat stuck on a rock and the force of the water turned it over and spilt us all into the river. The cadets all had on life jackets and were all right though I had to help one of them who failed to follow the instructions I had given in case this should happen: to allow themselves to go with the current and gradually make for the nearest bank. Unfortunately I lost my gun and fishing rod, and we all lost clothes.

It took us some time to repair the boat and collect what had floated ashore, and then we had a second upset and were overtaken by darkness before we got out of the gorge. We decided to tie up the boat and climb the cliffs. We were lucky to find a village where they first took us for dacoits in our semi-nakedness, but eventually lent us a lantern, and one of the villagers guided us to Sun Saan two miles away where Jagut, a Nepali prince, has a house. I had told him that we would try to call on him on our way down, and we arrived as he was having dinner with Sir Edmund Gibson, my neighbour here, who was staying with him. We walked in, clad in next to nothing (I only had on a pair of swimming drawers), and pretty weary and cold. We were fed royally, given hot rum, and put to bed, so woke up the next day none the worse. Jagut has a charming villa on the edge of the cliff overlooking the river with channels of water flowing through his garden. He keeps a book in which visitors have written verses extolling the beauty of his home, and when I got back here I wrote to thank him for his most generous hospitality to us all and enclosed the following rhyme:

> Jagut Shamsher Jang Bahadur
> Kept a good cellar and a good larder
> Till Gibson Uppal, Ombir, Sinha
> Sood and Ranu came to dinner
> Out of the night, and drank and ate
> Dry every bottle and clean every plate.

Edmund described this as 'a very notable addition to his book of verses which already contains several masterpieces by me worthy of inclusion in the *Oxford Book of English Verse*'!

The next morning we walked back up the gorge to the place where we had upset in the hope of finding what we had lost. The local fishermen did their best to help, but the water was too deep and rapid. The gun, I'm glad to say, was insured. I have taken on the production of a show at the end of the month for our Visitors' Day, and we are trying to do the Waterloo campaign from Hardy's *The Dynasts*. It is proving very complicated and I wish I could get out of it, but I can't.

5.6.51. *J.S.W., Clement Town.* We did 'The Hundred Days' on the 28th April. We had had a good deal of discussion on what we should attempt, and this had narrowed down to a choice between the events culminating in the battle of Trafalgar or the Waterloo campaign. Then happened one of those unexpected incidents that sometimes influence action. A cadet was run away with by his horse. He rode it beautifully and brought it under control while I was watching. Tall and with an almost aquiline nose, I felt he must be Wellington and decided on 'The Hundred Days'. It was impossible to portray Hardy's vision of the Immanent Will in only an extract of *The Dynasts*, so we decided to take Napoleon's defeat at Waterloo out of its philosophic framework and present the events leading up to it as a pageant play.

The parts of the Phantom Intelligences were cut so as to make only a commentary on the action without reference to the working of the Immanent Will, and Hardy's commentary or stage directions were added to this. To distinguish the 'chorus' from the actors the commentary was spoken by 'Spirits of History' through amplifiers hung above the auditorium. The action took place either in the arena or amphitheatre, or on the fore-stage or proscenium, or on the ground at the sides of the stage, or as a shadow play cast on a screen stretched in front of the stage across which a curtain could be drawn—you can refer to the plan of our theatre attached to my account of *Julius Caesar*. The musicians were screened behind the left wing of the stage. The amphitheatre is large, and accommodated the musical ride with 20 horses that the cadets did some time ago.

The play opened with the Russian and Prussian or British national anthems (the band was excellent) as the Emperor of Russia, the Prince Regent and the King of Prussia walked down through the auditorium discussing the rumours from Elba (from Part 3, Act IV, Scene 8). The next scene was the first of Act V, Napoleon's escape from Elba, done as a shadow play with the Marseillaise played as he was rowed out to the waiting brig. The silhouettes of the ships and boats had been made in our workshops, and to give them the right motion they were pulled across the stage on eccentric wheels. We had some difficulty over 'then a feeble breeze, then a strong wind, began to belly the sails' until a cadet had the brilliant idea of agitating the screen itself. The scene in the Imperial Palace of Vienna was played on the proscenium and the meeting between Napoleon and Lessard took place in the amphitheatre, as did the scene at Schonbrunn. The House of Commons scene was done as a shadow play with voices, and the rustic scene at Durnover Green was played on the high ground to the right of the stage where Boney's effigy could be safely burned. This was followed by an interval.

We had made a map of the country over which the Waterloo campaign was fought from Brussels to beyond Charlerol in part of the amphitheatre in front of the auditorium. The villages were shown as clusters of painted matchboxes, and the forests with twigs; and each place, as it was named in the commentary, was illuminated with a torch bulb placed within it and connected with the commentator's switchboard. After the interval, with an aim that I have to admit was partly instructional, the commentator read a description, not from Hardy but from History, of the development of the campaign during the first fortnight of June, and, as a place was mentioned, it was lit up. This was pretty, but failed to show the actual movements of the armies, and, if we had had the time and money to prepare it, we would have done better to make a film and project it on to the screen.

Following this intrusion into drama, came the midnight ball in Brussels. While the band played, the dancers were shown as shadows on the screen, and as the dance broke up those players who were to speak wandered or strode onto the proscenium as if from the ball-room. Napoleon at Charleroi was also acted on the fore-stage, and we had intended, but eventually had no time to prepare, the 'little moral panorama' as a shadow play of skeletons and corpses. The most difficult shadow play to organise was the march out of Brussels. The fore-stage was the chamber overlooking the main street with its window the screen from which the Duchess of Richmond and her niece drew aside the curtain to watch the army pass. Behind the screen the regiments marched throwing their shadows on it. They had to march in modern threes very carefully sized with the tallest cadets nearest the screen. Four files made the nearest to the projector light at the back of the stage throw too large a shadow. Their entrances had to be timed with the crescendos of the march music, and the band had to time its diminuendos with their exit. The famous marches 'The Girl I've left behind me', 'Hieland Laddie' and 'British Grenadiers' were played, and we dressed the marching figures to throw the proper shadows: in tall plumed caps, kilts and bonnets, or with high busbies made of cardboard. They carried wooden rifles we had made to the correct contemporary shape and length. There were not enough actors for all the regiments, so the first column, having marched past, had quickly to change their head-dresses, double round behind the stage, and be ready to cross again. For several despairing rehearsals all was congestion and confusion till they had learned their exact places, to change plumed caps for busbies, to hold their antique firearms correctly, and to move so as to throw the right-sized shadows. The Field of Ligny was acted in the amphitheatre, while the Field of Quatre-bras was described by the Spirits of History in a darkened theatre. Then the scene in the Place Royale in Brussels filled the arena, and the body of the Duke of Brunswick was carried through the Place by an escort of Brunswickers in their black uniforms and silver death's heads to the Funeral March from Saul. This music was an anachronism, but I felt it was justified by its solemn beauty.

Up to now except for the commentary, we had kept close to Hardy's text, but Act VII as he wrote it was beyond us, and after several unsuccessful rehearsals that seemed to be getting us nowhere, I decided to remould it. I kept the theme of the play and counterplay of fortune, the shaping and nearing of crisis. Wellington was stationed commanding his army on the plateau to the right of the stage, Napoleon on the ground to the left. A search-light from the back of the auditorium picked out each of them with their group of officers and soldiers around them as it was their turn to speak. Both, and some of their officers, were on horseback, Napoleon on a white mare, and Wellington on a bay. At times, in complete darkness, the Spirits of History spoke. At times the chemists had their way with smoking and explosive powders, and there were noises of battle behind the stage. This was a mixture of realism and fantasy, but as the searchlight moved from one group to the other, and as messengers came first to Napoleon and then to Wellington demanding reinforcements, there was certainly a feeling of growing crisis. I shall long remember Napoleon on his white mare with his group of officers picked out by a beam of light which also faintly illuminated the audience of 2,000, as Heymes rode up with the message from Ney imploring reinforcements. Then followed the Aide from Colonel Kempt praying for the same from Wellington:

> 'Inform your General
> That his proposal asks the impossible!
> That he, I, every Englishman afield
> Must fall upon the spot we occupy
> Our wounds in front.'

Finally,

> 'Stand up, Guards!
> Form line upon the front face of the square!
> Now drive the fellows in!
> They will not stand.'

And there followed a charge behind the stage and gradually away out of the area. The lights were turned out, and the commentator read the lovely passage: 'The reds disappear from the sky, and the dusk grows deeper…In the vast dusky shambles black slouching shapes begin to move, the plunderers of the dead and dying.' We might have left it there, but in rehearsal this seemed an unsatisfactory ending. Napoleon was left unaccounted for and there was a need for a relief of tension; so we adapted an Epilogue from Hardy. To music and a relevant extract each group of players came on to the stage or into the amphitheatre to build up a final tableau, Napoleon last of all on Marengo, while the commentator read the passage ending:

> 'Great men are meteors that consume themselves
> To light the earth. This is his burnt-out hour.'

Looking back on this production I feel that it was well worth doing. I'm not sure that the ending with a tableau was dramatically fully satisfactory, though it made a splendid spectacle. It was undertaken at the last moment and the introductory verses written or chosen in desperation on the afternoon of the final rehearsal. We only had a fortnight to rehearse, and only three hours a day then, and on two days it rained. The cost of the dresses and uniforms for the 200 players which were magically conjured out of bazaar cottons and satins, cardboard and paints, by Dr. Verma, was less than £70. This, in a way, was my 'burnt-out hour' at the Joint Services Wing. Admiral Parry took the Passing-out Parade and ended his Address with these words: 'I am sure you would all like me to say a few words of appreciation of the retiring Principal, Mr. Gibson. He has indeed given a splendid example of how to combine deep knowledge of academic subjects, and also the great art of living dangerously. By this I mean that he thoroughly enjoys, and also encourages all of us to enjoy, expeditions in which there is an element of risk. You will be better officers if you can share his spirit of adventure.'

[I had handed over to Bhawani Shankar and flown to England]

During his time at the JSW – and even for a couple of years later – Gibson was also assisting the UK High Commission in Delhi in helping to resettle the 'remnants of the Raj' – the old, the infirm, the destitute and the needy among the British who wanted to go their home country but did not have the wherewithal to do so. Gibson interviewed these people, helped to sort out their paperwork and in the process also made no bones about how Britain was treating its nationals who did not belong to the civil service or the army.

16.4.49. From *the Office of the High Commissioner for the United Kingdom, New Delhi.* I am off again to Kashmir tomorrow to try and organise all the old ladies who want to leave. I have given your name as being prepared to interview the odd European who wants assistance. I think there'll be very little in it. John Taylor.

My offer 'to interview the odd European' proved to have more than 'a little in it'. In fact, between April 1948, and December, 1953, when I left Dehra Dun, I had carried out 41 interviews in Mussoorie and different places in the Doon between the Ganges and the Jumna, and had typed and sent to Delhi some 133 letters and reports. I had to deal with Anglo-Indians in distress, those who had failed to register as citizens of the U.K. in time, those who claimed to be citizens of the U.K. and wanted assistance to go there, and citizens of the U.K. who needed assistance to carry on living in India. A number of these were old ladies, unmarried or widows, who had made a living keeping boarding houses or rooms and who had been left more or less destitute after the British withdrawal from India.

The British Government was prepared to give assistance to the indigent European British subjects of U.K. domicile, subject to the execution of an undertaking to repay to H.M.'s Government in the U.K. any expenditure involved and I had to advise the High Commission in Delhi of the probable capacity of the applicant to settle and earn a living in the U.K., or the existence there of someone able and willing to take financial responsibility for the applicant. In doubtful cases a written guarantee of accommodation and maintenance was to be procured from those who offered it in the U.K., and every effort was to be made to dissuade persons from going to the U.K. who would be destitute on arrival. For those U.K. citizens who were practically destitute or were old or infirm and would be unable to earn a living in the U.K. and had no one there to support them, the British Government had to be approached to find out whether arrangements could be made for them.

By 1951, when there were 154 confirmed U.K. citizens in Dehra Dun and a number of others whose claims to this citizenship were doubtful, the High Commission had compiled a list of charitable funds and alms-houses in India supported by contributions from U.K. citizens and providing assistance to such citizens and others. There were 54 of these of which four were in Delhi, one in Mussoorie supporting between three and five people of pure or mixed European descent resident in that area, and one, the Dehra Dun Women's Benevolent Society, supported by subscriptions from residents in Dehra Dun, which provided grants towards school fees for European and Anglo-Indian children, for the sick and needy, and for funeral expenses. Those in Delhi were the Anglo-Indian Unemployed Relief Home which provided accommodation for up to ten transient poor Europeans or Anglo-Indians; the St. James's Church Home with four cottages for deserving Europeans, Indians and Anglo-Indians who were otherwise self-supporting; the Grant Govan Homes with eight alms-houses for old women who received Rs. 40 a month pocket money; and the Delhi Area Benevolent Fund covering Delhi, Punjab, Himachal Pradesh and seven Districts in the U.P. which included Dehra Dun. This provided money and the machinery to investigate and help cases of distress among civilian citizens of the U.K.

I had some correspondence with the first two of these, in Mussoorie and Dehra Dun, and a good deal with the last of those in Delhi, much of it sad. Before the passing of the British Nationality Act, 1948, some members of a family might have already emigrated to the U.K., and then, after the Act, the rest of the family, unless they could prove U.K. citizenship, could not be assisted. Sometimes all arrangements would have been made with relatives in England to send their ancient aunt or father, and then she would become too ill to move, or he would die. A number of genuine U.K. citizens, either through ignorance or inertia, failed to register themselves before the last date laid down for doing so (1.1.50), and their cases had to be dealt with.

21.10.49. *J.S.W., Clement Town. To the Office of the High Commission.* I have to spend a good deal of my time battling against the inter departmental walls and red tape of the government in Delhi, and it seems a pity that you people from home are becoming as bad. For the barren formality of getting a magistrate's signature I have had to spend four hours and a gallon and a half of petrol—neither easy to come by, and this was a serious interference with the plans of the Government of India by usurping time I had allotted to my grow-more-food campaign. However here is your Form R4 refilled and witnessed by the City Magistrate. Many thanks for the Instructions, I hope to be able to use them in exams here to the cadets on the subject 'How might this have been said more concisely and clearly?' By the way, on several occasions I have had to pay extra postal charges on overweight letters from your office. Would you ask your dispatcher to be more careful!

In December 1949 I heard from the High Commission that many of the wives of British soldiers who had gone to the U.K. disliked conditions there so much that they were asking for free passages back to India. I was once again asked to explain the difficulties of life in the U.K.: climate, food and housing shortages, and high prices, and try to get those applying to withdraw their applications.

15.12.49. *J.S.W., Clement Town. To the Office of the High Commission.* I hope you have had my message about Mrs. H. She would be admirable for one of the parts in the first scene of *Macbeth*. I fear that she doesn't think much of your Office, and since she reckons she'll not be making anything by accepting an assisted passage and paying back what it costs, she has decided to go on her own; so you can cancel the sanction. You might tip off Lord Woolton to fly her home in time for general election. I understand the Conservative Party spends a lot on transporting its supporters on these occasions.

16.11.53. *The Doon School. To Commander Galpin, R.N. (Retd.), The Delhi Area Benevolent Fund.* There are so many of these people who, whether they can prove U.K. citizenship or not, are nevertheless terribly hit as a result of the British leaving India, and I do wish something more could be done for them. I sometimes wonder if people at home have any idea of the undischarged responsibilities of the British in India. The Services and Civil Service saw to it that they were not too hardly hit themselves, but they left the camp followers to starvation.

18
BACK AGAIN TO THE DOON SCHOOL

Gibson was back at Doon School in August 1951. And for the Founder's Day put up a pageant based on the history of the Doon Valley from ancient times up to the British rule. Vacations this time involved a car trip to Central India for big game shooting, taking in Gwalior, Jhansi, the old haunt of Nowgong and Khajuraho with a duck shoot with the Maharaja of Chhatarpur [Chhokrapur of J. R. Ackerley's fine memoir *Hindoo Holiday*]. He was also elected president of the Rotary Club of Dehra Dun this year. The Roys with whom he had dinner, in the company of yogi Agehananda Bharati, were the eminent leftist M. N. Roy and his wife Ellen who had settled down in the city.

25.8.51. *The Doon School.* It seems almost incredible that it's only a day over a week since I left England. On arrival in London I deposited my trunk with Grindlays for onward passage by sea, and then went to St. James's Theatre to see Shaw's *Caesar and Cleopatra*. I popped in for some supper to a little restaurant close by and when I was asked 'By yourself, Sir?' I replied, 'Yes, alone and lonely.' Someone at the next table, whose name I never found out, dining with a very pretty girl, said, 'Then come and drink a glass of champagne with us.' I did—more than one—and then went on to the play. The next day I went alone once more to see *Antony and Cleopatra* (no champagne this time) and realized how much greater Shakespeare was than Shaw. But what a cast for the two plays. I don't suppose one will ever have another chance of seeing so many first-class actors together again: Laurence Olivier, Vivien Leigh, Robert Helpmann, Esmond Knight, Richard Goolden, Peter Cushing, to mention only a few.

The flight to Delhi was without incident, but I had next to me Eric Shipton and Tom Bourdillon on their way to explore a new route up Everest. Term starts tomorrow and we have had as much rain in the last three days as you get in Norfolk in a whole dry year: over 22 inches.

23.9.51. *The Doon School.* I went fishing last Sunday, but it's already too late for the Doon rivers. As soon as the water goes down to manageable depths all the pools are bombed—the military stationed in the district throw in hand-grenades—and everything is killed. It's tempting for them, no doubt, to collect so easily a splendid supper, but it's very short-sighted, for they kill all the small fish and it won't be long before there are none left. In the old days this sort of thing was stopped, but I fear since the war discipline isn't what it was.

14.10.51. *The Doon School.* Founder's Day is next Saturday, and I'm involved in producing a pageant for it, all my spare time being taken up with rehearsals. We are doing a history of the Doon which is so closely connected with India's great epics. The first half is largely legendary, and then we become historical. It has been a little difficult not to emphasise that the most prosperous time in the valley has been under British rule, but though that may be true, it isn't quite the place or time to say it.

21.10.51. *The Doon School.* We had Founder's Day yesterday and all went off well. John made a very good speech, followed by the Chairman of the Governors, Sir Chintaman Deshmukh, who is Finance Minister at the Centre though not a member of the Congress Party. He is very able, and though his speech was not great oratory, what he had to say was good. The pageant went off without a hitch: fifteen episodes in the out-door theatre. First we had a scene of primitive men hunting the primeval beasts whose fossils are found in the Siwalik Hills; then scenes from the Indian epics: Bhagirath calling on the Ganges to come down from heaven; Hanuman coming to the Siwaliks in search of healing herbs; Ram and Lakshman arriving in the Doon to do penance; Drona's youth in the Doon; the Pandavas passing through the Doon on their way to heaven. Then there were eight scenes from history: the inscription of Ashoka's edicts on the rock near Kalsi; the settlement of the Doon by the Banjaras—a gypsy folk whom we showed arriving with their cattle, building their village and rejoicing with folk dances; a Moghul general passing through the Doon and singing a poem in praise of its beauty, with his followers in lovely dresses; the arrival of Guru Ram Rai who founded Dehra itself; the period of disturbances when the valley was raided on many occasions—we showed the Banjara village being looted and the cattle driven off; the war between the Gurkhas and the British followed by an honourable peace treaty; the capture of the brigand Kalua by the first British Superintendent of the Doon, followed by peace and prosperity shown by the Banjaras in dance simulating the tilling of the soil, the spreading of seed and harvesting. The final scene was a Doon School class in which a map of the city was built up on the floor of the theatre with models of all the places of learning, training and research—the schools and colleges, the Military Wing and J.S.W., the Forest Research Institute, and the Survey of India. About 150 boys were involved and they will have learned more from taking part than they would have if we had tried to put across the same ideas in class.

19.12.51. *The Doon School.* The last week of term was the usual nightmare, but the boys are all now safely gone after a very jolly 'Golden Night'. Holdy has persuaded me to join him in a shooting venture in Central India—I heard too late that the Ski Club of India is at last again meeting at Gulmarg—and we are going to a place called Chanda said to be one of the best areas: tiger, bison, grey jungle, fowl, etc., and good fishing. We start on the 24th and go in his jeep.

20.1.52. *The Doon School.* We have had an excellent holiday. The drive through Delhi, Agra, Gwalior, Jhansi, Saugor, Seoni and Nagpur to Chanda took us through the country of Kipling's *Jungle Books,* and we stayed at the Forest Rest House at Wamanpali. There, though we didn't shoot a tiger, we had a very interesting time in the forest and saw bison, sloth bear, red dog, panther, and any number of different deer. We probably made a mistake in taking Prem Singh, our Dehra Dun

Shikari, with us, as he and the local shikari failed to work in agreement. There were several tigers in the block, including a very large male, but none of them gave us a chance of a shot. I particularly enjoyed my first grey jungle fowl shoot and have kept a number of their hackle feathers for making flies.

While in the F.R.H., we were able to watch the elections to parliament. The arrangements for these seemed very good, and their organization had called for a great deal of planning. There were places where the returning officers had to travel 100 miles by bullock-cart from the nearest motor road, so that even the primitive people of the most backward areas should be able to elect their representatives. The great experiment in democracy that India is making has no parallel in history and one watches it with interest, admiration, and sometimes a little doubt. From Chanda we came back via Jubbulpore, Khajuraho and Nowgong which it was good to revisit. We had a day's duck shooting with the Maharaja of Chhatarpur, son of the ruler described in Ackerley's *Hindoo Holiday.*

19.2.52. *The Doon School.* I was reminded today that I had promised an article for the *Doon School Weekly* so I sat down this evening and wrote one on interesting books and magazines in the Geography Library in hopes of tempting someone to read some of them, and then I wondered and felt what was the good of trying to drive to the water horses that would not drink, so I wrote the first bit that follows:

>Futile! Usher, sell your wares
>In the streets of Babylon?
>Those whose jaded palate craves
>Turmeric and cinnamon;
>Minds debauched by what they have seen
>Of Life distorted on the screen;
>Little reck they what you mean.
>
>Futile usher, no one cares
>In the streets of Babylon.
>As well sing to desert waves
>Your unresponded antiphon.

Transatlantic comic cuts,
Something appealing to their guts,
That's the stuff to give the mutts.
Sentimental fool to plan
Turning out a better man
From the Streets of Babylon.

Then I thought perhaps my article might encourage a few to make better use of the Library, so I added this second bit:

Scatter seed upon the ground:
Shout good tidings to the wind:
Cast your bread upon the stream.

If only once an echo sound,
If leaven work in but one mind,
Faith is not an idle dream.

Of the thousand seed you sow,
If only one should sprout and grow!

The King's death was a great shock to us all, but India's reaction was very touching. We have just come out of ten days' state mourning and his devotion to duty and happy family life seems to have made even those who are normally critical of England feel that the world has suffered the loss of a great and good example. Next week I'm off to Delhi to attend an Old Boys' Dinner and to hear Yehudi Menuhin who is giving two concerts in aid of the Prime Minister's Relief Fund.

26.3.52. *The Doon School.* I had a most enjoyable time in Delhi except that when I got there I heard that Bhawani Shanker had leukaemia and was desperately ill in Bombay. He has since died. Quite apart from the tragedy for his family, this is a blow of the first magnitude to the N.D.A. and indeed to education in India in general. I admired him greatly, and all he garnered from his tour in the U.K. and U.S.A. will now be wasted; and he was just settling down at the J.S.W. and implementing his ideas which were excellent. It will be very difficult to find anyone else with his qualities, and when found, whoever it is should again tour if he is to have the same broad outlook as Bhawani and to know what is being done in other training establishments. The Ministry of Defence wants me to take over again while another Indian is found and trained, but I have had to say that this would not be fair to the Doon School where I am now in the middle of various teaching courses, and have just got to know the boys in my house once more.

The first concert was as good as I had hoped it would be. I had written to ask whether there was any chance that he could be persuaded to play Debussy's *La fille au cheveux de lin,* and it was the first encore he played, so I was very happy. I haven't heard a good fiddle solo since Chillon College days when the last I heard was Kreisler playing the Kreutzer Sonata in Lausanne Cathedral.

The next morning I went with the twenty boys who had come for the concert to hear a session of Parliament: question time and both amusing and instructive. Then we heard part of a case argued in the Supreme Court, and after lunch were preparing to set out back here when one of the boys' parents who was in charge of the concerts rang up to say they were prepared to put in a row of special seats if we could stay for the second concert that evening, and that Menuhin was playing the Kreutzer Sonata. I said that we would stay, but that we should have to drive back through the night and must not miss school the next day. We did and it was more than worth it.

Nothing more but trivia to report. In the Flower Show I won the sweet pea cup from the Civil Surgeon, who had imported seed from Australia, by a short head. I helped judge the Flower Show and Garden Competition at the N.D.A. last Sunday. The junior Indian officers make a brave effort to keep up the enormous gardens they have inherited from the British on much reduced pay, but it will take a long time to put up the general standard of living as high as they aim. I have read Canon Tyndale-Biscoe's autobiography and found it very interesting. He was an extraordinary man, with an assurance I should never feel, but he certainly did a great deal for the people of Kashmir where he still has a great reputation. *The Autobiography of an Unknown Indian* is by N.C. Chaudhuri, and I hope you will be able to get it. I think you will find the first half very interesting and charming, but the second perhaps heavy going and to be skipped.

26.4.52. *The Doon School.* Last week I wrote an article for the *Doon School Weekly* on the Weather, 'Spring to Summer'. I began: 'It certainly has sprung. Less than three weeks ago snow was falling at 8,000 feet, hail lay on the ground all night unmelted at 6,000 feet, and we were still wearing winter flannel suits at 2,200 feet. Today it is too hot by breakfast time to sit out of doors in comfort. On April 13th, while the school was playing the J.S.W. at cricket (a game that Mr. Holdsworth holds worth playing in any temperature provided that there is not more than two inches of snow on the ground) the maximum shade temperature rose for the first time this year to 100 degrees.'

Holdy replied: 'I must beg Doon School cricketers not to pay any attention to Mr. Gibson's demoralizing remarks about the weather. If he had his way the weather would always be ruled either too hot or too cold for cricket, though never unsuitable for what he wants to do that day himself whether it is fishing or sweet peas. I have, as a matter of fact, played cricket—a three day match at Bombay—when the temperature reached 102 degrees. It was fairly hot, but not too hot for Vijay Merchant, who made over 150 runs against us. I actually played my Freshman's Trial at Oxford on a day when there were two inches of snow on the ground in the morning. It had melted by twelve o'clock, but the wicket was rather funny. Fortunately, the bowlers were frostbitten and I think I made fifty runs or so. The most desperately cold cricket I have played was at Mr. Gibson's own University...we were playing in a gale of wind blowing straight from the frozen wastes of Siberia. Don't go to Cambridge. The main point is to have a firm conviction that cricket is the only human activity that really matters and never mind the weather. It is never too hot for cricket.' So I have sent Holdy the following:

A suggested
ANTHEM
for a well known
PROPHET

Written with his tongue in his cheek
by an insignificant
SCRIBBLER.

It may be freezing cold,
But with one accord we hold
What R.L.H. has told:
    Whatever the wicket
    We *must* play cricket
    Stick it, boys, stick it!
It may be burning hot,
But it would just be rot
To suggest that we should not
    Whatever the wicket
    Get on with our cricket,
    Stick it, boys, stick it!

Never mind the weather,
We'll hunt the stricken leather.
Now, boys, all together:
    Whatever the wicket
    We must play cricket.
    Stick it, boys, stick it!

There's only one thing, rain,
That makes us all complain;
But don't mention it again;
    Whatever the wicket
    We'd like to play cricket
    Stick it, boys, stick it!

Oh, yes, and then there's light:
We can't play in the night;
Or do you think we might?
    Whatever the wicket
    We should have our cricket
    Stick it, boys, stick it!

Whatever kind of day,
We always ought to play.
With one accord we pray:
    Whatever the wicket

> Give us our cricket!
> Stick it, boys, stick it!
>
> We hold the firm conviction
> All's vanity and fiction
> Save devotional addiction,
> Say we fielders, bowlers, batters,
> Though you think us mad as hatters,
> To the game that really matters.

2.5.52. The Doon School. The Defence Ministry has asked the school to lend me to the J.S.W. for another two years, but the Board of Governors, and I think they are right, have said that they are not willing to give me leave. I had an accident last Sunday on the road up the Ganges gorge while driving Holdy's Jeep that I had borrowed. The road is restricted to one-way traffic, but as it was very early in the morning and we were 14 miles up it and wanted to move only two miles down. I never thought there would be anything else on it. Nor did the bus-driver coming up. No serious damage was done but it was very annoying to crash a borrowed car. I was thrown forward by the impact and cut my head on the top of the windscreen. The flowing blood softened the righteous anger of the bus-driver, so all was well. My first collision in 25 years' driving, and I hope I shan't have another for another 25 years.

Last week John and I dined with the Roys and met a sadhu friend of theirs, an Austrian who calls himself Swami Aghyananda Bharati. From his youth he had a feeling about India, a feeling of affinity for its philosophy, as though he belonged there, so he says; and he came out after the war and now teaches philosophy at Banaras University and wears a saffron robe. He is an extraordinary person – brilliant conversationalist, tall, fat, vulgar, amusing, a glutton who pretends to asceticism. I felt he might have come straight out of the pages of Rabelais.

22.5.52. The Doon School. Ten days ago Shanti Sahi produced *The Lady's Not For Burning* in the out-of-door theatre. I thought it would be too difficult—you will remember seeing it with me—but it was done very well and was a great success.

We plan to be off on June 8th—four Doon School boys, two cadets from the N.D.A., John and myself—to the Harki Doon with skis.

[My diary letter to my mother about our time in the Harki Doon apparently got lost]

25.7.52. *The Doon School.* The other morning I woke from a nightmare that an avalanche was coming down on me and sprung out of bed to hear the sound of crashing branches. My huge toon tree which I have always loved had collapsed. It was one of an avenue and had developed more to the open than the closed side, and this must have made it unbalanced. Then the weight of all the water in its leaves, and the soil having become waterlogged, it just fell without any wind.

19.9.52. *The Doon School.* Days are frightfully full. Apart from teaching I have boxing (I feel I'm getting a bit old for that) on Mondays and Tuesdays, gardening with the boys on Wednesdays, football on Thursdays and Fridays, and fishing at the weekends. The water has been excellent these last two Sundays, and last Sunday I had the best day of my life, catching 43 lb. of fish including a 17-pounder and six others. I was broken by two more, and if we could have landed them we should never have been able to carry the lot home. Holdy also caught several good ones. He likes to fish a pool until he catches one; I like to fish rapidly down or up a river covering as much water as I can and seeing the country.

8.12.52. *The Doon School.* I went out with the juniors for their cross-country practice the other day, thinking I could manage their short course of 1½ miles easily enough, and show them how it ought to be done. In fact I pulled a muscle about a quarter of the way round and had to limp painfully and rather ashamedly home.

12.1.53. *The Doon School.* Last term ended with the usual 'Golden Night' and a much les grand menu than we used to be able to manage: the falling value of money is telling on us all. After a visit to Delhi for a dinner to the Swiss climbers I went up to Simla to stay with the Khoslas where I was privileged to join a very happy family party. He is a judge of the Punjab High Court and a keen trekker. The idea was to have some skating, but as soon as I arrived it started raining which meant snow to finish up with. I wired for my skis and they arrived the day the snow first lay, and I had three good days on them. On New Year's Eve we had decided to go to bed at 12:30 but were still up frying eggs at 5:30, and I complained at being led astray by a parent, and he a Justice! I also had a morning's skating on excellent ice, the rink being four flooded tennis courts. Except for a few minutes one year at Gulmarg, it was 16 years since I had been on skates, and I found I could still do most of the turns.

20.2.53. *The Doon School.* Samuel now has seven children and can't possibly afford to feed and clothe them on what I can afford to pay him. He has at last been persuaded to have the new operation to close the gland duct, but was off work for nearly three weeks. The surgeon, a very good fellow, said there was nothing wrong but that his system had not reacted normally and he would soon be all right. However, this has not been a good advertisement to the rest of the school servants whose teeming families add a fraction to the frightful problem of overpopulation in India.

Jill writes about the tremendous rise in the cost of living. I have been hard hit too. When I joined the J.S.W. I was told that I would have to pay 5% of my salary as rent for my bungalow, and this was taken off all the time I was there. Now some blighter in the central accounts department has found a rule by which, as a civilian, I should be charged 10%. I have nothing in writing about the 5% and have to make up the difference.

15.3.53. *The Doon School.* An old boy, after visiting the school early this month, wrote a letter to the *Weekly* suggesting that the present boys, now that the school had become accepted as a good one, had not the same dynamic spirit as earlier generations. To this a reply in defence of the present was sent the next week and signed 'Three Blue Eyed Boys'. I have just sent off the following to the Editor:

Lines Suggested by 'Letters to the Editor'

(With apologies to W.S.Gilbert)

Yum-Yum, etc.
Three little Blue Eyed Boys are we,
Smug as only a pre can be,
Pleased as punch with our repartee,
Three little Blue Eyed Boys.

Fishing, first aid and climbing, three
Of our successes, and then P.T.,
And see how we did in the N.C.C.,
Three little Blue Eyed Boys.

Compared to the Old Boys, vis-à-vis
We're more than sure that you must agree
We're sixteen annas in the rupee,
Three Little Blue Eyed Boys

Pooh-Bah
I think you ought to recollect
You cannot show too much respect
Towards us Old Boys when we wonder
If the old school's going under
It can't be what it used to be
When we were there,
When we were there.

In our time you would always see
Us seek responsibility.
You'd never find us try to shirk
An irksome job of social work.
You can't be what we used to be
When we were there,
When we were there.

When we were there we took no pleasure
In slackness or in idle leisure
In our day no indiscipline
Made masters see incarnadine
How different it used to be
When we were there.
When we were there.

Chorus
Here's a state of things;
Here's a how-de-do;
To his view each clings,
The Old Boy and the New
But which is right
And which is wrong
Though day and night
Disputed long
We haven't got a clue,
We haven't got a clue!

Mikado
My object all sublime
I hope to achieve in time,
To make this school the undoubted prime,
This school the undoubted prime;
And make each boy there taught
Behave as he knows he ought,
A source of general good report,
Of general good report.

Chorus
His object all sublime
He hopes to achieve in time
Etc.

8.5.53. *The Doon School.* Our half-term expedition with some 40 boys was to Bodia and the limestone caves. We walked and Kay and the children rode along lovely paths through the hills. Here and there were patches of snow down which the boys and the children slid on their back sides. The caves were a new interest for most of the boys, but I found 90 feet up a rope ladder hanging in the void about as big an effort as I was ready for. My garden is now mostly dried up, but Kay has painted a lovely picture of part of it, and she and the children enjoyed arranging bowls, first of sweet peas, then of roses, and finally of carnations. I enjoyed having them enormously and have sent a little sonnet to Sally and Dilys:

> Now that you two to Bombay are gone home,
> You mischievous, sophisticated pair,
> In solitude, wishing you once more there,
> I sit, despondent, in my empty room.
>
> My house is still and silent as a tomb;
> Order restored, the tables polished, bare;
> An unpressed cushion neat in each armchair
> Each shelf-space filled with its allotted tome.
>
> Come once again and spread disorder wide;
> Bring your menagerie, your paints and clay;
> Wake echoes with your laughter, dance and song;
>
> Between Bombay and Dehra Dun divide
> Your time, and for return suggest the day,
> Or send a promise that you won't be long.

I have to take over as President of the local Rotary Club. I can't spare the time, but feel I ought to do it when asked. The Rotary movement does, I think, quite a lot of good, and I was impressed at the district assembly that I had to attend in Naini Tal by the reports from various clubs of what they were doing. The visit there woke many pleasant memories: the Cannings in 1937, and sailing when I went over from Almora.

We have had an S.O.S. from the Everest Expedition for 18 more pairs of crampons. I suppose they must have dropped a load down a crevasse or something. I have sent my four pairs which will be handicap if we go high in the holidays; but with boys only in my party, I don't expect we will, and anyway the expedition must come first.

2.6.53 *The Doon School. To Tensing.* Just a line of hearty congratulations. I was woken by a telephone call this morning at 3:30 from General Williams to hear the splendid news, and was so glad that you were one of the two to get to the top. Do you remember the dispute I had with Nandu Jayal when he wanted you to become his batman, and I told him I would never speak to him again if he interfered with what I expected would be a great climbing career? Well now you've done it, and all of us here, Holdy and John Martyn, send you our very warmest congratulations.

19
ATTEMPT ON 'BLACK PEAK'

The year 1953 was to be Gibson's last at the Doon where he had spent "seventeen happy years". During the summer of this year he, accompanied by a party of students and colleagues, made an abortive attempt to climb Kala Nag (Black Peak) in the higher Himalayas. They had made it up to 20,800 feet but just as the peak was barely 100 yards above, had to give up for a number of reasons including an inclement weather and lack of stamina among some members of the party. This year, he was also elected President of the Dehra Dun Rotary Club.

9.6.53. *Forest Rest House, Jarmola.* Here we are on trek once again, three days out from Chakrata. How I ever got away I shall never quite understand. For the last three weeks of the term I seem to have worked from 5 or 5:30 a.m. till 12 or 1 at night with perhaps 40 minutes shut-eye after lunch every day. In the middle of all this I was desperately ordering and sorting climbing equipment, skis, food and medicine for this trip, as well as writing letters to all sorts of people for help on the way. Mrs. Jill Henderson, who runs the Darjeeling Branch of the Himalayan Club, has been a very great help, as usual, with Sherpas and equipment. On Sunday the 6th we went by bus to Chakrata, stopping and eating a picnic lunch beside the Ashoka rock at Kalsi in the shade of ancient mango trees that overhung the stream in which we cooled our feet. We are going up by last year's route. Ringali F.R.H. was as usual shut and the chowkidar away in the nearest village, four miles off, so we had to break in. I had no time to listen to the coronation service on the wireless, but we were all very pleased at Everest being climbed, especially by Tensing. He would have been with us if he had not joined Hunt's party, but has sent us, through Jill Henderson, two very nice Sherpas, Pemba Norbu and a youngster named Chembe. The rest of the party is of boys from the school, the Kashmir House cook, and porters, and the mule men.

10.6.53. *Naitwar Forest Rest House.* We were just sitting down to an early supper last night when a panther called in the hills above us and a few minutes later one of the mule men saw it in the pine forest about 200 yards from us. I got out my rifle as quickly as I could and ran over to where he was. Then another man saw it behind us even closer to the bungalow. I ran back and was just in time to see it, a very large one, but I dared not risk a fleeting shot in the growing dark. We spent a somewhat restless night as I have Isabel, my Labrador bitch with me, and there is nothing a panther likes better than dog. The mule men were also anxious about their animals and lit fires at each end of the line along which they were tethered. It was too hot to sleep in, and we lay on the veranda with loaded weapons and torches. The latter flashed on several occasions, but the panther remained hidden, though we knew it was around as it called again a little way down the valley.

10.7.53. *The Doon School.* Here is my diary for the trip: the most enjoyable I have yet been on.

What follows are excerpts.

12.6.53. In Camp opposite Oshla. The bridge above Oshla was swept away last night and the path up the Bandarpunch valley is not possible for mules. It is difficult to decide what to do, but what we have re-sorted all the stores into three lots (1) for a fortnight in the Bandarpunch valley, (2) for a week in the Harki Doon, and (3) for our return. A thunderstorm started while we were doing this and we had to get up tents at full speed, but not much rain fell.

15.6.53. A rest day to wash and dry clothes. I climbed to about 13,000 feet exploring for a camp site from which we could ski and found the ice cavern from which the river issues at the foot of the Bandarpunch glacier, but saw nothing better than a place I had spotted yesterday on the way up, at the foot of a valley the other side of the river. After lunch I sent off 9 porters with loads to this new site. In the evening Kirpal Singh, the shikari, who had gone out with my gun and 10 cartridges, returned with two bharal and four snow pigeons. I wish I could do as well!

17.6.53. A wonderful day. Cheema, Deb and I went up on skis while the rest walked, and on the way we saw, quite close to us, four bharal and then a female red bear and cub. The view of Swargarohini straight down the valley was tremendous. We reached our col at 1230 at 15,900 feet. There we lunched and climbed a little peak 250 feet above. We all had a startlingly cold but most refreshing dip in the stream on our return, and then supper of roast bharal, green peas and tinned pears.

19.6.53. I had toothache all day. In the evening we played 'Indications' and I was given to act the first people to fly the Atlantic. I fear I was rather vulgar.

21.6.53. A wonderful day, though I was very tired at the end—perhaps partly because of the 7 sulfa pills and 6 aspirins I took during the night in an effort to kill my toothache. As we climbed I breathed in the cold air and my tooth went gradually numb and gave no more trouble. The pass at the end of the valley was at 16,400 feet and from it we could see Karsali, the Jumna, and away in the distance, across what we took to be the Mussoorie ridge, the plains. We got back to camp after nearly nine hours out in wonderful country. I issued rum and drank Venkata's and Adi's share myself.

22.6.53. This morning we set off with nine porters in a cold wind and drafting mists to move up the main valley. First we had to cross the torrent coming down Ski Valley II which we did above its glacier snout, cutting steps for the porters in the soft ice. Once on the glacier of the main valley we passed through fantastic scenery: a great row of giant tables, rocks poised on ice pedestals; crevassed and twisted ice; red and black medial moraines. We eventually made camp at 14,600 feet on the last bit of grass. Below us the main glacier, clear white ice in the middle, runs down the valley. Across it is the 'Black Peak' and the Bandarpunch ridge rising majestically in great rock cliffs. Looking the other way is Swargarohini, and between it and the 'Black Peak' there is probably a pass to Harsil.

23.6.53. Two porters arrived with welcome additions of food and wood. One feels rather ashamed to rely on the efforts of these men without whom no expedition could be carried out in comfort, but they seemed very happy at 8 annas extra for coming through such beastly weather.

24.6.53. Up at 0500 to see the sun catching the tops of the peaks. The 'Black Peak' looks possible and most tempting, but the snow is likely to be very heavy. Came down in rain and lay in my tent building castles in the air till it cleared in the evening. There were clouds below, but the 'Black Peak' and Bandarpunch were lit up in all their glory.

25.6.53. We were all up at 0500, but it was 0715 before we were away, the plan being to carry a tent and provisions for Cheema, Pemba and myself as high as we could, and for us three to try the 'Black Peak' tomorrow. All the boys went very well and showed excellent sense of balance. Eventually we got onto the glacier and made our way upwards across crevasses and through fantastic scenery. By 1100 we had reached 17,000 feet and an excellent place for a camp, though rather lower than I'd hoped. The weather was glorious and the 'Black Peak' appeared invitingly within our reach. We decided to have a crack at it there and then, and at 1130 Cheema, Pemba and I set off, leaving the others to climb a little peak, the top of the great black rock shoulder of the mountain, at about 17,400 feet, and then go down with Chembe. The snow was in excellent condition for climbing—a hard crust into which you could kick from stepholds. At about 19,000 feet we roped up and I led for a little, but found it very exhausting, so Pemba, who was in great form, took over the lead. Over the steep slope the snow became more deep and soft, and here and there we went in above our knees. Eventually, at about 1530 and 20,000 feet, we got onto the final ridge and saw the summit less than 1,000 feet above us and apparently within easy reach; but here we met with something unexpected: a tremendous wind blowing across our path. The snow was wind slab, generally firm enough to hold our weight, but here and there letting us through, which was exhausting. In spite of this it seemed that we would make it. We made steady progress, but the wind was icy cold and if the rope got loose it was bowed out by the wind and jerked us out of our steps.

I noticed Cheema's nose had turned a livid colour and tied my scarf round his face. I was horrified to find that he had left his windproof trousers in the tent and only had on a pair of grey flannels. At about 1615 he said that he felt very tired—his first expression of doubt after a wonderful climb. The top looked only about 25 minutes away, and we stopped for a little rest, huddled together for shelter against the wind, and looking down on Swargarohini. We went on for another 10 to 15 minutes, and Cheema said he could go no further. The top was perhaps 100 yards ahead and 100 feet above us and Cheema begged us to go on. Had there been no wind I would have done so, but I knew that Cheema must keep moving, I suggested to Pemba that he should go, but he replied that getting to the top was the sahib's pleasure, not his, and that there should be three on the rope for crossing the crevasses on the way down; so we all turned back with nothing but the wind to prevent our getting to the top. It had been a magnificent effort for a boy of 17 to have climbed in one day from 14,600 to 20,800 feet or thereabout.

27.6.53. After breakfast in the sun we all bathed in the lake—cold enough to take your breath away, but not as icy as at the ski camp. Kirpal Singh told the boys that it made him feel shy to see them with nothing on. We re-sorted clothes and stores into those to take with us to the Harki Doon tomorrow. I spent some time lying in my tent looking down the valley to the mountains the other side. I realized that a photo would not do the scene justice. It notes everything, whereas the mind picks and chooses, and that is the difference I suppose between painting and photography, and why the latter can be great only occasionally.

28.6.53. A very long but good day, on the march for 11½ hours. The boys were splendid. When I recall the early days of the Doon School, when you could hardly go out for an hour's walk without someone complaining that he must have a drink of water, it seems to me that the right sort of traditions really have grown up—and it also seems to me that right behaviour is very much a matter of custom and habit.

29.6.53. A pleasant day. We sat and smoked the hookah with some shepherds who gave us cheese made from sheep's milk to eat.

1.7.53. A beautiful clear and sparkling morning and we all had very cold bathes. The boys explored in the morning, while I wandered round with my camera, taking photographs of flowers, and after tea we practised rock-climbing on the great erratic boulders. Saw a Himalayan rosefinch and the redstarts were displaying. After supper we had a camp fire and singing. The first day without rain for a long time and a perfect one for our last in the Harki Doon.

7.7.53. An easy 8 miles up to Mandali which we reached at 1100. The bungalow book goes back to 1929 and contains many interesting entries including a visit by the Irwins when he was Viceroy. A pity so many of these books have disappeared.
[Note: The expenses of this expedition to the nearest rupee were: Food 1197; Daily Expenses on bungalows, milk, etc. 128; Cook 50; Sherpas, including travel, 557; Porters 746; Mules 1,382; Buses 149; Equipment 221; making a total of 4,430 and a share for each of us of Rs.554.]

An account of the expedition was published in the *Himalayan Journal* for 1954 which included the verses I had written on June 29th. These ran:

> First up the steep grassed mountain sides made white
> By the anemone which when the sun is down
> Folds up its petals and turns white to blue;
> Then by ravines and crags and jutting buttresses
> Where the *Paraquilegia grandiflora* clings
> In clumps of gentlest mauve or blue, and deep green leaves,
> And where a slip or foot misplaced on loosened stone
> Might spell headlong descent into the depths below;
> Up to the waste of boulders, glacier strewn.
> Then by a little ridge onto the pass

Beyond which lies the Harki Doon, our goal.
Here we have lunch: sardines, chapattis, cheese.
While our stout porters catch us up and smoke.
Then down into the misty depths glissade
Across some thousand feet of rotting snow,
Down to the alp where last year's ski camp was;
On through the dwarf, foot-catching rhododendron
To where the silver birch, bent by the winter's snows.
Trunk to the ground and then in curve uprising.
Brings us to forests and deep grassy glens
Through which pour streams along whose banks
The water-loving *Primula stuartii grows,*
And from lush grass rise spurs of heavenly blue
Here are the tracks of bear, their yellow turds,
And you may sometimes find the musk deer's slot
We reach the Harki Doon where the fierce torrent.
Runs in a wide and shallow bed, too swift to wade
Yet freer and less angry than below.
Where down a valley step it pours confined.
And roars between mighty boulders.
A group of these, huge slippery rocks,
Some twelve feet high or more,
Crashed from the crags above and ice born, now.
Made for the nimble-footed nature's bridge.
By this we cross, not without trepitude.
Those with nailed boots remove them and bare-foot
Spring from one smooth stone to the next
Deb slips; his arm is caught.
Adi is pushed up by his broad behind.
Up the last hundred feet or so
Of ancient, grass-grown, lateral moraine
Where the blue Himalayan poppy blooms,
We reach at last the chosen site to camp.
Enormous boulders perch along the ridge,
And ancient trees gnarled and fantastic, garlanded with moss.
We dump our loads.

16.9.53. *The Doon School.* I'm now President of the local Rotary Club, and this is part of my Address on my installation: 'I do not expect or wish for anything startling to happen during my year of office for I believe in and hope for quiet and steady growth. I have worked in places where the personnel were continuously changing and where every newcomer felt that he must make his mark. The result was that there was far too much planning and changing of plans, and too little permanent achievement. I have spent much of my life with boys and more and more I come to realise that what really matters for them is the formation of good habits and sound traditions; and these take time to grow. To illustrate this, may I tell you something of how the tradition of going on expeditions has grown up in the Doon School. Years ago, when we first came here, some of us on the staff felt that it was a pity that the youth of India took so little advantage of the wonderful mountains almost at their door-steps. We started to encourage trekking. My first expedition was with a party to climb a hill of about 1,000 feet. We never reached the top. A year or two later a party of the toughest boys considered it a great triumph at a half-term break to reach the top of Nag Tibba. Last term a party including boys in their first term climbed this hill of just under 1,000 feet, and in the trek that I have returned from last holidays, which was at times very arduous, I never heard any complaint of difficulties or discomforts. Now, these later boys were no different from their earlier predecessors, no older or stronger, but they were upheld by a tradition that has grown up in the school: a tradition that is bearing fruit, for some of the most enterprising young climbers in India today are old boys of the school. The point of all this is that I hope to be able to maintain the traditions of this Club: possibly to add a little to them in small ways that accumulate.'

The excitement of this week has been killing a cobra. I was attending to house business after lunch when a boy rushed into my study to report a large black snake under the spiral stairs outside the bathrooms. I picked up a hockey stick as the nearest handy weapon and a house bearer on the spot had a long pole. I told him to get up the stairs and pin the snake which was behind a dustbin with the pole while I hit it. He did this very skilfully, jamming it into the corner of the walls and stone floor, but as he did so it reared up and spread its hood giving out a fearsome hiss that almost took my breath away. However it wasn't long before it was dead.

21.10.53. *The Doon School.* Founder's day is on its way and I am in charge of the entertainment. We are putting on a series of little playlets or episodes in the various languages studied in the school: Hindi, Tamil, Sanskrit, Punjabi, Bengali, French and English; and that is leaving out others that are talked but not taught: Telugu, Malayalam, Kanarese, Urdu, and one might even add Doon School slang.

Gibson, always concerned about the students' development beyond academic studies, here he appends his annual letters to parents, excerpts from which follow:

17.6.39. *To parents of boys in my house.* Boys here all have open to them opportunities of living a very full life and of developing all sorts of interests apart from or in extension of their work in class. Among the boys in this house this term there have been scouts and cubs who are to be trusted to go out on their own and camp and cook and look after themselves, carpenters and metal workers, gardeners, photographers, painters, sculptors, modelers, lino-cutters, singers and instrumentalists, debaters, map builders, motor engineers, journalists, typists, bookbinders, leather workers and librarians, not to mention members of the Scientific, Historical, Literary, Naturalist, Film, Oriental and other societies which include Mr. Martyn's Crickets who discuss problems round the hearth. I would rather that a boy became a really good carpenter, or a skilled musician, than that he should be an indifferent performer at too many things, and I feel that parents must not expect their boys to do everything we encourage here, and that they can, by encouragement and criticism of and interest in what boys bring home, help them to attain higher standards. I find half the boys in this house are more interested in reading 'comics' than anything else. With the School Library full of splendid books more easily accessible than many of the boys may ever find again, this seems to me a disaster. I do not believe that reading with the studious determination to increase one's general knowledge is the right approach to reading, which should be a pleasure, and the problem is how to turn what some boys think will be a bore into an enjoyment, and how to train their tastes so that they can appreciate the more subtle humour of say Pickwick at its higher value than the humour of 'Film Fun'.

16.12.39. *To parents.* A suggested innovation for next term is that some form of social service should be made compulsory for a period of 90 minutes each week. Already there are large numbers of boys who give this service in various ways: as prefects, librarians, gardeners, workers in the museum, helpers in rural reconstruction at Tunwalla, teachers in the Adult School for the servants and so on; but I feel that the lesson should be enforced that all members of any society are not only entitled to enjoy its benefits but owe a duty to help it in what ways they can. The regeneration that is taking place in India can only happen through and with the help of the country's citizens given not for gain, but as a service they owe to their society, and I believe that it is not unreasonable to demand this service from those who may not be old enough to realise that they owe it. If the suggestions being considered materialize boys will be able to learn to build irrigation channels, walls and gates, prune trees and plan gardens, estimate and control expenditure, and many other thing which will give them experience which will be useful when they leave school. I write all this because I sometimes wonder how many parents realise what we are trying to do here. The envelope in which this letter comes to you will be full of slips of paper reporting on your son's progress in class, but you will not know much of his progress in the art of living unless you find it out from him in conversation or through his letters home. I often wonder how many boys write interesting letters to you, their parents. I don't know, because we don't read them; but I have sometimes been shown parents' letters to their sons, and some have been extremely dull, containing no news, no comments, nothing for the boy to think about. It is in your hands to see that your boys write to you full and interesting letters.

16.6.1940. *To parents.* There are still too many boys blind to what they could see and deaf to what they could hear. They leave their minds blank, to be filled by the unbeautiful and untruthful, by unscrupulous propaganda, by debased public taste, by flattery and by appeals to fears and prejudices, to which a person without a mind of his own turns for second-hand and usually second-class opinions. When they leave school they will join the ranks of those whose opinions are made for them by dictators, party leaders, bankers, or the writers of advertisements for patent medicines: it will depend on what rut they get into. So I appeal to you again to do all you can during the holidays to excite and widen your boy's interests in what goes on around him, and when he leaves home insist that he writes and tells you about things.

21.12.1940. *To Parents.* I am sad at the high regard in which the cinema and 'comics' are held by a number of boys in the house. The problem with the cinema is much the same as with the garishly coloured papers, though it affects more people. Both are forms of 'escape', of living in our imagination a different life from our own. This is not objectionable, as long as we realise what we are at. The danger is when the escape is to something objectionable, as in the lurid stories of one of the papers I came across this term, or where we come to believe that the escape life is the real life or the best kind of life, when it is not. This is a very serious danger to which unthinking and enthusiastic cinema-goers expose themselves, and its influence is insidious and difficult to guard against. Before a boy has developed his critical faculties, he is exposed to film after film made by people whose ethics are controlled by the need to make a profit, and whose art is reduced to what the crowd will swallow. It is not surprising that he loses the power to distinguish the true from the false, good value from dross; and there are people who have so drugged themselves by the enjoyment of other people's emotions on the screen that they have apparently become incapable of enjoying real life and of discovering the excitements and interests of what goes on around them. Will you help by discussing the films you see with your boy?

22.12.1941. *To parents.* This term I suggested to my tutorial that they should keep diaries, and for a long time they were dismally uninteresting, written up at the last moment to satisfy me, lists of trivial events brought to me with the ink hardly dry. However, before the end of term we managed not only to get some interesting comments on events written in some of the diaries, but also to have discussions about them at tutorial meetings. The diary habit is worth forming because to jot down each day's interesting events and one's reactions to them not only orders one's ideas, but may later become a record of times it is fun to look back to.

December 1947. *To parents.* Several of you have asked me what the school intends to do about the official language. It is early to say anything definite yet and the remarks that follow are my own views. We shall probably see that the standard of Hindi in the school becomes progressively higher, but shall continue to teach subjects other than languages in English. English is likely to remain the most important second language of the educated and commercial classes of the country. Provided that the boys who come to this school can speak their own language fluently, it will be a very valuable asset to them to be expert at English, and India is likely to need large numbers of people who are so. For those for whom Hindi is not their mother-tongue there may be a requirement to know three languages: their own, Hindi as an all-India language, and English for international contacts. This is no more than the three languages usually required of boys in Europe.

December, 1948. *To parents.* I asked a large number of boys from Bombay this term how many of them had done any of the following: been out with the fishermen of one of the local villages for a night; visited Bassein, Korlai, Kolaba near Alibag, or any other fort along the shore; climbed Bawa Malang or been to Sagargarh in the hills; or indeed done anything more adventurous than visit coffee shops and cinemas. Not one of them had done any of these things, and surely this is a condemnation of the way many of your boys are growing up. India wants young men with an objective outlook and a spirit of adventure, and if your boy grows up without these he will be left behind by others, or India will not achieve the future that is hoped for her. We try to keep boys physically fit, and this is difficult when they come back here badly out of condition. The record is held by—I will not name him—but he put on 27 lb. between May and August, and has taken off each month 9, 6½ and 1½ during this term.

20
TO MAYO COLLEGE

In October 1953 Gibson accepted the offer to join Mayo College, Ajmer, as Principal, the former incumbent and Gibson's former colleague Vyas having left. Despite Vyas's efforts which Gibson praises highly, the school was at this time dogged by low finances and very few boys. Parents still seemed to believe, six years after India's independence and the phasing out of the princely states, that it was meant solely for the royalty. And he was the only Englishman left on the staff, though in subsequent years a number of English worthies were to arrive for tenures of one or two years as teachers.

Before joining Gibson bought a Jeep at an "awful cost" of £1,000. His early efforts were aimed at increasing savings, cutting costs as subsidies from the princes of Rajasthan had stopped, improve the level of instruction and add new courses. Agriculture was one such course since Gibson realized that a number of children from the landed gentry might have to rely on earnings from their lands with the dawning of a democratic India. He also came to know Nehru just before leaving the Doon.

With the Himalayas having been left behind by Gibson, his spirit of adventure and wanderlust seemed to have hardly died down since he managed to discover ever new diversions in the arid state of Rajasthan by way of forays into the countryside, shooting trips at the invitation of the princely states in their twilight years and occasional visits to Dehra Dun for fishing and mountaineering jaunts. Geoffrey Kendal's roving troupe Shakespeareana also began to visit during his time at Mayo though for some reason he does not mention any of its cast by name – people who were to find fame in their own right or as actors later in life.

From Ashfaque Husain, 15.9.53. Vyas has now gone to the J.S.W. The Principalship of Mayo College is now thus open and a meeting of the General Council has been called on the 25th to discuss the question. I have renewed my acquaintance with the Mayo College, being on the General Council since the beginning of this year. I feel that there is nothing seriously wrong with the school except (1) its bad name, no longer deserved, and (2) lack of dynamic leadership. I am convinced therefore that you can make a good job of it, and I am writing this letter to ask you if I may suggest your name.

21.10.53. *Doon School.* The main news of the past few weeks is that I have been offered the headmastership or as it is called there, the post of Principal, at Mayo College, Ajmer. I have accepted. It will be more than sad to leave the Doon School, but it is a job that needs doing, and I think I ought to have a crack at it. The school buildings and grounds are magnificent. All they need is more boys. To get them I shall probably have to see that the standards of teaching are improved, and try to attract middle-class boys with brains. In the past most boys there have come from princely families and the standards of scholarship have not been very high.

16.12.53. *Doon School.* This coming to an end of seventeen very happy years has been a great strain. There have been farewell parties from the servants, the staff, the clerical staff and the boys. Such nice things have been said, and I am one of those sentimental people who get lumps in their throat even in the cinema, and I have had great difficulty in not behaving like old Mossadeq. The boys have given me the most lovely silver set of tray, teapot, coffee pot, milk jug and sugar basin. Silver is one of my weaknesses, and when these were handed to me last night it so took my breath away that I think I forgot to say 'Thank you'. Jagjit Singh, Gurdial's younger brother, who has come climbing with me on several occasions, won the Sword of Honour and Gold Medal at the Military Wing. I was introduced to Nehru who had come to take the parade.

8.1.54. *Delhi.* Here I am, on my way to Ajmer. The last few days at Dehra Dun were all packing and farewells. Since then I have been scurrying round Delhi seeing various people and buying a jeep. The cost is awful--£1,000, half my provident fund from the Doon School, but a jeep is really solid and it should last me a long time. At the moment I am waiting for it, and as soon as it comes shall start by road for Ajmer, 250 miles at 20 m.p.h., as it is not yet run in. I do hope I shall like and be able to make a success of Ajmer. I think I was right to try and to resist the temptation to go on happily at the Doon School, I have exchanged the certainty for the chance, and I hope that is right.

25.1.54. *Mayo College.* Here I am safely arrived though hardly settled down in my new home. My dear, it's an absolute palace. My study is 30 feet by 20, the drawing room and dining rooms the same. There are ten bathrooms enough to float in, with bedrooms and dressing-rooms to go with them. The drawing-room has a beautiful wooden floor and when I play my records of the Pope's choir singing in the Sistine Chapel they sound as if they were really singing there. The room is so high it resounds like a church. A certain amount of furniture is provided by the College, but it would cost a fortune to hang the place with the curtains it deserves and furnish it as it should be. I sleep in a bedroom fit for a king (indeed almost built for one, for in the old days the Principal of Mayo College was a very important person with the power more or less to make or mar the fortunes of the young princes who came to him), but I sleep on a wooden charpoy or cot as found in the simplest peasant homes. I'm not sure what the size of the garden is, but estimate about three acres; the College grounds cover 300. The main college building is of unpolished white marble, and very fine in a rather fairy castle way. There are numerous other fine buildings and houses put up by the various States: I have so far counted 16, but I may have missed some. In my garden I have what is said to be the finest tennis court in India, and the main college cricket ground has just been borrowed to play an inter-zone Ranji Trophy match, corresponding to a country match at home. All this, of course, is an inheritance from the past. But the college has been losing money steadily for the last several years, and part of my job will be to try to make ends meet. One thing that will greatly help to do this is to get more boys. At the moment we are just over 150. We have room for another 100, residential room for more, but classrooms are rather small and few. There are several classes with only five to eight boys in them: ideal for the teacher, but uneconomic. I think I should be able to attract more boys. One of the reasons they have not come in greater numbers up to now, has been the general idea that the college was still only for princes and the landed aristocracy. There is a big task ahead, but well worth doing, as this is a wonderful place for a boy to grow up in with its beautiful grounds.

I had a very pleasant drive here from Delhi, stopping at Alwar and Jaipur on the way, and including a diversion to see a ruined city and perfect little Moghul castle on the way, some 25 miles off the direct route. The country is very different from the Doon, but has character, and the college is about 1,700 feet above sea level, surrounded by the Aravalli Hills. At present it is cold at night or in the shade, and the temperature has been below freezing on several nights. My garden has some good flowers, but no sweet peas and no roses. I hope to put that right by next year.

I seem to have a very good staff, and they have all been very helpful and kind. Large numbers of old boys have called to inspect the new Principal, and I hope I have gone down all right. We had a house-warming party on Saturday for about 50 people with which Samuel and his wife coped well. I get Rs.100 a month entertainment allowance, but at the present rate it does not look as though it will go very far.

There is no other Englishman on the staff here, but from what I have seen so far I think I shall like my colleagues very much. Some of the boys are older than those at the Doon School, and some not nearly so bright. But there are good ones coming on, and Vyas has done very good work in introducing scholarships and in turning the school into an ordinary public school. Most boys still come from families who have lost much of their land, but who still have large farms on which they will have to live, and I am considering starting an agricultural section.

Extract from Mayoor, *the Mayo College Fortnightly, 21.1.54.*

PRINCIPAL'S INAUGURAL ADDRESS

Fellow students, and in this expression I include both boys and teachers for I believe that learning is something that goes on throughout our lives, I hope that we look on our work at this college, not as something that has to be got through and put behind us, but for the boys as the beginning of an interesting and happy life, and for those who teach as an absorbing interest from which one derives the same pleasure as a gardener who watches his fruit and flowers ripen and bloom as the result of his careful attention.

A person who has no interests is very seldom happy, and here we offer to introduce you to many. I hope that this will enable some of you to turn into scholars: historians perhaps, who know about India's past and can apply the lessons of history to the problems of the present; or scientists who will help to win for the people of our country freedom from want. Others, I hope, will learn to become honest and efficient administrators, or fit themselves for a life in the defence services; and yet others farmers and businessmen.

And there are, as well as learning, the many other activities in a school like this: painting and modelling, music, reading, acting, carpentry and metal work, games, hiking, nature study, scouting, shikar and so on. When you grow up you will never regret it if you have developed a hobby—an interest beyond the earning of your daily bread. I hope you will take full advantage of such activities and interests as we can offer you here.

To the new boys I offer a welcome to our family. Like them, I am new, and perhaps somewhat overawed by new surroundings. As we look around this hall we see the portraits of those who have been here before us, and of those through whose generosity this college has its being. May we be able to live up to their expectations and hope that this will be and remain a good and great school. Those of you who have been here before I would ask to welcome the newcomers and make them feel at home.

26.2.54. *Mayo College*. I am gradually settling down here, though there is an endless amount to do. I hope I haven't taken on more than I can manage. It is a more difficult job than I realized, but if I can pull it off it will be more than worth while. Many of the buildings are very decorative, but they are not functional and they are expensive to keep up; and many of the boys are not remarkable for their scholarship. I have got to attract boys from other classes and from other parts of India than Rajputana (now Rajasthan). It will be difficult to do this until the College gets a reputation for better scholarship, and meanwhile I have got to save a very large sum of money in our annual budget, for we no longer get the considerable help from the Princes that we used to. The problem is how to improve instruction, and at the same time save money. I work longish hours in the office as well as trying to do a fair amount of teaching. Actually there isn't time to do as much teaching as I would like to; I ought to be nosing round and thinking and planning, but I think I'm a good teacher, and feel that if I can make some impression that way it will be valuable in the long run. I want the staff to see what I do, and perhaps eventually pay me the compliment of copying me. Also I get to know the boys, and they are our most influential ambassadors. If I can give them ideas, that will be important. I have already discovered that our prep department isn't as good as it should be. I wish I knew more about teaching very small boys: they come from six years old, and if I can only get the teaching at the bottom of the school as good as it should be, then that will bear fruit all the way up the school.

However, I shan't worry you with all this any more, for in spite of work to do, I have managed several outing on Sundays, and I have had the best games of tennis on my court since I came out to India. I was asked to a big duck shoot by a local Maharaja one Sunday, but did anything but distinguish myself. It is very different from jungle fowl shooting, but I hope I shall get used to it. I have already taken some boys rock-scrambling. The cliffs round here are fine for climbing, and there are all sorts of things to do, and interesting places to visit. Two weeks ago we went to a most romantic castle on top of a hill. This is typical border country rather like what we drove through in Wales when I was last home; the scene of the same sort of wars and the same sort of fortifications.

Last week we had our annual Prize Giving—the college big day. It seemed to go off all right, except that some of the princes did not come. They have been used to sitting on the dais, and I was told that the ministers of the government of Ajmer should sit there too. This would have made too great a crush, so I put the princes and ministers in the front row of the stalls, and the Governing Body and staff on the dais. Some of the princes seem to have heard of this plan and absented themselves.

Principal's Report at Prize Giving, 20.2.54.

Excerpts

It is inevitable, I suppose, 'that I should compare Mayo College with the Doon School, if not aloud, at least to myself, and I have been told that I shall be expected to say what my impressions of Mayo College are. They are bound to be coloured by my past, and I shall not hide the fact that I love the Doon School and shall continue to feel part of it whatever happens to me here. When I was appointed to it seventeen years ago I was called by Lord Halifax, whom many of you knew as Lord Irwin, and I was told by him that I was going out to work of very great importance. 'India', he said, 'is likely soon to become independent and you schoolmasters have the responsibility of helping to train boys who should become, in coming time, some of India's leading citizens.' It is perhaps too early yet to know whether this will be true of old Doon School boys, but of Mayo College, which was earlier in the field, it already is.

In spite of the need for economy the General Council has been able to improve the salary grades of the clerical staff and the lower-paid servants. The teaching staff has also been promised that when we make ends meet their maximum pay will be raised to Rs.550 instead of the present Rs.350. You cannot expect a teacher to maintain himself and his family in conditions of decent culture on less ...

Mr. Vyas, who has gone as Principal of the J.S.W., is an old friend and colleague of mine, and I should like to pay a tribute here to what he did for Mayo College. He took over at a time of change and had to meet and deal with a number of exceptional difficulties. He was responsible for the establishment of the College Stores, Workshop and

Museum, and for the introduction of many new hobbies and of Science as a subject boys can take in the Intermediate examination. In these and other ways he built soundly, and the success with which I hope that the College will progress in the future will owe much to his planning and hard work.

19.3.54. *Mayo College. To Aamir Ali.* How are you liking Bangkok? I once—intimate moments with royalty!—saw the King of Siam and his brother with no clothes on. As small boys they were staying with their mother in the same hotel in Morgins as we were, and one evening they came rushing down the passage naked, pursued by an ayah. They were trying, I think to escape from a bath.

India needs more good schools, and here is one not well known enough. It would be very wrong if it had, as has been threatened, to close down. Mr. Fyzee (some sort of uncle to you, isn't he?) was here the other day, and told me you were thinking of coming back to teaching. My dear Aamir, if you would join me here it would be lovely, but school-masters are terribly badly paid, and we here, while our budget remains unbalanced, worse than many. My own salary is little more than I should be getting in an ordinary state secondary school in England had I remained an undistinguished member of the assistant staff; but it covers me with embarrassment every time I sign the tiny cheques for my colleagues at the end of the month.

24.3.54. *Mayo College.* In Delhi I got the encouraging impression that the Government of India was really interested in the Public Schools and felt differently about them from the days when they were inclined to look on them as snob institutions. They now seem to realise that they may be valuable for developing an all-India feeling. I have hope that the central government will help to tide us through our difficulties. They have given us a grant of Rs.50,000 to be matched by a collection of a similar amount by our old boys. I am feeling more settled and think I shall like this job. Of course I miss the high hills, the forests and most of all the rivers of Dehra Dun and all my old friends there, but Ajmer has many compensations. There are lovely lakes or tanks within easy reach with plenty of shooting and sailing, and there are numerous rock cliffs with excellent climbing.

27.7.54. *Mayo College.* The chief excitement of the past days has been the All India Congress Committee meeting. When I was approached about this before I came on leave I had felt that the argument against letting it happen at the school was that an educational institution should not be tied up with any particular party, while the argument for was that it would bring all sorts of people from outside Rajasthan to see the place, which would be valuable publicity. I agreed, provided the request to use the school came officially not from the Congress Party, but from the State Government on the grounds of security, convenience, etc. I expected them to use our polo ground, which we no longer use, and various buildings we could temporarily vacate for them. When I found that they had used our main cricket ground I was horrified..

On another ground there was an industrial fair and an exhibition of cottage industries with various aspects of India's five-year plans. One was strongly impressed that India was on the march. Its problems are vast, but they are being tackled with keenness and a good deal of efficiency. One difficult one, which I feel up against myself, is the employment of the semi-educated products of some Indian Universities. Of course the universities turn out many first-class students, but they also give degrees to a large numbers of halfwits who find it almost impossible to get jobs. A frustrated and cynical section of the population, they are a danger to the well-being of the state.

In the end the P.M. did not stay with me as he wanted more room for secretaries than I had after putting up my other guests. Dr. Katju came, and Pandit Pant, one of the strong men of the party. The Working Committee of most of the well-known Congress leaders met in my study. I took the P.M. round the college in my jeep—as also, at different times, various other celebrities—and he talked to the boys in Assembly. In conversation with him I found that he had an open mind about flying saucers and read all he could find on them. I feel he is a very great man, and that there is no doubt about it if you read his books.

I think all went off well and the school created a good impression, though some of my predecessors would have been horrified. The old outlook is typified by a story I was told last night by an old boy. When a boy at school was asked who he thought was the greatest living Indian, and when he answered 'Gandhi' he was given a good beating!

What unnecessary difficulties stupid Englishmen, and probably stupid Indians too, made for themselves.

8.8.54. *Mayo College.* It has been great fun having Holdy who returned to the Doon School last Monday. He helped coach football and gave a lecture on Kulu, Lahul and Spiti. His last Sunday we went to Masuda and the Raja showed us round his old fort and new farm. The former is gradually decaying. I wonder what will be the result of the sudden removal of power from these people. There is a certain sadness in the old order changing. There was a debate in the school last week that 'This House supports the abolition of Zamindari' and it was interesting to find among boys, most of whom are likely to suffer from zamindari abolition, more than a third of them supporting it, and I was very pleased at the sincerity and growing confidence with which many of them spoke.

26.8.54. *To Peter, my young nephew.* I was just going to sit down to write this letter when a college servant came and told me that there was a cobra coiled round the gate of one of the boys' houses. I went and shot it. Have you read 'Rikki-Tikki-Tavi' in *The Jungle Book* by Kipling? Last Saturday we had a holiday as it was Krishna's birthday. Krishna was a real man like Christ, though less is known about him.

I spent the holiday, Saturday and Sunday, taking a party of boys to stay in a village in what used to be Jodhpur State with the father of one of them. The drive in my jeep of 90 miles there was interesting as we crossed the Aravalli Hills. These are some of the oldest in the world. When we got to the boy's village, a place called Khejrala, we stayed in his father's castle. The barons, or thakurs as they are called, lived in castles and ruled their villages, and their wealth came from what they took from their farmers: sometimes one-third of what they produced, but often more. Now this system has been abolished. The castle had first an outer wall enclosing the whole of a low hill. Inside the wall were various shops and dwellings, and on top of the little hill was the old main castle, like an English keep. Next to it were more modern and comfortable buildings. The keep has now been turned into the women' quarters known as the zenana, and there are still many families where the women live shut off from the outside world. For the night we were there I slept on a walk that went round the battlements. The wind blew, so it was pleasantly cool, and in the morning I was woken by the sound of hundreds of wings. A huge flock of pigeons had come down into the courtyard to be fed, and there was a peacock standing on the wall beside me. Later I went to look at the thakur's farm. He is an enterprising man and has done much to develop his land: sinking wells and installing pumping machinery, and sowing good-quality seed. We had some good shooting, and the whole school was fed on venison the day after we returned.

2.9.54. *Mayo College.* I sat down last night to write to you and then found myself trying a sonnet on your 80th birthday. All my spare time last week was spent doing an internal audit: a beastly job because if it's to be at all effective you have to suspect everyone of inefficiency or dishonesty and poke about trying to find mistakes in their books, stock in hand, and so on. Though there were some shortages of food and clothes in the school store, which is the most likely place to find things go wrong, and the most important and difficult department to keep straight, fortunately all other departments seemed to be running well. There is such a lot to do here to get the school as good as I want it that I could go on working all day every day for months. But I don't. I get up at 0630, work for forty minutes or so before breakfast, and then go to office where I am, or in class, till about 1400. Then I come back for lunch, read the papers, and sleep till about 1600. I get through a bit of work between tea and games at 1745, and then more in the evenings, unless I have to go out. I seem to be keeping very fit.

Every Monday evening a master teaches a class in front of the rest of the staff, a practice that I have introduced. Then we send the class away and criticize his methods. This is quite fun and the staff seem to have entered into the spirit of the idea, though some didn't like it at first. Several have very little idea of how to get their stuff across, and I am hoping this experiment will lead to improvements. I also want to check their correction of boys' exercise books as some don't pay nearly enough attention to this. There is lot to do before we can consider ourselves a really good school. I have been reading through and making suggestions for corrections in all the 'projects' that boys wrote during the holidays. This gives me an idea of each boy, his home circumstances, and so on, but it takes the devil of a time.

25.9.54. *Mayo College.* On the 29th I take four or five boys with me to Dehra Dun where they can see the sights, and I hope for two or three days' fishing. There are no mahseer near Ajmer. Term starts again on October 11th.

21.10.54. *Mayo College.* I arrived back here two days before term, happy but tired and expecting two days of comparative test, only to find a telegram waiting for me to say that 'Shakespeareana', a company of players, were arriving the next morning. The two days went in hectic arrangements: advertising, printing and selling tickets, and hiring a hall. The staff, both teaching and office, were a wonderful help. A total of about 2,000 tickets were sold to students and 500 to adults, which was not bad for a hall that could only accommodate 400 and that was not filled till people realized how good the players were. For the week they were here, they stayed with me. It was great fun, and they were very pleasant people, but I never got to bed before 0030 and several evenings not till after 0100.

Since 'Shakespeareana' left I have been trying to get square with school work that has accumulated while they were here. I was going to write to you last night but this was upset by the arrival of a boy's relations. His father is dead, and he was looked after by his grandparents. The grandfather died last week and the widow, only 40 years old, committed sati, that is burned herself on her husband's funeral pyre. Too ghastly. It is said to be the first time it has happened in Jodhpur for 100 years. The boy was taken off home in spite of my protests.

19.11.54. *Mayo College.* The edge of this letter has been eaten by a rat! I have had a plague of them, and they have destroyed some clothes, but they seem to be diminishing now after strenuous efforts to catch or poison them. The grey squirrel or tree rat also does a lot of damage in my garden, nipping off the tops of my seedlings and digging up the garden peas as I plant them. I gathered my first sweet peas of the year two days ago. During the week October 24th to 30th we had Diwali, the festival of lights. The college buildings looked lovely with lamps, earthenware saucers filled with mustard-oil feeding cotton wicks, ranged all along the windows and over the roofs and domes at night. On the holiday I took out the boat for its first wetting. There was a good wind and we had great fun. It sails quite well. But is very lively and I shan't be able to let boys go out in it alone until they know a lot more about how to avoid being upset. The next weekend we had a visit from Rajkot who came to play us at cricket. Their headmaster, Wynter-Blyth, his wife and two daughters, and another of their staff stayed with me. Though they won, it was a frightfully exciting match. The meeting of the General Council, or Board of Governors, was held on Saturday and Sunday and I had a house full of them staying with me. It went off well enough, but there are bound to be difficulties while our income does not meet our expenditure, which it will not until we get more boys, and I feel that cutting down expenditure too much is not a way to attract newcomers. During this year we have saved about Rs.19,000 on estimated expenditure, so I don't think we have done so badly. Sahgal, who is a splendid Bursar, should get the credit.

23.12.54. *Mayo College* Christmas cards are pouring in from many I haven't sent to. My sweet peas are beginning to flower on long firm stems. My roses are in full bloom, and the annuals are all well up. I would like to lie back in the sun and do nothing, but there is our syllabus to revise, weak members of the staff to see or write to, an entertainment for next Founder's Day, early February, to be planned, an article on the school to be written for the *Statesman,* and so on and so on. I shall think of you all on Christmas Day. I'm not ploughing a lone furrow. The staff is good, particularly the older ones; the boys are a very pleasant lot, better mannered than many I have met; and we're all keen.

21
A HEADMASTER'S YEAR

At the end of his first year at Mayo, the college had an overdraft of Rs. 200,000, despite having sold 100 pounds worth of cauliflower grown on the college estate during the year! Gibson had now begun to act as an ambassador of the school while on official trips across India. His efforts included making business contacts to help place old boys in jobs. Among the visitors to the school this year were Dr Rajendra Prasad, then President of India, and Shakespeareana of course. During the summer break Gibson also fulfilled his wish to finally climb the Black Peak, though his journal of this trip is fairly dull.

This was a time of enthusiastic optimism. At the end of 1954, in my Christmas Circular to my friends, I had written: 'We have at the moment an overdraft at the bank of Rs.200,000. We can hardly carry economies further without loss of essential efficiency, but we have room for another 70 boys without increasing the numbers in our classes to over 20 in each, and without having to increase our present teaching staff—so we draw a useful profit on each additional boy we get. To achieve the better results in public examinations that will attract more boys we are doing all we can to awaken interest and stimulate minds— good films, active school societies, interesting and often distinguished visitors who lecture on Saturday mornings to the older boys, and so on.

We are also trying to make our lessons more interesting and thought-provoking.'

From letters to my mother

    Mayoor is our fortnightly publication. We have started competitions in it similar to, but not as difficult as, those in the *New Statesman*. We have also started gramophone music at our morning 'Assembly', using Indian, Western and Folk Music records; and all the boys now chant the prayers in Sanskrit and English instead of their being read by Shastriji or me. In these and other ways I am trying to get more interest and participation by the boys. We have started a College Conclave with a representative of the parents, five members of the staff, and fifteen boys 'to consider all activities carried on in the College and make suggestions for their improvement'. It can pass rules that do not conflict with those laid down by the General Council, but I, the Chairman, can exercise a veto if I feel it necessary. The chief object is to interest the boys in the problems of planning and administration, so it has a number of Committees dealing with Games, the Store and the Mess. Of these perhaps the most interesting for a boy to be on is the Stores Committee for, from time to time, the boy members accompany the Stores Superintendent to the bazaar and check up on his purchases. They also visit the various dairies and help decide which is the most reliable.

    All senior boys do an hour a week of Estate Labour—not perhaps very popular, but much useful work has been done. Over an acre of seedlings of the lately imported improved snowball cauliflower was planted, and selling some of these in Delhi and Bombay has made a useful contribution to college funds. Boys also helped in ploughing and sowing wheat, carrying cauliflower stumps to compost pits, and what they most enjoyed, gathering ripe chillies. We have also all helped to returf the main football field, planting grass rootlets by hand: an arduous job, but one that will give great satisfaction when completed. On Independence Day last year I took the Bursar and five boys to a Tree Planting ceremony, and now we plan a census of all the trees on our campus and further planting.

    We had our Prize Giving on February 24th with Sardar Panikkar as the Chief Guest. I had expected him to be very good, but he was disappointing and he made an attack that many of us thought mean on the past of Mayo College. I had moved the function to the Bikaner Pavilion to avoid last year's disputes about sitting on the dais, and to have more room. In spite of all this activity, I sometimes feel a bit lonely with no one quite on the same wave-length as myself, as there used to be in Dehra-Dun. Being a headmaster is a bit isolated.

I have been to an old-style Rajput Wedding: elephants, white horses, swords, and wonderful brocade dresses and jewels. I wish I had a magic carpet at my command—it would have fitted in well with the scene—and I would have fetched Jill's children to it.

24.4.55. *Mayo College.* Next Sunday I drive to Jaipur, fly to Madras, train to Ooty, and drive to Lovedale for a conference of public school headmasters; and then return by air for another conference here on the 7th. John will be with me all the way so I expect to enjoy it. I shall have three or four days here to get ready for our expedition, and then jeep to Dehra Dun and Chakrata from where the boys from here and I will set out for the snows, to be joined there later by others from the Doon School when their holidays begin at the end of the month. How I shall ever complete all the arrangements I don't know.

However, the arrangements were finally completed and, starting out on 10 May, Gibson and party conquered the Black Peak – "a narrow crest of snow over a cornice" - on 8 June 1955, returning to Doon School on 22 June. Since it was familiar territory, terrain and landscape for Gibson, and by now he was a veteran of climbing in the higher Himalaya, his diary does not have the sparkle and detail evident in a first impression. Albeit he did a good amount of skiing on this trip.

Giving a brief statement of the costs of this expedition, Gibson writes: "The most expensive item was mule transport: Rs.1,624. Next came food: Rs.1,449; then Sherpas: Rs.878 and Porters: Rs.865. The total, including the drive from Ajmer and back, came to Rs.5,737. This according to the time spent in the hills, worked out at shares from Rs.537 to Rs.776 for each of us."

1.7.55. *Mayo College.* It is difficult to imagine, unless you have experienced it, the wonderful relief brought by the advent of the monsoon. Doors and windows, long closed against the heat and dust, are thrown wide open; naked and almost naked children run into the downpour; and where there has been a brown desert green grass springs up within a week.

21.7.55. Mayo College. The rains have ceased for the last three weeks and we are all praying for them to start again. Here we had transplanted our early cauliflower (we sold over £100 worth in Bombay last year) and sown our maize, and we have lost the lot. There was good rain for three days, then another three or four days of cloud and breeze, and then one night, a gale rose and blew all the clouds away. Since then it has been dry, but there had been enough rain to fill the lake we sail on, and although the water is now going down rapidly, we have had great fun in my little boat.

During the last week of the holidays there was a meeting in the College of the All India Women's Association and a number of women well known in public life came down. I had them all to breakfast one day. At the moment I have staying with me a Miss Stock who is very interesting. She took a first at Oxford and then went into Adult Education under the Workers Educational Association. She came out to Dacca University as Professor of English just before the British left India, and is now working in a College of the Punjab University. She leads a hard life, but seems happy, and is certainly a most stimulating person. I hope to pick her brains on how to improve our teaching of English here. She knows Jomo Kenyatta well and has given us all a most interesting talk on the problems of East Africa.

8.8.55. Mayo College. Miss Stock has left. I enjoyed her visit very much, though I felt I was a bit dull confronted with real scholarship. It was fun to listen to intelligent talk. My dear, it has just started raining really hard. I must undress and go and stand in it—the best cure for prickly heat.

26.8.55. Mayo College. Early in September I have go to go Hyderabad to inspect a school and I plan to stop in Bombay on the way to make business contacts that may help place old boys in jobs, and also to see if we can't draw more boys from there.

30.11.55. *Mayo College.* Shakespeareana have been again, the whole company staying with me for eight days when I ever got to bed before midnight: both refreshing and exhausting. The boys all enjoyed their plays which were of good repertory standard, and I enjoyed having them. We have had visits from parties of 15 and 25 military cadets and one of 48 teachers on an educational tour. Among General Knowledge lecturers have been the Steuart Wilsons and Krishna Chand Secretary to the Planning Commission, who spoke on Community Projects. We celebrated Gandhi Jayanti by giving all the servants we could a holiday and feeding them and their families that night, and by helping to build a garden for children as our share of Shramdan. The garden had been well planned out, and tools, stones for the paths, water and roller were ready for our use. However, the number of workers had not been foreseen, and no sooner was a bed prepared for plants than the pathmakers trod over it; and before those cleaning the paths could get all the weeds out, the stone spreaders were upon them. There was lots of enthusiasm, but Shramdan needs careful organization and direction. Dr. Rajendra Prasad, the President of India, visited us at the end of October and spoke in a friendly and encouraging way.

At the beginning of this month I had to go to Bhopal for a rather dull educational conference, but I managed from there a visit to Sanchi with its magnificent Buddhist monuments; and just before that the Steuart Wilsons had been to stay with me. He was Musical Director of the BBC and then of Convent Garden, while she is a well known 'cello player. They agreed to give a little concert in my drawing room to which I invited about 40 people. I borrowed a 'cello for her from a man who works in the railways, and when she was tuning it the C string proved to be rotten and broke. I suggested we might try her nylon washing line, and this was fitted and promised very well; but at the last moment, getting it up to pitch, it pulled the neck of the 'cello out. I was afraid that she was going to burst into tears as she had been working very hard to get the instrument into condition, but the lender explained that this had happened before. All went well in the end and we enjoyed Steuart's very lovely singing. Yesterday, after lunch, I took the afternoon off and went to see the great fair at Pushkar to which people come from far and wide to sell and buy camels, cattle and horses which have blocked the roads for miles around for the past few days. Pushkar is the other side of a little pass from which you have views of the desert in front and Ajmer behind, and the road, all the way, was full of peasants on foot, animals, and every sort of conveyance: buses, tongas, bullock wagons and ancient cars dug out for the occasion. We passed a dead pony and smashed tonga and a bus upside down, but arrived safely to a most picturesque outing. The people in this part of India are both better looking and more colourfully dressed than in the U.P. India is full of visitors and tourists. The welcome given to the Russians seems to have caused apprehensions abroad, but on the whole I think it is a good thing. They gave Nehru a wonderful welcome, shown all over the country in cinemas, and I expect India wanted to show it could do as well, and let them see what a free country can manage.

In Assembly this morning I spoke about Guru Nanak. I said: 'Some days ago I was speaking to you of the prayer we use written by Shankara and asking God to pardon three errors: thinking of Him as limited to some form, trying to describe something that cannot be put into words, and forgetting, when we use some special place of worship, that God is everywhere.' I pointed out that many people use an image as an assistance in concentrating their devotion, but that Islam and Christian Puritans among others, were afraid that simple people would mistake the symbol for what it stood for, and had therefore forbidden any representation of God. I also said that many men and women who had devoted themselves to spiritual exercises although belonging to different religions had experienced the same sort of union with a spiritual force which we may call God. I went on: 'It was, I take it, this sort of evidence that led Gandhiji to say that all religions are true, but that no religion is the whole truth; and we, in our Assembly here perform a daily act of worship suitable to whatever particular religion we may personally follow.'

20.12.55. *Mayo College*. I got back here on the 13th to finish off reports and Mrs. Joshi of the Ministry of Education, an old friend, arrived, and then the Zatopeks from Czechoslovakia who were to be guests at the Agra University sports which are being held in Ajmer. They were a charming couple and it was great fun to have them. He runs about 15 miles a day to keep in training, and did a demonstration 5,000 metre run at the athletic meet at a speed of over 12 miles an hour, which is about as fast as I can bicycle! She is expert with the javelin, and they both sang very well and after dinner we had folk songs which carried me back to evenings in Alpine huts. After Christmas I'm off to Calcutta to carry out the same sort of visits there as I did in Bombay.

22
GROWTH OF MAYO COLLEGE

Since Mayo could count the rulers of nearly all princely states in Rajasthan among its alumni and many had their sons at the college in Gibson's time, the doors of hospitality by the maharajas were always wide open for him. Thus the winter of 1956 began with an invitation from the Maharana of Udaipur for a panther shoot and Gibson did manage to bring one down. This was followed by a trip across the Aravallis in his Jeep – with some of the schoolboys for company as always – to Jodhpur and a stay at the palace before it was turned into a hotel. The following winter there was Imperial Sand Grouse shooting in Gajner where, to his shame, he could bring down only nine as opposed to 98 by the Maharana of Kotah next to him! Between camping and fishing expeditions with boys there was visit to Jaisalmer and another to Jaipur at the invitation of the maharaja for a dinner with Clement Attlee, former British premier, and Krishna Menon. Among the visitors to the college was Dr. Zakir Hussain.

The number of boys at the college was by now steadily on the rise and within the first 30 months of Gibson's tenure 100 new boys had joined. So much so that soon Gibson had to oversee the building of many new blocks and facilities. Some more teachers from the UK and elsewhere too were joining on short term, fascinated by the college pedigree, including a couple from New Zealand. There was a performance of "A Midsummer Night's Dream" with dialogue in a mixture of English and rustic Hindi. Twice there was a severe flue epidemic which overran the college stretching its facilities to the limit. And on the personal front, Gibson won the shield for the best private garden at the Ajmer Flower Show. Gibson had also introduced an annual feature involving a large number of college boys who had to play-act an adventure up a hill not far from the college on a moonlit night, with names such as 'Escarpment Escapade'.

During summer vacation Gibson chose to go on a trekking trip to the Baspa Valley beyond Simla with college boys, teachers, sherpas and mules as usual and his journal of this expedition makes very interesting reading. There was trekking, skiing and climbing up to the snow line.

10.1.56. *Mayo College.* The past three weeks have been extremely full and gone like a flash. I left here by train on Christmas Eve and arrived in Delhi on Christmas morning. The flight to Calcutta was uneventful and on arrival I was greeted by a message over the loud hailer, 'Would Mr. Gibson come and answer the telephone.' This was to let me know that Gulab Ramchandani, ex-Doon School, was coming to pick me up. Good staff work, as all the information I had been able to send was that I hoped to arrive on the 26th. The old boys had also made arrangements to meet trains. The four days in Calcutta were very full, and I think there will be plenty of openings in the future for the right sort of people, if we can produce them. I stayed with the Burdwans who were very good to me, and I managed a concert by Peter Pears and Benjamin Britten, and a ballet by Martha Graham's dancers—modern and experimental, but colouring and decor both lovely. I was back in Delhi for New Year's eve and on the 1st caught the train here with John.

Two very heavy days catching up with school business, and then we went off for a short holiday. We started a party of four, but as we were leaving I caught sight of a little boy from Assam who is here for the holidays and thought it was a good opportunity for him to see something more of India, so suggested that he should come too. That meant others wanted to come, and in the end we were nine in my jeep and trailer, off to Udaipur where H. H. had asked us to stay. On the way we lunched at Deogarh where the Rawat has three boys here. They live in an enormous castle in the middle of their village or township, very interesting with its Rajput architecture and paintings. You have to climb endless flights of narrow stairs (narrow for defence in the old days) and you get a wonderful view from the top. They showed us two of their fighting rams. I can's say I really liked their charges and the awful thuds with which their heads met, but the rams didn't seem to mind and had to be pulled apart. We spent three days in Udaipur which is out of this world. H.H. is an old boy of Mayo College and has a son there at present, and is a very modest and charming person. But what an awful responsibility he has. His income is much reduced and I don't know what he will do with all his palaces, two of them rising out of the waters of the lake and all the retainers who still look to him for a livelihood.

One evening we were taken out for a panther shoot to a village where a cattle-lifter had killed. We spread ourselves along a ridge and Mahendra, H.H.'s son, and I were given the best position and I was offered first shot if it came out in our direction, as expected. I told the boy to shoot first, and eventually we sighted it coming slowly along the hillside. When it got almost below us at about 80 yards Mahendra shot. Probably out of politeness he missed. The panther took no notice and I fired and missed not out of politeness. Then it started to gallop, and using my second barrel, H.H. had lent me a Purdey rifle, I got it in exactly the right place, just behind the shoulder. I would have been considered an excellent marksman if I hadn't given the game away with my first shot.

From Udaipur we drove across the Aravalli hills to Jodhpur where we stayed at Umed Bhavan, a palace finished only a few years ago and built partly as famine relief. It cost over a million pounds and is now, I suppose, a white or rather pink, for it is of the local red sandstone, elephant. It may well be the last palace to be built in India. Air-conditioned throughout, with more than 150 guest rooms or actually flats of several rooms, it has been inherited by a small boy of about 10. He was away, but we were very well looked after by various Doon School old boys and Swarup Singh, the present head boy of Mayo College. The old fort, described I think by Forster as looking like a dragon, does indeed do so from the air, for we visited the Air Force Academy and they took me up in a helicopter from which I got some lovely pictures—or so I hope.

25.1.56. Mayo College. The new term has started and our numbers are up to 200. There is little let-up in the continuous stream of events. For four days I have had a house full of parents, and this morning General Daulet Singh, who has three boys here, has arrived. Last Sunday we took all the new boys up Taragarh by the narrow and romantic 'Happy Valley'. The ruins of the Moghul fort, and the very fine mosque at the top, and the view of four or five lakes, various ridges of the Aravalli Hills, and the white city of Ajmer below were well worth what was quite a climb up and a tiring descent, which the boys did very well. That afternoon I had to attend the district sports, a convocation at a local college, and then a dinner to the Chief Minister of Rajasthan. Tomorrow is Republic Day and our N.C.C. cadets are taking part in the parade, and the artists producing a historical tableau. The same evening the Gautreys from the U.K. High Commission arrive for two nights. They want to meet the U.K. citizens in Ajmer so there will be a tea party on my lawn for about 50: mostly foremen and their wives in railway service. On Friday Christopher Smith arrives from Haileybury for five days, and on Saturday an educational mela for all the state schools is to be opened by Dr. Katju, Minister of Defence. Next Sunday a party of 30 students from the U.S.S.R. are visiting the college, and I have just heard that February 16th has been fixed for Prize Giving when I shall have a house full of guests, and for which we have little time to prepare.

7.3.56. Mayo College. I have just got my Leica back from Germany where I had sent it for overhaul, and they have made a wonderful job of it. The camera and three lenses are as good as new—recovered with new leather, lenses cleansed of any fungus, exposure timings all checked. Father had it in East Africa before he passed it on to me, and I have had it all my time out here.

Adam Arnold-Brown has just come out to take over the Hyderabad Public School. I found him very interesting. He was at Gordonstoun with Prince Philip. We took the boys rock-climbing and I have found some excellent cliffs. Adam was followed by Colonel Prem Singh whose boy is here and who has just returned from playing polo in Central America, and who brought with him an interesting fellow called Gerald Russell, an Englishman with an American mother who left him a chateau in France. He was on the party that brought back a

Giant Panda from China, and last year among those who went to hunt for the Abominable Snowman. The evening of the day they left came H.H. Udaipur and the Yuvraj of Dungarpur, and then five tennis stars from Australia. Then I had another houseful for Prize Giving including Mr. Dandekar, father of one of my cadets at the J.S.W. and Managing Director of the Associated Cement Companies of India. He has joined the General Council and I hope will be a great help. It went off well and we did bits of Richard II—the first three scenes—the third with horses for the lists at Coventry; a Prep School play by Tom Gay; and a Hindi one by Ganju, another member of the staff. Most of my guests get shanghaied into giving a general knowledge talk to the boys, and we have had some very good ones so far this term. At the moment I have Rom Meades staying with me. He is a Football Association staff coach, has played for Blackpool and now plays for Cardiff City, and is in India under the Rajkumari Amrit Kaur Coaching Scheme. We are very lucky to have him for a short time. The Ajmer Flower Show took place while I was in bed with flu, but Buddhai, my mali, did all that was necessary and I won the shield for the best private garden and the first prizes for roses and sweet peas, so that cheered me up. In the school we have mumps, flu and suspected measles, and two of the best members of the staff have been offered headmasterships next term, so life has its little worries; but our numbers continue to go up.

4.4.56. *Mayo College.* While you were having a hard winter I was gathering sweet peas and enjoying the sun. Now the roles must be reversed. Here the temperature is already over 100, the garden drying up, and mosquitoes swarming while you must be enjoying the English spring. I wish I could get home this summer, but I can't possibly afford it. We have suffered a sad reverse. I had nine boys in for the School Certificate and I knew one must fail but hoped the rest would get through and that two would get first divisions. In the event four failed and none got firsts, and this is a serious set-back to my plans to improve our academic record. English language caused most of the trouble, and I taught them that.

There has been an outcrop of minor sexual troubles—boys between 13 and 15 fondling each other. This may be part of the explanation of the lack of zest I sometimes complain of, but I can't say I altogether know how to deal with it. Preaching high ideals and the clean body doesn't cure it, and punishment drives it under and does harm. I don't think the agonies of self-reproach I suffered as a boy at giving in to the temptations to masturbate were good for me, and medical opinion seems to be that it does no harm if not carried to excess; but where do you draw the line? The prefects are the ones to help by setting a decently high tone.

On Easter Sunday we all turned out—staff, boys, clerks and servants—at 7 a.m. to do two hours' harvesting. The corn is cut with hand sickles and there are 15 acres to reap. Everyone everywhere is hard at work on the same job, and it is difficult to get labour. We must get ours in before the grain begins to drop, so we all turned to. After reaping, the corn is threshed by treading it with cattle, and then winnowed in the wind: all very primitive but peaceful and curiously satisfying.

The Sunday before Easter was Holi, the Hindu Spring Festival. We had a holiday on Monday so I took a party of 11 boys and masters to Rajgarh on the Benas River 90 miles away for a weekend's camping and fishing. The river flows through a deep gorge with cliffs on each side and deep pools full of fish and gharial, the long-nosed fish-eating crocodile. We camped in an orchard beside a semi-ruined fort overlooking the river and from where we could hire a boat, and we shot enough duck and caught enough fish to make it unnecessary to open the tinned food we had brought. One afternoon we rowed up the river to an ancient temple under the rock cliff and lay on the floor and listened to a devotee chanting the *Gita* — very peaceful and pleasant.

I wrote to Dr. Zakir Hussain who is one of my heroes and who was to have been our Chief Guest at Prize Giving but who fell ill and could not come, to say how sorry I was, and to say that I had hoped to suggest how to make Basic Education pay. I have had a very good letter in reply in which he says: 'I cannot tell you how sorry I was at my inability to keep that engagement. I am more sorry, for my absence prevented you from making that valuable suggestion about distilling liquor in Chemistry Labs in order to make schools self-supporting! I would have thoroughly enjoyed it and in spite of being a fairly good Mussalman I would have endorsed your suggestions as something at least better than the intoxication with words to which our boys get addicted in schools and colleges.'

7.5.56. *Mayo College.* On the last full moon of April we had a scheme I called 'Operation Moonlight'. Half the Senior boys were dacoits and the rest the police. The dacoits had half an hour's start (except for six of the police who were on patrol) and had to get 10 kidnapped small boys to their Fort on top of Taragarh. There are about five routes up this hill which rises steeply for some 1,000 feet above Ajmer. It proved good fun for all of us.

I meant to start for the hills today, but couldn't finish my work in time. Then a prospective parent turned up and I showed him round the college. Then I paid the man who gathered the honey from the wild bees' hives that hang from the marble turrets of the main school building—a perilous job done at the end of a rope hanging over space. This produced 24 lb. of pure yellow liquid for which I paid nearly £3. Then four of us sat on my lawn in the falling dusk and watched the birds bathing in my bird bath. The crows I resent, but they did enjoy it. The golden-backed woodpecker with its crimson crest was the best.

Tomorrow I shall pack with the help of Charlie. It amuses me to think of all the preparations people make in England for a Himalayan expedition: endless lists, careful weighing, and so on. I have had no time so far to plan anything and you must imagine a room full of skis, ropes, ice-axes, tins, trunks, tents and goodness knows what. Having piled these into the jeep and trailer we shall wait till the evening and motor to Delhi through the night to avoid the heat. I have to spend two days in Delhi seeing people and then some days in Dehra Dun to watch the boys and Shakespeareana act Richard II. From there by a new road said to be jeepable through the foothills to Simla, 70 miles on to Rampur Bashir, then up the Sutlej on foot to its tributary, the Baspa, up which we go in search of skiing, our further movements depending on what we find.

For an account of our expedition to the Baspa see next chapter.

4.7.56. *Mayo College.* I have been back for just over a week and, what is sad, have already put back the three inches I took off my middle during our trip. I have been elected secretary of the Indian Public School's Conference this year, which will make more work, but while the holidays last I'm taking things easy and enjoying myself. You ask about books worth reading. I have lately very much enjoyed *The Founders* and *the Guardians* by Philip Woodruff. This is his pen name.

When he was out here I knew him as Philip Mason. He was in John Martyn's father's house at Sedbergh.

31.7.56. Mayo College. We've been at work for a fortnight now and it seems as though we only started yesterday. There has been a great influx of new boys and we are now as full as we can go without more building. We have added a century in 2½ years and I hope we shall prove worthy of the trust people are putting in us. Last Sunday I drove a visiting Swiss surgeon who had been medical adviser to their last Everest expedition to the opening of a village hospital about 43 miles from here. There is a great renaissance going on all over India, but I was sorry that a politician who made a speech thought fit to run down the British. No doubt there is some justification, but I said to him that bitterness over the past was not the best foundation for a happy future.

29.8.56. Mayo College. The air is filled with the noise of loudspeakers celebrating the birth of Lord Krishna. Modern progress has its frightful drawbacks. I'm in the middle of the annual internal audit, a boring and unpleasant business, and I'm inspecting exercise books from all classes. I fear there are several slackers on the staff who don't do as much correcting as they ought to. It's soul-destroying I know, but for the ordinary boy it is essential. This will mean unkind words, and what with 12 to 14 hours work a day I feel a bit worn out. However, next week I shall have a bit of a change, as I have to go to Bombay and Ranchi to inspect schools.

Last week we had a visit from Dr. Zakir Hussain, one of the great men of India. He was just back from a visit to Saudi Arabia and gave us a very interesting talk.

1.10.56. Mayo College. We have had a week of documentary films—four or five short ones each evening instead of prep. Some were very inspiring, and there is no doubt that India is taking great strides forward; but all is not entirely well. My particular worry at the moment is how to find funds to expand Mayo College. We are now as full as we can go without further building. We have plenty of room for this, and it would help us as we could then run parallel classes, the brighter boys separated from the slower so that they do not handicap each other.

Schools like the Doon and us, if there were many more, could improve things considerably, but the politicians have a prejudice against us, though, as in England, they send their sons to us. With about £50,000 I could double the output of Mayo College. If we take this money out of our endowment we shall not be able to keep our fees as low as they are at present; and if we put up our fees many of the middle class parents, whose sons are often the best, won't be able to afford them.

9.11.56. *Mayo College.* A large party of boys went to Bihar to see something of industrial India, but I could only get away for a day. The next excitement was having Peter Cooper to stay. He was touring for the Trinity College of Music, but wasn't able to give a concert in Ajmer. However he played to me and a few boys and was quite marvellous. Then there was a visitor from the U.K. High Commission, then Dinah Stock, now Professor of English at Calcutta University and as usual most refreshing. Next comes my General Council meeting, then a rock climbing and adventure camp for some 30 school-masters. There are other minor worries such as the boy who fell off his bicycle and broke his arm. A week later, with the arm in plaster, he got onto his bicycle again, fell off again, and broke the other arm since when he has been known as 'The armless wonder.' His parents are in Egypt where his father is Indian Consul General and today I've had a frantic wire to know how he is. I was tempted to reply 'Armless but wonderful' but decided this might frighten his parents that he had lost both, and anyway the Post Office won't accept telegrams for Egypt.

The bulbuls that come through the window into my bedroom every morning to feed while I have chota hazri are getting very tame and amusing to watch. The bigger—I can't make out whether it is the husband or a young giant, but she used to feed it some weeks ago till she gave that up as a bad job—comes onto my fruit plate with a good deal of fuss, but as soon as it is there she turns away and won't eat while it is feeding.

On November 1st Ajmer ceased to be a separate State and was merged in Rajasthan, an occasion for numerous and deadly dull farewell parties. The old State had promised us a grant of Rs.62,500 that we reckon was legally owed to us and that we had worked very hard to get. It had been approved, but the authority to pay the money was sent to Delhi late and the merger came off before the money arrived; so now we shall have to start again.

28.12.56. *Mayo College.* It was fun to have Tom Wyatt who was at Sidney with me and is now Joint Secretary of the Cambridge Syndicate to stay in the middle of last month. He talked to the boys, to the staff, and to the Rotary Club, so I fear we worked him hard. At the end of the month I went to Jaipur for the meeting of our General Council and stayed with H.H. who made me very comfortable. He asked me to lunch with the Attlees and that curious person Krishna Menon. I put on my O.H. tie for the occasion, and Lord Attlee reacted well. We had a long talk, not only about Haileybury but also about India. He told me that before Lord Linlithgow died he had congratulated him on what the Labour Party had done in India.

We had another General Council meeting on the 16th of this month and my plan for the expansion of the college has been approved. By the 22nd I was so worn out that I decided I must escape for a day or two, so collecting Charlie, Dwarka and Sukriti (a boy from Assam here for the holidays) we set off for Jaisalmer. We camped by a little lake beyond Jodhpur and cooked for supper four partridges we had shot on the way. Shortly after Beawar we had crossed the Aravallis with their rocks wind and sand eroded into fantastic shapes; then to Jodhpur the land was mostly flat with here and there a fortified hill-top. On the borders of Jaisalmer you come to uplands of tufted yellow grass and rocky outcrops and have a strange feeling of being on top of the world. Then you suddenly see the fort of Jaisalmer looking like a huge battleship. In yellow sandstone it covers the top of a great mound of rock and sand some 500 yards long—a continuous wall of semi-circular towers. Glowing in the soft afternoon sun it was more romantic and beautiful than I had ever expected. When you get inside the fort you see the wonderful carvings for which the place is famous—the most delicate lattice work in stone I have ever seen. There are 34 deserted townships in the State. A hundred years ago the people of these towns or villages—all with finely built stone houses with delightful carving and pillared courtyards, broad streets, splendid tanks for collecting water, great stone tables on carved legs, burial places with carved monuments and inscriptions—all fled one night from the extortions of the dewan, or prime minister of those days. Known as Paliwals, they were herdsmen, farmers and traders (Khyber, Multan, Jaisalmer, Surat route), and they left, abandoning all but the valuables they could carry. Today their ancient homes look as though only deserted yesterday, so well is the stone preserved in the dry air; but what a monument to the greed and wickedness of one man. On our last day we went out to H.H.'s farm where there is a great lake 5 to 7 miles long. It was covered with duck of all sorts, and I don't think I have ever seen so many together at once, but we could not shoot as there was too much water to cover, without many guns and several boats.

24.1.57. *Mayo College.* Term started a week ago with an unanticipated influx of new boys. We had expected 20; in fact 40 joined us, and they are really good value: bright eyed, intelligent, and all that one could desire. My house has been full of parents, and Samuel is wonderful. He always seems able to produce dinner for any number up to 14 at a moment's notice.

We were all much looking forward to shooting Imperial Sand Grouse at Gajner, H.H.'s preserve, to which he had invited us. We rose before dawn to find a fine drizzle falling, but we weren't going to miss this wonderful chance, so we set off in our open jeeps. By the time we had driven the 40 miles there it was raining hard, and there was no chance of the birds coming to water, which is how they should be shot. We lowered the windscreens and drove over the sand trying to get near enough to the flocks for a shot. It was very wet and bitterly cold, and having satisfied honour with two birds we withdrew. The next day we had to get back here. After nightfall we came to a river bed which had been dry on our way out, but which was now in full flood. We had all but crossed when the jeep started to stall. I got into four wheel drive and just got the back wheels clear of the water which had come over the floor boards, when it stopped. By moonlight we dried the battery leads and the plugs, and tried and tried to make it start. You can imagine with what relief we heard the engine purr after half an hour. On return I found a great pile of examination papers that I had to correct for the Union Public Service Commission: a frightful bore and absolute blood money only taken on in an effort to make ends meet, and in order to keep an eye on general standards over the country.

15.2.57. *Mayo College.* Term pretty hectic so far, though we are now well over double in numbers what we started with three years ago. Shortly after the beginning of term we had the hospital and one house full of boys with flu, and now we have thirty with measles. This evening a boy has had to have an immediate operation for appendicitis. A young couple from New Zealand, Allan and Pat Berry, have just joined us for a year. She is expecting a baby in March, so that will be another complication as they have a flat on my first floor; but they are a very pleasant couple. He is off to climb in the Hindu Kush in the summer, and it would have been fun to have gone with him, but I hope to get home. Prize Giving is in a week and we are working very hard with rehearsals of *A Midsummer-Night's Dream.* If any of the key players get measles it will turn into a nightmare.

8.3.57. *Mayo College.* I wish you could have seen the play. It is difficult to be objective about one's production, but I think it was good by quite high standards. Bottom and Co. said their prose parts in low class Hindi as used by the ordinary workman—a wrinkle I borrowed from the Maddermarket Theatre with their broad Norfolk. The Pyramus and Thisbe parts they said in English marred by the usual Indian mispronunciations. The rest was, of course, as Shakespeare wrote it, and said very well, and I am sure he would have approved of the workmen speaking their own language, and of the lovely Rajput dresses for the court. Puck, who tends to be a problem, was the best I have ever heard: a youngster from Assam with exactly the right face and voice. We did it out of doors in front of the pavilion with a forest of palms and ferns and white-ant hills in the background, and for Bottom's play the duke and court sat at the back of the audience at the top of the pavilion.

Pat Berry has had her baby. When it all started she thought it was dysentery, which she did have, and I only got the doctor just in time. The baby was born 10 minutes after they got to hospital.

27.4.57. *From my end-of-term letter to Parents.* When I had been here for a term I told the General Council that I estimated that it would be take three or four years to raise our numbers to 250, and about four years before we could expect satisfactory results in public examinations. The first estimate has proved right, and I think the second will too. In my last letter I mentioned our plans for expansion.

These are now in full swing. The new hostel is up to the first floor, the new central dining hall is nearly up to ceiling height, a new science lecture room is complete but for roof and fittings, and a large hole, growing in extent and depth as a result of the work of the boys, marks the site of our new swimming bath.

28.4.57. *To John Martyn.* Term ended three days ago with a wild bee comb being blown from the clock tower while we were all at 'Assembly' outside: and the bees came down and attacked us all. I gave the word to disperse, but a master who knew the bees better than I did said that we should lie on the ground and keep quite still. The boys behaved splendidly, and those who lay flat without movement, in spite of swarms of bees around them, were not stung. One little boy who lost his nerve and waved his arms about (and I am ashamed that I was no better) got stung more than 50 times. Rescue operations were carried out under sheets, and apart from a few high temperatures that night nobody, thank goodness, is any the worse. I have ordered four white bourqas to be hung in my office for rescue operations in future, in case this should happen again. I'm off this evening for two months in England.

21.7.57. *Mayo College.* This flu is a ghastly nuisance. On return here I learned that the Health Authorities of the State had ruled that the opening of schools was to be put off, but many of our boys were already on their way here. The evening they arrived half-a-dozen went straight into hospital, and now there are about 40 and several of the staff. The other day I had to go to Jaipur for a meeting and arrived there absolutely filthy after trouble with the jeep. Luckily I had some clean clothes with me, but there was no time to go anywhere to change, so I popped into a shop selling sanitary fittings (most suitable I felt) and astonished the shopkeeper by changing behind his counter. I hope he did not know who I was.

30.7.57. *Mayo College.* Still over 50 in hospital including the headmistress, housemistress and matron of the prep school and all but one servant. Nurses unobtainable. To add to these worries we have just been invaded by a mob of about a thousand schoolchildren. Fees in State schools in Jaipur, but not in Ajmer, have been increased, and this led to a strike there, and some of their students have come to Ajmer to stir up trouble here. I had hoped that we would not be worried, but this morning the band of hooligans who yesterday had smashed the windows and furniture of a school that had refused to close, arrived, and the police did nothing. My prefects wanted me to give out mosquito-net poles and repel them, but I decided that this could lead to greater trouble, so I got most of them to sit down, and with the help of Dwarka who is head of the school as interpreter, I told them that though we sympathized with their desire to have education made available to all, it would not further this if they made it impossible for us to go on teaching. A good many saw the point, but others were out for trouble, and stones began to fly. I chose discretion rather than valour, and agreed to close down classes for the rest of the day.

22.11.57. *Mayo College.* Tomorrow morning the Chief Minister of Rajasthan is opening our new house, and that is to be followed by the General Council budget meeting—always a fearful headache as they expect me to make bricks without straw. Last Sunday, I drove 230 miles to Pilani where I had to inspect a school for the Ministry of Education. Pilani is an astonishing place, miles from anywhere in arid desert country, but the birth-place and family home of the very wealthy business family of the Birlas. Try to get hold of a book called *India, Democracy and Education* by Hennessy, published by Orient Longmans. It tells you all about it and is a fascinating account. Starting in a small way with village schools, they have built up there a really splendid educational centre during the past 20 years.

We started a second round of flu just before I left Mayo College. By the time I reached Pilani there were over 60 in hospital, and we have had to use the new house that is being opened tomorrow as an emergency hospital. Fortunately, the boys seem to recover quickly. They have high temperature of 105 or over for one or two days and then get better, but are left very weak. I am counting so much on fairly good results this year. We expect to have the new dining hall finished for the start of the next term; the swimming bath is dug and the foundations started; the science block is being enlarged; our numbers are now 298 and we have more applications for next term than we can take; and I have collected some promising young masters, but what a blasted nuisance this flu is, and if you can have two rounds in one term, when will it stop, and when may it become deadly?

23

THE BASPA VALLEY

8.5.56. *Delhi* After packing in awful heat H.L. Dutt, Charlie and I got away at 1730. Twenty miles short of Jaipur we were stopped by a marriage party whose bus had run out of petrol and who were fearful of arriving with the bridegroom after the auspicious hour. They siphoned some out of my tank through the thinnest possible rubber tube, and it was ages before they were convinced that they had taken enough. Had ices in Jaipur and ordered and paid for chicken sandwiches for supper on the way, but forgot to collect them when we left. Arrived in Delhi at 0445.

10.5.56. *Doon School.* Breakfast in Meerut at the Wheeler Club, and then collected sugar and sweets from the Swarups in Muzaffarnagar. Lunched with Bill in Roorkee and borrowed boots, crampons, sleeping bag and lilo; then on to the Doon School. Spent a pleasant evening with Ellen Roy [Leftist thinker M. N. Roy's widow].

13.5.56. *Doon School.* In the evening watched *Richard II* by Shakespeareana and the boys. It was very good indeed, John asked me to write an account for the *Weekly,* and this kept me up till 0200. I am so often astonished at the universality of Shakespeare and his understanding of human character that changes so little in time and space. The nobles at the court of Richard II behave very much the same as the politicians here today who have to be called to Delhi for correction by the High Command, and for me the lesson of the play was that a state divided against itself cannot stand.

14.5.56. *Simla.* We found the Jumna at Rampur Mandi too big from the recent rain to cross by ferry, and had to go round by Saharanpur and Ambala. Inspected the brewery at Solon and were much refreshed by cold and excellent beer.

15.5.56. *Simla.* Held up by the usual frustrations at the start of an expedition, this time by conflicting reports on the position of the Inner Line and the state of the road, and I spent most of the day seeing officials of the Himachal Pradesh government. To Dr. Parmar I suggested that we wanted to find out whether his State had as much to offer as Garhwal. This put the Tourist Bureau on its metal, and they were very helpful indeed. We managed to convince them that the Inner Line went through Chitkal and not Narkanda or Sangla. Surely it would only encourage claims from the other side if it were moved farther from the frontier.

17.5.56. *Simla.* Packing completed and listened to Po Saw playing the piano in the evening—as much as I could through other people's conversation.

18.5.56. *Rampur Bashahr.* Up at 0500 and took Dutt, Charlie, Prem and the cook with half the baggage to the bus, and after that had started for Rampur Bashahr, loaded the rest of the stuff into the trailer and back of the jeep and Munna and myself in front and followed them. Here we are in the Raja's guest house and Negi, his Private Secretary, and Bishan Das, the Magistrate, have been most helpful arranging eleven mules for us tomorrow. Negi revived us on arrival with tea and excellent preserved local cherries and later with a spirit distilled from grapes also grown locally and pleasant to the palate. There is no food to be bought in the bazaar as the truck drivers went on strike some days ago, saying that the road was too dangerous. I can hardly blame them. Our bus was the first to come down for several days, so, so far we are lucky. The lovely old wooden painted palace, carved and of typical hill architecture influenced by Buddhist tradition, is gradually falling to pieces, having been replaced by a new one in stone. It should be scheduled as an ancient monument and repaired before it is too late.

19.5.56. *Sarahan.* A long day of 19 miles to Sarahan where we are in a beautifully situated P.W.D. Rest House, high up on the edge of the Sutlej gorge with fine views to the snows of the Kulu district. We share the bungalow with a party of wireless engineers on their way up to man a station at Chini.

20.5.56. *Paunda.* Another long day of 20 miles to start with level and pleasant walking through pine forests, and then a descent and long climb. Took photographs of a party of Tibetans on the way and fell in with the headmaster of the Sarahan School on his way to conduct an examination in Chini. He said that on the whole the new democracy did not yet suit the local people as well as the old direct rule of the rajas as they missed the personal touch, and it took so long to get anything done.

21.5.56. *Kilba.* Yet another 20 miles to Kilba where we are in a very pleasant Forest Rest House. I had thought I was getting old, but now begin to feel the joy of trekking. The cook makes very good parathas stuffed with potato, onion and sardines. We came down to the Sutlej at Wangtu where we made friends with the police picket. The rocks all around have 'Om Mani' carved on them and some people say that the Chinese claim as theirs anywhere where this has been done, though whether this is really so I have no idea. Though there are Buddhist and Tibetan influences in these parts, they are certainly preponderantly Hindu and Indian. All those crossing the bridge have to sign a book, I suppose to control infiltration from across the border. The police had wireless information of our coming, and all goes well. From Wangtu we walked along the Sutlej for several miles, bathing in its fierce waters dark with silt, then up from the river to Kilba, a longish but pleasant ascent.

22.5.56. *Sangla.* Expecting a mere 14 miles would be easy, we have all found today long and tiring. On the way beside the Sutlej we came to a wire rope bridge by which a boy of 14 and then a policeman crossed from the opposite side. The boy was bound to the bosun's chair by chains and handcuffs. He had apparently stolen about Rs.80 and was being taken to prison. I suggested to the constable that he was a bit young for this, and that a good beating should answer the case. Apparently this had already been administered. We offered to take him on as a servant so that he could earn enough money to repay what he had stolen, but the constable couldn't allow this on his own. The incident made us all a little sad.

Eventually we reached the confluence of the Baspa, both rivers in fine gorges with the sun lighting gnarled tress growing from their sites from behind, and with a path running across a cliff opposite us on a wooden floor support. As someone remarked, it was like a Chinese painting. We turned up the Sangla gorge and as we broke out of it into the flat valley we were met by a very beautiful sight: the shining river splitting up into silver webs here and there and flowing through green fields. I wish you could enjoy it all with me: not only the forests and crags and high mountains, but the valley with its singing birds and flowers and flowering shrubs and scents and the blue smoke of fires, the great herds of laden sheep and all the charming people.

24.5.56. *Rakcham.* The Lambedar of Rakcham, forewarned of our coming by the police, was there to meet us, and sent for porters who carried the loads in relays to a delightful camping spot about ¾ of a mile beyond the village, and here we pitched our tents on a grass alp with a clear stream. 'Loveliest of trees, the cherry now is hung with bloom along the bough.' One stands between us and the simple school building, and its beauty against the snow peaks and blue sky brings a lump into my throat. We have said goodbye to our muleteers and rewarded them for carrying our skis, though we noticed that the impossibility of putting them on the mules was gradually solved during the march. They were a hardy, happy, willing lot, typical of the Punjabis who are pushing their way up into the hills clad in their under-drawers, with their usual capacity to find a job and do it well.

26.5.56. *Camp at 13,000 feet in Shaone Gad.* We didn't get away till 0930 with a mixed party including ten women and a donkey. Any doubts about the women were rapidly dispelled and we all felt humbled by what they happily carried. Round our camp are fields of *Adonis chrysocyathus* from which the porters have made bunches for their caps and garlands for us all. The women sang folk songs to us before they left – an open-faced smiling lot, different from the women of Garhwal.

29.5.56. *Camp at 13,000 feet.* Up with the sun and we all climbed a little peak the other side of the valley—15,700 by aneroid—with fine views. This is a large valley and the end of it is several miles away. There are three large tributary valleys all filled with glaciers, but no snow is lying on their lower ends. On the way we found an ideal place for a camp a thousand feet above our present one which is homely and pretty, while this was more austere, less sheltered, and more a real mountain camp site. A very enjoyable day, and an icy bathe, hot tea and brandy revived us all. Shaitan Singh had belied his name and brought up a sheep for Rs. 25. Food so far has been simple but good, and there is no doubt that it pays enormous dividends to have a good cook.

30.5.56. *Camp at 13,000 feet.* Shaitan Singh today lived up to his name and caused trouble with the porters.

31.5.56. *Camp at 14,000 feet.* Here we are in a wonderful mountain camp at the confluence of all the great tributary valleys with views of the high mountains in all directions. South of us is one very reminiscent of the Matterhorn. Beside us flows a turgid stream with a pool offering opportunities of a swim if we are brave enough.

1.6.56. *Camp at 14,000 feet.* We had great fun skiing and the 'Shinka Handicap Straight Race' was won by Munna from me by about ten yards. Charlie, Munna and I all tried a steep schuss of about 100 feet with deep waves in it, and none of us could stand it. After skiing we went down for wood and I found the carry-up rather a fag and wished I was as shameless as Prem who moved about enough to fill a match-box.

2.6.56. *Camp at 14,000 feet.* A long but very happy day. We went to what on Map 53 I is marked as the Shinka Pass. The Old Forest survey, Bengal Presidency, sheet 347 of 1901 calls it the Barga Ghati, while the Rakcham men say it is the Lamiya. Anyway it was a good pass, 16,300 by aneroid, with a number of cairns on it. It took us seven hours to reach it, and this included wading a river and a lot of deep soft snow. We came down by a very steep snow slope for which we all roped, up but as soon as it was safe we all sat down and glissaded, Munna, I fear, losing the seat of his trousers.

5.6.56. *Camp 14,000 feet.* We have had another good day and climbed the mountain overlooking Rakcham, height by aneroid 17,600 and a pleasant exposed little summit after an easy walk up. On the way down we had excellent glissading, and Munna's other trousers are, I fear, now seatless, though the decencies are preserved by a pair of my best thick wool underpants which only have small holes made in them by moths. The snow was just not hard enough for us to glissade on our feet, so we had to come down on our bottoms.

6.6.56. *Camp 14,000 feet.* It rained and blew hard during the night and the morning was misty and cold. I spent a quiet day mending rucksacks, boots and clothes, and reading. An attempt to make salt shortbread was unsuccessful, though it might have been edible had I put in less salt. The rest of the party were less rude about it than I should have been had any of them produced it.

8.6.56. *Camp 14,000 feet.* After a cup of tea I set off to take photographs and had to climb about 1400 feet more than I expected, to get the view I wanted; and then, owing to the cold, the film stuck in my camera. Charlie, Munna and Prem descended to Rakcham so that they can visit Chitkal tomorrow, and to make sure that porters come up to bring us down. Their departure brings to an end what has been a most happy successful camp.

10.6.56. *Sangla.* A delightful walk down through orchards coming into fruit, walnut trees, deodars and spruce, with birds singing all round. Prem and I picked up an 'Om' stone each, mine for the Mayo College museum. We inspected Sangla village on the way. There is a pleasant Buddhist temple with a huge prayer drum inside it, covered with bronze and silver, and outside the walls are circled by little prayer drums, many covered with tin from old kerosene tins.

11.6.56. *Kilba.* An easy walk down the Baspa, then hot along the Sutlej and up here. I wonder if anyone has thought of fixing a cine camera somewhere with a good open view to include, if possible, a fruit tree, a bit of field, a stretch of a river, and a mountainside, and taking photos at some sort of intervals—say a minute each day of the year—the opposite of slow motion, to show the change of seasons. We are sad to have left the Baspa which Conway in *Sunlit Waters* calls 'the most lovely of all Himalayan valleys.' This is a very big claim, but it is certainly in the top class. The F.R.H. has some *Illustrated London News* and *The Queen* of 1916 vintage. How far off and long ago it all seems.

12.6.56. *Nichar.* Again down to the Sutlej and along it to Wangtu, the river now a roaring, tearing tide. Lunched at the little shop by the bridge and picked seven flies out of my cup of tea. On arrival here we were so captivated by the place that we decided to stay and do a really long day to Sarahan tomorrow. The F.R.H. is a dream, a two-storied white building like a miniature French chateau, surrounded by an orchard of apples, pears and plums. The village temples too are charming and fascinating with much Tibetan influence. All very content. Chicken, apples and apricots cooking for supper.

14.6.56. *Rampur.* We decided to shorten our march by a mile or so by taking the new motor road that is being built as a National Highway along Sutlej not far above the level of the river. Ever since I started walking in the Himalayas I have looked forward to the time when they would be available more quickly and easily by roads, and this now seems really to be coming. If the villagers can develop handicrafts to fill their long idle winter hours, there is no knowing what wealth may be produced. Their houses show the same skill in wood carving that you find in Switzerland, and perhaps, one day, this too will be turned to manufacture of watches and precision instruments. I talked to the engineer in charge of the bridge and asked him why there were not thousands more men working on the road. The difficulty is apparently not lack of funds, but shortage of labour, and what labour there is seems to spend much of its time making tea, playing cards, and sitting round.

Arrived at Rampur we had refreshing baths in Negi's quarters in the palace. We wanted to sleep out on the lawn in front of the palace but Negi wouldn't hear of this as he thought it would be a reflection on his hospitality, so we had to share the heat of the Guest House with a party of teachers from Allahabad who had just completed a course for local schoolmasters in adult education. We attended their final function after supper and only just managed to keep awake till it ended a little before midnight. The District Magistrate made a good but over-long speech, and when the local M.L.A. rose to wind up there was a general exit that had to be stopped by the N.C.C. cadets on duty. But, as with the road, it was thrilling to see the changes that are gradually taking place in the lives of the people. Among a large audience were a number of women who looked as though they had come from Tibet, and they sat and watched enthralled.

15.6.56. *Simla.* The drive back provided its excitements. At places we had to pass down-coming trucks, and the hunt to find a bit of road wide enough to do so took time and patience. Our starting handle was ineffective and the battery run down, and the driver would back the bus to the very edge before the engine got going. Half-way between Narkanda and Simla a front spring broke, and we finished the journey with a block of wood in its place. The life of a driver on this road must be hard, and we were full of admiration of ours. Among the passengers was a Sikh who had been working on the road as a foreman. He had thrown his hand in as the life, he said, was too hard and lonely, and provisions were so difficult to come by. Shall suggest to Parmar, the Chief Minister, that some sort of canteen service might be organised for workers on the road. Before we left the Sutlej valley we had given lifts to several children on their way to school—another change in ways of life. We whiled away the time composing limericks:

> There was a young fellow called Jha
> Who shocked his poor doting mamma.
>   When he left her his tum
>   Was as big as his bum;
> On return it was smaller by far.

There was a young man from Narkanda
Who reminded us much of the Bandar,
   For the seat of his bags
   Was in tatters and rags
As glissading had torn it asunder.

18.6.56. *Dadahu.* Gopal told me that it brought bad luck to take an 'Om' stone away.

20.6.56. *The Doon School.* Crossing an Irish bridge we took an unexpected bump, and the bracket attaching the trailer to the jeep cracked and bent. The 'Om' stone was blamed. With the help of a doctor who stopped to offer assistance, and some villagers, this was shored up on a beam of wood, and all seemed well. We were warned by a bus driver that there was too much water in the Jumna to cross by the ferry at Rampur Mandi, so we continued down to Jagadri. Five miles short of Saharanpur there was a loud bang, and the trailer broke completely adrift to cries of 'The stone, the stone'. Luckily we were going slowly at the time, or there might have been a bad upset: The local Cane Crushing Officer, who was just behind us, was very helpful and took me to a man in Sarahanpur who sent out a truck and brought the baggage and trailer into a garage. Four strong men lifted the trailer bodily onto the truck. [Note: The following term we had a lot of illness in Mayo College, and there were continual murmurs of 'The stone, the stone'. At the end of the term I arranged with a boy from Simla to take the 'Om' stone and replace it on the wall from which we had lifted it. That evening I was rung up from the station by him to be told that he had lost his ticket.] It took seven long hours of riveting and welding to put the trailer right.

24

A HALF-CENTURY

In 1958 Gibson turned 50 which explains the title of this chapter. And even at this age Gibson's spirit of adventure had not faded since he took time off during summer break to take a group of boys and teachers to make an attempt at the Swargarohini peak in Garhwal. The year began with a duck shoot at the invitation of the Maharana of Kishangarh. And concluded with invitation from the Maharaja of Jaipur to a private dinner with Prince Philip. Arthur Hughes, ex-ICS and 'The Times' correspondent also decided to come over and teach for a time. The year had begun with 340 boys and by the following year it had 392. The school standards were improving and so were its finances. The Gibson touch was slowly beginning to change the college fortunes and lift its profile. Gibson's visits to schools such as the Scindia in Gwalior and others across India as part of his duties as a senior member of the country's educational community also enabled him to compare notes and seek improvements.

21.1.58. *Mayo College.* Term started a week ago. All goes well and we are about the 340 boys we wanted for this term. I spent the New Year in Bikaner at Charlie's place and we had some very enjoyable shooting. It was my first experience of Imperial Sand Grouse over butts, and I didn't do too badly. We came back in my jeep via Jodhpur,

300 miles in the day, not what you would call a rest cure. The chief anxiety was to get the roof onto the new dining hall. It would have been ready in plenty of time if the railway authorities hadn't delivered the steel girders to their workshop instead of to us. It took a month to find out what had happened to them, and after we got them work went on day and night. On the 13th, as I was going to the station to meet a parent, I found the workmen (and the women), having downed tools, making off home. I asked what was up, and apparently some man had made love to some woman, not his wife, during the night shift. Knives had been drawn and work ceased. Fortunately I am on good terms with most of them as I go round and ask how they are getting on from time to time, and was able to persuade the whole crowd to return to the job—in spite of my Hindi which everyone laughs at—and I felt rather pleased with myself. We are now using the new hall, roofed without a ceiling. The new boys look a good lot, and our standards are really going up, I think.

I'm very delighted that the Everest Foundation have made us a grant of £200 to buy climbing equipment. I wrote to the P.M. to ask if I could import this free of duty and had a letter back within two days from the Finance Minster to say 'yes'! Later I had another letter from the P.M.'s secretary asking whether I would have bothered Churchill over such a small matter, and I replied that it probably would not have been necessary. Here, if you want something quickly, you have to go to the top. Our annual Prize Giving is fixed for February 21st and the Chief Guest will be Admiral Sir Stephen Carlill.

23.2.58. *Mayo College.* Shorty Carlill and his wife were a terrific success. They arrived the day before P.G. and went all round talking to the boys from the six-year-olds in the Prep School to the grandfathers of the senior houses. I had three tents in my house. Just after lunch on the big day I was rung up by the Assistant Magistrate and told that Maulana Azad had died and asked whether we would cancel our function. I said that life must keep going, that we would fly the flag at half-mast, cancel the band and garden party, but otherwise carry on. The flag was lowered, I rang up the Grenadiers and told them not to come, and all the tables were being moved, when the news came through that the Maulana was still alive. Up went the flag. Out came the tables, and the band was telephoned for. Everything was just ready on time. The Admiral's address was the best I have heard for a long time. The matter was good, and the delivery splendid. Then we had tea during which I was told that the main switch-board was on fire. This would have ruined the concert, but it too was put right in time. The concert, over which I had been very anxious as the idea was mine and I was not sure it would work, and knew we had not had enough time to rehearse properly, went off very well. Maulana Azad, one of the strongest and best of Nehru's advisers, died on Saturday morning. He will be a great loss to the country.

6.3.58. *Mayo College.* Last Saturday I went to Kishangarh for a duck shoot, and as usual I could not bring down the high ones. I can't think what is wrong with my shooting these days, I seem to have lost all confidence. I was given an excellent butt next to H.H. Kotah and while he, certainly with the advantage of two guns and a loader, brought down 98, I had to confess to a bare 9! Monday was my fiftieth birthday, and except that none of you were here, it was. I think, the happiest birthday of my life. The boys and staff were very kind to me and presented me with one of Gue's paintings I have long wanted to buy. I had a supper party on my lawn for all the staff, teaching and clerical, and the monitors, all in fancy dress, and many dresses were very good indeed. I understand that one uninvited boy dressed as a veiled woman and came to see what it was all about, for which I give him full marks for initiative. Today has been the festival of Holi when everyone throws colours and I have stuck indoors. It's like snowballing. Once or twice is enough. There descended upon me the *Times* Correspondent, a Special Correspondent of the *Economist* and a retired I.C.S. officer, Arthur Hughes—all very interesting.

14.3.58. *Mayo College.* Arthur Hughes who left after Holi soon came back and has decided to stay and teach here for a bit. He is great fun and a scholar much above my level, and it is amusing finding him wondering whether he will be able to manage classes; but he seems to enjoy them and the boys to find him stimulating.

27.4.58. *Mayo College.* Our School Certificate results arrived at the beginning of the month—at last good news: 57% first divisions, 29% second, 14% third and no failures. When I admit that only seven boys took the exam this may not sound so good, but it does at least show that we can get first divisions, and in years to come I expect five times as many more boys to compete.

On the 7th of April we had our Full Moon operation. The staff, known as Magistres Lunatici Mayonenses or Abominable Moonmen (the fattest of the Fullmoonman), had to escape to the top of a local hill from where they could take off for the moon before midnight. The boys had to capture them for the local Zoo. Unfortunately the moon was obscured and rose later than expected (it was three days after full) and most of the moonmen found it easy to remain hidden in bushes rather than expose themselves climbing the hill.

Now we are suffering a fearful heat wave—well over 110 degrees. No one in Ajmer can remember anything like it in April, and I long to get up into the hills. The poor birds sit around gaping, and I have put out dishes of water for them. Two owls came yesterday afternoon as well as three lovely woodpeckers, gold down their backs, wings and breasts green and with scarlet crests on their heads. I'm now reading reports on boys before writing 345 of my own. I specially liked two: 'He can only spell four-letter words' and 'His geometrical drawings are improper'.

During the summer vacations of May-June 1958 Gibson and a group of Mayo boys and masters made an attempt at the Swargarohini peak. The party consisted of seven boys from Mayo College, five masters: Allan Berry and Alby Clough from New Zealand, Shiv Ganju, H. L. Dutt and myself; Mrs. Berry and Mrs. Clough; and Dr. John Moor from England. They could not afford Sherpas. Beyond Chakrata they left for Lake Camp with 42 porters who insisted on sitting down for a smoke about every half-mile and once they had arrived at the lake in driving snow, all the porters deserted them, saying that it was inauspicious to try to climb Swargarohini! Eventually, the group divided themselves into two parties, one of which tried to climb the peak and even reached 19,000 feet but gave up due to bad weather and defeated by the rocks. Those who stayed below did skiing in the valley. Even Gibson's party made it to 17,000 feet but turned back on account of very steep snow. While the two New Zealanders made another attempt, the rest of them, including Gibson, crossed into the Harki

Doon. There they practised rock-climbing on great boulders on which our old cairns still stood.

29.6.58. *Mayo College.* We returned a fortnight ago. On the way we visited the Moghul castle of Kankwadi where Aurangzeb imprisoned his brother Dara. We hoped to find ornaments or coins in its tank dropped by people drawing water. Though the water was as we expected, very low, we never got down to it, as we found it protected by wild bees. Our results in the Board examinations were quite good, and we now seem to have a good reputation as there are far more applications for admission than we take.

28.8.58. *Mayo College.* Peter Lloyd arrived three weeks ago and promises to be a tremendous success. He is a master from Uppingham and has come on exchange for a year with Gupta, our Science senior master, who flies to England tomorrow, I have asked Jill to have him to stay in the holidays. Arthur Hughes, also a great success, has promised to stay for at least a year, and half-way through September we add another from England—Maclean from Eton where he was captain of football, in Pop, and a regular 'blood'. He goes to Cambridge in September next year, so will spend about a year with us. With these native English speakers on the staff I hope to lay the foundations of correct expression, and that once laid, these foundations will remain firm. Next week we have a visit I am much looking forward to from Minoo Masani and his wife. His two very stimulating books, *Our India* and *Our Growing Human Family,* have given me many ideas for my teaching.

19.10.58. *Mayo College.* Just back from a very happy and refreshing visit to the Scindia School, Gwalior. We arrived in Agra four hours late as we had to pass through an area where there had been unusually heavy rain and the flood water was well over the axles of the carriage wheels, so the train had to go very slowly. As we had missed our connection I had to ring up to let our hosts know that we should be late and the telephone operator was fearfully slow till the station-master suggested that I should tell him that I was the superintendent of police with urgent news about dacoits. Then I was put through at once. All the games we played were very exciting.

16.1.59. *Mayo College*. I got back from a short holiday in Udaipur, where H.H. very kindly had my old jeep repainted as a Christmas present, a fortnight ago.. I sometimes wonder if we have bitten off more than we can chew with this rapid expansion of the college. It means improvisation all the time. We have had over 120 applications for 35 vacancies this term, and they still pour in at the rate of six or seven a day, though some, thank goodness, are for the dim future. Sahgal, the Bursar (and how lucky we are that he is also an engineer), has done wonders expanding dormitories, turning thunderboxes into flush system lavatories, building bathrooms with running water, etc. Our next problem is to expand classroom accommodation. Parents arrive tonight and tomorrow in large numbers, and I have visitors from the British High Commission. I live pretty simply when by myself, but all this entertaining costs me more than I earn, and though the school makes me a fair allowance, it is not enough. However I can't ask for more while my staff are all so underpaid. If we put up the fees further, the parents of many of the best boys can't afford them. We have thought of fees graded according to income, but income is impossible for us to assess, and I doubt if we ought to become a taxing authority.

14.2.59. *Mayo College.* We now have 392 boys, with one or two more to come. On the 23rd January I jeeped to Jaipur to have lunch with Prince Philip. It was very good of H.H. Jaipur to have asked me. Not knowing that the Duke was coming to Jaipur, I had mentioned to Jai that I was disappointed not to have been able to spare the time to go to two receptions in Delhi to which I had been invited to meet him. Jai replied, 'Well, he is paying us a private visit, Come over and stay with us.' We all lunched together at a small table in Jai's garden, and what an admirable person the Duke is. He has gone down very well indeed in India, and must have done a great deal for cordial relations. We all hope that he will bring the Queen one day. He talked to me after lunch about schools, the Outward Bound movement and so on, and I asked if he minded if I smoked. As he said, 'Go ahead' I lit my pipe, and later an officious A.D.C. said that I should not have done so. Who was wrong?

On January 30th we had a visit from Lt. General Bahadur Singh, an old friend with whom I used to shoot in the Doon, and now Adjutant General. He talked to the boys on the armed services as a career, and went down very well; and one of the things he pointed out was that by joining the N.D.A. they became independent of their parents much earlier than if they went to college. He also said that they escaped from the tyranny of their school-masters. A small boy at the end, when asked for questions, caused much amusement by saying: 'Sir, you told us about escaping from the tyranny of our teachers; but what about the tyranny of our senior officers?' We are rehearsing Galsworthy's *Strife* translated into Hindi by one of the staff.

10.3.59. *Mayo College.* Prize Giving went off well, with a record gathering of Old Boys and parents. *Strife* in Hindi was not bad, but I wished I could have been able to help more in rehearsals. I am ashamed that after 22 years out here I still can't speak it, but I never seem to have a moment or the energy to get down to learning the language properly. On the Wednesday following Peter Cooper arrived to give a concert in the Assembly Hall on the piano I persuaded the Government of Rajasthan to give us. It had been lying unused in the Circuit House since that ceased to be the residence of the Chief Commissioner. He played a splendid programme really beautifully—Byrd, Gibbons, Bach, Brahms, Chopin—and you must go to hear him if you ever get a chance. The same day Sir Julian Huxley gave the general knowledge talk to the upper school. It too was very good, and it was a great compliment to us that he agreed to speak. I told him about your skating with his father those years at Morgins. From February 27th to March 1st we had Vinoba Bhave here. He is an old disciple of Gandhiji and is going round India trying to persuade those who have more land than they need to give it to him to be divided among the landless. I am not sure that this Bhoodan (giving of land) will do much to solve the economic problems of the country, but there is plenty of room in the world for more generosity, and if he can stir people to this, so much to the good. I was a bit worried because his visit was expected to attract thousands of visitors and villagers who were all to camp on our polo ground. I was afraid of diseases and endless noise. However the Chief Minister of Rajasthan got round the General Council to allow it and the whole 50 acres was covered with a bamboo and grass-mat township. The boys helped in the camp, complained of the dust, the smells and the flies, but generally did a good job. I was not wrong about the disease and we have had an epidemic of flu, caused, the doctor says, by all the dust, and the movement has been rechristened Fludan by its critics. One of Vinoba's followers, Cherian Thomas from Kerala which has a communist government, stayed with me for some days recovering from the flu. I liked him very much and found him very interesting. He had just returned from a visit to China, had walked from Cape Comorin to Kashmir in the interests of Bhoodan, had been parliamentary secretary to the Congress party, and had had part of his education in the U.S.A.

26.4.59. *Mayo College.* Surjit Singh Majithia, the Deputy Defence Minister, officially opened the new swimming bath, the hole for which was largely dug by the boys. After supper they put on a mock parliament for us with some of the boys taking part: question time, an adjournment motion, and the introduction of a bill—all interesting, instructive and amusing. My dog turned up and Jaipal Singh complained 'I spy strangers'. Pattabhiraman, who was acting as Speaker, immediately ruled 'Every dog has his day'.

On March 19th we had a terrible tragedy. Mahabir Dayal, the senior assistant master, suddenly felt a pain. The Civil Surgeon and school doctor happened to be together in the school hospital and were called. I arrived shortly after them. Mahabir looked pale and was sweating and said he thought he had indigestion. The Civil Surgeon put him in his car and drove him to the civil hospital. There he had a very severe, and what must have been a second heart attack, and died within ten minutes. I liked him very much and he will be a great loss to the school.

Our exams have shown that we are not getting across nearly as much as we should be. The little blighters still write off the point, spell words wrong that are spelt for them in the questions, and fail to read and follow instructions—all the obvious things that one has told them so often.

Last night's scheme we called 'Escarpment Escapade' and it was suggested by the escape of the Dalai Lama to India. The Nag Pahar ridge between Foy Sagar and the Pushkar valley north-west of the village of Hathikhera was the boundary between the countries of Foy Nag and Pushkar. The boys of one house were the people of Foy Nag and had a traditional respect for the Head of the State, but a number were dissatisfied and ready to help the Peoples' Liberation Army; the majority were to assist the escape of the Head of the State and the transport of his treasure across the border into Pushkar. The ridge is one on which we have found a number of good rock-climbs, but there are a few tracks across it. The boys of another house were the forces of the country of Pushkar, and the rest of the senior school the People's Liberation Army, of whom 15 were allowed to be deployed as scouts while the rest had to remain south of Hathikhera until informed that the Head of the State had fled. Orders by the government of Pushkar for their military commanders and political officers were that unrest across the border made it possible that the Head of the State might seek asylum in Pushkar, and that should he do so, every assistance was to be given him once he had crossed the border, but under no circumstances were any of the forces of Pushkar to enter the friendly state of Foy Nag, and the border was to be protected from entry by undesirable people.

The scheme went very well and there were various amusing incidents: one of the boys who had gone out to reconnoitre the area had told the villagers of Hathikhera that there was some danger of an attack by dacoits on the night of the scheme, and those in the opposing party, and the umpires, found themselves chased by angry men with lathis on the night; another boy, climbing the cliff of Nag Pahar, got stuck below a hive of wild bees. I was called to his assistance. I couldn't get down to him, even on a rope, because of the bees, and I had to shout to him to hang on for as long as he could while I went down another way and climbed up to him. The saddest thing was the fate of the 'treasure'. I had filled an old ammunition box with papayas from my garden. This was safely carried up by the 'Head of the State of Foy Nag' and his companions and was meant to refresh us all at the top of the ridge, but they, thinking the content was only stones, emptied it down the cliff when they had reached the top.

25
A CROWDED PROGRAMME

The summer vacations of 1959 were spent on a trekking and skiing trip to Chamba and the outlying areas in what is now Himachal Pradesh. And of course there were trips within Rajasthan – to Jaisalmer and Jodhpur. This year Gibson also delivered a radio talk on mountaineering in India. He was also elected President of the Ajmer Rotary Club. Sadly, owing to the low finances of the college, he had been working on the same salary since the time he had joined in 1954 and the rest of the staff hadn't received any raise either. Conscious of this, Gibson had brought up the issue of staff salaries at the meeting of the College General Council and his efforts had borne fruit. He was also writing in the national Press on the future of public examinations in India and found himself having to defend the status of public schools in India which at this time were coming under attack as places which only produced an elite class and snobs. With a passion for mountains, he was also trying to save the Calcutta-based Himalayan Club at this time which was on the verge of extinction. Amid all these worries he was invited to attend the marriage of the daughter of the Maharao of Kotah – the first time a daughter was getting married in the family in 200 years – and greatly enjoyed the occasion.

1960 was the year when Gibson for the first time introduced an entrance test for the college, such was the demand for places in it now, and the idea was to be picked up by Doon School two years later. Among the distinguished visitors to the college this year was Arnold Toynbee.

In 1961, during the visit of Queen Elizabeth to India, it was decided to honour Gibson with an OBE in recognition of "A valuable contribution over a long period to the prestige of the United Kingdom in India." Gibson also met the Queen twice within a space of a week – first as a guest of the Maharajah of Jaipur when he took along the entire college boys in nine buses packed beyond the limit, and the following week at the ceremony in Delhi where the Queen pinned the OBE on his lapel.

11.5.59. *Chamba.* We spent the 8th sorting equipment and packing, and that evening caught the train to Delhi where we arrived the next morning covered in dust and smut from the engine. I cleaned up and had breakfast at the Gymkhana Club and then went off to the Ministry of Education to discuss various problems: scholarships, examinations, financial help for the school, and so on. Then I called on Thimmy, now Chief of the Army Staff, and told him of our difficulties in getting bookings to Pathankot, the rail head for our expedition. He very kindly arranged for us to have berths in an army coach. We got our supplies into the carriage, but there was no room for us, so we squeezed in elsewhere, separated from our beddings and luggage. We arrived the next morning and picked up some tents and other equipment on loan from the army, boarded a bus and started for Chamba, having been joined by an army doctor, Waryam Singh, who is coming with us. I am very glad to have him as it relieves me of anxiety about illness or accidents. We are a party of twelve including Peter Lloyd, Lowry Maclean, H. H. Dutt – who has been with me for the last two expeditions and is now doing most of the organization of this one – Guinness, the Doc and myself. The equipment from the army is stuff on which they want reports, and the sleeping-bags are rather heavy and bulky, but it will all be most useful.

The drive here was hot but interesting. We crossed the Ravi by a suspension bridge so narrow that we had to take care not to stick our elbows out of the windows. Our original plan was to cross the Sach Pass into Pangi but we are told it is deep in snow, and it would take us too long and be too expensive, so we are going to a place called Tissa which can be reached in one day, partly by bus and partly by mules; then we turn up a valley at the head of which we hope to find good skiing and climbing. There is nothing over 17,000 feet, but there is a long series of ridges all over 15,000 with valleys coming down that look, on the map, as though they should be good for skiing. Chamba is only 4,000 feet above sea level and is pretty warm, but it is a most attractive place with a long history. The Raja's family, no longer ruling, goes back in direct descent to before A.D. 600 and has very interesting records. His three boys are at Mayo College, and he lives what I imagine must be a rather aimless and lonely life in a great palace that dominates the little town. The District Commissioner, C.P. Singh, is an old boy of Mayo College whose son is coming to us next term, so we enjoy splendid local assistance. We have visited the museum, full of good things. The Rest House, where we are sleeping, has an ancient piano that makes a horrible noise.

12.5.59. *Chamba.* Everything now ready for a start tomorrow. We all lunched with H.H. the Raja. If he is lonely, he certainly has a wonderful cook. The Raja's mother, a very small merry-looking old lady, entranced us.

Between May 13 and June 8 Gibson and party went on a trekking and skiing trip in the ranges beyond Chamba on heights not exceeding 15,000 feet. This was to form the basis of a talk he delivered on radio in Ajmer.

8.6.59. *Chamba.* Here we are all safely back in Chamba where it is fearfully hot. On our last evening at Tissa the school gave us a camp fire and entertainment, one item of which was a skit in which a clerk employed a porter to carry his luggage across the Sach Pass. By the time they got to the top the clerk was carrying the load and the porter had persuaded him to give him all his warm clothes. Many of the children must be related to porters or even themselves carry loads; others were no doubt sons of clerks. It was fun to see them laughing at themselves, and no doubt incidentally at us. We have invited the headmaster to bring a party to Mayo College in the winter. We have found the people of Chamba charming and full of good humour and friendliness. The elected head of the panchayat in the valley we went up was one of the Muslim Gujars who were as generous to us with deep draughts of lassi when we passed through their settlement as we have always found such people. As far as we could make out this area is not much visited by climbers although there lie within it the Pir Panjal peaks of over 20,000 ft., valleys and mountains narrow and sharp that do not take long to reach and that are not beyond the Inner Line. They are very beautiful and offer wonderful climbing at comfortable attitudes. This has been an expedition of lots of fun, though I find I get more quickly tired than I used to. I suppose I must face it now that I'm over 50.

17.10.59. *Mayo College.* I don't seem to have had a minute free for ages. Apart from teaching and all the correcting involved, and work in the office, I have a continual round of visitors—most of whom I enjoy. At the moment I have three of the staff of the Scindia School who are with us for our annual matches. Gerald Guinness, and Commodore Lele arriving tomorrow but that is nothing to the party I had a fortnight ago for the Rajasthan University Youth Festival which was held this year in Ajmer and for which I put up nine of the judges including the Chatterjees and Sondhis, old and valued friends. Since then we have had our half-term break for which Dinah Stock joined us. Arthur Hughes, I and others, took 92 boys in two great buses and my jeep to Jodhpur and Jaisalmer. At Jodhpur we stayed in great comfort at Umed Bhawan and went over the ancient fort, round the old city, and visited the Air Force College from where we were flown over the town. One evening we had drinks with Hanut Singh, the great polo player, and he told us how his father had taken him to England when he was 15 in the first world war, had insisted on seeing Kitchener, an old friend, and had arranged for him to go to France and serve—so he had never been to school. He has a very interesting photograph of Churchill as a young subaltern when he came to play polo, with a very square jaw and looking even more determined than he did later in life. On the way to Jaisalmer (179 miles) we ate a picnic lunch at Pokaran from where the three boys came to the Doon School. In Jaisalmer bathed, rode camels and horses, shot sandgrouse, and explored the fort and town and visited the famous underground Jain library with manuscripts nine hundred years old, and, most interesting we were invited to the Dassera Durbar, which is something that is coming to an end. The Maharawal sat on his throne decked in jewels and fanned with yak tails, and surrounded by his courtiers wearing swords. The mares were blessed and danced on their toes, while goats were sacrificed—one blow of a sword and the head was off. A bit primitive perhaps, but with the music of pipes and drums and the colour, all very stirring.

31.10.59 Diwali, the festival of lights. It is also the Indian equivalent of November 5th and everyone lets off fireworks. This fills me with terror. What I know I ought to do is to have a professional who takes the risks on behalf of the rest of us. What in fact happens is that every boy in the school gets a parcel of anything from the most frightful bangs called atom bombs, to rockets that may go off in any direction. They all gather on the main field and let them off indiscriminately. A star goes up and by its light you can see small and larger groups and individuals all over the place: some bending over to light a rocket, others running away from one due to go up—groups rather like those in Dutch painting of villagers on the ice. Why no one gets hurt or blinded I can't imagine. When someone does I shall have to make a new arrangement. Till then I suppose it will go on in the traditional way which always frightens me.

3.11.59 Went over to the short-wave transmission station seven miles out of Ajmer to record the talk on mountaineering in India that you listened to. I am glad to hear that you were at least able to recognize my voice. I talked, not about international expeditions competing for the highest peaks, but tried to interest foreign visitors in a pleasant climbing holiday with a mountain of perhaps about 20,000 feet as their goal and gave advice about food, clothing, porterage and so on.

5.11.59 Peter Walker, another school leaver with us for a year, this time from Tonbridge, arrived.

9.11.59 Captain Harvey, Captain Superintendent of the Training Ship *Dufferin*, arrived in the evening after I had held a meeting of the Board of Directors of the Ajmer Rotary Club of which I am President this year. Harvey stayed for two days and gave two very good talks to the boys, one on his ship and the other on the Merchant Service as a career. I hope some of them will think of this as a way of life.

20.11.59 Much of the morning taken up with a trial landing of an Otter to see whether it is safe for Air Marshal Mukherjee to land on our polo ground now that part of it has been ploughed up for wheat and the grow-more-food campaign. It was decided that it was not long enough for a fully loaded plan, and that the Air Marshal would have to come by helicopter. This was what the boys wanted as Otters have been before, but so far no helicopter has landed here. In the event he did not come at all, but had to stay in Delhi. China business I suspect.

21.11.59 The meeting of the General Council went off well. The Chief Minister of Rajasthan came, which was encouraging as it showed that in spite of political criticism of this sort of school, he realized that it was doing good work. Also present were Jai, H.H. Mewar, and others. I was able to report that, with our numbers at 407, we now had about 180 boys more than it was considered the college had accommodation for six years ago. Our new buildings include Rajasthan House, the double-purpose dining hall and theatre with store rooms and kitchens, the new swimming bath, the partly completed new teaching block, four new laboratories and a lecture room, the metal workshop and extension of the carpentry shop, the music school, new dormitory blocks for Ajmer and Jodhpur houses and bathrooms and lavatories for these and Bikaner and Tonk houses, a new ward for the hospital, a common-room for the staff, and various other minor alterations and improvements. These have added Rs.80,000 to our overdraft, but have cost Rs.7,60,000, and would have cost much more if Sahgal, our wonderful Bursar, had not done such splendid work. I can take credit only for being the stimulus; but I feel we haven't done badly. We still have to complete the new teaching block, equip the new labs, provide bathrooms and lavatories in two more boys' houses and modern sanitation in masters' houses, and to construct more married masters' quarters. The staff are also paid much too little and I made out a strong case for raising this. As I have remained at the start of the Principal's pay for six years, I have been given another Rs.200 a month from next January, increasing each year by Rs.200 till I reach Rs.2,000 a month in four years time. I need it, but still feel guilty at getting so much more than my colleagues.

11.12.59. *Mayo College.* The future of the Himalayan Club is causing some concern as there is difficulty in finding, in Calcutta, members to serve on the committee, edit the *Journal* (a job I would very much like to have accepted but have not the time for), look after equipment, and so on. Trevor Braham, who has been so good an editor, was here for a day last week on his way home, and we talked things over. He has gone on to Delhi and Dehra Dun, and we agree that if the centre is moved to Delhi it will be easier to run the club. We must certainly not let it die.

For some time I have been trying, by articles in the *Statesman,* to interest the general public in the future of public examinations in India. It seems to me to be of vital importance, but no one appears ready to do anything much about it, other than accept a policy of wait-and-see.

7.1.60. *Mayo College.* I returned here from the Himalayan Club dinner in Delhi, where the paintings and sketches by Manvendra Panna, Mahavir Ghanerao and Ramesh Mathur were much admired, on December 21st, then worked in the office till late lunch on the 24th, after which Dan Mal, Arthur Hughes and I set off for Banera where we arrived shortly after dark to find the rest of the party sitting round a splendid fire in the open beside the lake. So far as I was concerned the Christmas Day shoot was not much of a success. I had a touch of flu, and, left on an island in the middle of a large lake with duck flying all around me, my gun jammed. The right barrel failed to eject and the ejector got behind the cartridge so that I could neither poke the spent cartridge out nor shut the gun to use the other barrel. All that was needed to put things right was a pen-knife or screwdriver, and I, stupidly, had neither, so while the birds almost landed on the water beside me, scared only by my language, I struggled ineffectually with my thumb nail, a reed as a ramrod, a spent cartridge as a level, all to no purpose. I sweated so much with anger that by the time I was rowed ashore in the boat that came eventually to pick me up after dark, my fever was gone. Christmas dinner was a memorable evening. We collected in an upper courtyard of the palace where again we sat round an open fire, this time burning in the hollow trunk of a huge tree. We fed on roast goose and, in place of plum pudding, carrot halwa covered in flaming blue local spirit. After the traditional toast of 'Absent

Friends' we all danced country dances, my contribution being my special skiing exercises which I called a Cossack dance. These went down well and I was asked where I had learned the steps! The Raja, a splendid person, was in full mess kit, while his great-great grandchildren were in pyjamas. It was a most enjoyable family party. The next day we had a beat for wild boar which failed to appear; however it was very exciting and a nilgai, four jackal and two jungle cats walked past me almost within touching distance. On the 27th we paid a rapid visit to Chittoor, and then on through Udaipur to Dilwara where we stayed the night and were shown some of the family treasures which include a letter from Rana Pratap. We did our morning duty from latrines opening through the walls from which the refuse fell more than a hundred feet down to waste land at the foot of the ancient ramparts. The cold blast up the funnel reminded me of the Britannia Hut above Saas Fee. Then we spent a pleasant day at Deogarh, and so back here.

26.2.60. *Mayo College.* On January 8th I drove to Jaipur, 82 miles that I get very tired of, for a meeting to consider better pay for the staff. This has been approved and though, by English standards still very low, is something that has been badly needed. We shall also put up the pay of the clerical staff and servants in proportion, which will mean that in the end we shall have to put up our fees. Term started on the 11th and among other parents I had Bachan (of Rampur, who was in Kashmir House and has now put his son here, making me feel a sort of grandfather) and his charming wife to stay. We were also joined at the beginning of term by Jonathan Hazell who is spending six months with us between Rugby and Cambridge, so I now have four English boys, two Indian boys, and Arthur Hughes living in my house. I sometimes look back regretfully to the more lonely, but more peaceful days when I had meals by myself with my feet on a table, leaning back in an armchair reading. For the first weeks of term we worked hard on *Twelfth Night* for Prize Giving. On February 5th, I again drove to Jaipur, this time for the annual meeting of the India Pubic Schools' Conference which was held at the Girls' Public School started there by Maharani Gayatri Devi. It was my last year as Chairman, and the Chief Guest was Professor Humayun Kabir, an old friend, now Minister for Scientific Affairs at the centre. The conference went off well and Humayun was encouraging about Public Schools. Most ministers feel they have to run them down, though they continue to send their children to them if they can. Lilian Lutter, the Principal of the school, was a marvelous hostess and ran everything very well. I got back from Jaipur late on the night of the 8th, and the next day we had a visit from Lt. General Taper, G.O.C. in C., Western Command. Four days later the Medleys arrived from the U.K. High Commission. I enjoyed both these visits, but they didn't make it any easier to get on with rehearsals of *Twelfth Night*. However, Richard Lea, the school-leaver from Haileybury, relieved me of much of this. Prize Giving was on the 15th, after the General Council meeting in the morning. The most important thing they had to consider was an offer by the Life Insurance Corporation of India for 23 acres of our polo ground. They wanted this at Rs.5 a square yard, which is too little, and a committee of three was appointed to discuss the matter with their representatives. I'm glad I'm not to have any responsibility for the bargaining, but I hope the sale comes off as we need the money to meet our increased salaries. General Thimayya was the Chief Guest in the afternoon and gave a very good address. *Twelfth Night* was voted a great success. We acted the 18 scenes straight through without any intervals, mostly in front of and partly from the pavilion where the audience was seated. Orsino came down from the balcony through them, unable to make up his mind about love and music, while Malvolio was cellared in the changing rooms beneath, his cries for help sounding properly sepulchral. The art exhibition was first-class.

On the 20th the four English boys, Dan Mal, Arthur Hughes, and two boys of the Kotah family set off with me in two jeeps for the Kotah wedding. This was to be something very special, as it was the first daughter of the Maharao to be married for some 200 years. And H.H. went a bust, saying that it was probably the last time a marriage with all the traditional finery and pageantry would be celebrated in Rajasthan. We had covered some 50 miles of the 120 there when the two boys in the back of my leading jeep set up a fearful howl and almost frightened me into the ditch. Then I heard one of them shout that the other jeep had overturned. I turned and drove back to it as far as I could. All one could see at first were the four wheels in the air, and we expected everyone to be dead, as we had been bowling along at a good pace. It really was a frightful moment. As we reached the wreck figures began to emerge from the far side and from underneath. The windscreen had been broken clean off, but the hood had helped save them. No one was worse than bruised and shaken except for Arthur whose right foot was badly crushed and broken. It was a miracle for them all, but hard on him, and he was wonderful. I got him into the back of my jeep and drove the 25 miles back to Nasirabad where Dr. Frances Milne took charge. I could see his foot was bad, and I was worried about shock. He was put into an ambulance and driven with Frances to Ajmer while I rang up the school and got them to lay on everything necessary for X-rays and so on .Then I returned to the scene of the mishap to find out what had happened to the rest of the party. They had turned the jeep right side up and driven on towards Kotah. When I caught them up we decided that as we could do nothing for Arthur we might as well get on to the wedding. We arrived in time for a late lunch and saw it all: certainly a magnificent show: elephants with solid gold headpieces, thousands of brightly clothed people in the streets, at least a hundred princes in all their glory, jewels, and swords in hand. After a late tea I set off back here where I found Arthur fairly comfortable, but the bones in his foot so badly smashed that they can't be set. They will have to mend up by nature, but the Civil Surgeon thinks that he will not be too much inconvenienced once the ends have mended together. Bed by midnight, reasonably tired after 300 miles by jeep and all the excitements.

The next day, another Sunday, I had to drive another 170 miles to Jaipur and back for a meeting with the Chief Minister, Vice Chancellor and others about Rajasthan College, and on Monday Their Highnesses of Bikaner came to stay. Thursday was a holiday for Shivratri and I had looked forward to a rest but this was not to be. Dan and I had to spend the whole day trying to sort out the problems of one of the staff who has been having wife trouble. Tomorrow the Doon School Cricket team with Holdy arrive for our annual match, and by Wednesday evening they will either have given us measles, for which they are in quarantine, or caught mumps or chickenpox from which we are suffering. On Thursday I leave for Bombay where I have to inspect the training ship *Dufferin* for the Government of India. I must be back the following Tuesday when Admiral Samson is paying us a visit, followed the next day by Sir Paul and Lady Sinker. He is Director General of the British Council and was a prefect in my early days at Haileybury. I'm reading Pope-Hennessy's *Queen Mary* and enjoying it. The German courts sound just like those of Rajasthan with all their jealousies and anxieties about marriages.

8.4.60. *Delhi.* Here I am, actually on my way home. Just before I left, Dr. Arnold Toynbee spent three days here: a visit we shall all remember. He gave the boys a brilliant lecture on apartheid, and one morning, before breakfast, climbed Taragarh to see the mosque and ruins on top. I hope I shall be as energetic when I reach his age. I am now staying with the Bharat Rams who last night took me to a piano recital at the German Embassy which was very lovely. Tomorrow I fly to Switzerland.

[I watched a good deal of T.V. in England and felt, in spite of all the rot on it, what a wonderful stimulus it can be, and how handicapped we are in India without it to help us understand all that is going on in the world. I got back to Delhi on the day that the General Strike was supposed to start, but as my jeep was at the airport to meet me I reached Ajmer all right. My drawing and dining rooms were being redecorated by Sakina, Bachan's wife, as a gift to the school, and they now look very lovely. In August Howard Thompson from Northampton Grammar School, and early in September John Edmundson from Rugby joined to help us as school-leavers. We all miss Arthur Hughes who has left to take over Rajasthan College in Jaipur, but Dinah Stock paid her annual visit while I was getting over my illness and cheered me up a lot. The General council budget meeting was not too argumentative. The grades of the staff and pay of the servants have all been improved, though my teaching staff still get considerably less than the new rates recommended for a policeman in England. Even so I fear that we shall soon have to put our fees up. They are only £150 a year at present.]

As an experiment I have started an entrance test for the school, and I hope that, in time, other schools will join in with us. It was a frightful fag sending off all the papers and making arrangements with centres all over India. Not long ago I had staying with me John Levy who was recording Indian music and went to Pushkar to collect their folk songs, and Peter Cooper who gave a delightful piano recital to the school.

26.11.60. *Mayo College.* One of the senior houses did *Arms and the Man*, much more ambitious than usual, and very good fun. The inter-house debate was also good on the motion that only the People's Car should be allowed for private motoring. There were good arguments about conformity and individuality, but the one I liked best was that it would help family planning as there would be no room in it for more than four people. This was answered by a boy who said that nothing would prevent Indians overcrowding their cars, and that it would only make driving more dangerous if a small car had to be stuffed with ten.

A new member of our General Council, Akbar Hydari, is a splendid person. Not only will his advice be good and sensible, but he brought with him six pairs of climbing boots from Aamir Ali in Switzerland. My heavy luggage from England has at last arrived. It was landed while I was ill and couldn't do anything about it. The duty and demurrage have come to nearly £100, which is disastrous!

6.12.60. from Sir Paul Gore-Booth, High Commissioner for U.K. I have had it in command from Her Majesty, The Queen to inform you that Her Majesty would be pleased to confer upon you the appointment of Officer of the Most Excellent Order of the British Empire (O.B.E.) in the coming New Year Honours List. Would you please let me know as soon as possible whether this intention of Her Majesty would be acceptable to you.

Christmas Eve, 1960. *Mayo College.* Here I am safely back from the Doon School where we had a wonderful weekend, but one thing in Dehra was very sad: the murder of my old friend Ellen Roy. I had been much looking forward to seeing her again, but she was done to death the week before. No one knows why, and the murderers have not been found.

1.2.61. Mayo College. On Sunday, January 15th, the Queen and Prince Philip visited Jaipur. Jai had kindly invited the college monitors, Dan Mal, Sahgal and myself to his reception for them. Everyone wanted to go, so I rang up and asked if the whole school could be found some place from which they could watch the procession. We were promised the courtyard where the royal party would alight from the elephants, so nine huge buses stuffed fuller than their regulation set off for Jaipur with all the boys, staff and wives on Sunday morning. We passed through the village that the Queen was to visit in the afternoon, and already it was full of villagers in yellows and reds packed in enclosures each side of the road, like formal beds of flowers. We had a picnic lunch in the house and garden of Raja Ram Singh of Khandela, an old boy and the parent of a present boy. Then there was a brushing and tidying up and the main party went off to their courtyard where they were very comfortable, seated in an excellent place for a view. The rest of us changed into formal dress and drove to the City Palace, a very lovely building, where we waited for the arrival of the royal party. There was some criticism of Jai's insistence on full dress—all the nobles of the state came in their traditional durbar clothes with swords and jewels, but most of us, and certainly I think the visitors, enjoyed the pageantry from the past which was very picturesque and beautiful. The Queen held on tight as the elephant knelt for her to get down, and as she came into the reception there were the ancient music and songs used in the days of great durbar. Jai, who always treats me very well, had put me in the special alcove with the V.I.P.s, so I had a good chat with Her Majesty and asked if I might introduce to her the Head Boy of the school. On her way in Jai had explained to her that as she could not get to Mayo College, the College had come to her, and she had given them a very pleasant smile and wave as she went past. She had a long talk with M. P. Jain, the head boy. She asked him what he wanted to be, and he told her a mining engineer. She had recently been down a mine and they exchanged experiences. Both she and the Prince were in splendid form and seemed to enjoy it all greatly.

On Tuesday evening I left by train for Delhi where I was met by Pearl Gautrey, wife of one of the U.K. High Commission with whom I was to stay. By 1030, I was changed and at the house of the Gore-Booths. He is a new High Commissioner and seems quite first class. There the High Commissioners of all the Commonwealth countries represented in Delhi were giving a joint reception to citizens of the Commonwealth, and there I was to receive my gong. This little ceremony went off well, though I wished you could have been there. I saw the High Commissioner for New Zealand knighted, and when the Queen pinned on my O.B.E. she gave me what I thought was the best smile of all, recognizing me from Jaipur—but there I probably flatter myself. Prince Philip said something about the boys at Jaipur while she was doing it—he was standing just behind her—but as I wasn't sure about the protocol of having a conversation over her shoulder I just smiled and kept silent. When I was offered the O.B.E. I had wondered whether someone working in India for India ought to accept such a decoration, but Dan Mal, whom I consulted in confidence, urged me to do so, and I was very pleased with the citation which could not have been more generous: 'A valuable contribution over a long period to the prestige of the United Kingdom in India'. After this, we all went on to the lawns of No.2 King George's Avenue and the Queen and Prince walked round shaking hands and talking with as many people as they could. It must be an awful strain, but she looked calm, graceful and happy all the time. I lunched with the Jameses and then went off to another reception, this time by the President of India in his lovely gardens. Again the Queen and Prince went round shaking hands and saying the right things. There were hundreds of people there and as I had had my share I kept in the background and admired the flowers.

The next day was Republic Day and the Gautreys took me to the Diplomatic Enclosure for the great march past, tanks, guns, contingents from all the different units and regiments of the armed forces, boys' brigades, girl guides, school children, pensioners, police, firemen—there seemed no end and they were all very smart. Finally came the Camel Corps, gun on mules, and the elephants, followed by folk dancers and tableaux by the different states and industries to illustrate their life and work. I greatly enjoyed the groups of dancers; from the primitives of the hills and forests to more sophisticated traditional dances. The finale was a fly-past by different jets in formation. The last group of three streamed from their wings and fuselages smoke or vapour in the three colours of the Union flag and ended up with a loop in formation over the War Memorial arch—very thrilling. The getaway for us was long and tiresome owing to traffic blocks, but we didn't mind that as it was fun to see the people enjoying their day.

The following day, the 27th, I had Tenzing and his daughter to lunch at the Gymkhana Club. I hadn't met him since he climbed Everest and it was a splendid reunion. He was quite unchanged and unspoiled and said the right thing when he exclaimed that I wasn't looking at all an old man. John, Bill Williams and the Gautreys also came, and we had a very enjoyable party. Tenzing's daughter was very pretty and spoke excellent English. She had just taken her Cambridge School Certificate examination.

That evening we went to Beating Retreat held on the broad avenue and square at its end between and below the Secretariat. It was magnificent and very moving. The playing of the massed bands was perfect as well as their individual playing and marching: the pipes, the low-pitched naval and higher pitched army bands. Along each side of the avenue and square were soldiers dressed in ancient uniforms, and on the ramparts of the secretariat the camel corps was drawn up. The bugles of the band were answered by others from the top of the towers of the secretariat—emotional and romantic. I could hardly keep the tears back when, before the actual sounding of Retreat and lowering of the national flag, the bands played what was a favourite hymn of Gandhiji's *'Abide with me.'* After this we went for a drink with the Mahadeo Singhs who had two sons in my house at the Doon School and now has to more here. Then after a swift supper, I caught the train back and arrived for a long day's work on Saturday. By the evening I was aching all over and worse the next morning—flu, of which there is a good deal about. This was a great disappointment as I was due in Udaipur for the Queen's visit. However, it allowed Dan Mal to go in my place, and he was introduced and greatly enjoyed it all, so perhaps it was as well. To those who have been out here for twenty years and more, and can remember the difficulties of 1942 and later, the success of the Queen's visit and the happiness that it is engendering are a very great reward and encouragement. It is not only those she meets who are happy that she is in India. I have been astonished to hear from all sorts of people, malis, porters at railway stations, servants, remarks of appreciation on her visit and of her charm.

Note: I appear not to have written more letters that term, or they have been lost; but reports in *Mayoor* show that life went on much as usual. There are accounts of the Rock Climbing and Adventure Course held during the holidays, of General Knowledge talks by the Education Minister of Pakistan, Narendra Singh of Sarila on the Indus Water dispute, Natwar Singh on the Foreign Service as a career, Professor G.C. Chatterji on Philosophy, Lt. General Nathu Singh on his days at Mayo College and the Army as a career, and Lieutenant Bharat Singh on his experiences in the Gaza Strip with the United Nations Emergency Force. At the annual Prize giving the Chief Guest was Rajyapal Gurmukh Nihal Singh who gave a friendly and thoughtful address, and the school performed Ibsen's *An Enemy of the people* translated into Hindi by one of the staff. I had expected this, with its obvious relevance to Ajmer's own water-supply, to go down well, but it was not a great success. In March we at last beat the Doon School at cricket on their ground.

The Moonlight Operation on the last full moon of the term was 'The Rescue of Sita' held at Sand Valley on the way to Srinagar, the valley being the sea between Bharat and Lanka and the sand ridge to the north-east the island of Lanka.

26

CHINI

In the summer break of 1961 Gibson and party decided to go on an expedition to Chini in the Himalayas. There were 13 members in the party and it was Gibson's 13th Himalayan expedition. Here are extracts from his diary:

11.5.61. *Simla.* We left Delhi at 0630 and it soon became obvious that the bearing in my trailer wheel had gone, and we had to stop at Panipat to have it changed. This was done at the side of the Grand Trunk Road by a very efficient mechanic while the rest, except Ramesh and me, went to order breakfast. He was to keep an eye on the jeep while I bought a fresh bearing from a nearby shop. This took me about five minutes and when the time came to pay for the repair I went for my attaché case between the front seats of the jeep and found that it had gone. There was the usual crowd of lookers-on, mostly school children, around us, but how it could have been taken without Ramesh seeing we could not think. It was a major disaster as it contained Rs.1,110 of expedition funds, my Leica camera, fountain pen, reading glasses, passport and other odds and ends. I made a report to the police, had a bad-tempered breakfast, and proceeded to the district police headquarters to make a further report. They seem to think that there is some chance of getting it back, but I feel very doubtful. Even an excellent supper and the loan of Rs.1,000 from Bhajji in Simla this evening has hardly cheered me up.

16.5.61. *Chini* [now called Kalpa]. There were only seven mules available this morning, so Raghu and I decided to take our jeeps, and Anokiram took Raghu's trailer behind his, my trailer being left behind. The Sherpas and Suresh came with us, while the rest walked, heavily loaded, with the mules carrying the contents of my trailer. I found the road a terrifying experience, especially as my hand-brake doesn't work and the fuel pump kept giving trouble, causing us to stop on what felt like almost vertical slopes which the jeep would anyhow only take in four-wheel bottom gear. Passang had to sit beside me holding a great rock, and jump out and put it behind a wheel when the jeep stopped. The road was so narrow that we had to remove spare wheels and footboards, and the overhangs were so low that we had to lower windscreens. Chini is very lovely, but Chini Kailash, the mountain that we had hoped to try, not only looks very difficult, and swept this side with avalanches, but is much further to get to than had appeared on our small-scale map. At 9,400 feet, we are 3000 above the river on its right bank, while the mountain rises precipitously the other side of the Sutlej: a magnificent spectacle, but how we shall approach it is difficult to see.

18.5.61. *Chini*. Shiv and several of the others went down to the Sutlej to find out what was involved in crossing to the other side and came back rather worried by the difficulties. I explored the village of Chini where there is a fine temple of carved wood, and the ruins of the High School, burnt down last year, stand stark against the background of the Chini Kailash range.

20.5.61. *Camp*. The sun rose at 0530 and an hour and a half later we were off to the snowfields, carrying our skis. We were joined by the headmaster of the school in Chini, Mr. Mitra from Bengal, whom we had seen, much to our astonishment, skiing, yesterday, and who had come to talk to us. He had taught in Jodhpur and knew Mayo College, had held a commission in the Garhwal Rifles during the war, and, having bought a second-hand pair of steel-edged skis, had taught himself how to use them from Vivian Caulfeild's *Skiing Turns* and a more modern book by Peter Lunn. I was filled with admiration, and with interest at seeing again, after nearly forty years, Caulfeild's classic book. The snow slopes were between two ridges, more or less at right angles and meeting at a peak of 17,000 feet, and promise excellent skiing.

22.5.61. *Camp.* I took a morning off, mending, cleaning up and bathing in the stream. At 0430 a party with Shiv and Dan Kumar set out to climb the 17,000 ft. peak. By noon we were expecting to see them on the summit, and by 1500 we were getting anxious, when they suddenly appeared on the final ridge, and we watched them to the top through glasses. A telegram arrived to say that my attaché case had been found with my passport and other papers safe, but all valuables removed. They had had a wonderful climb, and the summit by aneroid was 16,900 feet, quite high enough for those for whom it was a first expedition; but I told them that it was not first-class mountaineering. They should have turned back earlier, or taken the safe route down by the ridge eastwards.

29.5.61. *Chini.* Walked to Duni and took photos of the weaving training school and the Buddhist monastery with its nuns in purple; then on to Koti where the devtas [gods] were brought out for our benefit, after a good deal of swaying to and fro to find out whether they were willing to be photographed. The carvings in and on the temple were very attractive, as were the village school and its children. One of the children was holding his Hindi reader upside-down. Some of the locals complain that with the opening up of these mountainous areas illnesses that they had not known before and bad habits like thieving have been introduced, I suppose it must be to the advantage of the country as a whole, and who can measure the value of new learning, of lives saved, of the wheel in place of the human back, and of wider horizons. In the evening we packed the jeeps for tomorrow. I can't say I look forward to the drive, and I feel much sympathy for the forest officer who is said to have ridden his pony with two khalasis holding a sheet between him and the edge of the path, so that he could not see the precipice below. Unfortunately, here, there would be no room for sheet-carriers beside the jeep.

9.6.61. *Mayo College.* I enclose the diary of my thirteenth Himalayan expedition. Ill luck had started just before we left Ajmer when I had to have a tooth with an abscess under it removed to avoid possible worse trouble in the hills. It had to be extracted under gas and I came to as it broke. The dentist spent the next forty minutes getting out the root with hammer and tongs. Then came the loss of my attaché case and the expedition funds. Finally, as we passed the thirteenth milestone from Ajmer on our way back, and I remarked 'Thank goodness we're home and all is well' there was a fearful noise from under the bonnet and we stopped with a bump. Raghu drew up behind to find that he had a puncture, and I had to be towed home with a ruined clutch. Now that my unlucky number is past, I shall feel free to go on further expeditions without anxiety.

Six months after getting his OBE, Gibson's happiness was tempered by the news of the sad demise of his mother. This was also the year when, unusually for a college principal, he had to appeal to the Election Commission of India against the local collector who had been trying to requisition parts of college premises to put up poll booths! And the collector was promptly reprimanded. 'The Merchant of Venice' was performed on annual day with the cast wearing Rajasthani dresses. In 1962 Gibson could finally declare that the college was finally out of debt and there was a waiting list of 1,000. The Chinese invasion of India this year was to have its repercussions on the college functioning in a quirky way.

4.7.61. *Letter from my sister.* I have just been over to see Mum and found that she had had a fall in the garden. She was in bed, but the doctor had found nothing broken.

16.7.61. *Letter from my sister.* I'm sitting with Mum now. She looks lovely just sleeping peacefully, but she is much weaker and no longer able to take food. I'm so glad your letter came in time for me to read it to her the day before yesterday.

[My mother died last night and was buried in the churchyard of her old home, Marlingford. Unless otherwise stated, my letters from now on were addressed to my sister.]

28.7.61. *Mayo College.* I came back here to sort out a problem of getting back a house we needed this term for our growing, and I now hope full numbers—about 450. The tenants, two dear old ladies, had been holding on to it illegally, but had promised to clear out two days before the beginning of term. Two days didn't give us long to get it ready for the boys, but we thought we could do it. Then, on the day they were to leave, they said that it was not an auspicious day, and that they would go four days later. We started the term, as you can imagine, in a pretty good muddle. Nor was this the only difficulty. Six of the teaching staff were out of action. Two were away with their children desperately ill; the headmistress of the prep school broke her arm badly; Brian Bamber was hung up in the Mediterranean in a ship with engine trouble; our biologist had mumps; and a new master had to have his appendix out the second day of term.

5.10.61. *Mayo College.* I don't often have time for versification these days, but yesterday evening a boy, and rather a tough one, suggested in a meeting of the Conclave that the school should supply something more refined than Lifebouy, which is the soap I use myself; so after the meeting I sat down and wrote the following:

> Oh mother, pray send me a tablet of Lux;
> They tell me it wont hurt the skin;
> While the horrible stuff that the college provides
> Is patently made for the cleansing of hides
> And not for the delicate cov'ring I'm in.
> Oh, mother, please send me a tablet of Lux.
> and so on.

The term passes very quickly. We have been joined by Brian Bamber, a Yorkshireman and very good value, and Hope-Mason, another school-leaver from Haileybury. Shakespeareana have paid us another visit, and we have had very good General Knowledge talks by Admiral Katari, John Martyn, Roddy Cavaliero of the British Council and Joyce, the head of the U.S. Information Service in India. H. L .Dutt has left for a year at Oxford, and our old boys are beginning to distinguish themselves at their universities. There are twelve of them at the N.D.A. as well as two older ones on the staff there.

30.11.61. *Mayo College.* Last year I sent the Chief Minister of Rajasthan a tin full of gubbins collected out of our drinking-water pipes, and at last Ajmer has a water filtration plant. Shashi Kathpalia, one of the better, if not the best, of our younger staff has just left, lured to a business job in Bombay on three times the pay of a school master and one third of the importance to society. We have held a football coaching camp for local players on our grounds, conducted by Mr. Rahim, India's best coach, most excellent fellow and once a schoolmaster. He taught our boys what I have been trying to teach them for the last eight years in one month. Such is the fruit of renown, and I pulled his leg and told him it was because he had INDIA on his sweater.

October began with the celebration of Gandhiji's birthday when supper is served by the boys and staff to all the school servants and their children. We all carry round great dishes of food shouting what we have to offer in the way cigarette sellers do on railway platforms. The sad news is that Dan's daughter has died, and Gue's son cannot recover. Gue is one of the very best and keeps smiling in spite of this cloud hanging over him, but we all know the strain he is undergoing.

It is said that there is some danger of the duck and the geese this year being radio-active as they have arrived from Siberia after the Russians let off their bombs, and we have been advised not to eat them. I shall take no notice, and if I die you can write to K. and complain.

It is now three years since we last had to put up our fees from Rs.1,770 to Rs.1,920. Since then the cost of food has risen by nearly 25% and salaries and allowances have had to be improved to keep pace with the costs of living. We are now going to put up the fees to Rs.2,100 a year, and one can only hope that prices can be held stable in future.

25.1.62. *Mayo College.* On December 23rd John Martyn arrived and that afternoon we set off in my jeep for the meeting of the I.P.S.C. in Rajkot. There were five of us: Arthur Hughes, John, two boys from Assam who had been unable to get home, and myself. The end of term had been complicated by the Goa operations as the railway system of the whole of India was disorganized by troop movements. Just as our

N.C.C. Cadets were entraining for their camp at Cochin I had a message from Delhi that their connection there had been cancelled. I rang up the Adjutant General, who has his boy here, and he said he would do his best, and would anyhow send an officer to meet them on their arrival in Delhi. There they were told that the only possible way of continuing to Cochin would take them five days, and the master in charge very sensibly called off the camp. It took him four days in Delhi to dispatch the boys to their homes, and the two from Assam had to return here. Until they were able to get trains, the boys were very kindly put up in the Modern School, whose Principal, Mahendra Kapur, was once on the Mayo College staff. My only comment on the Goa business is that it was very well managed and quickly over without much loss of life; that it has lowered India's prestige among those who had hoped it meant what it said about peaceful solutions; and that it was ill-timed if it was not to be thought of as something of an election stunt. The Portuguese were pig-headed and stupid and India could not hold back its ardent nationalists.

On the way to Rajkot I towed my trailer loaded with tents, luggage and cooking utensils. We spent the first night with the Thakur of Ghanerao who took us the next morning to see the great fort of Kumbal Garh on the top of one of the Aravalli hills. We spent another night at Ghanerao where we were made very welcome, and on Christmas day set off for Mount Abu. I had imagined this to be a dull, dry hill, but it turned out to be most attractive with forest and lakes and extensive road where you can drive or ride for miles. We put up at the Bikaner Palace, now an hotel—the great houses of India go the same way as those of England—and they produced plum pudding. The next morning we explored what we could of Abu and visited the famous Jain temples which I did not think as attractive as those at Ranakpur. After lunch we pushed on through some very pleasant country over a bad road which ran between two parallel ranges of hills through Bhil country, and I was interested to see people with bows and arrows, walking along what is one of India's new highways. We camped for the night at a very lovely place called Balaram with an ancient temple and overlooking a river. The next day we had planned to reach Ahmedabad for lunch, but broke a front spring, fortunately near a large town. This took three hours to mend and we sent off a wire to Janak Singh of Limbdi that we hoped to get to him there by 2130. We did, but not without further adventure.

Some time after sunset we were stopped by a truck driver who warned us not to go further as dacoits had tried to block the road and had thrown stones and rocks at his truck. We were cold and hungry and decided to go on. The boys wanted to get out my gun, but we decided to keep it hidden as it was likely only to cause trouble. About a mile further on we came across the road block—milestones and rocks scattered across it—but my jeep, being used to that sort of obstacle, got through without more than a bump or so, and we heaved sighs of relief. Then, another mile or so further, we were stopped by another truck driver who told us that the road was again blocked some way on by two trucks that had collided, and that he would show us a diversion through the fields. He went ahead, and as we followed I remarked that this would be a good way of leading us into an ambush. I had no sooner said this than we saw lights beyond a hedge and found ourselves in a camp and surrounded by men with staves. What they wanted I don't know, but the truck went on and we followed with a great deal of horn-blowing. The driver must have been all right for he led us back to the main road and we were able to reach Limbdi in spite of our lights failing. We told Janak about it all and were glad that we didn't know before that some years ago he had been shot in the wrist and two people in his car killed by dacoits. I think it all has to do with the mad policy of prohibition, which not only loses the government huge revenue, but has bred, as it did in the U.S.A., a disrespect for law and order and a flourishing bootlegging industry with bribery and corruption everywhere.

People in Rajkot are a bit sad at the end of Portuguese rule in Diu as it means that supplies of smuggled brandy and wines have dried up. They say that the forces that went in came out with cases and cases of drink that they had bought, for there wasn't apparently much looting for Rs.7 a bottle—compared to Rs.70 which is what Scotch now costs in Ajmer, or Rs.100 in areas where there is prohibition. People like me can afford only Indian whisky at Rs.18 a bottle. It isn't all that bad, but one likes to offer the other to one's guests.

Back here on the 5th, I found an offer of Rs.8,000 for my jeep waiting for me—higher than I expected because of the coming elections, and I have sold it. It has done me very well for eight years; I shall have to pay Rs.16,000 for a new one, and I'm told they aren't as good as the old ones. I found a requisition by a local government officer for our main building as a polling booth for five days for the elections. This was too fantastic and had to be fought. The problem was that the Collector, who is a good man, felt he had to support his junior who I considered was swollen-headed and power-drunk. Endless visits and letters were exchanged. I explained that a boarding school couldn't close all its offices and half its classrooms in the middle of term, and offered other accommodation, but made no headway; so I eventually appealed to the Election Commission for India who was, so the college lawyer informed me, the only person to whom there lay an appeal in law. I sent him all the letters written and received and am told he was very angry and instructed the officials here not to be so foolish. My object now is to restore good relations with them, but the whole business has been a great worry and has left me rather shaken. I hope the old standards of sense and justice won't be destroyed by the young civilians now becoming senior officers, and that India doesn't turn into another Ghana.

I have just had 30 boys in, recording their parts for the *Merchant of Venice* which we are doing for Prize Giving on February 24th. Then they listened to themselves as I played the recording back, and finally I played a recording by the Marlowe Society. Being a headmaster leaves me too little time for this sort of thing and for teaching. I wish I could give up administration.

15.3.62. *Mayo College.* Prize Giving went off very well and the Gore-Booths seemed to enjoy their visit. He gave a very good address in which he enlarged on the words at the end of the inscription under Lord Mayo's statue: 'It was his hope that this college might promote among the youth of Rajputana the cardinal virtues of fortitude, temperance, justice and benevolence', and how these virtues were relevant to today. Later the boys acted *The Merchant of Venice* produced by John Hope-Mason and myself and played in the splendid dress of Rajasthan. Years ago I produced the same play at the Doon School in Moghul dress, and I am convinced that Shakespeare, who dressed his Romans in Elizabethan clothes, would himself have taken advantage of the beautiful costumes of India if he had had the chance. This time we acted indoors. Once again Bassanio, Antonio, Gratiano and their followers came on at the end of the play, in a procession carrying torches and lanterns. David, our Biology master, who has a lovely voice and composes music, sang 'Tell me where is fancy bred' to a tune of his own played by the college orchestra. For the masque in Act II fifteen of the junior boys performed a much appreciated dance across the stage.

15.4.62. *Mayo College.* On Saturday a week ago the School and I lost a friend when the Raja of Bhinai died of heart failure. He was an old boy, a parent of present boys, secretary of the Old Boys' Society and a member of the General Council, the school's governing body. I attended his cremation in Bhinai, about 30 miles away, and found his funeral a little bizarre, though very interesting sociologically. He was carried through his little town seated on a sort of throne with jewelled headdress and all his finery on, looking just as he did when alive. We all walked behind, breathing in the dust, while his people, who appeared to have had great affection for him, threw offerings over the body. It was macabre, but moving.

Last night we had our annual Moonlight Operation, once again on Taragarh, and one of the boys got hurt by a rock rolling down the hill. The X-ray hasn't yet come, so I don't know whether he too has a broken arm, but if it is it will not be more than a cracked bone. There was a very amusing incident during the scheme. I was on my way at speed in my jeep, to act as an umpire, when I was stopped by two policemen for going too fast. I was very angry at the delay and was using my best Hindi in hot argument when one of them said: 'Don't you recognize us, sir?' They turned out to be two boys who had made friends in the local police station and borrowed uniforms, and they were so well made with false beards and moustaches that I failed to recognize them. They were two of the police scouts who had been allowed to go forward early, and their plan had been to stop any dacoit bus using the road they were on, and to delay it as long as they could. I gave them full marks for their initiative and disguise.

One bit of cheering news lately has been last year's School Certificate results—good at last: 14 first divisions, 3 second, 4 third and one failure. One boy, Anil Khosla, got distinctions in all his eight subjects and Deb got his first division with three distinctions. I suppose you realize how lucky you are to have children of your own. Sometimes I think how lucky I am not to have the responsibility, but I have begun to reach the stage where I haven't the energy to care so much to achieve what I know I ought to do, and I think to myself how pleasant it would be to have someone in this huge house and lovely garden to walk round it with me and enjoy it. I have spent all my life bringing up other people's children and it has been exciting and absorbing work; but they come and go, rather like 'borders of sweet peas.' It would be nice to have something more permanent. That is partly why I take this interest in Deb Barua. I have watched him for the past six years, and I think he is someone rather special. I may be wrong, but I hope not. If he had to go to the sink that Calcutta University appears now to have become, it might be another good person lost. I would like to be able to feel that I have done something for someone that isn't part of my job; and I think you will be able to understand. I much look forward to arriving in London with Deb on May 3rd.

8.4.62. *Extract from my end-of-term letter to parents.* I think it may interest you to know how our internal reporting system works. Each month every boy takes a 'Report Card' to each master who teaches him and has it marked out of 10 for each subject under three headings: effort, achievement and a third assessment which includes punctuality, neatness and general efficiency. The housemaster sees all these cards when they have been filled, and sends on to me those boys whom he considers not to have been doing their best. I usually put them on daily reports: a card which is signed by the teacher at the end of every lesson, by the housemaster each evening, and by me at the end of a week. This card is renewed each week, until a satisfactory one is produced by the boy.

Our Radio Engineering and Automobile Engineering classes will start a new session next July. The fee for either course will be Rs.90 for the year, and the classes will be limited to 20 each. For holiday projects we are trying an experiment. New methods of teaching are in the air, and we would like to see if those who are taught here have any ideas of their own.

13.7.62. *Mayo College.* Here I am safely back. I had a hectic six days after leaving you: visit to the Foots with John Martyn; lunch with Charles Carrington and Arnold Toynbee at the Travellers; lunch with Don Soughan and Eric Shipton who told us all about Patagonia where he thinks Tibetan refugees would settle happily as it is very like Tibet:

dinners with Angela, John Levy and the Pickards: three plays; and some shopping. The worst bit of the latter was buying a woman's bathing suit at Dickins & Jones for our swimming coach here. She had asked for one without padding, but they all had a sort of stiffening to make the breasts stick out. At last they produced one from which, so they said, this could be removed; so we turned it inside-out to do this. When we found that the padding things were called 'Tweka' it was too much both for the rather charming assistant and for me.

15.8.62. *Mayo College, To Deb Barua.* About Mayo College, I feel that I have more or less done all that I set out to do and more than I dared to hope for. We are now out of debt, we have over 1,000 names on our waiting lists, and our academic results last year were really good: Khosla top in India in the School Certificate, Suresh Sharma second in Higher Secondary science and Arvind Caprihan fourth. In the universities too we are beginning to make a name. Anwar Siddiqi stood first in his subject in Aligarh, and there have been other good results.

14.9.62. *Mayo College.* Life as full as ever. The Doon School have joined in with our entrance test this year and this has involved many letters fixing up centres, informing parents, correcting proofs, and so on. Charles Clarke, another school-leaver from Rugby, turns out to be first-class. In Assembly we are playing folk music collected from all over the world by UNESCO. It is very interesting, but sometimes rather weird and apt to make the boys laugh. Why shouldn't they?

24.9.62. *Mayo College. To Adam Arnold-Brown.* Like you I used to think that cricket was a poor game for schools, taking up too much time, and leading to overmuch hero worship; but I have come to change my mind. I now think it is a very fine school for the training of character and leadership. Granted that there can only be two captains in the twenty-two players, but the captain of a cricket eleven really can win or lose the game by good or poor captaincy. On his decisions on changes of bowlers, placing of his field for different bowlers and batsmen, orders to his batsmen to hit or play safe, and so on, the whole game hinges, unlike in fast-moving games like football where he can certainly encourage and make changes in the field, but does not have time for real generalship. In cricket too, while fielding you have to be alert all the time, and it is a difficult exercise to remain so when the ball may only come to you now and again. The batsman also must concentrate all the time, and if he plays an innings lasting more than an hour or so, this too is good training; while there is endless scope for cunning by the bowlers. I hope you may change your mind about the game! I agree with you about basket-ball. It's a good game and splendid exercise, and we have four courts in full use here now. We think we have evidence that it is very good for those who want to grow taller.

I find myself very much in sympathy with what you say about religion. I cannot accept the dogmas of the Christian church and I think many of my staff feel the same about their religions, but we find that a boy who has no belief is robbed of a moral support for right action. In this secular state of India the need of some religious support has been found to be so great that the government appointed a high-powered committee to consider what should be done. They have gathered together extracts from the preaching of the prophets of all religions and published them as a book--but it doesn't meet the need. Exhortation cannot take the place of faith.

11.11.62. *Mayo College.* You have probably read all about the Chinese invasion in the papers. It has caused a tremendous, and to some people surprising, upsurge of national enthusiasm all over the country. What seems to me important is to carry on with preparations for a possibly very difficult time ahead, using this enthusiasm to get people to put more effort into their daily lives, and into making a success of the five-year plans. There is some danger that, instead, it may dissipate itself in useless processions and speeches. If the crisis is short then that would not matter, but if there is to be a long-drawn-out struggle then energies and enthusiasm should be conserved. I've told the boys here that their contribution to the national effort should be to make themselves physically fitter and mentally more alert, and I have told the District Magistrate that I would not allow them to take part in a procession of schoolchildren who would be wrong if they thought that that was assisting the war effort. I have, however, said that I would allow the N.C.C. to take part in uniform, as marching is part of their training.

While in Delhi I was to spend five minutes with the P.M. But Nehru was very worried about the Chinese. He has not been very fit lately, and it must all be a fearful disappointment to him, and a great strain. On the few occasions I have met Krishna Menon I have found him congenial, but a lot of people think he is a bad man. Life is full of problems. I suppose the responsibility for what is happening now lies with the P.M. and those of his advisers who trusted China and did so little about its rape of Tibet.

23.12.62. *Mayo College.* Uppermost in our minds for some time has been the Chinese attack and we wonder what will be the result of their 'peace offensive'. Mayo College has not been much affected, but we are rapidly building a new wing to what will become a third 'middle house' so that we can take in all those sons of people who are being shunted about at short notice: boys who were registered for 1963, but for whom, without more building, we should not have had room. At the meeting of the General Council I reported desperate letters from eleven officers who had been moved from family quarters, and got permission to build a temporary shelter for their sons. I did not realize that within a week there would be 25 more. A temporary shelter for such a number would have been a waste of money, so I decided to build what will cost about Rs.70,000 and permanently increase our numbers to about 500. There was no time to call a special meeting of the General Council, and I hope I shall not get into trouble for going ahead on my own. After their exams the leaving class all helped with the work which has made splendid progress. Within a fortnight the foundations were dug and the walls up to four feet or so, and now the doors and windows are in. We aim to finish it by the first of January: rooms for 36 boys and a matron, prep hall and common room, bathrooms and all. The boys from Assam are spending their holidays here, and help with the building every day, and it has been both a triumph and surprise to see the house rise to roof level within three weeks.

All women and children were evacuated from the tea gardens in Assam, and Charlotte [niece of my brother-in-law] and her three children, her brother Toby who was working with Tibetan refugees, and another girl are now with me. It will be fun to have a traditional Christmas all together.

27
EAST AND WEST

Now that Gibson had reached 55, perhaps he found it difficult to go on mountain jaunts. As a consequence the highlight of 1963 was a Jeep trip to central and eastern India taking in some of the newly-emerging industrial cities such as Ranchi and Durgapur, ancient places such as Vidisha, Cuttack and Konarak, the Rajkumar College in Raipur and Nowgong, the haunt of his early years. Prime Minsiter Lal Bahadur Shastri was the chief guest at the annual day this year.

8.3.63. *Mayo College, To V.A. Stow.* Prize Giving on February 3rd was one of our good ones. The Chief Guest was Karan Singh of Kashmir who gave an excellent address and was a most popular visitor. His father's stay here must have been before your time. The entertainment that evening was not a play but a series of scenes and skits after each of which the audience had to answer a question on their programmes. We had tried something similar five years ago, and this was an improvement. We were amused to find that the Vice-Chancellor of Rajasthan University didn't know the name of the castle in which Macbeth murdered Duncan. The first scene was a welcome to Karan Singh and the audience, first in English, then in 23 Indian languages and dialects, and finally in Sanskrit. Those speaking were dressed in their local costumes, and the audience had to name the language. All the main languages of India are now spoken as their mother-tongue by one or more boys in the school as well as two dialects from NEFA and three from Rajasthan. I don't think anyone in the audience got more than 16 correct even with the help of the clothes the speakers were wearing, and I felt that this emphasized the importance of English as a unifying force in the country. It will also give you an idea of how the school has expanded and changed in character, though about 33% of our intake is still from Rajasthan and we have many representatives of the old Mayo College families. I look back with a good deal of nostalgia to the old days when our numbers were less and it was possible to get away on most Sundays. Now we are over 500 and you would notice many new buildings. One of these we put up during the winter holidays, using some of the roofing of the old stables, polo alas being no longer financially possible. This saved time and expense. There are four dormitories for nine boys each, a matron's flat, bathrooms and lavatories, and a prep room and a common-room each to hold 75—the rest of the boys being accommodated opposite in Bharatpur House. Building this was fun. In spite of the cold this went on late into every night by electric light, and we were able to occupy it on the first day of term. We thus now have four houses for senior boys, 13 to 16½, at which latter age they leave us too early, to go on to a university, and three houses for 'middles' roughly 9 to 12½ or 13. The Junior House, for those who come younger is in the buildings, to which we have added, that used to be called New Jodhpur House. Of the housemasters I think you would only remember Garg whose house, Ajmer, won the Udaipur Shield last year; Raghubir Dayal of Jodhpur House who still loyally tells me how much better you were than I am when he disapproves of anything I do; and Gue, who is a most successful housemaster of Colvin, one of the Middle Houses, Datta has given up his house, and Dan Mal is Vice Principal.

On January 30th Bharatpur House was officially opened by the new Minister for Defence, Chavan, and now what was, a short while ago, a desert of stone chips and rutted mud, is a flourishing garden. We are all rather proud of this evidence of what can be done if there is a will to do it. After Prize Giving I was pleased to be able to hold Dr. Karan Singh to a draw at chess. When he was a boy in my house at the Doon School he used to beat me.

24.4.63. *Mayo College.* Shakespeareana, now much reduced in numbers, visited us last month. For many years they have been acting anywhere from Karachi to Hong Kong and they deserve all honour for bringing live plays to thousands who would otherwise have had no chance of seeing them. It was fun to have them for a week during which they were able to get a bit of rest for a while from their arduous travels.

Poor Gue's son died some weeks ago after seven years of almost continuous pain from the tumor on his brain. He was a very pleasant boy and met his suffering with very great fortitude. The ways of providence are difficult to understand.

Some day ago just as I was finishing my bath, I got an urgent telephone call from our hospital to bring as much ice as I could. Charles Clarke had taken some boys out rock-climbing in the very early morning and was half-way up a cliff with one of them when they were attacked by bees. He had climbed down to the boy beneath him and then down with the boy to the foot of the cliff and then jumped on Brian's motor bike, both of them with bees swarming all round them, a very brave bit of work. They got back here on the bike and more than 150 stings were taken out of the boy and over 100 from Charles. By the evening they both had very high temperatures, but, thank goodness, are now both all right, though Charles had a sprained ankle for some days. From the hospital I had to go off to fetch the rest of the party and wondered if I would find them stung to death. Fortunately, they had been on push bikes and had not arrived when the bees swarmed, so had escaped.

15.5.63. *Mayo College.* The journey to Dehra Dun was a nightmare. We had booked third-class but there were eight berths short. I got out at every station up to Alwar sorting things out and putting boys into first-class compartments where there was space. The conductor, who should have provided the berths we had booked, wasn't very helpful and when he wanted to charge me a full first-class fare for a boy sleeping on the floor, I called him a bloody fool, and he went off the deep end at such language 'from an English gentleman'. Fortunately, there was a very decent army officer in the carriage who told him that 'bloody fool' was not really rude and that there were much stronger expressions if you wanted to be so. At Delhi the buses were late and we had to wait for two hours in a very hot sun. When they did arrive they said that there was too much luggage. However, various stalwarts loaded it on while I held the conductor spell-bound with my Hindi agreeing to pay for nine maunds extra weight. On arrival back at Delhi we had another incident. On the way out we had had to employ two sets of porters, one to carry the luggage from the train to the station steps, and another to carry it from there to the bus stand, a matter of fifty yards. I wanted to avoid this so told the driver to go straight into the station yard. We were busy unloading when a policeman came up and pointed to a 'No parking' notice just in front of us. Remembering the incident in the train, I addressed him as Sardarji and explained in admirable Punjabi how hot and tired and late we were, all to no effect. I was just going to start in good forcible English when I remembered that our driver was also a Punjabi Sikh, so I slipped him Rs.10 and left him to sort the matter out. Later, we saw the policeman and the driver sharing a friendly pot of tea. So are one's morals undermined by the heat and the dust of the east.

I got back here on Tuesday to find an invitation from the Gore-Booths to a reception to Lord Mountbatten on Thursday, and as reports were not ready for me, I accepted and let myself in for another two nights in the train. I'm glad I went. They told me about the U.K. government assisting teachers to go abroad and work for period of two to four years, but they insist that their living conditions should be satisfactory: fridges, air-conditioners, etc. and pay at least as good as at home. I wonder how those of us who are already out here without these luxuries will view the newcomers. The reception was great fun. I met many old friends and had a chat with the P.M.

In spite of the heat I'm enjoying being here. I wake to bird song at 0530, have a mango and a cup of tea, bath, work till 0930, breakfast, work here till 1100, go to office till about 1400, beer, lunch, read the paper, sleep, tea at 1630, tennis at 1715, bath, write letters, sup, read, then sleep on the lawn where a blanket is occasionally needed in the early morning. In four or five days I plan to start for Kashmir with Ramesh Mathur and Anil Datta.

6.7.63. *Mayo College.* I did not get away to Kashmir as soon as I expected because the school party which had set off to climb in the Trisul area was turned back by red tape security regulations although

Charles Clarke had a valid pass. He came back here and fell ill with what he thought was heat-stroke, and this delayed my getaway. However, I was able to work on my account of the early years of the Indian Public Schools Conference which celebrates its jubilee next year. I read through some 27 bulky files of correspondence, agenda and minutes in my bedroom kept fairly cool by khas khas: a frame of thick, sweet-smelling grass roots kept wet from an overhead tap and put in front of the windows through which the wind blows an evaporation-cooled and scented draught. Schools out here owe a great deal to the hard work and planning of a group of exceptional headmasters: Smith-Pearse, Barry, Foot, Merchant and Shukla to mention some, and to Sir John Sargent, then Educational Commissioner, and Ashfaque Hussain.

Early in June five of us with Shankar the plate-breaker set off in my jeep and trailer for Kashmir. The first day to Delhi was so hot that we decided to drive by night and the next evening started at 1830, reaching Pathankot early in the morning. There we rested for two hours in an air-conditioned waiting room at the station, had breakfast, and went on to Udhampur which we reached at 1630. The army was very good to us everywhere and we stayed as guests in various messes. The first week we camped at 10,000 feet beside snow at the bottom of Mary's Gully above Gulmarg, in an alpine garden. We had 3,000 feet of splendid running above us from the top of Apharwat, but I only managed the full run twice, finding the climb harder than in the days when I could do it twice a day.

After this we made Srinagar our base and went out on excursions all round the country. On one of these, to Pahlgam, I gave a lift to a man in khaki. There were a lot of police about as the P.M. was also going there, and at a bridge we were stopped. When they saw the man to whom we had given a lift we were about to be arrested as he was a deserter. Explanations were made no easier as he also proved to come from Ajmer. However we were rescued by an officer who knew us. You know how lovely Kashmir is, so I won't enlarge on that, but one of the most attractive places we went to was Yus. I managed four days' trout fishing, but got nothing bigger than 1½ pounds. Several, landed before breakfast, were fried on the spot—delicious! Petrol was very expensive—more than a rupee a litre, but we saw much of the country, and the change has done me a lot of good. I found Kashmir very much changed from the old days. The peasantry are no longer so servile;

nearly all villages have good schools and are served by buses; on Sundays and holidays the locals come out with their wives and children for picnics in the many lovely Moghul gardens and other pleasant places. Fathers sit on the grass playing cards, while mothers tend their babies and the children jump and run around. The burkha has almost disappeared. The villagers are much cleaner than they used to be, and amenities for tourists are good and suited to all purses. Nedou's Hotel is little changed, with Willie and Crole still running it; and for those who want more modern luxury there is the Palace Hotel. There is said to be a good deal of nepotism and corruption in the administration, children still ask for bakshish, and the unwary are overcharged, but I felt that there was much more efficiency, and that India should certainly keep what it holds. If the valley went to Pakistan it would be filled by Punjabi Mussalmans and the local populations would revert to servility. I tried water-skiing, but was no good at it. You have to lean backwards as compared to the forward position on snow, and I kept on going nose dives. The drive back was pretty warm. We drove, altogether, some 3,560 miles and all went well except for six punctures which was bit unfair as all tyres were new.

3.8.63. *Mayo College.* At the beginning of term Brian Bamber returned from England with his bride, and shortly afterwards Dennis Woodman, a V.S.O. graduate from Cambridge, came to teach maths while O.P. Agarwal does a year at Leicester University, generously arranged by the British Council, learning about the 'new mathematics'. Dennis is very good, interesting the boys in using our large telescope for which Sahgal has made a shelter on the roof of the new teaching block.

I played soccer on Monday—staff against boys, no score—and feel I'm getting a bit old and stiff. I envy Jack Spelman retiring, and have been wondering how much more I can do for this place. I'm not as energetic as I used to be, but there are certain things I know I ought to do before leaving—one to get rid of one or two inefficient members of the staff. But I'm not beastly enough, and persuade myself that I can get them to improve. In government service you can always shunt on someone you don't want to some other job. Here, if you push a person out he may have nowhere else to go.

At the end of July Lal Bahadur Shastri, the Home Minister, spoke to the boys. He went down very well, starting by saying how pleased he was to be among people of his own size, and going on to tell them something about what he was like when he was their age. He had turned up at school in a torn shirt and been asked by his teacher why he did not get another. When he said that he couldn't afford one, the teacher told him that he could at least mend it. He produced needle and cotton and showed him how to do so. Shastri appealed to the boys to be thorough and to make the best of everything they could. I liked him very much. He is very human. When he came to my house for a cold drink I asked if I might offer his A.D.C. a beer. He replied, 'If this is an area of prohibition, No; but if not, certainly.'

6.10.63. *Mayo College.* Last week the Senior Science Society heard a first-class lecture by Dr. Narlikar, son of the Chairman of the Rajasthan Public Services Commission. He had just won the same mathematics prize at Cambridge as his father had before him, and is now a don at King's.

The next day we had the annual feeding of the multitude—all college servants and their children—on the evening of Gandhi Jayanti, an event I always enjoy. There was a full moon lighting Madar in the background, and a triangle of dark green cricket field pushing into the coloured lines of diners sitting on the ground. It would have made an excellent subject for a painting by Rembrandt.

On the 4th morning General Chaudhuri arrived by helicopter to speak to the Rotary Club that evening at our Bikaner Pavilion, and to the upper school yesterday morning. He landed on our central ground, and such a machine never having been seen in Ajmer before, thousands of the citizens and their children came to inspect it. We had expected this and laid on police and military to control them, and all went well, everyone being very friendly. On Saturday morning the pilot took up three parties of ten each for flights round Ajmer. I was in one, and hope to have taken some good photos of the school.

10.12.63. *Mayo College.* The rising cost of living is making finances very difficult, and we shall have to put the fees up again in 1965. Although it doesn't seem that there will be any difficulty in keeping the school full, increased fees are going to make things very difficult for the middle-income group from which so many of our good boys come.

I have just completed a letter to parents telling them of the experiment we intend to carry out next term with extra coaching. We have to have this because boys come, some knowing no Hindi, and others very little English. There are also those congenitally weak at maths. So far we have failed to get ahead as fast as we should in removing these weaknesses, and we have decided that we may be able to do better if, instead of giving a boy just general coaching in a subject, we are more specific. If we find a boy who does not understand how to convert decimals into fractions, or another who cannot recognize a phrase from a clause, instead of putting them down for extra coaching in maths or language, we shall send them to a teacher to learn just that specific skill within a limited period, and coaching will be much more closely related to the work actually being done in class. This all involves much planning and arrangements for time and remuneration.

Term ended three days ago, and as soon as I can get away I'm off on a tour to the east of India with Ramesh, Dan Mal's middle son, who has joined the staff—the third generation of the family to serve Mayo College—and his young brother, Suresh.

6.1.64. *Mayo College.* I have just completed the enclosed account of our journey.

Shortened

EAST AND WEST BY JEEP

Somehow reports and Christmas letters had been written and plans for next term finalized, provisions for the way bought, and packing completed by 1500 on December 18th when we set off. The back of the jeep had been made more capacious by attaching an expanded metal cage to the lowered tail-board, and into this extra space we had packed a second spare wheel, two of my mountaineering tin trunks full of food and utensils, four suitcases, two tents, a shovel, a gun and a rifle, an ammunition box, a primus stove, two attaché cases, a clothes bag, and warm coats and sweaters. We left the hood behind.

We had our first puncture some twenty miles out of Ajmer, and stopped for the famous puris at Sarwar, but otherwise drove uneventfully through Bundi, where we had to switch on the headlights and put on extra clothes, to Kotah. The last few miles were cold and it was very pleasant to be welcomed into the warmth and luxury of the palace.

Our start the next morning was delayed by the need to buy a new inner tube and we did not leave till 1100. The road to Baran was fairly good, but after that very uneven and dusty till we got onto National Highway No. 3. From Shivpuri, along N.H. 25 we had a good run to Jhansi, crossing the Sind River on the way, and arriving as it began to get dark. We found a room in the Circuit House and bought some eggs and opened some tins from which the cook there made us a reasonable supper. The night was disturbed by rats and mosquitoes. The former ate a large hole in Suresh's only respectable coat, which should teach him not to keep sweets in his pockets, and the latter kept us awake for most of the night. Not having expected mosquitoes in the winter, we had brought no nets.

We got away early the next morning and it was pretty cold in the open jeep. The ferry crossing of the Betwa took nearly an hour, and we arrived in Bundelkhand of which I have many happy memories from 1945. It was good to see again the irregular red-tiled roofs. In Nowgong we paid a call at the old Kitchener College and Colonel Sidhu took us to the Mess where we met a number of the staff of the Army Cadet School, and were given an excellent late breakfast of eggs, sausages, tinned prawns and reviving hot coffee. Then we visited the interesting state museum at Dhubela in the garden of which the very fine, more than life-size, bronze statue of Lord Kitchener stands leaning like the famous tower, slightly off the vertical, dumped by over-zealous remakers of history. Then on to Khajuraho, a very different place from what I remember twenty years ago. The temples are being cleaned and are now set in well laid lawns planted with bright flowering shrubs. The village is a hive of tourist industry. We called on H.H. Chhatarpur and found him in excellent form, though now living a very cut-off life in a small and rather shabby building. We had our second puncture before reaching Panna for tea, but the drive across the Ken and through the forested hills was very beautiful. Lokendra met and looked after us till Manvendra, who had been playing tennis, turned up. The palace is an attractive building with a long flight of broad steps leading up to a portico supported on high pillars.

The next morning we were up before dawn and drove off into the forest in a double jeep, made in the palace garage by joining the body of the second on to the first. I now have difficulty shooting with a rifle. Without glasses I can't see the sights, and with I can't see the target. I missed three chink, but both Manvendra and I, firing together, killed a sambar. After an excellent breakfast we did a long and pleasant drive to Dehri-on-Son, lunching on some fine rocks beside the road with a magnificent view down across the plains. We passed by Benares, now called Varanasi, and got onto the Grand Trunk Road (N.H. 2) where there was so much dipping of lights to do that ours died on us. A kindly truck driver, and there are many, though one curses them when they take up all the road, put them right. We could find no accommodation at Dehri, so pitched our tents on a little square of grass in front of 'Son View', a rather squalid little hotel with very primitive conveniences. However, they cooked us a good meal.

We were away again early on the 22nd to cross the river by the rail ferry; but owing to a very large new truck getting stuck and having to have its mudguards removed to free it, this took us three hours. Once on the road again we met long lines of new Ambassador cars driving west to Delhi. They were all going much above the proper speed at which a new car should be 'driven in'. At Ramgarh, after turning off N.H.2 onto N.H.33 to Ranchi, we found the road blocked by a huge procession in honour of Guru Gobind Singh. It was growing dark and we could not move forward, but appeals to a police officer that we had an appointment with the Commissioner of Chota Nagpur were successful, and a way was made. In Ranchi arrangements had been made for us to stay at the new and comfortable Circuit House. After leaving Ranchi, and lunch on a green bank beside a little river, we filled up with as much petrol as the jeep would hold at Lohardage, from where the drive up through the hills was very beautiful. Netarhat was very cold. In the evening we all had a picnic at 'Sunset Point', a very beautiful place with a magnificent view across hills down to a valley. A film company was shooting a sentimental scene of a woman leaning against a tree watching the setting sun. We also saw a party of men and women, some Americans, in saffron robes and with large cars. Somehow most pale face sadhus seem to me a little bogus.

The drive back to Ranchi, once we were out of the hills, was fast, and we covered 48 miles in just over 50 minutes. The place we chose to stop for lunch was a bit smelly, but the prawn patties and chicken sandwiches went down well. Shortly after dark we found a P.W.D. Rest House in a pleasant compound at a place called Raghunathpur and decided to stop there. We looked pretty disreputable, and a dusty open jeep isn't much of a status symbol. The chowkidar would not let us in; nor was he impressed by my addressing Ramesh as 'Maharaja Sahib'. Eventually we got a permit from the S.D.O. and started to cook Christmas dinner on the primus. We found the grapes we had bought in Ranchi too sour to eat, so we stewed them with lots of sugar, and they were excellent, cold, the next morning. After an adequate dinner we drank 'Absent Friends' and I thought of other unusual Christmas dinners I have eaten.

Durgapur was not far off our route on Boxing Day, so we decided to visit it. We had not realized the extent to which 'security' was in force. When we got there we were told at the Public Relations Office that we must have a pass from the Chief Security Officer, and that this should have been applied for a fortnight before we planned to come. However, on my plea that I was a British taxpayer who wanted to see how his money was being spent, he allowed me to ring up the Managing Director who kindly gave us permission to go round. A P.R.O. took us under his wing and showed us everything from the arrival of the coal and ore, through the smelting and casting of ingots, to the manufacture of steel sleepers and wheels. I was interested in the use made of by-products such as gas, and the conservation of power; but I was thankful I did not have to work there. The glowing molten metal, the noise and the smells, all made me think of hell, and the workers of the slavery of modern industrial life. It is sad that we can't have the conveniences and comforts of electric trains and motor cars without the horrid conditions from which their beginnings are produced. We spoke to a number of the workers, men and women, and though their pay was attractive compared to what they could have earned in the fields and markets, I thought that their lives must be very hard and uncomfortable. If Gandhiji could have prevented India from becoming a great industrial country and could have diverted the people from the mills and factories to cottage industries they might have lived more pleasant lives; but I suppose no country can cut itself off from the industrialization of modern life, any more than the people of the hills can remain simple and honest and be protected from the influx and competition and contamination of those from the plains; and would I like to do without my jeep?

From Burdwan into Calcutta we passed an endless stream of trucks which kept well on the crown of the road. They are so heavily loaded that it is dangerous for them to do anything else, and in the course of our tour we saw a number overturned by the sides of roads. Inside the city headlights are apparently not allowed, and as our side-lights had failed we had to proceed holding torches.

The next three days were very full. I watched polo and the races. It was all very enjoyable; but I fear that there has been a general lowering of standards and corruption seems to be widespread. There are so many controls and taxes, many unreasonable or difficult to enforce, that the temptation is to find ways of evading them, and when you get charged Rs.10 duty on a Christmas present that can have cost only half that, you feel like trying to get your own back. I began to wonder whether, if we want to train our boys for a successful life in business, we ought not to see that they can cheat without being found out. I found some of our old boys unhappy about their conditions of service and thinking they were worth a good deal more than they were earning. Part of the difficulty is the high standard of living in Calcutta, and I told them that if they could only make friends by offering them drinks that they could not afford, then those people were not worth having as friends. Also, parents having spent what they consider a lot on their son's education expect them to earn too much too quickly.

The drive to Bhubaneswar along N.H.5 and through the surrounding countryside was very attractive; but the road surface was not as it was under repair the whole way. We crossed the Brahmani and then the Mahanadi below the anicuts, and in Cuttack saw many more hundreds of new Ambassador cars, this time streaming south. The next day we all set off in my jeep, cleared of baggage except for a tent, and drove to Konarak to inspect the magnificent 'Black Pagoda'. Then we had a splendid bathe from a beach as good as that at Juhu, but much more extensive, and deserted by all but local fishermen. We pitched the tent for the girls to change in, and I wished I had had a surfing board.

After this we went out to sea in a local boat and watched the men hauling in their nets. There is a Rest House near the temple, a good place for a holiday, where we drank large quantities of delicious coconut juice. In the afternoon we drove to Puri, passing through villages with their walls brightly decorated in the traditional Orissa style, and there inspected the temple of Jagannath, myself from the outside as I was not allowed in.

Politicians were already gathering for the Congress session, and the following day we passed a number on our way back to Cuttack. We found a new definition for 'Democratic Decentralisation': 'When a large car flying the national flag and carrying a minister leaves room on the road for a passing jeep.' In Cuttack we called on the Sahus. Then we set off for Sambalpur and the Hirakud dam which we reached in the evening after passing through very pleasant country. We had an introduction to the Chief Engineer, but when we got to Hirakud we found that he lived the other side of the three-mile dam. After some delay we were given a permit by the security authorities to motor across, and while waiting for this I took a photo, probably forbidden, of the setting sun across the tremendous lake held up by the dam. Then we drove across the dam to meet the Chief Engineer who kindly asked his assistant to look after us.

Leaving Hirakud, we drove along N.H.6 to Bargarh where the weekly market was in full swing. Both there and at Barpali, which involved a diversion of 22 miles, we bought very attractive hand-woven cloth for curtains and bed-covers. We went on through fine scenery and splendid forests, and planned to spend the night at a Forest Rest House in the hope of seeing some big game, but the one we had thought of was under repair, so we drove on into Raipur. There we stayed at the Circuit House and ate at what we were told was the best restaurant; but the food was poor and the waiter in dirty uniform. When we found the Rajkumar College the next morning, and that it had an excellent Guest House, we were sorry we had not gone there. From Raipur we passed close to the Bhilai Steel Works and I stopped to take a photo from the main road. A man got down from a passing lorry and took the number of my jeep, and asked my name and address. I told him. Some people seem to have security on the brain. We reached Nagpur about lunch time, the road being good all the way: indeed N.H.6 is the best I have been on: a good surface, little traffic and lovely country; and many of the people, whom I took to be tribals, very good looking and handsome. We called at a house to ask where the Vivian Boses lived and were very hospitably treated by Mrs. Khaser whose son, it turned out, I had not been able to find room for in Mayo College. She not only saved my life with a glass of iced beer, but showed us round her lovely garden with a great variety of roses in bloom and grapes hanging from fine vines. We then had an interesting talk and a meal with Vivian and his American wife and set off again after tea. The road now led through very bare and desolate hill country, and when, at nightfall, we found a small but clean Rest House at a place called Pandhrana, we stopped there.

The next morning we found ourselves opposite a cotton ginning factory and the huge white piles of cotton with the factory chimney belching smoke made a fine picture. We drove on to Multai where we saw the source of the Tapti and then through more fine forest where we sighted several spurfowl, to Hoshangabad and across the Narbada. Just beyond the river were caves with prehistoric wall-paintings. Although these were declared Ancient Monuments, many had been blemished by the signatures of idiot visitors. We reached Bhopal about tea time and had a look at the buildings of the new capital; then, seeing the name 'Nagu' on a gateway, we called to find the I.G. Police whom I had met in Indore some years ago, and whose nephew had been a very good cadet at the J.S.W. He was good enough to ring up the Guest House at Sanchi and arrange for us to stay the night there. The drive there was cold and dark but we had hot baths. The bathroom, however, smelt unpleasant as the flush was not working properly: one of the more frequent discouragements to tourists in India.

We were up early the next day and drove to Vidisha, Ashoka's ancient capital, and looked round the caves of Udaigiri. Then we returned to Sanchi where my film ran out before I had taken all the photos I wanted. On the way back to Bhopal we had a puncture, and while we were changing the wheel the head of Buddhism in India stopped to offer help. We liked him. We had no time to do more than look at Hindustan Heavy Electricals from the outside, but got the impression of great advances in production in the country. We reached Aklera after dark.

Once on the road again for what we planned was our last day, we passed through Jhalawar and drove along a good new road to

Gandhisagar on the Chambal. The dam is a fine one, and the lake behind it stretched into the far distance. From there we continued to the dam at Rana Pratapsagar, in the course of building lower down the river. There were thousands at work, and it was interesting to see the construction, with waterways curving upwards to prevent erosion of the river-bed. After this we stopped to look at the romantic fort at Bhainsrorgarh, perched on a high cliff above the Chambal, and at the temples at Baroli, now tidied up by the archaeological department and less romantic than they were ten years ago. We drove on to Kotah, rapidly becoming a great industrial city, and crossed the river by the barrage to call in at Kunadi. There they made us very welcome and showed us the case full of prize books won at Mayo College by different members of the family. The drive back to Ajmer, with a stop for puris at Sarwar, was uneventful, and we arrived in time for supper. These have been a memorable three weeks in which we have seen and learned more of India, geographical, ancient and modern, than is easy to do in as many years. We have driven nearly 3,400 miles, but I feel refreshed and much more sanguine about the future.

8.2.64. *Mayo College.* Term started with a spell of exceptionally cold weather and at the beginning of this week flu set in. On the worst day we had 110 in the hospital and the pavilion, turned into a temporary ward, and 40 or so in bed in their houses. This is making the production of *Julius Caesar* for Prize Giving on the 22nd, when Chagla, the Minister for Education, will be the Chief Guest, very difficult. If we can't get it ready I plan to show *A Play in the Making.* The boys know their parts and I think it might interest the audience to hear how things can be said differently, and to see groups moved about and lighting altered.

Earlier this week I attended the wedding of Manvendra Singh at Dudu. The wedding was very splendid and we processed behind the bridegroom, who was on a gaily-painted and caparisoned elephant, through the Bride's village at sunset with all the villagers crowding round and much dust raised; but this made the setting sun, behind cupolas and minarets, glow even more gloriously. Jai was with the bridal party wearing magnificent emeralds.

Apart from teaching, for which I have less time than I would like, and dictating answers to letters, on which I have to spend much longer than I wish, we have been having a series of meetings of the 'Land Committee' of the General Council, trying to get our property in and around Ajmer properly defined, so that we can sell what is no use to us. This has been in a muddle for the last 25 years, and clearing it up involves troublesome legal disputes.

Paul Anderson is to join the staff from Australia in a few days, and after him, when he has had his honeymoon, Manvendra Singh, who is an old boy of the school. I am now counting the days till I sail for Europe and, at last, a proper six months' leave.

12.3.64. *Mayo College.* Prize Giving safely over. Chagla couldn't make it, but the Nepalese ambassador nobly took his place at very short notice. The play went well and Dinah Stock wrote a very interesting criticism. Next, we beat the Doon School by eight wickets at cricket. I sail from Bombay to Genoa on March 18th and shall spend some days skiing in Switzerland before I come on to you.

24.9.64. *Mayo College.* Safely back to find three school-leavers—John Blackburn, Andrew Richardson and James Turtle—doing good work, and Paul Anderson returned with a wife, all living in my house. This may mean that they don't see as much of the boys as if they lived in their houses, but it also ensures that they will get at supper at least one meal a day of the sort of food they are used to. This morning in Assembly I handed a silver tray to Mrs. Madan Raj from the boys and staff. She is off to work in Canada and will be much missed by the prep school boys after whom she has looked so well. Yesterday Buddhai, my mali, came running up to say that his wife was about to give birth to a baby, and I had to rush her to the hospital in my jeep.

12.11.64. *Mayo College.* The last fortnight has been fearful. Over 280 entrance tests for the next year to be looked through, of which at least 200 were well worth admission; but we only have 53 places. Endless letters from officers being shunted to the frontier, widowed mothers in hospital, divorced parents who want to shift their children from unhappy homes, and so on. Having sorted it all out as fairly as we could, now I am getting another flood of letters asking me to change my mind all, or most, for very good reasons. But I can't do so. Added to this are our own end-of-term chores, and this is the touring season in this part of India and guests arrive daily. On top of everything else the railways have written to say that they can't manage our special train on the last day of term because of the Eucharistic Congress and the visit of the Pope to Bombay, for which they need every available carriage and engine; so the boys go off, according to present arrangements, which may be changed again and have involved 520 letters or telegrams to parents, a day late. The food for that day costs the school over Rs.1,000, and our year's budget is already Rs.60,000 overspent owing to rising prices. However, I'm cheered up by the new library which is nearly completed, and at last we have a flock of sheep which I hope will not only improve the grass on the playing fields, but supply the school with better mutton.

28
THE YEAR OF THE DRAGON

In 1965 Gibson was honoured by the Indian government with a Padma Shri. He thus became one of the few Englishmen to have been honoured both by the Queen of England and the President of India. This year he was also offered the post of principal of a school in Thimpu, Bhutan, to be opened there under royal patronage but he declined the offer. However, he offered to advise if needed and the result was a trip to the Himalayan kingdom. He also invited Peter, his nephew, over to the college as a school-leaver teacher. The Indo-Pak war this year did not leave the college untouched and Gibson describes in some detail the headaches it brought. He also put the college General Council on notice this year to find a replacement for him by 1968.

26.1.65. *Mayo College.* I'm just back from the Ajmer Republic Day parade, commanded by an old boy whom I taught here and who is now in the Indian Police. Christmas I spent very pleasantly with H.H. Kotah who, now that Jai has resigned on appointment as Ambassador to Spain, has taken his place as President of our General Council. The Government of India has honoured me with an award called the Padma Shri that more or less corresponds to the O.B.E. This really ought to have gone to Dan Mal or Sahgal, but I feel a bit vain at being, I believe, the first citizen of the U.K. to be so honoured.

Prize Giving is to be on February 14th, the only day that Chagla, the Education Minister, who is to be Chief Guest, can come. If you remember, he was unable to make it last year as he had to attend a meeting of the U.N. This leaves us little time to prepare and for the production of *Macbeth* which is a play I have always wanted to try. It isn't an easy one and is being made more difficult by events. The boy who was to have acted Macbeth is in hospital with jaundice, so I have asked the old boy who took the parade this morning to do it. He is Devendra Singh who took the part of Bolingbroke in *Richard II* when he was here, what now seems many years ago, and I think he will be good, though as he is stationed some 30 miles away, rehearsals may be difficult.

24.2.65. *Mayo College.* Life has been very much a mixture of joy and sadness lately. Vanessa Anderson developed jaundice and had a miscarriage as a result which she and Paul have taken with great courage, and last week we had the news that Sunil Datta, who left us last year to join the N.D.A., had drowned in their lake. He was such a pleasant boy—always smiling and good-humoured.

Prize Giving went off well, and in spite of many difficulties *Macbeth* was, I think, a success. Devendra had been prevented from attending a number of rehearsals by a dacoity in his area, but came up to scratch on the day magnificently. Lady Macbeth was acted by the Rugby school-leaver, John Blackburn, very well indeed and with great conviction. At Rugby he had acted the part of her husband, and there can't be many people who have done both parts within a year. I was in two minds as to whether the ghost should appear or not, but eventually decided he should do so. There is a trapdoor in the middle of our stage and he rose up through this, the problem being to achieve this really quickly and without jerks; but we managed in the end, and instead of farce I think we accomplished drama. Chagla made a very encouraging speech, praising schools like Mayo College.

The next week we had a visit from Nari Rustomji who wanted me to take over a new school in Bhutan: very tempting, but I felt I must go on here while I can. I said I was too old, but would go and advise if wanted, after this term, and I suggested that John Tyson should be approached.

What about sending Peter [my nephew] out here as a school-leaver? Though a bit anxious about being responsible to you for him, I would love to have him. He would probably have a go of dysentery and might get jaundice, but so far no school-leaver has really suffered from coming here, and most, if not all, seem to have enjoyed their stay and to have benefited from the experience and enlarged their horizons. I am not sure that I could ask the school to pay him as I would not want anyone to think I was practising nepotism, but I would pay his passage, house and feed him, and give him enough pocket-money to travel around a bit. If he comes he should get here as soon after mid July as he can manage.

22.5.65. Delhi Gymkhana Club. In March I went to Delhi to bid farewell to the Gore-Booths who did such splendid work out here. Then I drove my jeep and trailer full of boys, and with Andrew Richardson, to Jaipur for a reception by Jai to Prince Philip. Andrew is working on the staff as a V.S.O. and has a gold award of the Duke of Edinburgh's Scheme. With his help we have started it at Mayo College, the first school in India, I think, to put it into practice, and the twelve boys I took were all working for awards. The Prince was very good, allowed them to be photographed with him, and shook hands with them all. The next day there was a cricket match against a party of M.P.s brought to the school by Jaipal Singh, followed by a 'Mayur Parliament'. Jaipal had made up an excellent list of Questions for Oral Answers on such subjects as the import of wheat, lessons through radio and television, newsprint quota for language newspapers, the shortage of railway wagons, merit-cum-means scholarships, famine in Rajathan, misappropriation of milk powder, unemployment among graduates, and so on. The questions were asked by the boys and answered either by the MPs or other boys acting as ministers. Later that week Shakespeareana came to stay with me and play to the school. They were making a film which I hear will be very good.

On April 12th we had our Annual Moonlight Operations, repeating the Magister Lunaticus scheme, but in a different area, and adding to the staff the Monitores Homonivori. The masters could only be captured by four boys touching, holding or sitting on them at the same time, and for the monitors there had to be five boys. The boys could be killed by any master or monitor touching them and naming them correctly. A dead boy could be revived by the Pandit at the temple if prayed to do so in good enough Sanskrit.

As soon as mark-reading was over at the end of term, I packed and set off in my jeep to attend the farewell function given by Rajasthan University to Dinah Stock who is going as Professor of English to the University of Uganda, Kenya and Tanazania. I shall miss her very much. The next day I drove on to Sariska where the Game Sanctury is looked after by Jai Singh, an old boy of Mayo College. We spent the next night in Delhi with General Bhagwati Singh who had arranged for us to buy the bus from disposals. Then we went on to the Khara Canal Rest House on the banks of the Jumna down which we spent a morning rafting from Rampur Mandi—a nostalgic reminder for me of old days in the Doon. On the last stretch of the road to Dehra Dun the bus broke down, and I drove to the I.M.A. to ask for help. Covered with filth and oil, I was ushered into the office of the Commandant, General Zorawar Singh, to find myself in the middle of a meeting of generals and brigadiers. Aid was generously and promptly sent, and we arrived at the Doon School on time, having driven over 500 miles in awful heat.

Reports finished, I came up here to Delhi, to receive the Padma Shri from the President. On the 19th there was a long rehearsal of the investiture ceremony, and I spent a very interesting evening with the Freemans (he is the new High Commissioner) and liked them both. The next day I received my Padma Shri and am a bit vain at having been decorated in Delhi by both the Queen and the President; but what pleased me most about the day was the news that the Indian team had climbed Everest. Last night I went to *Son et Lumiere* at the Red Fort and before the end there was a terrific dust-storm followed by lightning and heavy rain, the flashes and thunder much grander than man's efforts. I hope the wheat, lying out on the threshing-floor at Mayo College, wasn't rained on. We hope for 800 maunds; now have almost enough hens to keep the school in eggs, over 100 sheep, and are gradually building up a dairy herd.

The general situation in India is worrying. You've probably seen all about it in English papers: language difficulties, and trouble with Pakistan. The Pakistan business is eating up energy and wealth that ought to be being used on more productive activities. I feel that Pakistan has put itself very much in the wrong by its attacks in Kutch, and unless they withdraw there, losing face with their trouble-making politicians, it will be difficult for Shastri to control his. He is a good man, but has inherited all sorts of problems, and there is much pessimism about.

In two days I'm off to Calcutta, and then on to Bhutan with Arthur Hughes.

Condensed

BHUTAN DIARY

24.5.65. Arrived at Delhi station to find the train was three hours late. Had, as a companion in the train, a Poddar who has a paper factory in Dalmianagar and who described to me some of the methods, including forms of corruption, used in the trade. On the journey I read Reginald Reynold's *My Life and Crimes* and drank Poddar's generously offered beer and whisky.

25.5. On arrival at Calcutta was met by Dwarka and Mr. Mohan of the Bhutan Service. Tea with a party of old Mayo College boys, and then to stay with the Duckworths.

27.5. We were driven through the tea gardens, across the Inner Line, to Phuntsholing, just across the Bhutan border. There we had breakfast in the comfortable Rest House with the Chief Engineer, a Mr. Mathur, who had been at Government College, Ajmer, and knew Dan. After an early lunch we set off in three jeeps for Thimphu. Only three or four years ago this journey took six days by mule, but now the 130 miles of road can be done in twelve hours by jeep or bus.

29.5. Visited the school in the morning. A fine central hall was being built in the Bhutanese style: walls of earth that is rammed hard in sections between containing beams of wood, later removed, and floors beaten hard in the same way with wooden rammers by men and women dancing round to very pleasant chanting. No nails are used, and the windows of the upper story were being hoisted, pre-fabricated, into place. All the windows are made to the same pattern, each vertical section ending in a trefoil. We had tea with Nari at the Palace Guest

House where he is staying and then visited the ancient monastery at Wangdichhey. Later, Nari, who is an accomplished violinist, played Bach to us. The music surrounded by the brightly painted Bhutanese furniture and walls was an exciting mixture of cultures.

30.5. (Sunday). After breakfast Nari took us to the bazaar where there was talk of how it should be laid out. Two architects, Regge and Verdi, are up to make plans for the new township which is to be built now that Thimpu has been chosen as capital of the country. We then visited the Palace Workshop where Dasho Zorki Chichap is in charge, Great beams were being carved for the new Dzong, and anything is made there, from masks for the lama dances to those lovely little carved and painted tea tables. After that Nari drove us by the new road over the Dorchu La, a pass at 10,400 feet with a splendid long Om Mani Padme Hum wall, to a waterfall six miles short of Lumichowa where we had lunch. Only a few red, pink and yellow rhododenrons were still in bloom, but many trees were covered with orchids.

31.5. Most of the day we discussed plans for the school with O. P. Mathur, the Chief Engineer. I was keen that they should have more land for expansion and playing-fields. Another problem was efficient drainage. In the evening Nari showed us the monastery at Pangri Sampa where there was a chorten with lovely carved and painted slates let into its sides.

1.6. Visited the Queen-Mother at Dechencholing. She had a very lovely chapel, carved and painted with a number of images and lights burning from little bowls. She also employed women to weave the cloths that are made up into dresses for the men and women of Bhutan.

3.6. We went over the Paro Dzong in the morning. This is a splendid square building, as much a fort as a monastery: indeed the dzongs are both, and in addition the centres of local administration and education. We saw boys learning to write on white wooden boards covered with sticky ash. They used wooden styles which scraped off the ash covering and left the letters clear. There were also monks carving letters on long slabs of wood used for printing. The roof of the dzong is of wooden slats kept in place by great stones, and the building was several storeys high with room for many hundreds of monks. We saw one monk carrying a sort of cat-o-nine-tails of knotted leather thongs which is used for punishing offenders. Discipline is apparently very strict and harsh. In the afternoon we visited the Pyakar monastery, traditionally on the site of a place where Guru Rimpoche meditated.

4.6. Called on H.M. Jigme Dorje Wangchuk. He is an absolute ruler whose word is law, but he wishes to move with modern political theory and is behind the changes taking place in his country. In this he was supported by the late Prime Minister Jigme Dorji, who was assassinated a year ago, probably with the connivance of reactionaries who disliked these reforms. He is a most interesting person. Educated in Bhutan by, he told me, a 'failed matric', he has read very widely and has an extensive library. Life at his court, however, is traditional and formal. The King wants to send his son to the school he has started, and wants him to grow up in sympathy with the traditions of his people.

8.6. School in the morning. Entrance is by merit, though I suspect birth counts towards this, and it is hoped that it will produce, from the people of the country, the administrators, doctors, engineers, teachers, and other public servants the country needs, and who, for the present, are partly supplied on deputation from India. As there, Bhutan will have to solve the problems of scripts and languages. More than one Bhutanese dialect, Nepali, Tibetan, Bengali, Hindi and English in Roman are all in use at present for contacts outside Bhutan. After tea the King took me fishing at his orchard, after which champagne was served by one of the family in bare feet.

10.6. Nari took me to Simtoka Dzong where we saw classes in Bhutanese for the young monks or geylong. The wooden writing-boards, which can be cleaned and recovered with sticky ash, are much pleasanter to write on than the slates that used to be used in England. In the evening H.M. arranged traditional dances for us in his garden. One, in celebration of a victory over Tibet in 1624, and done in the costume of the time, was particularly graceful, with chanting in a low key.

11.6. The King presented me, for the Mayo College museum, with a sword, shield and helmet, and two masks.

13.6. I set off with the postal runner for Punaka, from Thinlegang where the bus took us. The walk of about nine miles was very pleasant, scented by the pines, but my rubber boots were too small and painful. We reached Punaka about 1800 to find an archery competition in progress. The target was about a foot in diameter and the range 130 yards. Those competing each put a rupee into a cap, and the winner took the lot. While I watched the target was hit several times, though there was a cross wind. The competitors were very skilful. They lent me bow and arrow and allowed me to try. My first arrow went about 10 yards, much to their amusement, but the second overflew the target, to my and their surprise. That was enough for me, as the string made great weals on my wrist.

16.6. Called on H.M. after breakfast to say goodbye. He presented me with a magnificent tanka of the 101 Buddhas and said that I should go down in his Land Rover.

17.6. During my short visit I felt I had recognized the Bhutanese respect for authority; their pleasure in beautiful things, whether wooden cups, hand-woven cloth, house decoration or traditional music and dances; their hospitality; and their joy in living. Many would probably prefer to continue in their traditional way of life, undisturbed by the rest of the world; but, faced with the alternatives of being overrun by China or developed with Indian aid, they have chosen the latter, and I was greatly impressed by the good work being done in lonely places and difficult living conditions by engineers, doctors and nurses, teachers, and forestry and agricultural experts from India. Much of the credit for this, I suppose, goes to Nari Rustomji, Adviser to H.M., and a person of tremendous drive.

7.8.65. *Mayo College.* Peter has arrived safely, it is very good of you to spare him, and splendid to have him here. The school has agreed to pay him the usual pocket-money that we give to school-leavers, Rs.200 a month, and as I have paid for his passage, I don't look on this as nepotism. He will be teaching 24 periods a week of 35 minutes each.

7.9.65. *Mayo College.* I expect you will feel anxious about Peter with this disastrous war having broken out, but there is no cause for immediate worry, and I hope it will stop before Pakistan and India ruin each other.

9.9.65. Last night the Pak air force dropped bombs on Jodhpur, about 120 miles from here, and one of their planes is said (probably only rumour) to have approached Ajmer. The boys were called out of their houses at 4 a.m. and slept no more, and I had been awakened at 2 a.m. by a telephone call from an anxious parent. I have had one or two requests to send boys home, but shall not do so until ordered to do it by competent authority. I am sending the following letter to all parents: "You are perhaps naturally anxious about your boy at this time, and I have had a number of telephone calls and telegrams asking what we are doing, and some suggesting that the boy concerned should be sent home. My view is that lines of communication should be kept open for really important messages in times like this, and that you can take it that all is well unless you hear from me. As to the question of going home, if you wish to remove your boy, I will of course send him: but he will not be welcome back next term. This is because I feel that an important part of our duty as ordinary citizens is to help maintain morale. If boys from Mayo College start drifting home it can only have a bad effect on the morale of the boys, school servants, and the general public. If the competent authorities were to advise that the school should be closed, of course, all boys would be sent home or removed to places of greater safety. Meanwhile all ordinary precautions are being taken: trenches for shelter against possible air raids have been dug, black-out is being observed at night, fire drill and first aid will be practiced, and we are having no difficulties over food. I can assure you that we are all in good heart.'

A large number of boys' parents, brothers and other relatives are engaged in the fighting and I dread every telegram, fearing I shall have to tell some boy that his father is dead.

10.12.65. *Mayo College.* In many ways this has been the most B term I can remember, and full of anxieties. Starting with Paul Anderson and a boy getting desperately ill within the first three days, at the end the father of the vice captain of the school, an outstandingly good boy, but with no money and a government scholarship, was murdered, and I had to break the news when he had finished his school certificate examinations. We also had our chief electrician and a mess servant in hospital, one with broken legs from a fall from a ladder, and the other very badly scalded. There is acute water shortage as well as of food; however we had a good wheat crop last year and can last till the next harvest, though it will be difficult to keep the boys satisfied with the rice, white flour and sugar we have.

At the top of the school we are too often reduced to uneconomic small groups: six boys want to read Biology; two for the School Certificate and four for the Higher Secondary because of different abilities in English and Hindi. Planning the time table for these and similar splinter groups is difficult, and sparing teachers for them expensive. Our great need is for a Prep School to relieve us from having to take almost illiterate youngsters from Rajput villages because they belong to old Mayo College families. I have put this up to the General Council, one member of which is getting on my nerves.

I have asked them to find a replacement for me by 1968 as I feel tired and not able to cope as well as I would like to. One problem that I feel I am not in a position to solve, but that an Indian headmaster should, is that of language. It seems clear that there are so many Indians who are not yet, and perhaps never will be, prepared to accept Hindi as the national language (partly the fault of the fanatical Hindiwallas who have tried to force the pace and want an over-sanskritized instead of an everyday sort of Hindi) that something else must be found. English has a great deal to be said for it, but is unacceptable to many on sentimental grounds, and would mean that there would be an elite who can speak it, and who, by virtue of doing so will be divided from the common man. But so are the pandits with their Sanskrit, and what society can do without an elite? If India had a dictator like Kemal Ataturk he would probably scrap all the different scripts and keep English till a national language evolved with words and expression taken from all the Indian tongues.

29

I BUY A FARM-HOUSE

Having savoured the beauty of Bhutan in the preceding year, in the summer of 1966 Gibson was off to Sikkim on a climbing trip – his last since he was 58 now. In anticipation of his retirement this year he also bought a house in Ajmer with land and garden for Rs. 20,000, expecting to spend as much to make it habitable. This was to be called 'Shanti Niwas' where Gibson was to spend the rest of his life. "I begin to feel desperately tired and in need of a rest or change," he writes, and looked forward to his retirement. At this time he also took two Tibetan refugee boys under his wing.

21.1.66. *Mayo College.* The start of term was made sad by the death of Shastri and Thimmy's death in Cyprus was another blow. He was an old friend and I have one of his nephews here. This is my thirteenth year at Mayo and I am hoping that it will not be a bad one! One bit of good news is that Mrs. Pandit has agreed to come to Prize Giving as the Chief Guest. We are going to have a variety show with different masters responsible for each item, so I have less to do but am working hard on a report for the General Council. For the past ten years the school has developed in rather a haphazard way, to start with dependent on the demand for places, and then on our being able to afford to build enough to meet the growing demand. This has meant *ad hoc* improvisation, and it is now time for long term planning. I am suggesting that we should start a pre school, and make arrangements for 600 boarders in the main school. This will mean that we can have classes of 100 divided into sets of 25, a possible and economic number to teach together; and for this we will have to add accommodation to our present four senior houses, as well as build a prep school, and turn the present junior house into a fourth middle house.

28.2.66. Mayo College. Peter, thank goodness, has recovered from his go of jaundice, and John Thomas, the Rugby school-leaver, has so far escaped. They are a good pair to have, and Rugby has certainly sent us a very excellent lot indeed. Prize Giving went off well. Items included a durbar by Saraswati at which the speakers of eighteen languages put forward their claims to be recognized, an extract from Bernard Shaw, the trial of a Mayo College boy in Hindi, Bengali folk music, Rajasthani dancing and some excellent tumbling and acrobatics. Since then Dr. Zakir Hussain has paid us a visit, and tomorrow an Afghan general, President of their Olympic Association, is coming to watch the boys at games. Raghubir Dayal leaves us on Thursday to take over as Principal of a School in Delhi. He is head of our History department and housemaster of Jodhpur House, and has been in charge of all arrangements for the School Certificate examinations for a long time. He has always been very efficient though, what may be a good thing, sometimes critical of my ideas; and he will be much missed. Shiv Ganju will take his place as housemaster.

10.4.66. Mayo College. Early in March the Governor of Rajasthan, Dr. Sampurnanand, delivered a speech with various criticisms of so-called Public Schools, and I was asked by Anil Bordia, the Additional Director of Education, to comment on them. I'm not sure that argument over firmly held prejudices does much good, but I spent some time setting down the usual defence of independence, and answers to the old accusation of producing snobs. I asked how many of the sons of our State and Central Ministers, although uncontaminated by Public School education, had shown sacrifice or spent their lives in social services and claimed that certainly some boys from Public Schools had done this and had been moved by different forms of idealism. I also pointed out that the state itself ran special and more expensive schools and institutes: the Sainik Schools, the Institute of Technology, the N.D.A. and so on for those they considered merited this education, and I said that the Public Schools were ready to take more and more merit scholars if the state would pay for them. I admitted that schools that were exclusive except to a ruling class, were a danger and undesirable, and that this was once largely true of some schools in the U.K., but said that I thought that this was no longer so, and that it did not follow that if the state could not afford good schools for all, it should allow none. Every good school helps to raise the general standards, and drops in the ocean are not to be despised. If there are a few flowers in the desert it is better to cultivate them and sow more, than let them wither for the sake of uniformity. I ended that if money is the root of all evil, envy is the fertilizer of a great deal of disapproval.

Narendra Singh brought Hella Pick to visit the school towards the end of March and to talk to the boys on the U.N. and India. Several of the boys asked her why England was opposed to India, and she followed up her visit with an article in the *Guardian* (March 26th) on relations between the two countries, which I hope may do good. Though it makes no difference to me personally, I am sad at the strained relations. I have been trying to get people in England to move the Ministry of Education to make grants to those with OPOS Scholarships that will enable them to go on from doing their 'A' levels to universities without difficulty. I am sure that this would be money much better spent than on some of the publications and advertisements it goes on. Plans are in hand to take a party of boys and masters to climb in Sikkim in the holidays at the invitation of their Principal Administrative Officer whose boy, Vivek Haldipur, is a very promising member of the school. Major General Sagat Singh, who is in command up there and is an old friend, also has a boy here, so we are hoping there will be no difficulty about passes for Peter and John Thomas.

Gibson and party left for Sikkim on May 5 but his diary for this trip is rather uneventful.

I returned to Delhi by train in a berth numbered 13. I wondered what my berth number portended, and learnt on arrival in Delhi. The rupee that night had been devalued, and if I want to change my provident fund into sterling I shall lose over £1,000! Fortunately, I spent my Doon School provident fund on moving to Ajmer and furnishing the house, so I am not as badly hit as I might have been a saver. John has more or less decided to settle in India, so he won't be very seriously affected, but the cost of his air tickets to England and on to Australia, where he is spending part of his leave, went up by Rs.4000 overnight. I don't understand enough of economics, which anyhow strike me as no more of a science than astrology, to be able to prophesy about the result of this devaluation, but I do know that when I came out to India Rs.8 would buy a bottle of whisky, and now it won't buy a peg. There is so much in India to cause continued hope, and so much to caution disquiet (as a tribe the politicians, or too many of them, seem only out for their own ends) that one does not know what to expect.

7.8.66. *Mayo College. To my nephew, Peter.* So glad you have got home safely. It rained hard at the beginning of last week, but we are still very short of water. We have had to buy a tanker and trailer and have hired the water in a good well some three miles away. The tanker is towed by our tractor three or four times a day to the well and brings back 12 to 18 hundred gallons of really good water. Till this was arranged we had unofficial help from the army. Nothing official could be arranged because we would have had to get the Collector to ask the Home Department of the State Government to ask the Home Ministry to ask the Defence Ministry to lay help on in aid of the Civil Power! We are also starting to dig a well in a spot recommended independently by Vivian Bose, a Franciscan Father, also a water-diviner, and a geologist. We have gone down twelve feet so far, and the diggers are enthusiastic and say the signs are all good for water.

I don't know how successful I am at improving our standards. At the staff meeting at the start of term I drew attention, not for the first time, to various things that I think teachers should take for granted: the importance of keeping 'Work Logs' reasonably fully and taking them to faculty meetings; of collecting effective evidence for end-of-term reports, both adverse and encouraging, by noting down weaknesses and strengths against boys' names in mark books; and of making sure that monthly reports do not differ widely from evaluations when a boy is on daily reports. I have to go on pointing out that written exercises must be quickly corrected and returned, that a spattering of ticks and crosses in coloured ink is of little value, and that our 'ABC' of corrections should be used to eliminate 'deadly sins' by choosing five or six, not more, in each exercise, drawing attention to them, and seeing that the boy corrects them himself. I feel that not enough of the staff try to improve their teaching by reading the articles in publications available in the library and staff room, and keeping in mind the 'Teaching Aims' laid down in our Syllabus Book. This term, instead of taking a class before the rest of the staff on Monday evenings, I am asking each master to read us a paper or give us a talk on his subject, on teaching methods, or on anything relevant to what we are all aiming at. For myself, I find that taking a class of 50 as an experiment is easy to manage with programmed lessons, but that the programmes take me longer to make up than I have time for; and when I set them an exercise to see whether they have really learned anything, it takes too long to correct in such large numbers. I am still teaching Elementary Geometry to these large classes in the Middle School in the hope that it helps them to think logically, and in the upper school I am going on with practice in Faster Reading: some boys, last term, improved their speed, without a deterioration in comprehension, from some 250 to over 1,000 words a minute.

9.9.66. *Mayo College*. It had hardly rained here at all till Thursday this week, and the water shortage was getting more and more desperate. Then it started on Wednesday night and when I went to early school on Thursday morning I found that several housemasters had very sensibly told their boys to stay in bed. The rain was coming down in torrents and the roads were all deep in water. Those who had come to school were soaked through, so everyone was sent back. Breakfast was taken by many in wet shorts or even bathing slips, shoes were discarded as the water came over their sides, and we were unable to have any teaching or games that day. Two great trees were blown down, and nearly six inches of rain fell; so we now hope there will be enough water till next year.

Public life in India seems in a bad way at present, partly because, with the elections due next February, the government is afraid to do anything that might make it unpopular, while the opposition parties are doing everything they can to discredit it. Their tactics include scenes in Parliament and the State Legislatures, without which, they say, they can't draw attention to the abuses of the government, and stirring up trouble wherever they can in the country: strikes and student indiscipline. I haven't a great deal of sympathy for most of the politicians of the Congress Party which has not a clean record in administration and should have been much firmer in punishing ministers and members guilty of corruption; but there doesn't seem any alternative to the Congress.

John Thomas leaves us this evening. He as been a very good person to have here and was a very pleasant companion for Peter. We now have Mark McCormick from Yale helping us, and he too is very good value. On the 1st of the month Lt. General Moti Sagar gave a very interesting talk to the senior boys on India's defence.

23.10.66. Mayo College. I wrote to the Editor of the *Statesman* to say that I had read a short paragraph in his paper and headed 'Joshimath to Hardwar by Raft' stating that five young men were planning to make an attempt to do this down the Alaknanda. I said that this would be suicidal, that my letter was not for publication, but should be shown to the members of the expedition. I could not write to them myself as I did not know their address, and I had no reply from the *Statesman*, and forgot about the matter, thinking that when the party saw the state of the river they would realize that the proposed voyage was out of the question. When I opened the *Statesman* of September 17th I was horrified to see a picture of the launching of the raft and a large heading 'An Adventure that ended in Tragedy'. Two of the party had embarked on the raft and both had been drowned within minutes. I wrote again to the Editor of the *Statesman* asking whether he had been able to send my warning of August 19th, and got a reply from the Resident Editor, New Delhi, that he had been unable to forward it. I wish I had wired to someone in Joshimath.

On September 18th the Woodin family from America came to stay with me at the start of their exploration of the deserts from India to the Atlantic. They were great fun and their boys attended some of our classes and reported the standards high. I was intrigued by their clothes-washing machine: a sealed tub on top of their Land Rover. By the time it had shaken about all day the clothes were spotless.

I have had two good letters from old boys in England. The boy (Ashok Mahadevan) who went to Tonbridge is off to the U.S.A. and his final report was very encouraging indeed: 'He has had a splendid career here and has become a notable figure in the school ... as popular as he is respected.' That from an English headmaster cheers me up, and my only regret is that the Kent County Council was not generous enough to give me a grant that would have made it possible for him to go on to Cambridge or Oxford.

I have bought, or rather am in the process of buying, a house on the outskirts of Ajmer, an ancient and dilapidated farm-house with an adequate bit of land for a garden, for Rs.20,000. For this I am selling some of my capital in England, and it will probably cost me about the same, which I hope to meet out of my provident fund, to put in water and electricity and make the place habitable. Goodness knows whether I shall ever live in it, as I can't make up by mind whether to retire out here or come back home. One old headmaster friend has written that I would be wrong to retire so near my old stamping-ground, but my view of a school is that it should be like a family and if wanted by my successor I should like to help, and if not wanted, would certainly not interfere. I think I could easily resell the house which has the potential of being very lovely, if I decide to come back to England, and if I am to do this, the quicker I do it, the better it would be; but I don't want to leave before they have found a good person to take my place, and I don't want to run away from the considerable difficulties that are piling up in India. On the other hand I begin to feel desperately tired and in need of a rest or change.

23.1.66. *Mayo College.* The 'ban cow-slaughter' campaign is worse than sinister religious revivalism. As fast as pasture can be improved, scrub cattle multiply—rather like growing more food for an exploding population. Apparently there are 90 million beef-eaters in India: Muslims, Hill tribes, Christians and others, and the other day the Finance Minister was asking friends what these millions would eat in a country already short of food, if they were not able to get beef.

A fortnight ago we had our General Council budget meeting, and have had to put up the fees by Rs.250 a year to meeting rising costs, making the total Rs.2,750. By English standards this is very little for what we offer, but it is an awful lot for majors, young I.A.S. officers and those of the working middle-class from whom so many of our good boys come. We could easily keep the school full with even higher fees, taking mainly the sons of rich businessmen, but that I want to avoid.

Two Sundays ago the admissions committee sat from 10 a.m. to 4.30 p.m. without a break, making up our minds to whom we ought to offer places.

A member of a distinguished Mayo College family and of the General Council has caused me a lot of extra work: the production of 19 pages of typescript comparing our present constitution with a new one he has proposed. The current one provides for a Board of Governors to work as a sort of committee of the General Council; but in practice, with the approval of the President, the General Council functions as both bodies, cutting down the number of meetings that would otherwise have to be held, and avoiding possible disagreements. I'm a little anxious that the new proposed constitution might eventually lead to the school being controlled by too restricted a body of people; and I can see no good reason for changing what has worked well for the past twelve years.

The proposal is to constitute a body similar to the Indian Public Schools Society which founded the Doon School and elects its governors. I am all for this, but am suspicious of the proposals for membership of the Society; and it has not been made clear whether the new Society will control the Board of Governors, or the Board the Society. It is suggested that the latter, to start with, should consist of 100 members, each of whom is to contribute at least Rs.100. I feel that a sum of perhaps no more than Rs.10,000 is much too little to collect from those who may become responsible for property worth crores; though there are various suggested arrangements for bigger contributions from Patrons ('All Ruling Princes who contribute Rs.5000' and who would elect the President), from those entitled to nominate students, and so on. The whole thing is not clearly thought out, and needs much more consideration. I shall play for time, and hope to leave this problem to my successor.

30.11.66. *Mayo College.* I took last weekend off for a duck shoot at Shahpura. To start with all went well and I got my goose and several duck, but on the last morning a fearful thing happened. There were two people with me, and as the duck shoot was over, I said I would try some snipe. I told them to keep behind me on the bund while I walked through the swampy grass beyond it. As I did so a snipe got up and flew towards the bund, and I fired at it. The two, who had got ahead and were hidden by bushes on the bund, got the full load of the shot. Thank goodness, no permanent damage seems to have been done, and I have just had a wire to say 'Both in excellent spirits. Do not worry'. It gave me an awful fright, and I kept on trying to wake up from the nightmare.

Dilys (my god-daughter, Dilys Spelman, on her way to Australia), who arrived after my return, has seen the house I have bought and approves.

2.66. *Mayo College.* I have two refugees, Tibetan boys, with me. At the end of term I spoke in Assembly and then wrote to all parents on three matters that exercise me; the importance of Endeavour, the need not to waste food in a time of such shortage, and the difference between true learning and mark-grubbing. Whether because the staff has become more vigilant, or because of an epidemic of dishonesty, I don't know; but some 14% of the boys were discovered in some form of cheating during the term. Perhaps this is a reflection of the adult world which seems to have adopted a money standard instead of a value standard.

I took a holiday of five days round Christmas, and spent the first two with Raghu at Badnore. In the garden of Raghu's Guest House is a Muslim shrine at which village women come to offer prayers in the evening. As they walked down the path in their red, green, blue and yellow pyjamas and dupattas, they looked like a bed of moving flowers. It was good to find Muslim and Hindu living peacefully and happily together in Badnore. On Christmas Eve we drove out to the cultivated bed of a tank. This fills up with several square miles of water during a good monsoon, and then is gradually drained for irrigation. Wheat, barley, gram or linseed are sown as the bed dries, and the last two crops are a great attraction to barheaded geese. We planned to shoot some for Christmas dinner, and as the sun set and the moon rose we spread decoys and took up position where, from their feathers and droppings, we could tell the geese came to feed. Within an hour we had shot enough for ourselves and friends, and we returned to Dan Mal who had been waiting for us at a village close by, talking to the villagers, sitting round a fire. They were well clothed and looked well fed, and one sees evidence of increasing prosperity. In one village we passed through, one that I remember from only five years ago as little more than a cluster of houses, we found, this year, thriving shops, and were able to buy torches, forgotten in the haste of packing, and films for popular cameras were on sale.

On Christmas Day we drove through a countryside green with young crops wherever water was available from well or tank, to stay with Naru at Deogarh. The walls and pillars of our bedroom were inlaid with glass and shone like silver, and the borders of the arches were studded with old European round glass paperweights inside many of which were flower designs glittering like fresh-cut bouquets. High on the walls were priceless Rajput paintings.

On our way we had noticed a large crowd of men seated by the roadside and thought it must be a meeting being addressed by some politician seeking their support in the coming elections. But the following evening, returning to the fort after dark, we met a succession of ghostly figures in white khadi, hand-woven cotton pacehwaras or shawls. We stopped to ask one of them what they had been doing all this time, and found that they were Bolas, members of a caste who skin dead animals. Apparently one of them who lived in a village had stolen a girl from those who lived outside, and there had been a meeting of the clan to decide what should be done about it. Eventually the young Lothario had been told to marry the girl and pay a fine of Rs.4,000. I wondered where he would collect so much money, and was told he would borrow it from a money-lender and probably spend the rest of his life paying the interest.

The evenings were very lovely. The time of *godhuli*, dust raised by cattle returning from their pastures for the night has often been described in Indian poetry. A child of four or five will be driving a herd of great beasts, and you have to stop your jeep to let them by. As we did so on one country track the bell in a nearby temple was being rung for what might correspond with vespers. It was Purnima, the night of full moon. The sun was sinking behind a ruined fort on a ridge. The changing yellows, oranges, reds and plum colours in the west, and the greys and silvers as the moon rose in the east; the silences broken by beating wings and the cries of water-fowl; the raucous call of a sarus crane with its slow wing-flap against the sky: all was a restoring change, and I wondered if I was right to have a gun in my hands and why we accept ugliness and greed and fighting in a world that can be so beautiful, kindly and peaceful.

30

UNCERTAINTIES

From the first letter in this chapter one gathers Gibson had toyed with the idea of going on a round-the-world trip which he now abandoned for good reason. During his return from a trip to England he was forced to return on a ship which came via the Cape due to the Suez crisis and he enjoyed it greatly. In January 1968 the college made an attempt to choose his successor but it failed due to a procedural goof-up which Gibson describes in high dudgeon.

   29.1.67. Mayo College. To the Berrys in New Zealand. I feel I've about shot my bolt as Principal of Mayo College and that it's time there was a new 'tiger in the tank'. I have told the General Council that I want to retire within next year and have bought a house, partly as a move to emphasise this. I shall therefore only be able to take a short leave this year, and I'm afraid my proposed trip round the world via you is off. Once I escape from here I hope to take a year travelling, and will visit you; and after that I would like to go on teaching. I hope the new man here, whoever he is, would like me to do so in Mayo College. I am aware of possible difficulties, and shall not resent it if he does not want me, but I don't think I would interfere or be a nuisance. The house is great fun, and at present is being repaired and altered according to the genius of old Sahgal. I wish you could see some of the buildings he has put up since you were here: the new library really is a gem. A lot of friends at home think I'm mad to retire in India, but England has become frightfully overcrowded, while there are still many wide open spaces in India. The main problem is whether the politician will make the country impossible to live in or not. Most of them are corrupt and inefficient. At one time I thought that the Swatantra party might become a possible opposition to the Congress, but I've lost faith in them because of their support of the 'ban cow-slaughter' movement as a vote-catching stunt. They can't believe in it, and must know that it is economically disastrous.

Term is now under way with nearly 560 boys in the school: we plan to stop at 600. Arrangements have been complicated by the telegraph people 'working to rule' and telegrams arriving either not at all, or after the letters confirming them. On the first Sunday I went up Taragarh via Happy Valley and down via Government College with the sixty or so new boys: a good lot and no one shed tears. More or less weekly my sister writes of someone's death at home. What I used to look on as the older generation is now quickly becoming the past, and we are becoming the passing one. Life is sad, but I continue to enjoy it.

22.2.67. From Raja Ram Singh, an old boy of Mayo College. I was reading a very interesting book the other day, given to me by an educated young man. Entitled *No Ten Commandments,* the writer, S.T. Hollins, was a senior police officer from the time of Queen Victoria's death to 1947, serving at the end as Dewan of the former Tonk State. I have copied out a thought-provoking extract concerning Mayo College. 'One day when we arrived in camp we noticed a great white house like a fort on a hill nearby. I asked who lived there, and was told it was the home of a Thakur of the Gwalior State. I decided to call on him, and after lunch I rode to the house, escorted by two of my mounted police. … The Thakur's secretary took me into a well furnished room where a stoutish man was reclining on a divan. He rose at once and greeted me in excellent English … "Come and sit down", he invited, "and tell me who you are. I heard that a camp was pitched this morning about a mile from my house, but I did not know whose it was. The land on which the tents were erected is mine, and no one asked my permission to pitch them there." I apologized for trespassing, and said that I had sent a copy of my tour programme to the Gwalior Darbar and asked that

copies might be sent to any of the State nobles through whose estates I would pass. "I am only a petty noble in the Gwalior State", he said, "and the Darbar does not worry about me…" Then without warning he told me the story of his life. As a young man, he had been good-looking and full of ambition. His father had sent him to the Mayo College in Ajmer, founded in 1875 for the education of the Princes and nobles of Rajputana. At the College the Thakur mixed with the young Princes of Rajputana on equal terms. He was very good at cricket and tennis, and a fair polo player. He received a liberal education, and was fond of reading the English classics. He took a degree in economics, as his father thought the subject would be of advantage to him when he inherited the estate. He left Mayo College when he was twenty-four, and for a year he was A.D.C. to the Maharaja of Gwalior. At Court he picked up expensive habits and learnt to drink. He used to accompany the Maharaja to Sipri, where he entertained large parties on his houseboats and mixed a good deal with Europeans. Then his father died, and he returned home. The Maharaja did not approve of absentee landlords, so he had to spend most of his time on his estate. "I am bored to death living in solitary grandeur, he burst out, "and I blame you British for my unhappy condition." "But why put the blame on the British, Thakur Sahib?" I asked. "If you had not insisted on the education of Princes and nobles at institutions like the Mayo College at Ajmer, and the Daly College at Indore, there would not be misfits like me. Here I am, highly educated by Western standards and buried alive in this God-forsaken place. There is not an educated man within a hundred miles of my estate, and there is no one near me with whom I can converse as I am now talking to you. I have been driven to the usual refuge of the frustrated intellectual—drink and women." I suggested that his education might add to his enjoyment of life, and reminded him that he had just said that he enjoyed the English classics. I asked him why he did not fill his library with these and browse on them when he had finished his estate duties every day. He replied only that it was too late, and that he could not live without drink and women. And when I tried to distract him by asking him how he administered his estate, he said: "I have a first-class Kamdar (agent) and I leave everything to him."
…As I rode back to camp I wondered if perhaps he was right when he said the British were to blame. I recalled that people of India were highly cultured when the ancestors of the British rulers of India were

savages. Were we right, I wondered in grafting the culture and education that we had evolved on to an oriental people. Primitive peoples deteriorated by contact with European and Americans: do cultured people suffer in the same way? Was the Hindu of today superior to his ancestors of two thousand years ago? I could not find satisfactory answers to these questions.'

9.3.67. Mayo College. From the 24th to the 26th I had a house full for Prize Giving which went off well. Dr. Nagendra Singh gave an excellent address and added splendour to the scene in his academic robes. On the 27th Brigadier Gyan Singh gave a very good illustrated talk to the boys on climbing. On my birthday I lunched with the boys of the Junior Mess and had a quiet dinner when we ate the delicious plum pudding you sent me.

28.8.67. Mayo College. To Professor Hiren Mukerjee, M.P. Owing to the activities of President Nasser I am back a month later than planned, but I must say that I am very grateful to him, as far as I am concerned, for having made it necessary for me to come round the Cape: a most interesting and enjoyable voyage. I see that schools like this are under fire again. I had a look at various comprehensive schools while I was in England, and I don't think they solve the problem of eliminating an elite. I am reprobate enough to think that there should be an elite, though I agree that it should not be largely dependent on wealth or birth. What I found in England was that the top stream in comprehensive schools is just as conscious of being an elite as the old Grammar or Public schoolboy. I would be sorry to see a school like Mayo College, which I hope has done something to combat parochialism, turned into a neighbourhood school, or robbed of its independence and freedom to experiment, and, dare I say it, set an example. In fact we have done much to make a contribution to both sport and learning in the locality. Our swimming-bath and playing-fields are regularly used by other schools, and the senior boys teach in local schools once a week.

29.8.67. Mayo College. To John Martyn. I came back by the *S.S. Cathay* round the Cape: a lovely voyage, but I made an awful mistake on leaving London. I washed after lunch with Bill at the 'Senior' and forgot to replace my teeth. He did his best to get them to me before we sailed, but I was without them all the way to Cape Town, where they caught me up by air, and until then I had to watch people putting away delicious steaks, lobster, pheasant, while I had to make do with pulps. Too frustrating! However the passengers were a very pleasant lot, including a bishop. On one occasion, when the ship heeled over violently and the chair I was sitting in slid across the deck and bumped into his, I exclaimed 'Nearer, my Lord, to thee' which he didn't take amiss. I spent an hour or so most mornings learning to read and write Hindi, but I don't think I shall ever remember the joint characters. My memory gets worse and worse, as my mother's did. Can I put it down to inheritance?

It is time we began thinking of our centenary here and I've been writing to various old boys suggesting that if enough of them would put aside one rupee a month (and many could afford more) we would collect a very reasonable sum that could be used for scholarships.

31.8.67. Mayo College. (Extracts from a letter to three headmasters, Khanolkar, Rogerson and J.M. Dar, who had asked me what suggestions I had to make about criticisms in the Press of Public Schools.) We have always since the I.P.S.C. was founded, been alive to the danger of class exclusiveness, and though we have not been able to do away with the advantages wealth gives in gaining admission to our schools, we have done much to encourage entrance by merit and we should demand more merit scholars from the Central and State governments. If the Centre says it can't afford their fees, we should ask how much they spend on a cadet at the N.D.A. I think that we can prove that our schools are producing students well trained academically, and physically fit. It is more difficult to measure character, but this might be judged by finding out how many of our ex-students have taken part in student riots, or conversely, have done good work as secretaries of societies, captains of games, etc. in their colleges, institutes, the N.D.A., etc.

14.11.67. Mayo College. Prices continue to rise and servants, clerical and teaching staff all want more pay. The Central and State Governments have granted this, and for the first time we are behind them; but neither they nor we can afford it. I need cheering up. Did I ever tell you that when I was very young I kept having frightful nightmares in which my bed slowly turned over revealing tigers and enormous spiders? I've always remembered this awful dream because I had it again and again, and when I took the job at the Doon School I wondered whether the dream had been a warning not to go to the land of tigers! Whether it was or not, I've had a long, happy time in the country and do not regret having come; but the future does look rather sinister. There is labour unrest or student indiscipline or communal killing almost daily somewhere. Poor India. We seem to have to suffer either from drought and famine, or from floods and ruined crops.

Mayo College. Extracts from a letter to parents dated 1 December, 1967. 1967 was the first year of our present fees which we said we would not increase for three years. In this year, we have a credit balance, after including our endowment of about a lac, of nearly Rs.56,000; next year we expect to have a smaller one of perhaps Rs.33,000; in 1969 we shall be lucky to break even. To pay the same D.A. to all our employees at the rates laid down by the governments of Rajasthan and the Centre for their employees would cost us an additional Rs.1,78,000 a year. The General Council has therefore had to decide that we can no longer keep in step with these government rates. The lowest paid servants in the school will draw next year a minimum of Rs.90 a month and are provided with free quarters, but I do not know how they can support a family on this. The teaching staff earn less than lecturers at a university college, but have to work much longer hours and cannot add to their salaries by tuitions. Some schools in the U.K. faced with the same financial problem have instituted a sliding scale of fees calculated according to the parents' income. I feel that this amounts to a sort of extra income-tax, but it may be the answer to the accusation that schools like this restrict their intake to the rich. Would you consider the following idea? If all parents with an income of more than Rs.1,500 a month would voluntarily contribute 1% of their income over this amount up to a maximum of, say, Rs.500 a year, then I estimate that we could continue with our present fees and increase the pay of our staff and servants to what it ought to be. It would mean only Rs.60 a year for someone with an income Rs.2,000 a month, and from the number of parents who are wiling to spend quite large sums on birthday parties for their sons (one, this term, sent me a cheque for

Rs.300!) I think many could afford this; which reminds me that fruit or a cake costing up to Rs.10 is now the maximum we allow a boy to spend on his birthday. We are trying to cut down all extravagances.

After drafting this letter, but before it went to print, I received the following very generous donation and letter from a parent with whom I had discussed our difficulties. '... my conscience told me that I must do my bit in assisting good teachers and other staff members, and I therefore have great pleasure in enclosing a demand draft for Rs.4,000. I feel that if another 50 parents follow this example the problem of your school for the coming year would be solved.' It would indeed, but I do not know how many parents could afford so generous a donation. However, if any who can afford to help, even in a small way, will do so, we should, by that amount, be able to increase the D.A. that we can afford to pay.

11.1.68. *Mayo College.* On the 20th I had to go to Delhi for a meeting of the committee to select my successor. General Kumaramangalam had me fetched from the station and I had breakfast with him and Piloo. Nawab Ali Yavar Jung, Chairman of the Selection Committee, and other members were agreed on one candidate, but two strongly backed another, so the whole General Council is being called later this month to make a final decision. I shall blow up if the right person is not selected. The other had not applied officially, and had canvassed the two members who brought him, uninvited, to the meeting. He should not even have been considered.

The Pattersons from Australia have arrived for this term, and tomorrow two school-leavers, Michael Sidney-smith from Canford, and Charles Bland from Westminster, come too. The first is the son of a boy I taught at Chillon College. Through a miscalculation I have admitted seven more boys than we have beds for. I must go and try and find room for them.

31
MY LAST YEAR AT MAYO COLLEGE

The second attempt in March 1968 to choose a successor was successful and Shomie Das, a grandson of the Doon School founder, was selected. President Dr Zakir Hussain came as chief guest for annual day. And looking forward to years of retirement, with a couple of like-minded people he decided to form a society to help local farmers. It was to be called REWARDS – Rajasthan Emergency Water and Agricultural Development Society. Evidently getting wind of his retirement, Yavar Abbas arrived with crew to make a film onstensibly on the college but largely focusing on him. His faithful cook Samuel decided to go back to Dehra Dun after 30 years of service with him and a former cook of the Jaipur Palace, grandiloquently named Salvador Fernandez, showed up for an interview. Kendals of Shakespeareana too came and gave a private performance of 'Dear Liar' – based on Shaw's letters to Mrs. Patrick Campbell – as a birthday present. During May and June he was on another Himalayan trip, taking in both Sikkim and Bhutan this time round. And reminiscent of his old days of adventure, the year closed with sailing on the lake in Chhota Udaipur in his folding boat.

4.3.68. *Mayo College*. On January 19th I had to go to Kotah for the meeting of the College General Council to select my successor. This, at the time, was even more frustrating than the earlier meeting of the Selection Committee in Delhi. Both candidates and their wives were there as guests of H.H. for the weekend, the journey of one pair costing the school over Rs.2,000, which would have been well justified if they had been selected. The members of the General Council were divided and eventually decided to appoint another; so in my opinion, losing a very good man with an attractive wife. I was given the unpleasant business of breaking this news to them. However, it was then decided to offer the post to Shomie Das, grandson of the founder of the Doon School. I had taught him there, and he had come on Holdy's expedition to South Chander with us. He has degrees from Calcutta and Cambridge, and has been for seven or eight years on the staff at Gordonstoun. Chew, his headmaster, had written praising him highly and I had hoped he would be considered; but the selection committee had thought him too young. He is no younger than the headmaster of Rugby, and I think he will be just what we need. I very much hope he will come here in December.

On January 27th a party of 45 boys and staff arrived from Bhutan. We all greatly enjoyed their visit and the Bhutanese songs and dances they performed for us. There is a faint possibility, only at present in the discussion stage, that the King of Bhutan might send his son here next term. If he does Shomie will have helped to educate two princes.

Meanwhile the school was preparing for the visit of Dr. Zakir Hussain for Prize Giving on the 24th. We had been asked for a minute-to-minute programme, and he had promised to spend two hours with us. We had no sooner rehearsed down to the last moment than we had a message from Delhi that his visit had been cut down to an hour and a half. Rehearsals started again. We had decided to try to show as many of the activities that go on in the school as we could: rather a bit of window-dressing, but we wanted to justify our sort of education and to counter the attacks being made on it. We had to leave out clubs and societies: the Hindi Sahitya Parishad, the English Literary Society, the senior and junior Science Clubs, the Adult Education Society, the Collectors' Club, the Historical Society, the editors of *Mayoor* and bodies like the Games Committee, the Stores Committee, and the Conclave which advises me; but we managed to show coaching in football, hockey, cricket, athletics, tennis, squash, boxing, basket-ball, gymnastics and riding; displays of diving and life-saving in the swimming-bath; the obstacle course where the record time for a team of eight over a nine-foot wall is 12.5 seconds; social services: first aid, teaching children from local schools (gathered here for the day), and serving in the Tuck Shop; cubs and scouts in camp and training; the N.C.C. Army Wing shooting, Navy Wing knotting and splicing, and Air Wing aero-modelling; the rock-climbers' club climbing the wall of a house and rapelling down (easy, but spectacular); the musicians in the Music School; the Photographic Society at work; the Geographical Society at the outdoor relief map of India; the natural History Society skinning and setting up birds; the museum which I think R. N. Chatterjee has made what must be the best school museum anywhere; metal work, carpentry, radio engineering and motor mechanics in their different workshops; painting, lino-cutting, sculpture, book binding, leather work, cardboard modeling in the Art School; the library; the college farm; the Astronomical Society with its telescope; classes being taught modern mathematics, a programmed lesson, and practicals using Nuffield Foundation methods in physics, chemistry and biology; the Junior School at games, handicrafts and singing; two senior classes at rehearsals of Julius Caesar; and a very moving Hindustani play written by K.L. Kaul, a member of the staff, about a Kashmiri village. Finally we ended with our daily Assembly. The few boys not used up in one activity or another were to act as guides. We didn't expect anyone but the President's party, who went round in a car, to see everything, but we hoped everything would be looked at by some. We had just got this all planned for the hour and a half—the President's route, and the security police familiar with where they had to be—when, on the 17th I went down with flu. I was able to get up two days before Prize Giving for a final rehearsal of timing—my report, prizes, the President's address, dispersal of the boys to their various activities while the guests took tea, the President's tour while the other guests wandered where they liked, and finally the collection of all the boys for Assembly while the President was in the Art School next door. Our chief anxiety was what would happen if he wanted to stop anywhere to watch or talk for longer than we had allowed, and another complication was what to do with all the V.I.P.s: H.H. Kotah, President of our General Council, Sardar Hukam Singh, lately Speaker of the Lok Sabha and now

Governor of Rajasthan, the Chief Minister, etc. etc. There were all sorts of problems of precedence and security, but they were all sorted out eventually, poor Dan Mal nearly killing himself working out seating and so on late each night. On the day I felt very weak still, but all went well. Zakir gave a very encouraging address, and his tour round worked out to the last minute. After he had gone, the 700 guests remaining went to a full performance of Kaul's play, followed by a buffet supper for parents, boys and old boys. There were over 2,000 guests at the Prize Giving including 137 old boys, some with their wives, and 360 parents or relatives. Most of the parents and old boys were put up in the school, boys sleeping on the floor and parents in their beds. The numbers at Prize Giving are getting almost more than we can manage, but it was all made very worth while when I got a letter from Zakir saying that 'it was a great joy for me to see the expectation has become a reality'.

On Thursday I had a meeting organized by Dr. John Wells and the Rev. Ewing Smith of farmers and people interested in improving agriculture in this area. We hope to start a society to help local farmers to be called REWARDS—the Rajasthan Emergency Water and Agricultural Development Society.

On March 2nd the Kendals and Marcus Murch, the remaining members of Shakespeareana, arrived. As well as acting excerpts from *Julius Caesar* and *The Merchant of Venice* for the school, Geoffrey and Laura, as a birthday present to me, acted in my drawing room *Dear Liar,* based on the letters between Bernard Shaw and Mrs. Patrick Campbell. From the school I had asked members of the English Literary society and the staff, and a few friends from outside—over 100 in all, and there was just room for chairs for each. It was a very lovely present, amusing in parts and moving in others, and greatly enjoyed.

16.4.68. Mayo College. Jagut came to stay for three days. He is an old boy of Mayo from the days when a number came from Nepal, and I knew him in Dehra Dun where he has a very pleasant retreat on the banks of the Jumna. You may remember my telling you, about 18 years ago, how I turned up there with a party of J.S.W. cadets one dark night, most of us wearing no more than bathing slips, after we had been upset, rafting down the rapids. When we arrived we found him dining with Edmund Gibson, and I like to think they were in dinner jackets, but he denies it. It was fun to have him here and I think he enjoyed his visit except that he was distressed that the Honours Board from 1880 to 1937 has disappeared from the Assembly Hall. He won the Viceroy's Medal for Academic Work in 1918 and had hoped to see his name recorded. We have looked up the records and are having them repainted.

Salvador Fernandez, at one time a cook in the Jaipur palace, came for interview. Samuel, after more than 30 years service with me, wants to return to Dehra Dun before his uncle dies, so that he can inherit his property; he leaves me to, I think, our mutual regret at the end of this month. Fernandez, I fear, has too big ideas and would run me into even worse debt than Samuel with his multiplying family.

On Thursday we had a visit from about 50 girls and mistresses of the Welham Girls' School. My drawing-room was cleared for dancing and games, and their brothers, cousins, uncles and nephews, and the monitors, came to an evening party with dinner on the lawn. It seemed a great success: neither over-boisterous nor spoiled by shyness. Their head girl is the cousin of two of my boys and the daughter of Bula Senapati who was head of Kashmir House and is now doctoring in Nigeria. On Saturday two girls who had come to India overland by Jeep turned up. One was a singer and entertained the Western Music Club. What fun Mozart is when well sung; I did enjoy it!

April 1st passed uneventfully. Some boy had tied a whistle into the exhaust pipe of my jeep, but it failed to blow an audible note. On Tuesday morning Ken Mehta, India's Ambassador in Ethiopia, gave a very interesting talk to the senior boys, and that afternoon Yavar Abbas who made the film *India my India* and had rung me from Delhi to ask if he could make a film here, arrived, not alone, but with eight others. That evening he showed *India my India* to the school. I found it very moving He wanted, I was sorry to learn, to make a film centred more on me than the school, and the next four days were all cameras and tape recorders and disturbances to our routine. There are too many people who fear that my giving up my job here will not be good for the school. While I have been a fairly successful catalytic agent, Mayo College could not be what it is without a first class team working for its aims and I am very anxious that my colleagues should be properly appreciated. Dan, Sahgal, Gue, Naidu and others have all worked as hard as I have, but without public acknowledgement, and I have asked

Abbas to make this clear in the film. His team was fun. Mrs. Wordsworth had let her flat in London for two years so that she could come to see India, and Abbas had roped her in with her car to drive them here. I liked her very much and Bryan Langley, their chief camera man. Sunder Lal, the second camera man, had been in the Indian Navy and is now here again to finish up various shots. They were all good value, if rather a houseful. On their last evening we all went over to Kishangarh for the festival of Ganghor when women celebrate the return of their warriors. Held in the great courtyard of the fort, the women danced, carrying on their heads urns from which flames leapt up, among many other dances in wonderful dresses and jewellery and with much music. It was all very lovely. Round the platform were gathered people from the town all in coloured but mostly red dresses, and from the windows of the fort facing into the courtyard more spectators looked down on it all. This will be best part of the film!

On Saturday, the night of the full moon, we held our annual moonlight scheme. The briefing was as follows: 'Various Rajasthanis, citizens of Ajmer and people of Jodhpur, Bikaner and Tonk are gathered for a meal at Budha Pushkar. Unfortunately there are a number of bad characters among the crowd who are trying to smuggle gold bars. More unfortunately still, it is suspected that the Superintendent of Police, Shri Abhimanyu, and three of his Deputy Superintendents (Shriman Rakesh, Nizamuddin and Misra) have been bribed by the smugglers and are prepared to help them. While their orders must be carried out or at least appear to be carried out by the Police Force, the rest of the force, except for one constable, are honest and will try to arrest the smugglers. Meanwhile, a group of honest citizens, led by Shri Suri have formed a Committee to stop smuggling and root out corruption. The police, of course, know this and the corrupt ones may try to plant their spies in the Citizens' Committee, but it is up to honest citizens to defeat this. They must club together, elect their own leaders in secret meetings, and make plans to capture the smugglers and expose corruption in the police force. Police constables—all boys in Higher Secondary I and II. Smugglers—as nominated by the S.P. and D.S.P.s. Citizens' Committee—as nominated by Rajan Suri.' The scheme was held in the desert sands round Budha Pushkar. The smugglers had hidden six 'gold' bars (heavy steel ones) the day before, and had to retrieve them and get them to a rendezvous. Two, buried near a well, were found on the day to have been dug up by local villagers and pinched: one down to the smugglers! The camels hired by them failed to turn up, and various other things went wrong: a bus broke down and the start was delayed by an hour. This, however, was just as well, as during that time a sandstorm blew up and the moon was totally obscured. One boy, who should have been able to read the map supplied, strayed out of bounds, fell into the lake, and was nearly drowned in the mud. Poor fellow, he shouted for help but no one could hear him in the storm. Anyway, he extricated himself in the end, and it is rather a coincidence that I wrote a report on him some days ago starting, with apologies to La Fontaine, 'Le buffle s'etant vautre...' In spite of these mishaps the scheme was good fun till I had a puncture near midnight on the way back.

Term ends tomorrow week, and I hope to pay another visit to Sikkim and Bhutan.

10.5.68. *Mayo College. To Deb Barua.* Some days ago I was partly woken up about 3 a.m. by what I took to be a dog fight. I wondered why the chowkidar didn't chase them away, but turned over and went to sleep again. I was just off to early school the next morning when I was called by Tansukh who said he could not wake the chowkidar up. He was lying dead on my veranda. Poor fellow, he had had a heart attack and the noises I had heard were his death rattle. He was a friendly person, but a bit of a drinker and leaves no dependents. I had to pop his body, very heavy, into the back of my jeep and take it to the hospital and later to his home. I was late for school, which I am not often.

I have considered a means test for fees, but do not think it would work. First it is a sort of double income-tax, and then it would be difficult to know who declared their incomes correctly. My request to parents with an income of more than Rs.1,500 a month at the end of last tem brought in about Rs.17,000: generous from many of those who contributed, but not enough to make a worthwhile difference.

I'm very glad you were able to go to Gordonstoun and meet Shomie. I'm not worried about his youth. Everyone here seems happy about him and to agree that a young man is a good idea; but I am little anxious that he will find the change from the comforts of the U.K. to the inefficiencies of Ajmer—water shortages, fluctuations in the electric current when it's working at all, and so on, hard to bear.

I have also been a bit anxious that you might be suffering from all the trouble about immigrants, and I do hope not. I'm ashamed of some of my countrymen. Not perhaps at their colour prejudices—you will understand these as India is by no means free of them—but of their unwillingness to do an honest day's work. They get West Indians, etc. to labour at pay they themselves won't accept, and then complain that their standards of living are different. What a state the world is in! I begin to wonder if I was wrong to think it was right that the British Empire should be wound up—but this was made inevitable by the jealous Americans.

Garg has completed his term as housemaster of Ajmer House this term, and will be followed in July by Sahajwala. During his eleven years as housemaster Ajmer have won the Udaipur Shield ten times—an extraordinary effort, as I have tried to even things up by not giving them quite their share of the better new boys and those from middle houses. Gupta, Gue and N.C. are all due to retire from their housemasterships next year and I wonder whether we shall find as good people as they have been to succeed them. Your old housemaster, now in Delhi, has helped me very much by finding me a secondhand air-conditioner for Rs.800, a real bargain I am assured by the mechanic here, who had no part in selling it, but says it is worth at least Rs.2,000. I now hope to be able to be reasonably comfortable when the rains start, and eventually to move it to my new house.

[In May-June I visited Sikkim and Bhutan but the letters then written to my sister have not survived.]

20.7.68. *Mayo College.* My tummy trouble in Bhutan went on and off most of the time and was rather a handicap to full enjoyment. We did no trekking, partly because of it, and partly because the boys I was to go with only arrived shortly before I had to leave and the weather broke. I did, however, manage some ten days of interesting fishing, though Holdy would not have approved of what he calls my shark tackle. I had no fly rod, but I enjoy casting and trying to drop the spinner into exactly the right place. This, however, meant that once I got into any but a very large trout little if any art was required to land it.

Wading, waist deep, in cold water was, perhaps, not the best way to cure my complaint, and I caught nothing bigger than 3 ½ pounds; but I explored long stretches of both the Thimphu and the Paro rivers and had a lot of fun. I lived largely on every variety of boiled and fried trout, and even made fish-cakes of them, which must be a sort of sacrilege. I ate one memorable lunch with a delightful couple: German missionaries who run a leper settlement away in the wilds. She boiled the most delicious *truite au bleu* I have eaten for a long time.

The King has planted very lovely roses round the buildings in the courtyards of the Thimpu Dzong. He asked me to have a look at the school, which I did several times. He gave me two very attractive brass and silver trumpets which telescope from five feet open to two feet closed; and I bought in the bazaar two silver and gilt boxes, one rectangular to contain pan leaves, and the other smaller and round for the lime that is spread on the leaves.

The well we have been digging is now 130 feet deep, mostly through solid rock, and has so far cost over Rs.30,000. It has no water in it, except what poured in when it was raining. I fear it will be known as 'Gibson's Folly'.

4.9.68. *Mayo College.* We had a most enjoyable staff picnic last Sunday to a place called Chota Udaipur where H.H. Kishangarh has some buildings, now more or less in ruins, beside and above a little lake surrounded by hills. You could dive into the lake from the principal rooms, and we had some adventurous sailing in my capricious folding boat. There was a good wind with heavy gusts, and we were nearly upset several times.

26.10.68. *Mayo College.* You will probably have heard of Arthur Foot's death a month ago. He was a great headmaster and a big man in every way. There were occasional storms both with those in authority over him, and with those over whom he was in authority; but he was nearly always right in any stand he took, and even those who did not always agree with him, respected him and recognized the rectitude of his views. No one can be great without arousing occasional opposition, and many of us owe much of any success we have had as teachers, housemasters or headmasters to the example he set of integrity, justice and hard work.

I'm back from Bombay where I went to attend the launching of India's first warship to be built there since the days of the Wadias and their great wooden vessels, many of which sailed under R.N. colours. The prime Minister broke the coconut and the ship slipped into the water majestically.

10.1.69. *Mayo College.* The Dases are now with me: a delightful family of three children, two boys and a girl, and Pheroza who will be a great addition to Mayo College Society. Term starts in four days, and the General Council wants me to stay on for two or three weeks till Shomie finds his way around, so there will be two Principals acting in concert for a short time. Meanwhile I am moving my belongings in jeep and trailer and clouds of dust to Shanti Niwas.

A letter marked 'Registered acknowledgement due' was delivered at my house, signed by someone who called himself 'A prominent businessman of Ajmer' who wrote that he thought it his duty to bring certain things to my notice. He made a number of allegations against college employees, and said that he was sending a copy of the letter to the O.B. I reported all this to H.H. The Chairman, and wrote: 'This is an unhappy way to come to the end of my tenure as Principal, and I do not wish to hand over to my successor and leave him to be treated in the way I have been, until the whole matter is cleared up.' We have been unable to find out who wrote the letter, the address given proved to be bogus, and all the accusations, which I asked a senior government servant to enquire into, were spurious. I have now written to the O.B. 'Surely it is time that you admit that you have been misinformed and were wrong to take any notice of anonymous letters and ill-conceived tittle-tattle,' but the whole business, involving endless enquiries and letters, and sixteen more pages of reports to H.H., has not made my last few weeks over-cheerful. No one has so far suggested that I have made money corruptly, but I am responsible if anyone else has. Apart, perhaps, from some thieving from the messes, which we do our best to make impossible, I am as sure as I can be that there has been no material loss of money or supplies to the school. To make quite sure, I have asked the Director General of the Works at Army Headquarters if he would be so good as to depute a senior officer off-duty to estimate what all the building that has been done in my time should have cost, and he is sending the Commander Works Engineers when he can be spared. (This enquiry gave an estimated cost for those buildings very much higher than what we had actually spent).

From *Mayoor* of 10.2.69.
Speech delivered by his Highness
Maharao Bhim Singh of Kotah,
President, General Council, Mayo College,
At the farewell banquet of Mr. J.T.M. Gibson
On 1st February, 1969, in the College Assembly Hall

Mr. Gibson, your Highness, Ladies and Gentlemen, We have gathered here this evening to bid farewell to Mr. Gibson who is relinquishing the Principalship of the Mayo College after fifteen years of distinguished and very devoted service to this great institution. Mr. Gibson had already a varied and rich experience of Public School education, both in India and abroad, before he joined the Mayo College as Principal, in January 1954, and I am sure you will agree with me that, during this period of fifteen years, this institution has made phenomenal progress and great all-round improvement which are all attributable to his able guidance and untiring efforts.

The Mayo College was founded during the last century with the specific purpose of giving exclusive education to the Princely order and the nobility of the Indian States. With a change in the political atmosphere of the country and growing emphasis on the democratic nature of society, it became necessary to steer the educational trends of the College into a different channel to make our students play a useful role as citizens of the Republic of India. To achieve this purpose, the College was fortunate to have as its Principal such a far-sighted and dynamic personality as Mr. Gibson.

The College was also facing numerous other difficulties. Our financers were causing anxiety, the number of students had fallen low, the standard of scholarship had to be raised and, above all, the Mayo College had to be given its proper place and recognition as one of the pre-eminent Public Schools of India. During Mr. Gibson's stewardship, the College has been able to get over all these hurdles and I would like to thank Mr. Gibson, on behalf of the General Council, and the Old Boys of the College, and say how much indebted we are to him for this signal service to the College and his numerous achievements, which have brought fame to this institution. Our finances are on a sound footing, the number of boys has risen from 140 to 586, with a long waiting list, and the College is attracting boys from an excellent cross-section of society, including Government of India Scholars, and the high standard of scholarship attained is evident from our consistent good results, for the last several years, in the Indian School Certificate and Higher Secondary Examinations. With the introduction of progressive methods of teaching, there is greater emphasis on extra-curricular activities like mountaineering, sailing, life-saving, manual work, etc. which help in character-building and bringing out talent for leadership. Our boys are doing well in several all-India competitions and there is a greater demand for them in the commercial and industrial concerns in the country. With this all-round progress and increase in the number of boys, the staff had to be expanded and there has been an unprecedented progress of expansion of buildings, costing nearly 15 lakhs of rupees.

All this development has been primarily due to the zeal, devotion and single-minded purpose which Mr. Gibson has brought to bear on his work as Principal of the Mayo College. In him, we always found a gentleman who tried to give more than he received. He endeared himself to the staff as well as to the boys by taking personal interest in their welfare and looking after them, even after they had left the College, by helping them to get suitable situations and making good careers. It was, therefore, a matter of great pleasure and happiness to all of us when Mr. Gibson was honoured both by the British Government and the Government of India by conferring on him the titles of 'O.B.E.' and 'Padma Shri', for his meritorious services to the cause of education. It is one of the few examples of a person being honoured by both these Governments.

To me personally, Mr. Gibson's friendship has been one of the real joys of life. Separation from a friend is always sad, but the pain in bidding goodbye to Mr. Gibson is much mitigated by the thought that he has fallen in love with Ajmer and has decided to settle here as a 'Rajasthani'.

On behalf of the General Council and the Old Boys, as well as on my behalf, I wish you, Mr. Gibson, many years of good health, happiness and a comfortable retired life and assure you that your period of Principalship will always be considered a glorious chapter in the history of Mayo College and your name shall rank high amongst its builders.

Your Highness, Ladies and Gentlemen, it is also my pleasant duty this evening to extend to Mr. and Mrs. Das a most hearty welcome to the Mayo College and to say that in Mr. Das we have the promise of an able successor to Mr. Gibson. We have every hope and reason to believe that the Mayo College will continue to flourish under his wise stewardship and he and Mrs. Das will find their stay here happy and enjoyable. May I now request you to rise and drink to the health and happiness of Mr. Gibson.

7.2.69. Shanti Niwas. To His Highness the Maharao of Kotah. Please forgive this paper. I have not yet had time to buy any writing paper! I meant to suggest to you when we met that I feel it would be right for the School to provide my successor with a car. It is almost impossible to do one's job without one, and while it was possible for me as a bachelor to buy my own, a married man with three children cannot easily afford this. I believe most public schools do provide the Headmaster with a car, and I hope that Mayo College will be able to do the same, and that you will not mind my suggesting it.

398 *An Indian Englishman*

1. At Haileybury 1926

2. Skiing at Morgins 1936

3. With teachers early in his tenure as Principal at Mayo College

4. Prize Giving Mayo College 1966. Chief Guest Vijayalaxmi Pundit meeting monitors. Yogen Dalal is 4th from the right.

5. With Indian President V. V. Giri at Mayo College

6. With Indian President Zakir Hussain at Mayo College

7. Driving Indian Prime Minister Jawaharlal Nehru through
Mayo College grounds

8. With Governor of Kashmir Dr. Karan Singh at Mayo College

9. Shanti Niwas

10. With Deb Barua

APPENDIX

I suppose the most boring of all the chores of a teacher is the correction of exercises, but I believe it to be a very necessary duty if one's pupils are to be helped to clearer thinking and correct expression. To reduce the labour of correction I have long used the 'ABC' below to point out mistakes and shortcomings. A pupil learns much more by himself correcting his mistakes than by reading, or neglecting to read, corrections made by the teacher. The 'ABC' may seem a bit childish, but I have found it to bear fruit. I do not use it for every mistake in an exercise full of errors, but point out perhaps half a dozen of the worst to make sure that these have been put right by the time the next exercise is submitted. If they have not been, no credit is given for the following exercise. This means looking back, and more work, but is as valuable as hoeing after ploughing.

- O (a circle round the word) this word is unnecessary or should not have been used.
- X Spelling mistake.
- A A necessary word has been omitted here.
- A Ass. Read the question and answer IT.
- B Badly expressed, or sentence not properly framed. Rewrite it.
- C Condense and express more shortly. Be concise.
- D Dictionary. Is this the best word to express your meaning? Use your dictionary to find the meaning of the word you have used, or to find the right word.
- E Be exact. Be accurate. Draw this figure, make this measurement, or do this calculation again.
- H Heading. What is this about? What is its title?
- I Incomplete answer. Give the answer in the required form.
- K Keep to the point. This is irrelevant.
- L Logic. This does not follow.
- M Map or diagram needed for illustration.

N Number of verb or pronoun wrong.
O Obscure. Meaning not clear.
P Punctuation mistake.
R Reference. What does this pronoun stand for or relate to? Or relative pronoun and antecedent wrongly placed.
S Steps? Steps have been omitted. Show working.
T Time. Is this the correct verb tense? Or correct your sequence of tenses.
U Untidy. Be neat. Use a sharp pencil. Write better.
V Verb. Where is the main verb? This is not a sentence.
W Why? Give reasons.
Y Why have the mistakes in your last exercise not been corrected? No marks for this work.
Z Read through your work and correct slips before showing up.